Financial Services in India

Financial Services in India

Concept and Application

Rajesh Kothari

SAGE www.sagepublications.com

Los Angeles • London • New Delhi • Singapore • Washington DC

First published in 2010 by

SAGE Publications India Pvt Ltd
B1/I-1 Mohan Cooperative Industrial Area
Mathura Road, New Delhi 110 044, India
www.sagepub.in

SAGE Publications Inc
2455 Teller Road
Thousand Oaks, California 91320, USA

SAGE Publications Ltd
1 Oliver's Yard
55 City Road
London EC1Y 1SP, United Kingdom

SAGE Publications Asia-Pacific Pte Ltd
33 Pekin Street
#02-01 Far East Square
Singapore 048763

Published by Vivek Mehra for SAGE Publications India Pvt Ltd, typeset in 10/12 pt Palatino by Star Compugraphics Private Limited, Delhi and printed at Chaman Enterprises, New Delhi.

Library of Congress Cataloging-in-Publication Data

Kothari, Rajesh.
    Financial services in India: concept and application/Rajesh Kothari.
       p. cm.
    Includes bibliographical references and index.
    1. Financial services industry—India.   2. Banks and banking—India.   I. Title.

HG187.I4K68   332.10954—dc22   2010   2010033657

ISBN: 978-81-321-0507-7 (PB)

The SAGE Team: Rekha Natarajan, Sonalika Rellan, Vijay Sah and Umesh Kashyap

Contents

List of Tables

List of Figures

Abbreviations

ABS	Asset Backed Security
ADRs	American Depository Receipts
AI	Approval Inter-median
AIC	Agro-industries Corporations
AIG	American Insurance Group
ALM	Asset Liability Management
AMC	Asset Management Act
AML	Anti Money Laundering
AOP	Association Of Person
ARC	Asset Construction Company
ARCIL	Asset Reconstruction Company of India Ltd.
ASE	Ahmedabad Stock Exchange
ATM	Automated Teller Machine
BFS	Board of Financial Service
BFS	Board of Financial Supervision
BIFR	Board for Industrial & Financial Reconstruction
BIS	Bureau of Indian Standard
BOLT	BSE Online Trading
BPO	Business Process Outsourcing
BSE	Bombay Stock Exchange
CAMELS	Capital Adequacy Asset Quality Management Earnings Appraisal Liquidity and Systems
CAPM	Capital Asset Pricing Model
CARE	Credit Analysis & Research Ltd.
CASE	Computer Aided Software Engineering
CBDT	Central Board of Direct Taxes
CCI	Controller of Capital Issues
CD	Certificate of Deposits
CDO	Collateralized Debt Obligation
CDSL	Central Depository Securities Ltd.
CGSL	Citigroup Global Services
CIF	Cost Insurance & Freight
CIP	Carriage and Insurance Paid
CIS	Collective Investment Scheme
CLO	Collateralized Loan Obligation
CMO	Collateralized Mortgage Obligation
COF	Cost on Freight

CP	Commercial Paper
CPF	Customer Protection Fund
CPT	Carriage Paid To
CRA	Credit Rating Agencies
CRAR	Capital to Risk Weighted Ratio
CRISIL	Credit Rating Information Services of India Ltd.
CRR	Cash Reserve Ratio
CVC	Card Validation Code
CVV	Credit Verification Value
D/A	Document Against Acceptance
DAF	Delivered At Front
DBOD	Department of Banking Operation & Development
DBS	Department of Banking Supervision
DCR	Duff & Phelps Credit Rating India
DDV	Delivered Duty Unpaid
DEQ	Delivered Ex-Quay
DES	Delivered Ex Ship
DFHI	Discount & Finance House of India
DFI	Development Financial Institution
DMA	Direct Market Association
DNPD	Derivative & New Product Department
DRR	Debenture Redemption Reserve
DRT	Debt Recovery Tribunal
DSA	Direct Sales Association
DWBS	Department of Non-banking Supervision
EB	Exchange Board
ECB	External Commercial Borrowing
ECGC	Export Credit & Guarantee Corporate
ECS	Electronics Clearing System
EFT	Electronic Fund Transfer
ELA	Equipment Leading Association
ELSS	Equity Linked Saving Schemes
EOS	Electronic Point of Sale
ETF	Exchange Traded Fund
EXIM	Export Import Bank of India
EXW	Ex Works
FAS	Free Alongside Ship
FCCB	Foreign Company Convertible Bank
FCD	Fully Convertible Debentures
FEDAI	Foreign Exchange Dealers Association of India
FEMA	Foreign Exchange Management Act
FIIs	Foreign Institutional Investors

FITF	Financial Inclusion Technology Fund
FOB	Free on Board
FPO	Follow-on Public Offer
FVCI	Foreign Venture Capital Investment
GDCF	Gross Domestic Capital Formation
GDP	Gross Domestic Product
GDRs	Global Depository Receipts
GDS	Gross Domestic Saving
GIC	General Insurance Corporation
GIR	General Index Register
HDFC	Housing Development Finance Corporation
HFC	Housing Finance Company
HSBC	Hong Kong and Shanghai Banking Corporation
HUDCO	Housing and Urban Development Corporation
HUF	Hindu Undivided Family
ICAAP	Integrated Capital Adequacy Assessment Process
ICAI	Institute of Charted Accountants of India
ICICI	Industrial Credit and Investment Corporation of India
IDBI	Industrial Development Bank of India
IDFC	Infrastructure Development Finance Corporation
IFCI	Industrial Finance Corporation of India
IPF	Investor Protection Fund
IPO	Initial Public Offering
IRDA	Insurance Regulatory and Development Authority
ITEs	Intra-group Transactions and Exposures
KYC	Know Your Customer
LAB	Local Area Bank
LIC	Life Insurance Corporation
LPG	Liberalization, Privatization, and Globalization
M&A	Merger and Acquisition
MA	Member Affiliates
ME	Member Establishment
MF	Mutual Fund
MIBOR	Mumbai Inter-bank Offer Rate
MIFOR	Mumbai Inter-bank Forward Rate
MIRSD	Market Intermediaries Registration and Supervision Department
MISU	Market Intelligence and Surveillance Unit
MMMFs	Money Market Mutual Funds
MPSE	Madhya Pradesh Stock Exchange
MRD	Market Regulation Department
MSIM	Morgan Stanley Investment Management
NAV	Net Asset Value
NBFCs	Non-banking Finance Companies

NCD	Non-convertible Debenture
NDS–OM	Negotiated Dealing System–open Market
NHB	National Housing Bank
NPL	Non-performing Loan
NRE	Non-residential (External) Rupee
NRI	Non-resident Indian
NSDL	National Security Depository Ltd.
NSE	National Stock Exchange
NSIC	National Small Industries Corporation
NYSE	New York Stock Exchange
OTC	Over the Counter
P/E	Price to Earning
PCD	Partially Convertible Debentures
PDs	Primary Dealers
PFRDA	Pension Fund Development & Regulatory Authority
PMAC	Pricing Market Advisory Committee
PMS	Portfolio Management Scheme
PSB	Public Sector Bank
PSU	Public Sector Undertaking
PTC	Pass-through Certificate
QIB	Qualified Institutional Buyer
RBI	Reserve Bank of India
RDCB	Rupee Denominated Convertible Bond
REIT	Real Estate Investment Trust
RNBC	Residual Non-banking Companies
ROA	Return on Total Asset
ROE	Return on Equity
RRB	Regional Rural Bank
RTGS	Real Time Gross Settlement
SAR	Stock Appreciation Rights
SCB	Scheduled Commercial Bank
SCRA	Security Contract Regulation Act
SEBI	Securities and Exchange Board of India
SFC	State Financial Corporation
SHCI	Stock Holding Corporation of India Ltd
SIDC	State Industrial Development Corporation
SIP	Systematic Investment Plan
SKO	Superior Kerosene Oil
SLR	Statutory Liquidity Ratio
SMC	Small and Medium Sized Companies
SML	Security Market Line
SPN	Secured Premium Notes
SPV	Special Purpose Vehicle

SR	Security Receipts
STP	Stock Throughput Policy
TB	Treasurary Bills
TRA	Trust & Retention Account
UIN	Unique Identification Number
ULIP	Unit Linked Insurance Plan
UTI	Unit Trust of India
WDM	Whole Debt Market
WFE	World Federation of Exchanges
WMA	Ways and Means Advances
WOS	Wholly Owned Subsidiary
ZCCN	Zero Coupon Convertible Notes

Preface

The contemporary business environment emphasizes on learning as well as getting exposure to newer area of knowledge. It is a fact that financial services have assumed a very significant role in Indian economy during the last couple of years as service sector contributes to the major part of national income of the country.

Financial services involve conversion of intangible into tangible; as such these services are, by and large, in the shape of intangible. Unlike in the past when these services were offered, they were offered only as intangible: not to be seen, not to be touched, and not to be realized. The process of technology, communication, and intense competition have forced the service providers to convert them into products and, therefore, the service providers like bank call them saving products, loan products, etc.

The work *Financial Services in India* is, therefore, an attempt to educate the readers about the conceptual aspects of financial services available in India as there is a long-felt need of such publications because of dearth of concise literature. The book has been done in 15 chapters, precisely written and lucidly arranged by keeping common readers in focus.

The book starts with the concept of financial services and goes on to explain the regulatory framework for financial services in India. An attempt has been made to provide latest information and data so that the readers can find themselves in comfortable position to assess the reality of financial services in general, and in particular services like insurance, mutual fund, and Forex.

The book is suitable for the students having opted for papers in financial services at the level of BBA, M.Com., MBA, CS, and other professional courses.

I am sure that this book will prove its utility to students as it serves the purpose of learning with comfort.

Acknowledgements

This book would not have been completed without the blessings of my teachers and the support of my fellow colleagues, as well as, the support of bankers, insurers, fund managers and other service providers through their active cooperation and meaningful discussions across the table. I wish to acknowledge the cooperation of my research scholars, Dr. Saket Mathur, Dr. Narendra Sharma, and Dr. Sonal Jain, to name a few, for their valuable support.

Last but not the least, the contribution made my family members, namely, my wife Preeti and daughters Priyanka and Chhavi is equally important to highlight.

1

Introduction

Learning Objectives

- To know about Indian financial system.
- To learn about institutions, instruments, and intermediation and recent developments.
- To be familiar with impact of globalization and Indian financial system.
- To understand the concept of financial services.

THE INDIAN FINANCIAL SYSTEM: A REVIEW

An economic system consists of various economic agents like households, producers, government, and consumers. These agents undertake various economic activities like production, exchange, and consumption for the purpose of sustaining themselves resulting into mobilization, allocation, utilization, and generation of funds.

However, as we know, "need is the mother of all inventions." So there is need of a mechanism which should facilitate the flow of funds between surplus, and deficit units in an economic system known as financial system. A financial system comprises various financial institutions, markets, instruments, and regulatory bodies and helps in the flow of funds from the areas of surplus to the areas of deficit. See Figure 1.1 for more details.

The financial system performs the following functions:

1. **Facilitates Savings**

   Financial system helps in the mobilization of savings from households, public sector and private sector units and makes them available to the producers. This is done through

Figure 1.1   Reflects an Overview of Markets, Institutions, Intermediaries, and Instruments Operative in the Indian Financial System (IFS)

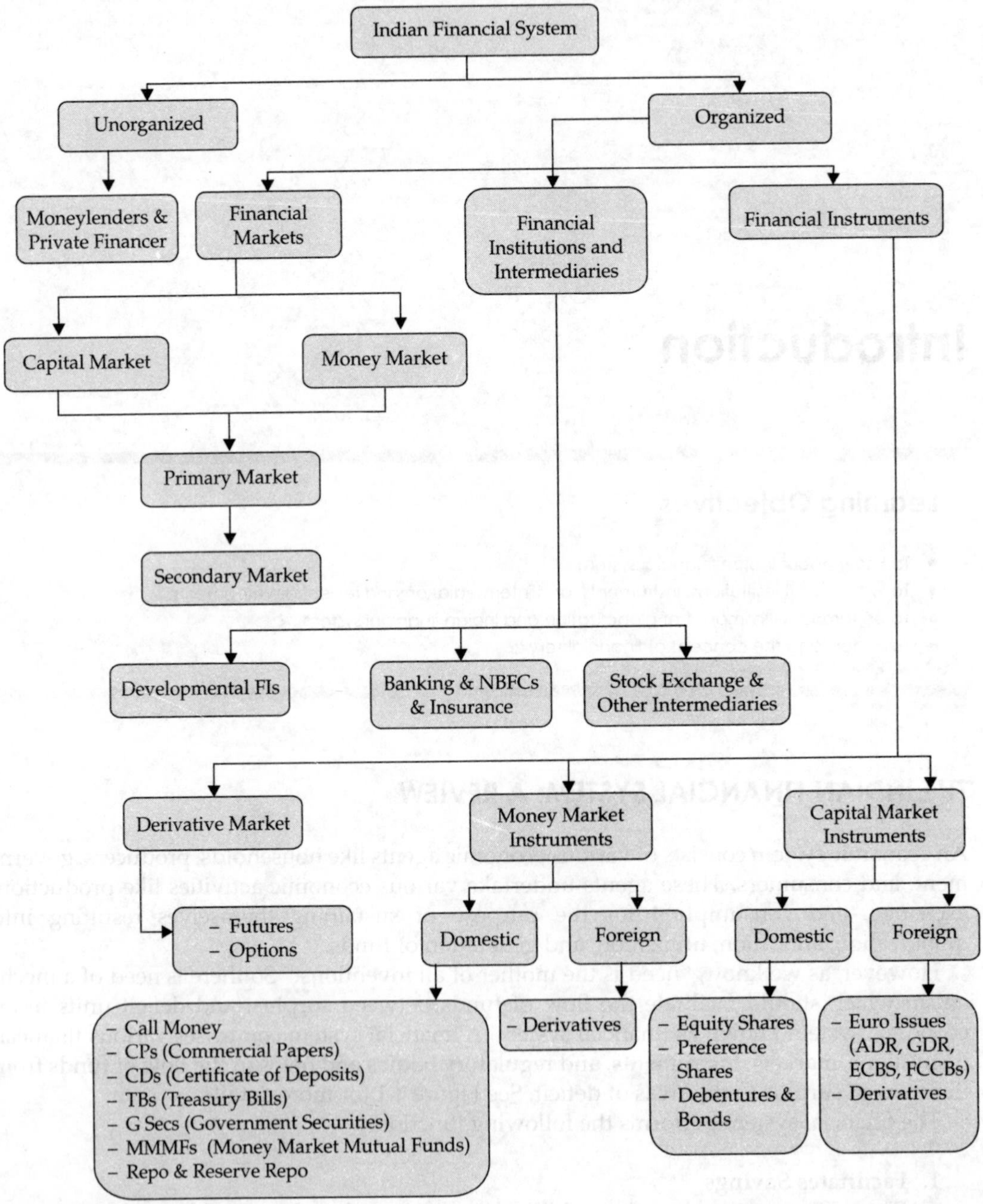

```
                          Indian Financial System

           Unorganized                              Organized

Moneylenders &      Financial          Financial              Financial Instruments
Private Financer    Markets            Institutions and
                                       Intermediaries

        Capital Market        Money Market

              Primary Market

              Secondary Market

Developmental FIs      Banking & NBFCs      Stock Exchange &
                       & Insurance          Other Intermediaries

Derivative Market       Money Market            Capital Market
                        Instruments             Instruments

   – Futures         Domestic    Foreign     Domestic    Foreign
   – Options

                              – Derivatives   – Equity Shares    – Euro Issues
– Call Money                                  – Preference         (ADR, GDR,
– CPs (Commercial Papers)                       Shares             ECBS, FCCBs)
– CDs (Certificate of Deposits)               – Debentures &     – Derivatives
– TBs (Treasury Bills)                          Bonds
– G Secs (Government Securities)
– MMMFs  (Money Market Mutual Funds)
– Repo & Reserve Repo
```

Source: Author's compilation.

issuing various financial instruments in the money and capital markets. Mobilization of savings and their utilization has a direct impact on the investment activity in the economy. If industries need fresh investments, they need adequate funds, as inadequate availability of funds may hamper the industrial growth.

2. **Provides Liquidity**

   Money is the most liquid financial asset. Money has time value and inflation erodes its value. That is why one always prefers to invest the funds in financial instruments like stocks, bonds, and debentures. However, these instruments are relatively more risky and less liquid. Financial system provides an opportunity to the investor to liquidate the investments whenever the investor desires.

3. **Facilitates Exchange**

   The financial system facilitates exchange of money and financial claims by offering a very convenient mode of payment for goods and services. Cheques, demand drafts, credit cards, and debit cards are the easiest methods of payments.

4. **Risk Management**

   A well-developed financial system helps in managing risk by providing various instruments, tools, and techniques of risk management.

5. **Regulates Markets**

   Regulation is essential for nurturing and developing any system in an organized stream. Thus, a financial system invariably has well-developed regulatory mechanism which regulates the financial markets in a systematic manner. In India there are many regulators like Reserve Bank of India (RBI), Securities and Exchange Board of India (SEBI), Insurance Regulatory and Development Authority (IRDA), Pension Fund Regulatory and Development Authority (PFRDA), and Board of Financial Supervision (BFS).

The organized financial system is one which comes into being by an Act and legislation. It works under preset rules, regulations, and norms and adopts transparency and accountability. On the other hand, unorganized financial system represents monetized and non-monetized sectors especially in rural area. It operates at local level, on local needs and local collaterals. It is a fact that there is significant presence of unorganized financial system in the country.

The following sections discuss:

1. Financial markets.
2. Financial institutions, banks and mutual funds, and NBFCs.
3. Intermediaries and instruments.

FINANCIAL MARKETS

A financial market is defined as the market in which financial assets are created and exchanged for a consideration. Financial assets represent a claim to the payment of a single sum of money at some point of time in the future and/or multiple payments in the form of interest or dividend spread over many time periods. Financial markets can be classified as:

1. Primary market.
2. Secondary market.

The financial markets are further classified into:

1. Money market.
2. Capital market.
3. Forex market.
4. Derivatives market.

Money Market

The segment of the financial markets, which deals with transactions in short-term instruments (with a period of maturity of 1 year or less like treasury bills, and bills of exchange) is called the money market.

Money market participants

The money market is a wholesale market. The transactions that take place in the money market are of high volumes, and involve large amounts of money. Hence, only large institutional players participate in the market. The major players in the money market are:

1. Government.
2. Central bank.
3. Commercial banks.
4. Financial institutions.
5. Corporates.

The government is active and the biggest borrower in the money market. It needs funds to meet the fiscal requirements.

The central bank of the country, that is, the Reserve Bank of India (RBI) operates on behalf of the government. It issues government securities to finance the deficit and sometimes also underwrites the issues of the government. Commercial banks act as borrowers/lenders in the money market. Banks are required to maintain statutory liquid reserves and cash reserves with RBI.

Financial institutions like Life Insurance Corporation of India (LIC), General Insurance Corporation of India (GIC), and Industrial Development Bank of India (IDBI) also act as borrowers or lenders in the money market depending upon the requirements. In addition to these institutions, mutual funds and foreign institutional investors (FIIs) also participate in the money market as investors or lenders. The level of participation of these players is mainly dependent on the limits prescribed by the RBI. For instance, FIIs can participate in the Indian money market by way of investment in government securities only. Corporates participate in the money market as borrowers of fund for working capital requirements.

In addition to these players, there are some specialized institutions like the Discount and Finance House of India (DFHI) and some primary dealers which also participate in the money market. DFHI provides the much needed liquidity by acting as a financier whereas primary dealers act as market makers by providing two-way quotes for the instruments traded in the money market thus enhancing the liquidity in the market.

Capital Markets

Capital market deals with transactions related to long-term instruments (with a period of maturity of above 1 year like corporate debentures and government bonds) and stock (equity and preference shares).

Market structure

The capital market consists of the primary market and the secondary market (see Figure 1.2). The primary market is used to create long-term instruments through which corporates can

Figure 1.2 Structure of the Indian Capital Market

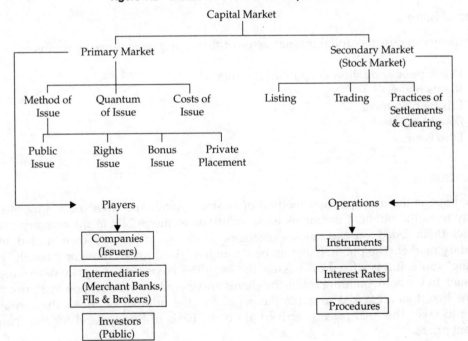

Source: Kothari and Dutta (2005).

raise capital/loans from the capital market. On the other hand, secondary market provides liquidity and marketability to these instruments. An active and buoyant secondary market attracts investors to the new issue market, thereby facilitating easy access to corporates to raise capital from the market.

Primary market

Capital Issue Control Act, 1947 controlled the issue and pricing of the capital issues by companies till 1992 when the CCI Act was repealed, and SEBI was made the apex regulatory authority in the capital markets.

SEBI has issued elaborate guidelines on matters relating to public issues, rights issues, bonus issues, issue of debentures, underwriting, private placement, pricing of issues, and so on. These guidelines virtually affect all activities relating to capital issues. Under the new guidelines, no prior approval of SEBI is required by the companies for raising capital through public issues/rights issues subject to the fulfillment of certain criteria.

A company, while raising its capital through issues in the capital market, must comply with the guidelines, and clarifications issued by SEBI and the provisions of the Companies Act, 1956. According to the Companies Act, 1956, a company should comply with the provisions relating to prospectus, allotment, issue of shares at premium/discount, further issue of capital, and so on.

Types of issue

A company can raise its capital through issue of shares and debentures by means of:

1. Public issue and follow-on public offer (FPO)
2. Rights issue
3. Private placement
4. Bought-out deal
5. Euro issue.

Public issue

Public issue is the most popular method of raising capital, and involves raising of funds directly from the public. Companies issue securities to the public in the primary market, and get them listed on the stock exchanges. These securities are then traded in the secondary market. The public issue can be through a "fixed price" route or through "book-building" route. If it is a fixed price issue, the securities are issued at a price determined by the issuer. In the book-building route, the shares are offered for subscription in a price band, and the investors are asked to quote the price, and the number of shares they would be willing to take. The final price is arrived at on the basis of the demand for the shares at different prices.

Rights issue

According to Section 81 of the Companies Act, 1956, when a firm issues additional equity capital, the existing shareholders have a pre-emptive right on such capital issue, on a pro rata basis. The rights offer is to be kept open for a period of 60 days, and should be announced within one month of the closure of the books. It is proposed that 60 days should be reduced to 43 days. The shareholders have the option to renounce their rights, in favor of any other person at the market-determined rate. The cost of floating the rights issue is comparatively less than the public issue, since these securities are issued to the existing shareholders, thereby, eliminating the marketing costs and other relevant public issue expenses.

Private placement

The private placement method of financing involves direct selling of securities to a limited number of institutional or high net worth investors. As the company is not approaching the public at large, it saves on various statutory and non-statutory expenses, and also saves a lot of time, as in private placement the maximum time required is 2–3 months. This avoids the delay involved in going to public and also reduces the expenses involved in a public issue. The companies appoint a merchant banker to network with the institutional investors and negotiate the price of the issue.

Bought-out deals

Bought-out is a process whereby an investor or a group of investors buy out a significant portion of the equity of an unlisted company with a view to selling the equity to public within an agreed time frame. The company places the equity shares, to be offered to the public, with a sponsor. At the right time, the shares will be offloaded to the public by way of a public issue.

Euro issues

Indian companies have been permitted to float their stocks in foreign capital markets. The Indian corporates, which face high rates of interest in the domestic markets, are now free to tap the global capital markets for meeting resource requirements at less costs and administrative problems. The instruments, which the company can issue, are global depository receipts (GDRs), American depository receipts (ADRs), euro-convertible bonds (ECBs), foreign currency convertible bonds (FCCBs).

Secondary market

The secondary market is that segment of the capital market where the outstanding securities are traded. The secondary market imparts liquidity to the long-term securities held by the investors. The secondary market operates through stock exchanges. The stock market is a pivotal institution in the financial system. A well-ordered stock market performs several economic functions like translating short-term and medium-term investments into long-term funds for companies, and directing the flow of capital in the most profitable channels.

Capital market participants

Capital market participants include brokers, underwriters, registrars to issue (one who takes care of applications, share certificates, allotment, refund, and subsequent transfer of shares and securities), bankers, advisors, institutions (domestic and foreign), depositories, and custodian.

Forex Market

Let us consider a transaction involving supply of bed sheets and cotton skirts from India to Germany. The Indian exporter will price the bed sheets and skirts in such a manner that he would make profit in terms of Indian rupees. He would like the customer abroad to pay him in terms of rupees only. The purchasing power available with the German buyer is in the form of German marks. Thus, he would like to know how many German marks he has to part with, to buy the bed sheets and/or cotton skirts.

There is a possibility that both the seller and the buyer may agree to settle the transaction in a third currency, say, the US dollar. In that case, the buyer first needs to convert his currency into US dollars. On receipt of the payment, the seller would again convert the dollars into rupees. The market, which facilitates such transactions, is called the forex market. The rate at which one currency is converted into another currency is the rate of exchange between the two currencies concerned. The exchange rate between two currencies can be obtained from quotation in foreign exchange rate market.

According to Section 2(b) of the Foreign Exchange Regulation Act (1973), foreign exchange is defined as:

1. All deposits, credits, balance of payments in foreign currency, and any drafts, travelers' cheques, letters of credit, and bills of exchange expressed or drawn in Indian currency and payable in foreign currency.
2. Any instrument payable at the option of the drawee or holder thereof or any other party thereto, in Indian currency or in foreign currency or partly in one and partly in the other.

The international foreign exchange market geographically extends from Tokyo and Sydney, through Hong Kong, Singapore, Bahrain, the European centers, New York to the west coast of the United States. This is the world's largest market, and is operational for virtually 24 hours a day, as different countries are in different time zones. However, there is no physical location for this market where traders can get together and exchange currencies. The traders sit in their dealing rooms and communicate with each other through telephones, computer terminals, telexes, and other information channels.

Participants in the forex market

Anyone who exchanges currency of a given country for other, or who needs such services, is a participant of the forex market. Commercial banks are the main participants of the forex market. Next in importance are the large corporates with investments abroad or foreign trade activities. Lastly, central banks play an important role in maintaining the foreign reserves and payments.

1. **Commercial Banks:** Commercial banks deal with international trade transactions and offer services of converting one currency into another. Usually, the commercial banks act as intermediaries between importers and exporters, who are situated in different countries. A commercial bank, which offers services, would sell foreign currencies to importers and buy foreign currencies from exporters.

2. **Corporates:** Large corporates may participate either as exporters or as importers. Exporters may require the services of banks to convert their foreign currency receipts into domestic currency (which they obtain by means of selling the goods and services). Importers requiring payments for the goods imported by them may utilize the services of banks for converting the local currencies into foreign currencies (which they need to make payments for the goods and services they have imported).

3. **Brokers:** The forex brokers bring the seller and buyer banks together, without disclosing the name of the counterparty bank, before the deal is finalized. The forex brokers are governed by the rules framed by the Foreign Exchange Dealers Association of India (FEDAI). Brokers also render their services, by giving market information to the banks. The foreign exchange brokers in India are prohibited to deal on their own account which means they cannot acquire any position.

4. **Central Bank:** The central banks in most of the countries have the responsibility of maintaining external value of the currency of the country. If a country is following fixed exchange rate system, then the central bank has to take necessary steps to maintain the rate, even if the country is following a floating exchange rate system; the central bank needs to ensure orderliness in the movement of exchange rates by intervening in the forex market.

   In India, the responsibility and authority of administration of foreign exchange is vested with the RBI under Foreign Exchange Management Act (FEMA). Due to the vast geography and foreign exchange received and required by large number of importers and exporters, it would be impossible for the RBI to deal with everyone individually. Therefore, a provision has been made in the Act, enabling RBI to delegate its power or functions to authorized dealers or money changers, with prior approval of the central government.

5. **Authorized Dealers in Foreign Exchange:** The institutions which have been authorized by RBI to deal in foreign exchange are called authorized dealers. For example, authorizations have been granted to banks, certain financial institutions (to undertake specific types of foreign exchange transactions incidental to their main business), certain state co-operative/urban co-operative banks and scheduled commercial banks (to open and

maintain ordinary Non-Resident Rupee Accounts [NRO Accounts] and Non-Resident [External] Rupee Accounts [NRE Accounts] on behalf of non-resident individuals of Indian nationality or origin).

6. **Authorized Money Changers:** In order to facilitate the encashment of foreign currency to visitors from abroad, especially foreign tourists, RBI has granted licenses to certain established firms, hotels and other organizations permitting them to deal in foreign currency notes, coins, and traveler's cheques subject to directions issued to them from time to time. These firms and organizations are known as "authorized money changers." The money changers can be of two types:

   i. Full-fledged money changers, who are authorized to undertake both purchase and sale transactions with public.

   ii. Restricted money changers, who are authorized only to purchase foreign currency notes, coins, and traveler's cheques, subject to the condition that all such collections are surrendered by them in turn to an authorized dealer in foreign exchange.

Derivatives Market

The word "derivative" means something, which has been derived from the other. Hence, derivatives market has no independent existence without an underlying asset. The price of derivative instrument is dependent upon the value of its underlying asset.

Derivatives are designed to manage risks. The derivatives market enable institutional investors, bank treasurers, and corporates to manage their risk more efficiently and allow them to hedge or speculate on markets.

Participants in the derivatives market

Generally banks, corporates, financial institutions, individuals, and brokers are seen as regular participants. The derivatives market allow the participants to hedge, speculate, or arbitrage in the markets. The participants can be classified into three categories based on the motives and strategies adopted.

1. **Hedgers:** Hedging is an act whereby an investor seeks to protect a position or anticipates a position in the spot market by using an opposite position in derivatives. The parties, which perform hedging, are known as hedgers. In the process of hedging, parties such as individuals or companies owning or planning to own a cash or commodity (such as corn, pepper, wheat, treasury bonds, notes, and bills) are concerned that the cost of the commodity may change before either buying or selling it in the cash market. They want to reduce or limit the impact of such movements, which, if not covered, would incur a loss.

2. **Speculators:** Speculators are basically traders, who enter the contract with a view to make profit from the subsequent price movements. They do not have any risk to hedge; in fact, they operate at a high level of risk in anticipation of profits. The speculators

also perform a valuable economic function of feeding information, which is not readily available elsewhere, and help others in analyzing the derivatives market.

3. **Arbitrageurs:** The act of obtaining risk-free profits by simultaneously buying and selling similar instruments in different markets is known as "arbitrage." The person who does this activity is referred to as an "arbitrageur." For example, one may always sell a stock on National Stock Exchange (NSE) and buy on Bombay Stock Exchange (BSE). The arbitrageurs continuously monitor various markets and whenever there is a chance of arbitraging, they buy from one market and sell it in the other and make riskless profit. They keep the prices of derivatives and current underlying assets closely consistent, thereby performing a very valuable economic function.

Types of derivative instruments

Derivatives can be classified into two categories based on the nature of the contract:

1. Futures.
2. Options.

Futures

A futures contract is a contract which conveys an agreement to buy or sell a specific amount of a commodity or financial instrument at a particular price, on a stipulated future date. A futures contract obligates the buyer to purchase the underlying instrument and the seller to sell it, unless the contract is sold to another before settlement date, which may happen in order to make a profit or limit a loss.

Futures contracts are highly uniform, and well-specified commitments for a carefully described commodity to be delivered at a certain time, and in a certain manner. It also specifies the quantity and quality of the commodity that can be delivered, to fulfill the futures contract. The quality specifications become less relevant, in case of futures on interest rates or currencies. The futures contracts are always traded on an organized exchange, with standardized terms of contract. The trading is usually done through brokers. A trader can trade on his own account also. However, most of the traders act as brokers, and trade on behalf of clients.

The clearing house ensures smooth and effective functioning of the futures market. It guarantees that all the traders in the futures market honor their obligations. Though, it does not take any active position in the market, it interposes itself between all parties to every transaction. It insists on margin and daily settlement, for safeguarding the interests of both the parties to perform their contractual obligations.

Options

Option is a contract that confers the right, but not an obligation to the holder to buy (call option) or to sell (put option) an underlying asset (the asset may be a stock, currency, commodity, financial instrument, or a futures contract) at a price agreed on a specific date or by a specific expiry date. The seller or writer of the option has the obligation to fulfill the contract, if the holder wishes to exercise the option, for which a premium is paid.

Every exchange-traded option is either a call option or a put option. Options are created by selling and buying, and for every option there is a seller and a buyer. The seller of an option is also known as option writer. In option contracts, all the rights lie with the option buyer.

As is obvious from the Figure 1.3, the seller always acquires an obligation and the buyer always acquires a right. Hence, the buyer pays the seller a certain amount upfront, which is known as premium.

Figure 1.3   An Overview of Option Trading

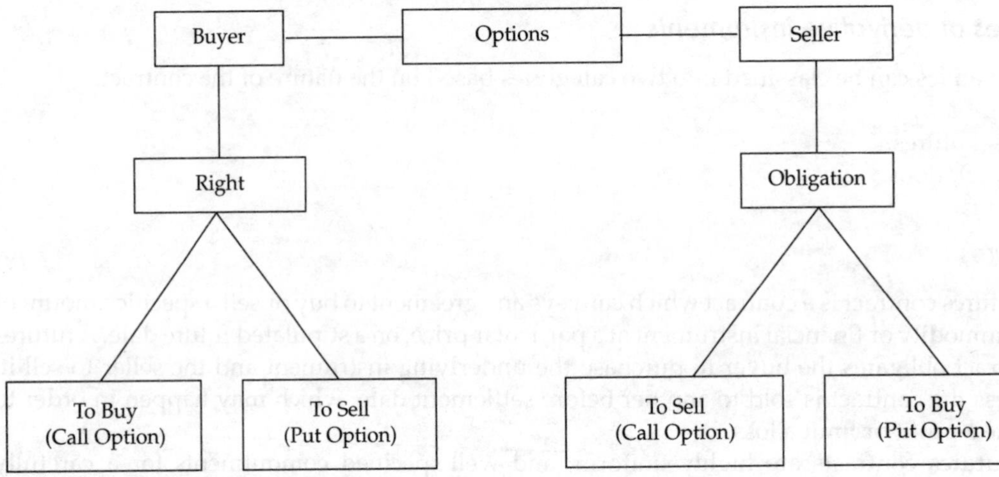

Source: Kothari and Dutta (2005).

FINANCIAL INSTITUTIONS, BANKS AND MUTUAL FUNDS, AND NBFCs

Developmental Financial Institutions (DFIs)

DFIs work as catalyst for growth. Some of the prominent DFIs working in India are as follows:

1. **Industrial Development Bank of India (IDBI)**
   Industrial Development Bank of India (IDBI) was established in 1964, as a subsidiary of the RBI by an Act of the parliament, and was made a wholly owned Government of India undertaking in 1975. It was established with the main objective of serving as an apex financial institution to coordinate the functioning of all other financial institutions. IDBI provided financial assistance for the establishment of new projects as well as for expansion, diversification, modernization, and technology upgradation of existing

industrial enterprises. IDBI was vested with the responsibility of coordinating the working of institutions engaged in financing, promoting, and developing industries. It had evolved an appropriate mechanism for this purpose. IDBI also undertook/supported wide-ranging promotional activities including entrepreneurship development programs for new entrepreneurs, provision of consultancy services for small and medium enterprises, upgradation of technology and programs for economic upliftment of the underprivileged. Recently, IDBI has merged its subsidiary IDBI Bank with itself.

2. **Industrial Finance Corporation of India (IFCI)**
At the time of independence in 1947, India's capital market was relatively underdeveloped. Although, there was significant demand for new capital, there was a dearth of providers. Merchant bankers and underwriting firms were almost non-existent and commercial banks were not equipped to provide long-term industrial finance in any significant manner.

It is against this backdrop that the government established the Industrial Finance Corporation of India (IFCI) on July 1, 1948, as the first DFI in the country, to cater to the long-term finance needs of the industrial sector. The newly-established DFI was provided access to low-cost funds, through the central bank's Statutory Liquidity Ratio or SLR, which in turn enabled it to provide loans and advances to corporate borrowers at concessional rates.

This arrangement continued till the early 1990s, when it was recognized that there was need for greater flexibility to respond to the changing financial system. It was also felt that IFCI should directly access the capital markets, for its funds needs. It is with this objective that the constitution of IFCI was changed in 1993, from a statutory corporation to a company under the Indian Companies Act, 1956. Subsequently, the name of the company was also changed to "IFCI Limited" with effect from October 1993.

3. **Industrial Credit and Investment Corporation of India (ICICI)**
The Industrial Credit and Investment Corporation of India (ICICI) was established in 1955, with the objective of providing finance to the industries in the private sector. It was incorporated under the Companies Act. Even though the IFCI existed at that time, the need was felt for a separate financial institution to provide finance to the private sector, especially in foreign currency. The ICICI was started as a private sector financial institution, unlike the IFCI. However, as the banks and insurance companies that were holding the shares were nationalized, the central government came to own a substantial holding in the company through them. The ICICI is widely known for its flexible approach in financing. It has ventured recently into leasing, guaranteeing for export obligations, and performance guarantees. It was merged with the ICICI Bank in May 2002.

4. **Industrial Investment Bank of India (IIBI)**
The IIBI first came into existence as a central government corporation, with the name Industrial Reconstruction Corporation of India in 1971. Its basic objective was to finance the reconstruction, and rehabilitation of sick and closed industrial units. Its name was

changed to Industrial Reconstruction Bank of India and it was made the principal credit and reconstruction agency in the country in 1985, through the Industrial Reconstruction Bank of India (IRBI) Act, 1984. The bank started coordinating similar work of other institutions and banks, preparing schemes for reconstruction by restructuring the liabilities, appraising schemes of mergers and amalgamation of sick companies, and providing financial assistance for modernization, expansion, diversification, and technological upgradation of sick units.

In March 1997, in line with the ongoing policies of financial and economic reforms, IRBI was converted into a full-fledged DFI. It was renamed as Industrial Investment Bank of India Limited, and was incorporated as a company under the Companies Act, 1956. Its entire equity is currently being held by the Government of India. Its activities include, providing finance for the establishment of new industrial projects as well as for expansion, diversification, and modernization of existing industrial enterprises. It provides financial assistance in the form of term loans, subscription to debentures/equity shares, and deferred payment guarantees. IIBI is now also active in merchant banking and its services include, inter alia, structuring of suitable instruments for public/rights issues, preparing prospectus/offer documents, and working as lead manager. It also offers its services for debt syndication, and the entire package of services for mergers and acquisitions.

5. **Infrastructure Development Finance Corporation (IDFC)**

   The Infrastructure Development Finance Corporation (IDFC), established in 1997, is a specialized financial institution, set up to provide credit enhancement to infrastructure projects, and to extend long-term loans and guarantees that existing institutions may not be able to provide. IDFC provides loans and guarantees worth USD 17 million to five projects.

   IDFC has also broadened its initial focus on power, roads, ports, and telecommunications to a framework of energy, telecommunications and information technology, integrated transportation, urban infrastructure, health care, food and agri-business infrastructure, education infrastructure, and tourism. In its sectors of engagement, IDFC has been awarded lead arranger mandates and key advisory assignments.

   The Asian Development Bank and the International Finance Corporation are shareholders in the IDFC. A comprehensive funding package for infrastructure projects has been developed by the IDFC and the Power Finance Corporation (PFC). At the state level, the PFC is primarily focused on public sector projects, while the IDFC concentrates on the private sector.

   See Table 1.1 for more details on DFIS.

Specialized Financial Institutions

The Export-Import Bank of India (EXIM Bank)

The Export-Import Bank of India (Exim Bank) is a public sector financial institution, created by an Act of parliament, the Export-Import Bank of India Act, 1981. The business of Exim Bank is to finance Indian exports that lead to continuity of foreign exchange for India. The bank's

Table 1.1 Development Financial Institutions (Year of Establishment)

All-India Development Banks
1. IDBI (1964)
2. ICICI Bank (formerly ICICI) (1955)
3. SIBDI (1990)
4. IIBI (1997)
5. IFCI (1948)

Specialized Financial Institutions
1. EXIM Bank (1982)
2. Infrastructure Leasing & Financial Services (IL&FS) Venture Cap. (1988)
3. ICICI Venture (1988)
4. Tourism Finance Corporation of India (TFCI) (1989).
5. IDFC (1997)

Investment Institutions
1. UTI (1964)
2. LIC (1956)
3. GIC and Subsidiaries (1972)

Refinance Institutions
1. National Bank for Agriculture and Rural Development (NABARD) (1982)
2. National Housing Bank (NSB) (1980)

State-Level Institutions
1. State Financial Corps.: 18 nos.
2. State Industrial Development Corps.: 28 nos.

Other Institutions
1. Export Credit Guarantee Corporation of India (ECGC) (1957)
2. Deposit Insurance and Credit Guarantee Corporation (DICGC) (1962)

Source: Indian Finance Review, BSE Publication, 2003.

primary objective is to develop commercially viable relationships, with a target set of externally oriented companies by offering them a comprehensive range of products and services, aimed at enhancing their internationalization efforts.

Exim Bank provides a range of analytical information and export-related services. The bank's fee-based services help identify new business propositions, source trade and investment-related information, create and enhance presence through joint network of institutional linkages across the globe, and assist externally oriented companies in their quest for excellence and globalization. Services include search for overseas partners, identification of technology suppliers, negotiating alliances, and development of joint ventures in India, and abroad. The bank also supports Indian project exporters and consultants to participate in projects funded by multilateral funding agencies.

State-level Financial Institutions

1. **State Financial Corporations (SFCs)**
   At the beginning of the 1950s, the government found that for achieving rapid industrialization, separate institutions should be set up that cater exclusively to the needs of the small and medium sector. Consequently, legislation was promoted by the Government

of India, for the setting up of financial corporations and the State Financial Corporation Act, 1951 came into force on August 1, 1952. The SFC's were closely modeled on the line of IFCI, but were intended to serve the financial requirements of small and medium sized enterprises. The SFC's provide finance in the form of term loans, by underwriting issues of shares and debentures, by subscribing to debentures, and standing guarantee for loans raised from other institutions and from the general public.

2. **State Industrial Development Corporations (SIDCs)**
   The state industrial development corporations (SIDC's) have been set up to facilitate rapid industrial growth in the respective states. In addition to providing finance, the SIDC's identify and sponsor projects in the joint sector with the participation of private entrepreneurs. For example, Rajasthan State Industrial Development and Investment Corporation (RIICO) in Rajasthan, Gujarat Industrial Development Corporation (GIDC) in Gujarat, and Punjab Industrial Development Corporation (PIDC) in Punjab are SIDCs and are promoting industrial development in respective states.

Investment Institutions

1. **Life Insurance Corporation of India (LIC)**
   The LIC was established in 1956, by amalgamation and nationalization of 245 private insurance companies by an enactment of the parliament. The main business of the LIC is to provide life insurance. With the opening up of the insurance sector, the monopoly of LIC has ended.

2. **General Insurance Corporation of India (GIC)**
   The entire general insurance business in India, was nationalized by General Insurance Business Nationalization Act, 1972 (GIBNA). The Government of India, through nationalization, took over the shares of 55 Indian insurance companies, and the undertakings of 52 insurers carrying on general insurance business. General Insurance Corporation of India (GIC) was formed in pursuance of Section 9(1) of GIBNA. It was incorporated on November 22, 1972 under the Companies Act, 1956 as a private company limited by shares. GIC was formed for the purpose of superintending, controlling, and carrying on the business of general insurance.

   On April 19, 2000, when the Insurance Regulatory and Development Authority Act, 1999 (IRDA) came into force, it introduced amendment to GIBNA and the Insurance Act, 1938. An amendment to GIBNA removed the exclusive privilege of GIC, and its subsidiaries from carrying on general insurance in India. Now many general insurance companies in the private sector are there, like Allianz Bajaj, Tata AIG General Insurance, and ICICI Lombard General Insurance. With the General Insurance Business (Nationalization) Amendment Act, 2002 (40 of 2002) coming into force from March 21, 2002, GIC ceased to be a holding company of its subsidiaries. Their ownership was vested with Government of India.

3. **Unit Trust of India (UTI)**

The impetus for establishing a formal institution came from the desire to increase the propensity of the middle, and lower groups to save and to invest. UTI came into existence during a period marked by great political, and economic uncertainty in India. Earnest efforts were required to canalize savings of the community, into productive uses in order to speed up the process of industrial growth. The UTI was founded in 1964, under the Unit Trust of India Act, 1963. Initially 50 percent of the capital of the trust was contributed by the RBI, while the rest was brought in by the State Bank of India and its associates, LIC, GIC, and other financial institutions. In 1974, the holding of the RBI was transferred to the IDBI, making the UTI an associate of the IDBI. In January 2003, UTI was split into two parts: UTI-I and UTI-II. UTI-I has been given all the assured return schemes, and Unit Scheme 64, and it is being administered by the central government. UTI-II is entrusted with the task of managing net asset value (NAV)-based schemes. UTI-II is being managed by State Bank of India, Punjab National Bank, Bank of Baroda, and Life Insurance Corporations.

Mutual Funds

Mutual funds serve the purpose of mobilization of funds from various categories of investors, and channelizing them into productive investment. Apart from UTI, mutual funds sponsored by various bank subsidiaries, insurance organizations, and private sector financial institutions have come up. These mutual funds operate within the framework of SEBI regulations, which prescribe the mechanism for setting up of a mutual fund, procedure of registration, its constitution, and the duties, functions, and the responsibility of the various parties involved.

Banking System

Banking in India has its origin as early as the Vedic period. It is believed that the transition from money lending to banking must have occurred even before Manu, the great Hindu Jurist, who has devoted a section of his work to deposits and advances and laid down rules relating to rates of interest. During the Mogul period, the indigenous bankers played a very important role in lending money and financing foreign trade and commerce. During the days of the East India Company, it was the turn of the agency houses to carry on the banking business. The General Bank of India was the first Joint Stock Bank to be established in the year 1786. The others which followed were the Bank of Hindustan and the Bengal Bank. Today the commercial banking system in India may be divided into (see Figure 1.4):

1. Public Sector Banks
   i.   State Bank of India and its associate banks called the State Bank Group.
   ii. Twenty nationalized banks.
   iii. Regional rural banks mainly sponsored by public sector banks.

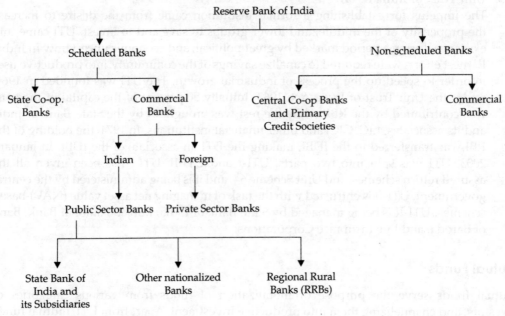

Figure 1.4 Structure of the Banking System in India

Source: Kothari and Dutta (2005).

2. Private Sector Banks
   i.   Old generation private banks.
   ii. New generation private banks.
   iii. Foreign banks in India.
   iv. Scheduled co-operative banks.
   v.   Non-scheduled banks.

Non-banking Finance Company

A non-banking finance company (NBFC) is one, which cannot accept deposits like a banking company. NBFC's can be classified as follows:

1. Investment trusts or investment companies.
2. *Nidhis* or mutual benefit funds or mutual benefit finance companies.
3. Merchant banks.
4. Hire-purchase finance companies.
5. Lease finance companies or leasing or equipment leasing companies.
6. Housing finance institutions (companies).
7. Venture capital funds.
8. Factors or factoring companies.

Investment trusts or investment companies

Investment trusts are close-ended organizations, unlike UTI, and they have a fixed amount of authorized capital, and a stated amount of issued capital. Investment trusts provide useful services, through conserving and managing property for those who, for some reasons or other cannot manage their own affairs. Investors of moderate means are provided facilities for diversification of investment, expert advice on lucrative investment channels, and supervision of their investment. From the point of view of the economy, they help to mobilize small savings and direct them to fruitful channels. Most of these companies are not independent; they are investment-holding companies, formed by the former managing agents, or business houses. As such, they provide finance mainly to such companies that are associated with these business houses.

Nidhis

Mutual benefit funds or *nidhis*, as they are called in India, are joint stock companies, operating mainly in south India, particularly in Tamil Nadu. The sources of their funds are share capital, deposits from their members, and the public. The deposits are fixed and recurring. Unlike other NBFCs, *nidhis* also accept demand deposits to some extent. The loans given by these institutions are mainly for consumption purposes. These loans are usually secured loans, given against the security of tangible assets such as house property, gold, jewelry, or against shares of companies, LIC policies, and so on. The terms on which loans are given are quite moderate. They are incorporated bodies and are governed by the directives of the RBI.

Merchant banks

Merchant banks mainly offer financial advice, and services for a fee, unlike commercial banks, which accept deposits and lend money. When merchant banks do function as commercial banks, they function essentially as, wholesale bankers. They provide a range of services like management, marketing, and underwriting of new issues; project promotion services and project finance; syndication of credit and other facilities; leasing, including project leasing; corporate advisory services; investment advisory services; bought-out deals; venture capital; mutual funds and offshore funds; investment management including, discretionary management; assistance for technical and financial collaboration and joint ventures; investment services for non-resident Indians; and management of and dealing in commercial paper. In India, the merchant banking services are provided by the commercial banks, all-India financial institutions, private consultancy firms, and technical consultation organizations. Apart from these institutions, professional merchant banking houses are slowly coming up in India.

Hire-purchase finance companies

Hire-purchase involves a system under which, term loans for purchases of goods and services are advanced to be liquidated in stages, through a contractual obligation. The goods whose purchases are thus financed, may be consumer goods or producer goods or they may be simply services, such as air travel. Hire-purchase credit may be provided by the seller himself or by any financial institution. Hire-purchase credit is available in India, for a wide range of products and services like automobiles, sewing machines, radios, refrigerators, TV sets, bicycles, machinery and equipment, other capital goods, industrial sheds; services like educational fees, medical fees, and so on. However, unlike in other countries, the emphasis in India is on the provision of installment credit for productive goods, and services rather than for purely consumer goods. Suppliers of hire-purchase finance include retail and wholesale traders, commercial banks, IDBI, ICICI, National Small Industries Corporation (NSIC), National Small Industries Development Corporation (NSIDC), State Financial Corporations (SFCS), State Industrial Development Corporation (SIDCS), Agro-Industries Corporations (AIC's), and so on. In the recent past, banks also have increased their business in the field of installment credit and consumer loans.

Lease finance companies

Lease finance companies provide finance to acquire the use of assets, for a stated period of time without owning them. The user of the asset is known as the lessee, and the owner of the asset is known as the lessor. Lease financing organizations in India include NBFCs like Infrastructure Leasing and Financial Services Ltd. (IL&FS), ICICI, certain SIDCs and Small Industrial Investment Corporation (SIICs), and other organizations.

Housing finance companies

These companies provide finance for construction/purchase of land and buildings. Housing finance is provided in the form of mortgage loans, that is, it is provided against the security of immovable property of land and buildings. Basically, housing finance loans are given by the Housing and Urban Development Corporation (HUDCO), the apex co-operative housing finance societies and housing boards in different states, central and state governments, LIC, commercial banks, GIC, and a few private housing finance companies like Housing Development Finance Corporation Limited (HDFC), Deewan Housing Finance, and *nidhi*s.

Venture capital funding companies

Venture capital is money provided by professionals, who invest alongside management in young, rapidly growing companies that have the potential to develop into significant economic contributors. Venture capital is an important source of equity for start-up companies. Professionally managed venture capital firms generally are, private partnerships or closely held corporations funded by private, and public pension funds, endowment funds, foundations, corporations, wealthy individuals, foreign investors, and the venture capitalists themselves.

Factoring companies

Factoring is a financing technique in which, a business sells invoiced receivables at a discount to a bank or a financing house or to an internal finance company. The factor may or may not accept the incumbent credit risk. This is a service offered by a factoring company that enables companies to sell their outstanding book debts for cash. Factoring is an ongoing arrangement between the client and the factor, where invoices raised on open account sales of goods, and services are regularly assigned to "the factor" for financing, collection, and sales ledger administration. Usually it is an arrangement used when the buyer, and the seller have long-term relationships. At times even the whole turnover of the company may be assigned to the factor. In India, factoring business is still in its nascent stage. Some of the firms offering factoring services include CanBank Factor, SBI Factors, and Hongkong & Shanghai Banking Corporation (HSBC).

FINANCIAL INTERMEDIARIES AND INSTRUMENTS

Financial intermediation in the organized sector is conducted by a wide range of institutions, functioning under the overall surveillance of regulators like RBI, SEBI, IRDA, and Pension Fund and Development Regulatory (PFDRA). In the initial stages, the role of the inter-mediary was mostly related to ensure transfer of funds from the lender to the borrower. This service was offered by banks, financial institutions, brokers, and dealers. However, as the financial system widened along with the developments taking place in the financial markets, the scope of financial intermediation is also widened.

Some of the important intermediaries operating in the financial markets include invest-ment bankers; underwriters, stock exchanges, registrars, depositories, custodians, portfolio managers, mutual funds, financial advisors, financial consultants, primary dealers, satellite dealers, and self-regulatory organizations (see Table 1.2). Though the markets are different, there may be a few intermediaries offering their services in more than one market, for example underwriters. However, the services offered by them vary from one market to another market.

Table 1.2   A Summarized View of Intermediaries

Intermediary	Market	Role
Stock Exchange	Capital market	Secondary market to securities
Investment Bankers	Capital market, credit market	Corporate advisory services, issues of securities
Underwriters	Capital market, money market	Subscribe to unsubscribed portion of securities
Registrars, Depositories, Custodians	Capital market	Issue securities to the investors on behalf of the company and handle share transfer activity
Primary Dealers	Money market	Market making in government securities
Satellite Dealers	Capital market	Securities
Forex Dealers	Forex market	Ensure exchange in currencies

Source: Author.

Financial Instruments

Instruments are documentary evidence of financial transaction. They represent values. The following section discusses the instruments in money and capital market.

Money market instruments

Call money/Notice money market

The money market is a market for short-term financial assets that are close substitutes of money. The most important feature of call money market instrument is that, it is liquid and provides an avenue for equilibrating the short-term surplus funds of lenders, and the requirements of borrowers. The call/notice money market forms an important segment of the Indian money market. Under call money market, funds are transacted on overnight basis and under notice money market, funds are transacted for a period from 2 days to 14 days.

Participants in call/notice money market currently include banks, primary dealers (PD's), DFI's, insurance companies, and select mutual funds. Of these, banks and PD's can operate as both borrowers and lenders in the market. However, non-bank institutions, which have been given specific permission to operate in call/notice money market, can operate as lenders only (Table 1.3). Eligible participants are free to decide on interest rates in call/notice money market.

Table 1.3 Eligibility for Transactions in Call/Notice Money Market

Borrowing	Lending
1. Scheduled Commercial Banks	1. Scheduled Commercial Banks
2. Co-operative Banks	2. Co-operative Banks
3. Primary Dealers (PDs)	3. Primary Dealers (PDs)
	4. Select All-India Financial Institutions
	5. Select Insurance Companies
	6. Select Mutual Funds

Source: Kothari and Dutta (2005).

Treasury bills

Treasury bills (T-bills) are issued by RBI on behalf of Government of India, to meet the short-term funds requirements of the government. T-bills also help RBI to perform open market operations, which help in regulating the money supply in the economy.

T-bills can be issued in physical form or credited to investors' Subsidiary General Ledger Account (SGL) in electronic form. They are issued for a minimum amount of Rs 25,000 and in multiples thereof. They do not carry any coupon rate, and are issued at a discount to their face value and redeemed at par.

Earlier RBI used to issue 14-day, 91-day, 182-day, and 364-day T-bills. However, as per the monetary and credit policy of April 2001, the 14-day and 182-day T-bills have been discontinued. Instead, the notified amount of 91-day T-bills auction has been increased to Rs 250 crore w.e.f. May 14, 2001. The notified amount of 364-day T-bills has been increased from Rs 750 crore to Rs 1,000 crore w.e.f. April 3, 2002.

Types of T-bills:

  i. **Ad-hoc T-bills:** These T-bills were issued in favor of RBI, whenever Government of India needed cash. They were neither issued nor available to public. These bills were purchased by RBI, and were held in its issue department.

Ad-hoc T-bills had a maturity period of 91 days and carried a discount rate of 4.6 percent. However, subsequent to an agreement between Government of India and RBI in March 1997, ad-hoc T-bills were replaced by Ways and Means Advances (WMA) for financing the government deficit.

ii. **On tap T-bills:** These T-bills were issued on all working days and there was no limit on the amount of investment in these securities. The maturity period was 91 days and discount rate was 4.6 percent. They were redeemable at par value on maturity.

State governments, banks, and provident funds used these T-bills as a liquidity management tool. However, these were also discontinued w.e.f. April 1, 2001.

iii. **Auctioned T-bills:** The 91-day T-bills and 364-day T-bills are auctioned w.e.f. January 1993. The 91-day T-bills are auctioned weekly on Fridays whereas 364-day T-bills are auctioned every alternative week on Wednesday. RBI announces the date and notifies amount of auction in advance. Bidders who participate in these auctions can be competitive or non-competitive. Non-competitive bidders like state governments submit only one bid. These bids are accepted at the weighted average of the successful bids if the notified amount is not fully subscribed.

Commercial paper (CP)

Commercial paper (CP) is an unsecured money market instrument issued either in the form of a promissory note (Schedule I) or in a dematerialized form through any of the depositories approved by and registered with SEBI. CP is issued at a discount to face value as may be determined by the issuer. No issuer can have the issue of CP underwritten or co-accepted. CP, as a privately placed instrument, was introduced in India in 1990 with a view to enabling highly rated corporate borrowers to diversify their sources of short-term borrowings and to provide an additional instrument to investors. Corporates and primary dealers (PDs) and the all-India financial institutions that have been permitted to raise short-term resources under the umbrella limit fixed by RBI are eligible to issue CP.

A corporate would be eligible to issue CP provided: (a) the tangible net worth of the company, as per the latest audited balance sheet, is not less than Rs. 4 crore; (b) company has been sanctioned working capital limit by bank(s) or all-India financial institution(s); and (c) the borrowed account of the company is classified as a standard asset by the financing bank(s) or institution(s).

All eligible participants are required to obtain the credit rating for issuance of CP from either the Credit Rating Information Services of India Ltd. (CRISIL) or the Investment Information and Credit Rating Agency of India Ltd (ICRA) or the Credit Analysis & Research Ltd. (CARE) or the FITCH Ratings India Pvt. Ltd or such other credit rating agencies as may be specified by the RBI from time to time, for the purpose. The minimum credit rating should be P-2 of CRISIL or such equivalent rating by other agencies.

CP can be issued for maturities between a minimum of 15 days and a maximum of up to 1 year from the date of issue. The maturity date of the CP should not go beyond the date up to which the credit rating of the issuer is valid. CP can be issued in denominations of Rs. 5 lakh or multiples thereof. Amount invested by a single investor should not be less than Rs. 5 lakh (face value).

CP may be issued to and held by individuals, banking companies, other corporate bodies registered or incorporated in India and unincorporated bodies, non-resident Indians (NRIs), and FIIs. However, investment by FIIs would be within the limits set for their investments by SEBI.

Certificate of deposit (CD)

Certificates of deposit (CDs) is a negotiable money market instrument and issued in dematerialized form or as a usance promissory note, for funds deposited at a bank or other eligible financial institution for a specified time period.

CDs can be issued by (a) scheduled commercial banks excluding regional rural banks (RRBs) and local area banks (LABs) and (b) select all-India financial institutions that have been permitted by RBI to raise short-term resources within the umbrella limit fixed by RBI.

Minimum amount of a CD should be Rs. 1 lakh, that is, the minimum deposit that could be accepted from a single subscriber should not be less than Rs. 1 lakh and in the multiples of Rs. 1 lakh thereafter. CDs may be issued at a discount on face value. Banks or financial institutions are also allowed to issue CDs on floating rate basis. The issuing bank or financial institution is free to determine the discount/coupon rate.

The maturity period of CDs issued by banks should be not less than 15 days and not more than 1 year. The FIIs can issue CDs for a period not less than 1 year and not exceeding 3 years from the date of issue.

CDs can be issued to individuals, corporations, companies, trusts, funds, associations, etc. NRIs may also subscribe to CDs, but only on non-repatriable basis which should be clearly stated on the certificate. Such CDs cannot be endorsed to another NRI in the secondary market.

Physical CDs are freely transferable by endorsement and delivery. Dematted CDs can be transferred as per the procedure applicable to other demat securities. There is no lock-in period for the CDs.

Repurchase agreements (Repo and reverse repo)

i. **Repo:** Repo means repurchase agreement or a ready forward sale, the term for a sale and repurchase agreement in money markets. It is a transaction where banks and other financial institutions raise and invest short-term funds. Under this transaction, a holder of securities, generally government bonds, sells them to investor with an agreement to repurchase them at a fixed price and date. The security "buyer" in fact lends the seller money for the period of the agreement and terms of agreement are structured to compensate him for this. Thus, while the party who sells securities with a promise to buy them back is actually borrowing money, the purchaser of securities in the first instance finds the repo in a money market investment. Whereas reverse repo is first buying a security to be sold at fixed price and fixed date. In India, repos are done in gilts. The government has limited the number of players to banks and primary dealers. Repos are much safer as the lenders hold government securities in their names and it is, therefore, a zero risk transaction, and has banks for meeting their requirements for investing in government securities. In case of repo there is no explicit rate of interest rather than an implicit interest cost in the form of higher repurchase price. The interest on repo is calculated by dividing the difference between sale and repurchase price by initial sale price. The Securities Contract Regulation Act says that any agreement for purchase of securities cannot be carried forward beyond 14 days, for lack of legal clarity it assumed that every repo transactions have to be over in 14 days. RBI makes use of repo to remove excess funds from the market. Sometimes RBI repo rate provides an indication about what interest rate should be. RBI conducts reverse repo to infuse liquidity in the market.

ii. **Repo and Reverse Repo Rates:** The repo and reverse repo rates are the overnight rates of interest that a bank pays or earns for borrowing and lending money, respectively to the RBI against/for government securities. These rates set the floor and ceiling for risk-free overnight borrowing and lending. Any loans to corporate/individual will have to be done by adding the risk premium depending on the credit rating of the borrower. The repo and reverse repo rates set the direction for other lending rates.

A rise in the reverse repo rate translates into a higher cost of borrowing for ordinary customers because if banks have the option to earn say x percent by lending risk-free to RBI, they will want to earn more when they lend to others. Also when RBI raises the reverse repo rate, it may reduce the overall liquidity available for lending to borrowers as some banks may find it attractive to lend to RBI.

Gilt edged securities

"Gilt edged" securities mean securities of the best quality. The securities issued by central or state governments, semi-government organizations like municipal corporations, autonomous institutions like port trusts, public sector units, and other quasi-government agencies are referred to as gilt edged securities. This is so because government itself guarantees the interest payments as well as principal repayment on these securities.

G-secs have a maturity period ranging from 1 to 30 years and they carry a coupon rate which is paid semi-annually. They are issued both in demat and physical form. These securities can be classified into three categories depending upon their maturities, namely, long-dated, medium-dated, and short-dated. Long-dated securities have maturities exceeding 10 years from the issue date, medium-dated securities have maturities ranging from 5 to 10 years, and short-dated securities are those, which mature within 5 years.

Government securities can be held in three forms:

1. Stock certificates.
2. Promissory notes.
3. Bearer bonds.

Normally in the money market, government securities are held in the form of promissory notes. Besides these principal forms of government securities, there are other types of securities which are floated by the government from time to time, for example, National Defense/National Savings/National Deposit Certificates, Deposit Certificates, Annuity Certificates, and Social Security Certificates.

Types of G-secs:

1. **Dated Securities:** They have fixed maturity and fixed coupon rates payable half yearly and are identified by their year of maturity. For instance, 12.50 percent GOI 2007 is a G-sec carrying a coupon of 12.50 percent and maturing in 2007.
2. **Zero Coupon Bonds:** These bonds are issued on discount and redeemed at par.
3. **Floating Rate Bonds:** They are bonds with variable interest rates with a fixed percentage over a benchmark rate. There may also be a cap and a floor rate attached, thereby fixing a maximum and minimum interest rate payable on it.
4. **Capital Indexed Bonds:** They are bonds where the interest rate is a fixed percentage over the wholesale price index. Redemption is linked to the wholesale price index.

Money market mutual funds (MMMFs)

Money market being a wholesale market, huge amounts are required for participating in the market, the minimum being Rs 10 lakh. As a result the market was beyond the reach of individual investors. MMMFs were set up to make available the benefits of investing in money markets to small investors.

MMMFs are mutual funds that invest primarily in money market instruments of very high quality and of very short maturities. MMMFs can be set up by commercial banks, RBI, and public financial institutions either directly or through their existing mutual fund subsidiaries. The guidelines with respect to mobilization of funds by MMMFs provide that only individuals are allowed to invest in such funds.

Earlier these funds were regulated by the RBI. But RBI withdrew its guidelines, w.e.f. March 7, 2000 and now they are governed by SEBI. The guidelines on MMMFs specify a minimum lock-in period of 15 days during which the investor cannot redeem his investment. The guidelines also stipulate the minimum size of the MMMF to be Rs 50 crore and this should not exceed 2 percent of the aggregate deposits of the latest accounting year in the case of banks and 2 percent of the long-term domestic borrowings in the case of public financial institutions.

Capital market instruments

A corporate can raise long-term funds through following instruments:

Equity share capital

Equity shareholders are the first to contribute to the capital, and the last to receive any return, say dividend. And even the declaration of dividend is not mandatory. However, equity shareholders enjoy voting rights, and because of voting rights, they elect the management of company, that is, board of directors who, in turn, make policy and ensure operation of the company. Equity shareholders are the main investors in the business. In practice, share-holders are the main suppliers of capital. Equity shareholders have maximum risk as neither dividend is assured nor there is any redemption of capital, since equity share is undated investment or investment for "sine die.". Investors in equity shares primary invest for capital appreciation, that is, market price is more than issue price and for dividends. Their liability is restricted to the amount of share capital they contributed to the company. Since dividend payment is not mandatory, equity capital provides the issuing firm the advantage of not having any fixed obligation but offers permanent capital with limited liability for repayment. However, the equity capital is a costlier source of finance as it is relatively more risky, the equity dividends are not tax deductible, and cost of issue is also relatively high.

Preference capital

Preference shareholders enjoy "preference" over equity shareholders on the post-tax earnings in the form of dividends; and assets in the event of liquidation. In other words, if directors decide to pay dividends to shareholders, first it will be paid to the preference shareholders and if any profits are left after that, then only equity shareholders are paid. Thus, there is no obligatory payment to the preference shareholders; and the preference dividend is not tax deductible. However, the preference shareholders earn a fixed rate of return for their dividend payment. However, they don't confer any voting rights on the preference shareholders. The Companies Act, 1956 restricts the issue of preference shares with voting rights only in the following cases:

1. There are arrears in dividends for two or more years in case of cumulative preference shares.
2. Preference dividend is due for a period of two or more consecutive preceding years.
3. In the preceding 6 years including the immediately preceding financial year, if the company has not paid the preference dividend for a period of three or more years.

Preference shares can be of following types:

1. Cumulative or non-cumulative preference shares.
2. Redeemable or perpetual preference shares.
3. Convertible or non-convertible preference shares.

For cumulative preference shares, the dividends will be paid on a cumulative basis, in case they remain unpaid in any financial year, due to insufficient profits. The company will have to pay up all the arrears of preference dividends before declaring any equity dividends. While on the other hand, the non-cumulative shares do not enjoy such right to dividend payment on cumulative basis.

Redeemable preference shares will be redeemed after a given maturity period, while the perpetual preference share capital will remain with the company forever. However, now with amendments in the Companies Act, only redeemable preference shares with a maximum maturity of 20 years can be issued.

Cumulative convertible preference (CCP) shares are issued as cumulative preference share, with 10-year maturity from the sixth year and onward, so 10 percent of CCP share would be converted into equity share every year. CCP share carries 10 percent rate of dividend.

Loan

A loan is a contractual obligation, in which the company agrees to pay a fixed rate of interest, and repayment of principal on fixed date. What share is to capital, "debenture" is to loan.

A debenture is a marketable legal contract whereby, the company promises to pay its owner, a specified rate of interest for a defined period of time, and to repay the principal at the specific date of maturity. Debentures are usually secured by a charge on the immovable properties of the company. However, the charge so created is not on certain specific assets but a floating charge.

The interest of the debenture holders is usually represented by a trustee, and this trustee (which is typically a bank or an insurance company or a firm of attorneys) is responsible for ensuring that the borrowing company fulfills the contractual obligations embodied in the contract. If the company issues debentures with a maturity period of more than 18 months, then it has to create a debenture redemption reserve (DRR), which should be at least half of the issue amount before the redemption commences. The company can also attach call and put options. With the call option the company can redeem the debentures at a certain price, before the maturity date and similarly, the put option allows the debenture holder to surrender the debentures at a certain price before the maturity period.

Debentures can be classified on the basis of conversion and security. The major types of debentures are as follows:

1. **Non-convertible Debentures (NCDs)**
   These debentures cannot be converted into equity shares, and will be redeemed at the end of the maturity period. During the life of the debenture, the investors receive semi-annual interest payments at a pre-specified rate.

2. **Fully Convertible Debentures (FCDs)**
   These debentures are converted into equity shares after a specified period of time at one stroke or in installments. These debentures may or may not carry interest till the date of conversion. In the case, of a fully established company with an established reputation and good, stable market price, FCDs are very attractive to the investors, as their bonds are getting automatically converted to shares, which may at the time of conversion be quoted much higher in the market compared to what the debenture holders paid at the time of FCD issue.

3. **Partly Convertible Debentures (PCDs)**
   In these debentures, a portion is converted into equity share capital after a specified period, whereas the non-convertible (NCD) portion of the PCD will be redeemed as per, the terms of the issue after the maturity period. The non-convertible portion of the PCD will carry interest right up to redemption whereas, the interest on the convertible portion will be only up to the date immediately preceding the date of conversion.

4. **Secured Premium Notes (SPNs)**

This is a kind of NCD with an attached warrant that has recently started appearing in the Indian capital market. The warrant attached to the SPN gives the holder the right to apply for, and get allotment of one equity share for Rs 100 per share through cash payment. This right has to be exercised between one and one-and-half year after allotment, by which time the SPN will be fully paid up. For example, Tata Iron and Steel Co. Ltd (TISCO) issued SPNs aggregating Rs 346.50 crore to existing shareholders on a rights basis.

Besides the above mentioned instruments, new instruments are making their presence felt on the Indian financial market. Table 1.4 presents a glimpse of these new financial instruments.

Instruments for raising financial resources from foreign countries

1. **Global Depository Receipts (GDRs)**

A negotiable financial instrument issued by a bank to represent a foreign company's publicly traded securities is called a depository receipt. The depository receipt trades

Table 1.4   New Financial Instruments: A Glimpse

- **Non-voting Shares:** Useful for companies seeking to bolster net worth without losing management control. Similar in every respect to equity, the sole exception being the absence of voting rights.
- **Detachable Equity Warrants:** Issuable with NCDs or other debt or equity instruments. Ideal for firms with growth prospects, which would prefer equity coupons to convertible debentures (CDs).
- **Participating Debentures:** These are unsecured corporate debt securities which participate in the profits of a company. Potential issuers will be existing dividend-paying companies. Could appeal to investors willing to accept risk for higher returns.
- **Participating Preference Shares:** Quasi-equity instrument to bolster net worth without loss of management control. Pay-outs linked to equity dividend, and also eligible for bonus. Will appeal to investors with an appetite for low risk.
- **Convertible Debentures with Options:** A derivative of the convertible debentures with an embedded option, providing flexibility to the issuer as well as the investor to exit from the terms of the issue. The coupon rate is specified at the time of the issue.
- **Third Party Convertible Debentures:** Debt with a warrant allowing the investor to subscribe to the equity of a third firm at a preferential price vis-á-vis the market price. Interest rate here is lower than pure debt on account of the conversion option.
- **Mortgage-backed Securities:** A synthetic instrument, otherwise known as the asset-backed security (ABS), for securitization of debt. An ABS is backed by pooled assets like mortgages, credit card receivables, and the like.
- **Convertible Debentures Redeemable at Premium:** Convertible debenture issued at face value with a "put" option entitling investors to sell the bond later to the issuer at a premium. Serves a similar purpose as that of convertible debt, but risks to investors is lower.
- **Debt-equity Swaps:** An offer from an issuer of debt to swap it for common stock (equity). The risks: it may dilute earnings per share in the case of the issuer; the expected capital appreciation may not materialize in the case of the investor.
- **Zero-coupon Convertible Note:** A zero-coupon convertible note (ZCCN) converts into common stock. If investors choose to convert, they forgo all accrued and unpaid interest. The risk: ZCCN prices are sensitive to interest rates.
- **Dutch Auction Note:** The interest rate is fixed and refixed for every 35 days.

Source: Author's compilation.

on a local stock exchange. Depository receipts make it easier to buy shares in foreign companies, because the shares of the company don't have to leave the home state. When the depository bank is in USA, the instruments are known as American depository receipts (ADRs). European banks issue European depository receipts, and other banks issue global depository receipts (GDRs). Thus, in other words, GDR is a bank certificate issued in more than one country for shares in a foreign company. The shares are held by a foreign branch of an international branch. The shares trade as domestic shares, but are offered for sale globally through the various bank branches.

Usually, a GDR is denominated in US dollars whereas, the underlying shares would be denominated in the local currency of the issuer. GDRs may be—at the request of the investor—converted into equity shares by cancellation of GDRs through the intermediation of the depository, and the sale of underlying shares in the domestic market through the local custodian. GDRs, per se, are considered as common equity of the issuing company, and are entitled to dividends and voting rights since the date of its issuance. The company effectively transacts with only one entity—the overseas depository—for all the transactions. The voting rights of the shares are exercised by the depository as per the understanding between the issuing company and the GDR holders.

2. **American Depository Receipts**

Introduced to the financial markets in 1927, an ADR is a stock that trades in the United States but represents a specified number of shares in a foreign corporation. ADR's are bought and sold on American markets just like regular stocks, and are issued/sponsored in USA by a bank or brokerage.

There are three different types of ADR issues:

i. **Level I:** This is the most basic type of ADR where foreign companies either do not qualify or do not wish to have their ADR listed on an exchange. Level I ADR's are found on the Over the Counter (OTC) market, and are an easy and inexpensive way to gauge interest for its securities in North America. Level I ADRs also have the loosest requirements from the Securities Exchange Commission (SEC).

ii. **Level II:** This type of ADR is listed on an exchange or quoted on NASDAQ. Level II ADRs have slightly more requirements from the SEC, but they also get higher visibility trading volume.

iii. **Level III:** The most prestigious of the three, this is when an issuer floats a public offering of ADRs on a US exchange. Level II ADRs are able to raise capital and gain substantial visibility in the US financial markets.

The advantages of ADRs are twofold. For individuals, ADRs are an easy and cost-effective way to buy shares, in a foreign company. They save considerable money by reducing administration costs, and avoiding foreign taxes on each transaction. Foreign entities like ADRs allow them to get more US exposure, and to tap into the wealthy North American equity markets. In return, the foreign company must provide detailed financial information to the sponsor bank.

Euro convertible bonds

Euro-convertible bonds (ECBs) are quasi-debt securities (unsecured) which can be converted into depository receipts or local shares. They are targeted at non-institutional investors. ECB's offer the investor an option, to convert the bond into equity, at a fixed price after a minimum lock-in period. The exchange rate for the conversion price is fixed, as is the conversion price. Investors are offered a put option, which allows him to get his money back before maturity. A call option allows the company to force conversion, if the market price of the shares exceeds a particular percentage of the conversion price.

Types of ECBs

1. Ordinary convertible bonds.
2. Deep discount convertible bonds.
3. Euro coupon convertible bonds.
4. Bull dog bonds; issued in sterling in domestic UK market by non-UK company.
5. Yankee bond: domestic US dollar issue made by non-US entity.
6. Samurai bond: long-term, domestic yen debt made by non-Japanese entities.
7. Bunny bonds: investors can invest their interest income into more bonds on same terms.
8. Dragon bonds: issued in dollars, yen, etc., to attract Asian investors.
9. Bonds with equity warrants.

Foreign currency convertible bonds (FCCBs)

The holder has the right to convert the bond into equity shares; it carries fixed rate of interest, conversion takes place on specified dates or any time between two specified dates, and cost of issue is less. An FCCB has the attributes of both equity and debt-fixed rate of interest, and capital appreciation potential. It can be issued in different currencies also.

RECENT DEVELOPMENTS IN FINANCIAL INSTRUMENTS AND MARKETS IN INDIA

Equity Linked Saving Schemes (ELSS)

Equity linked saving schemes (ELSS) are open-ended, diversified equity schemes offered by mutual funds. They offer tax benefits under the new Section 80C. This means one can invest a maximum of Rs 1, 00,000, and that entire sum can be deducted from taxable income.

Besides offering the tax benefit, the scheme invests in shares of frontline companies, and offers long-term capital appreciation. This means unlike guaranteed return-assured return schemes, like Public Provident Fund (PPF) or National Savings Certificates (NSC), the investors gets the benefit of rise in equity markets.

Lock-in Period

There is a 3-year lock-in period for investments made in these schemes. Investors planning to build wealth over the long term and save on tax can use these schemes.

Inverse Float Bonds

Inverse float bonds are structures where the return to the investors rises with a fall in the market rate. The papers are linked to various debt market benchmarks like the Mumbai inter-bank forward rate (Mifor) or Mumbai inter-bank offer rate (Mibor).

Functioning of Inverse Float Bonds

A corporate ties up with an arranger to float a 5-year paper, where the return is say 14.25 percent minus Mifor. Thus, when the Mifor rises, the return comes down for the investor, and vice versa. Since the rates are reset every six months, the investor takes a short-term view on a transaction which is actually for five years. With the 6-month Mifor at 6.10 percent, the investor thinks that the return is 8.15 percent (14.25 percent–6.10 percent), where 14.25 percent is the return on inverse float bond and 6.10 percent is the return expected at six months MIBOR. Which is more than what any paper will offer. But there is a catch. The investor cannot afford to keep the exposure unhedged simply because the return will shrink as Mifor starts moving up.

Asset Reconstruction Company

An asset reconstruction company (ARC) acquires bad loans better known as non-performing assets (NPAs) at a steep discount from banks. For banks and financial institutions, the sale of financial assets to an ARC enables the bad loans known as NPA's to be taken out of the loan books of the former. This improves the balance sheets of banks and financial institutions. This is different from the corporate debt restructuring process. While both aim to realize value from the non-performing distressed assets, the ARC route has the advantage of taking the asset from the banks book and creating a secondary market for it.

The ARC acts as the trustee and managing agent for the same, for eventual sell off to bidders. The company holds these financial assets in a fund floated by the trust, for the benefit of investors, usually, qualified institutional bidders. Against the assets, the trust issues security receipts (SR) to the investors, who shall subscribe to them. The ARC, in turn, uses the money realized to make the payment for the assets bought from the banks and financial institutions. The transaction between an ARC and bank is cashless. Banks receive cash only after SRs are redeemed, and this depends on how successful an ARC is recovering money from the borrower.

Security Receipts (SRs)

Security receipts represent the undivided rights, title, and interest of the investors in the financial assets held by the trust. The SRs are redeemed only out of realization from the financial assets held under the trust and carry no fixed returns. SRs can also be sold in the secondary markets, which make them an attractive window for investment by the big investors including FII's. At present, SRs are unlisted, and there is no trading. If the government allows listing of SRs on stock exchanges, then the SRs would be junk bonds. If an ARC controls 75 percent of the bad debt of defaulting firm, it can take management control of the company.

Securitized Instrument

Securitization allows lenders to realize liquidity from future receivables. The "originator" of such a transaction transfers its assets or future receivables to a special purpose vehicle (SPV). The SPV, in turn, bundles these assets and repackages them as securities called pass-through certificates (PTCs).

The PTCs are sold to investors at a certain coupon, based on the tenor, and quality of the assets. This measure allows the originator (original holder of the assets) to offload assets from its books and realize upfront cash. The originator may also make a spread if the interest received on the assets is higher than the interest paid on the securitized paper. So, now we have personal loans (credit given to customers for education, marriage, or buying durables like TVs, refrigerators, and even mobile phones) being bundled up and sold as securitized papers. Some of the popular securitized instruments are described as follows:

1. **Collateralized Debt Obligation (CDO):** CDOs, another form of securitization, are typically issued by banks and financial institutions. These are securitized interest in pools of the underlying assets which are usually bonds or loans. If a CDO holds only bonds, it is known as a collateralized bond obligation (CBO). If it comprises only loans, it is called a collateralized loan obligation (CLO). The structure in a CDO is similar to a securitization deal, except that with a CDO different varieties of loans or other assets are pooled together and sold to investors.
2. **Cross-border Securitization:** Typically in such transactions assets based in one market are securitized in another. Such transactions involve exchange, political, and currency risks.
3. **Future Flow Securitization:** In such transactions, the assets transferred to the SPV are not based on assets in the originator's books. They are based on future claims against future borrowers or other obligators. This could take the form of export, airline tickets, future royalties, health care, insurance premiums, sports events, and so on.
4. **Collateralized Mortgage Obligations (CMOs):** This pools together several classes of bonds, backed by the same mortgage collateral. Mortgage-backed bonds are secured

by the cash flow from a pool of mortgages sold by a housing finance company. In a CMO, the principal and interest payments made by borrowers are separated into different payment streams. Several bonds are branched out from the principal and interest components and sold at different rates.

Differential Voting Right Shares

Companies will now be allowed to issue shares with differential voting rights including non-voting shares, to the extent of 25 percent of the total share capital issued provided it had distributable profits as defined in the Companies Act, 1965, in the 3 years preceding such issue. However, companies will not be allowed to convert its equity capital with regular voting rights into shares with differential voting rights and vice versa. Issue of such shares will have to be approved by the shareholders' resolution in a general meeting. Further, listed companies will be required to obtain the shareholders' approval through postal ballot.

Companies which have defaulted in filing annual returns during the preceding three years or have failed to repay its deposits or interest thereon on due date or failed to redeem debentures on due date or failed to pay dividend,—will not be eligible to issue shares with differential rights. In addition, the companies should not have defaulted in addressing investor's "grievances." The issue of such shares will have to be authorized by the articles of association of the company. The conditions put down by the government further states that those companies proposing to issue shares with differential rights should not have been convicted of any offence under the Securities and Exchange Board of India Act, 1992, Securities Contract (Regulation) Act, 1956, and Foreign Exchange Management Act, 1999.

Preferential Allotments

Preferential allotment is a bulk allotment to individuals, companies, venture capitalists, or any other person through a fresh issue of shares. The entire allotment is made to pre-identified people, who may or may not be existing shareholders of the company, at a pre-determined price. Generally, preferential allotments are made to people who wish to take a strategic stake in the company like venture capitalists or existing shareholders like promoters who wish to enhance their stake in the company, financial institutions and buyers of the company's products or its suppliers. The rationale is to provide a route by which the company can secure the equity participation of those who it feels can be of value as shareholders, but for whom it may be inordinately costly and/or impractical to buy large chunks of shares from the market.

Preferential allotments are made by means of a special resolution which is passed by existing shareholders. This means that three-fourths of the shareholders should agree to the issue of shares on a preferential basis. The number of shares to be issued, their pricing, the consideration for issue of shares, and the identity and background of the persons or companies to whom the shares are proposed to be issued on preferential basis are taken upfront. SEBI, under its guidelines has prescribed a minimum pricing formula under which the preferential allotment can be made. Under this, an average of the highs and lows of the 26 weeks preceding the date on which the board resolves to make the preferential allotment is arrived at and this is the minimum price at which the allotments can be made. Till recently, all preferential allotments were exempted from the applicability of the takeover code. However, the latest amendment has brought preferential allotments of more than 15 percent of the equity under the ambit of the takeover code, implying that any allotment above this limit will necessitate an open offer to the existing shareholders.

Press Note 18

Press Note 18 sets out the government's policy for approval of new projects for companies from abroad when they already have an existing joint venture running in India. The guidelines were set out in a note numbered 18 by the Department of Industrial Policy and Promotion, for Public Information; hence it came to be known by the phrase Press Note 18. It says that if a foreign company has entered into a joint venture or embarked on a technology transfer/trade mark agreement with a domestic company in a particular field of operation, then the foreign company will not get an automatic approval from the RBI to open another such venture in the same field. This will be irrespective of whether the new venture is with a new company or on its own.

Instead the company would have to route its application for a fresh foreign direct investment (FDI) through the Foreign Investment Promotion Board (FIPB). The restriction will operate irrespective of whether foreign investments in the sector operate under the 100 percent automatic route. How much of a difference does this make to a foreign investor. The introduction of such a case by case approach puts brakes on foreign investments, which want to sidestep the existing joint venture. An application into FIPB means, the foreign investors have to give the detailed circumstances in which they find it necessary to set up a new joint venture or enter into new technology transfer, including that of trade mark.

Convertible Bonds

SEBI would allow public companies to issue shares to qualified institutional investors, which will create a market for rupee denominated convertible bonds (RDCB) in India. These new instruments would be attractive for foreign or domestic holders because it could help them in their tax planning. Merchant bankers will be allowed to structure instruments with up to 5 years tenure and will have the flexibility of conversion with no lock-in. Merchant bankers say under the new guideline, if RDCB is issued and converted, it may be seen as a long-term investment and may not attract capital gains.

Hedge Funds

Hedge funds are primary movers of hot money. In India, hedge fund activity has risen sharply in the past 2 years, thanks to low US interest rates, high domestic growth, and strong corporate performance. It is believed that close to 50 percent of the FII investment in India, at any given point in time, is through participatory notes (P-notes) and could be reasonably considered hot. The portfolios of hedge funds in general are leveraged and have much larger exposure to derivative securities. Hedge funds also alter their stance in the market frequently and decisively as they actively search to exploit transient opportunities of earning excess returns that do arise in the markets from macroeconomic and geo-political developments, and changes in the expectations and risk aversion of investors.

Phantom Stocks

Multinational companies (MNCs) in India are using exotic compensation tools like phantom stocks, also known as stock appreciation rights (SAR). SAR is a contractual right for a notional equity allotment to the employees. The allotment is notional as no actual shares are transferred to the employees. Under this contract, the employee is entitled only to the value of the stock appreciation during the specified period agreed under the contract.

For example, if a SAR is granted when the value of the stock is Rs 100 and five years later the SAR is exercised when the stock is worth Rs 150, the SAR would be worth Rs 50 at exercise. Depending upon the terms of the contract, the Rs 50 could be paid either in cash or in stocks. The shares referred to here are MNC shares listed on foreign houses like New York Stock Exchange (NYSE) or NASDAQ. The idea is to reward Indian employees with an instrument which is in some ways akin to a stock option.

When-issued Market

A when as and if issued (commonly known as "when-issued") security refers to a bond whose issue has been announced but not yet taken place. By inference, a when-issued market is one where such "when-issued" instruments are traded. In India, the "when-issued" market in government securities is expected to take off shortly with transactions taking place on RBI's Negotiated Dealing System-Open Markets (NDS-OM), an online trading platform for government securities.

A when-issued market will enable bidders to get an idea of how many investors are interested in buying. Reduced volatility will draw more investors and lead to further development of the bond market. In a when-issued market, trade can take place only from the day an auction of government securities is notified up to the date of the auction. During this period, there will be a kind of a book building with buying and selling of the "to be issued security" going on simultaneously. Once the securities are issued through the auction, there will be a settlement of all these buy–sell transactions that has taken place earlier.

Reverse Mortgage Products

Banks and housing finance companies are readying themselves to bring out their reverse mortgage products. Reverse mortgage will enable senior citizens to mortgage their property with a bank/finance company and receive monthly payments. At the end of the term or on the death of the person opting for the reverse mortgage, the bank/finance company is free to sell the property to realize the amount due to them.

The first step in reverse mortgage is to approach a bank or housing finance company (HFC) and express willingness to pledge one's home for the reverse mortgage scheme. The HFC will assess the value of the house by independent valuation. Then, the HFC will arrive at the loan amount depending upon the age of the person opting for the reverse mortgage and the prevailing interest rate. However, the loan amount will be on the basis of current value of the property and not on possible future appreciation. Currently, as per industry estimates the loan to value ratio is fixed at 45–60 percent of the value of the property based on the age. The spouse will be a co-borrower of the loan. This will give him/her the right to live in the house after the death of the borrower and get monthly payment till he/she continues to live.

Exchangeable Bonds

Exchangeable bonds (EBs) will enable large corporates with several group companies to reap the benefit of a float without actually selling shares at the time of issuing the bonds. A company can issue EBs to raise resources by offering the investor the option of converting the bonds into shares of one of its group companies at the time of maturity. The bonds will be tradable and will carry a competitive coupon rate. EBs are different from FCCBs, which can be redeemed only for shares of the issuing company and not for shares of a group company in which it has a stake.

Call-linked Bonds

Companies issue bonds to banks offering a spread over call money rates. Banks borrow money in the inter-bank call money market and deploy them in these instruments (see Table 1.5). For the issuing company, it is simply an avenue for low cost working capital funds. Banks which are essentially lenders in the "call market", deploy their surplus funds in these investments.

Table 1.5 Call-linked Bonds

And a Bond is Born

	Issuer	Investor
Step 1	• Needs cheap short-term funds—eyes call money market • Issues floating rate instrument with spread over call rate	• Interested as spread is assured over call • Worried about long tenor, seeks put option
Step 2	• Agrees to put option • Puts cap on maximum interest payable	• Worried about downside, asks for a minimum floor
Step 3	• Issuer agrees to floor • Introduces call option to exit if costs become prohibitive	
Result	• A mature floating rate instrument linked to call rate, and having the crucial ingredients—cap, floor, call, and put	

Source: Author's compilation.

A 1 year borrowing will cost the best rated company around 11–12.5 percent. A call-linked bond offering even 250 basis points over call (9.5 percent, with call rates currently at around seven percent) is still a cheaper option.

Structured Finance

While traditional bond issues would take days or even months to conclude through the private placement, top corporate issuers and investors are striking deals across the table in a matter of hours in complete secrecy. In structured finance, payers raising money through this route are mostly triple-A rated corporates. The two routes available to the merchant bank managing the issue are to take the entire float on its books and warehouse them until they find buyers. The second alternative is to fix couple rates, with the arranger given the mandate to scout for investors.

Press Note 1

The term "Press Note" is used because FDI guidelines are issued in the form of press releases by the government. The number is then written as a suffix to show the order of the press note issued in one calendar year, with the beginning of a new calendar year.

Real Estate Investment Trust (REIT)

A real estate investment trust (REIT) is a company that owns, operates income-producing real estates such as apartments, shopping centers, offices, hostels, and warehouses. In most cases, REITs own and operate the real-estate property. But some REITs also finance real estate. The shares of many REITs are freely traded, usually on a major stock exchange.

To qualify as a REIT, a company must distribute at least 90 percent of its taxable income to its shareholders annually. A company that qualifies as a REIT is permitted to deduct dividends paid to its shareholders from its corporate taxable income. As a result, most REITs remit at least 100 percent of their taxable income to their shareholders and, therefore, owe no corporate tax.

Debt Swap Scheme

In early 2003, the finance minister announced a scheme to replace the relatively high cost debt of states with lower cost borrowings, taking advantage of falling interest rates. The scheme envisages states pre-paying that portion of their outstanding debt to the center in which the interest rate is 13 percent and more, contracted during the mid 1990s when general interest rates were high. All collections from small savings, which include post office deposits, Kisan Vikas Patras, National Savings Certificates, and the Public Provident Fund (PPF) flow to the public account. After adjusting for repayments to the depositors of these small savings instruments, the entire net collections are on lent to the states. Of the amount apportioned to each state based on the collection in the respective states, 70 percent is made available as cash transfer, while the remaining 30 percent is used for repaying the high cost loans.

Participatory Notes

Participatory notes (commonly known as p-notes) are instruments used by foreign funds and investors who are not registered with the SEBI but are interested in taking exposure in Indian securities. Participatory notes are generally issued overseas by the associates of India-based foreign brokerages and domestic institutional brokerages.

They are, in fact, offshore derivative instruments issued by FIIs and their sub-accounts against underlying Indian securities. P-notes are issued where the underlying assets are securities listed on the Indian bourses. FIIs who do not wish to register with the SEBI but would like to take exposure in Indian securities also use participatory notes. Brokers buy or sell securities on behalf of their clients in their proprietary account and issue such notes in favor of such foreign investors.

Perpetual Bonds

A perpetual bond is a hybrid security somewhere between debt and equity. Although perpetual bonds are debt instruments, they do not have a maturity date. The investor will receive a stream of interest payments for perpetuity. The bonds are liquid as they can be sold in the secondary market through stock exchanges. The oldest perpetual bonds that continue to be in existence are those issued by the British government in 1814 to fund the Napoleonic wars. According to sources, the banks are looking at the option of issuing perpetual bonds—one of the new instruments likely to be approved as Tier I capital (i.e., equity and free reserves).

Preferred Ordinary Shares

Preferred ordinaries, a hybrid of ordinary and preference shares, have the following features:

1. These shares are redeemable within a specified time frame from the date of issue.
2. The option for conversion of these shares into ordinary shares at the end of the stipulated period is available to investors. The conversion takes place according to a pre-determined formula laid down at the time of the issue.
3. These shares earn a cumulative, annual, participating variable dividend as declared by the board, or linked to the profits of the company on the basis of a pre-determined formula spelled out at the time of issue.

Preferred ordinaries, as the name indicates, would be placed next to preference shares in terms of risk and returns but a notch above ordinary shares. The advantage with preferred ordinaries is that it permits a green field project to raise funds offering variable returns even before the scrip is listed in the bourse through an initial public offer.

Preferred ordinaries are

1. Redeemable within the period specified at time of issue.
2. Carry a conversion option.
3. Earn a variable dividend.
4. Carry no voting rights.
5. More risky than preference shares but less so than the ordinary ones.
6. Considered ideal for financing start-up, first phase, and second.

IMPACT OF GLOBALIZATION ON INDIAN FINANCIAL SYSTEM

Globalization means free cross-border movement of information, goods, services, capital, and people. Globalization is more than just about economics. It is also about culture, society, politics, and people. In the current wave of globalization, India started off in hyper-growth mode. It is the fifth largest economy in the world and in the last 3 years, the ratio of exports of goods and services to gross domestic product (GDP) has increased up from 14.6 to 20.5 percent. India's share in global merchandise exports had doubled from 0.5 percent in 1990–91 to 1 percent, and its share of global services exports has doubled in the last 2 years to 2.5 percent.

Globalization in India, was an undertaker because of its prevailing adverse economic condition. However, the outcome of globalization has been a complete transformation of Indian economy, as evident by:

1. India is now the second fastest growing economy in the world and is expected to be the third largest economy by 2020, after the USA and China.
2. GDP grew at 9.4 percent in 2007–08. It is expected to be at the rate of 6.7 percent in 2008–09 and 7.2 percent in 2009–10.
3. Forex reserve was around USD 215 billion at end of financial year 2007–08.
4. Buoyant capital market and rupee being best performing currency against dollar in 2007, the capital market is bouncing back from slowdown in September 2009.
5. India is ranked 23 in Global Competitiveness Index ahead of China (54), Brazil (64), and Russia (62).
6. Foreign trade (export and import) was 32 percent of GDP.
7. FDI is increasing at USD 25 billion per year mark. Exports are around USD 160 billion mark. Software and BPO exports are expected to be double from current USD 30 billion to USD 60 billion by 2010.
8. The economic growth is through enhanced consumption which forms 78 percent of GDP and service sector contributes over 60 percent of GDP. India is now emerging as a hub of manufacturing excellence, new growth engines like IT, automobile, pharma,

Table 1.6 Growth Rate and Sectoral Composition of Real Gross Domestic Product
(Average. 2000–01 to 2008–09)

Sector	Growth Rate						Share in Real GDP				
	Average 2000–01 to 2008–09	2004–05	2005–06	2006–07	2007–08*	2008–09#	2004–05	2005–06	2006–07	2007–08*	2008–09#
1	2	3	4	5	6	7	8	9	10	11	12
1. Agriculture and Allied Activities	**2.8**	**0.0**	**5.8**	**4.0**	**4.9**	**1.6**	**20.2**	**19.5**	**18.5**	**17.8**	**17.0**
of which:											
a) Agriculture	..	0.1	6.0	4.1	5.0	..	18.5	17.9	17.0	16.3	..
2. Industry	**6.5**	**8.5**	**8.1**	**10.7**	**7.4**	**2.6**	**19.6**	**19.4**	**19.5**	**19.2**	**18.5**
of which:											
a) Mining and quarrying	5.0	8.2	4.9	8.8	3.3	3.6	2.2	2.1	2.1	2.0	1.9
b) Manufacturing	7.1	8.7	9.1	11.8	8.2	2.4	15.1	15.1	15.3	15.2	14.6
c) Electricity, gas, and water supply	4.5	7.9	5.1	5.3	5.3	3.4	2.3	2.2	2.1	2.0	2.0
3. Services	**9.0**	**9.9**	**11.2**	**11.3**	**10.8**	**9.4**	**60.2**	**61.1**	**62.0**	**63.0**	**64.5**
of which:											
a) Construction	10.2	16.1	16.2	11.8	10.1	7.2	6.6	7.0	7.2	7.2	7.3
b) Trade, hotels, and restaurants	8.8	7.7	10.3	10.4	10.1	9.0	15.5	15.6	15.7	15.9	28.6^
c) Transport, storage, and communications	13.9	15.6	14.9	16.3	15.5 (12.4)^	..	10.2	10.7	11.4	12.1	..
d) Financing, insurance, real estate, and business services	8.7	8.7	11.4	13.8	11.7	7.8	13.5	13.8	14.3	14.6	14.8
e) Community, social, and personal services	6.4	6.8	7.1	5.7	6.8	13.1	14.2	13.9	13.4	13.1	13.9
4. GDP at factor cost	**7.2**	**7.5**	**9.5**	**9.7**	**9.0**	**6.7**	**100**	**100**	**100**	**100**	**100**

Source: RBI (2006).
Notes: * means quick estimates.
means valuable cover, expenditure made on acquisition of valuables, etc.
^ means projections.

bio-tech, nano-tech, and agri-business coming up in a big way. Innovations are driving enterprises and services especially financial services which are effective channel partners in mobilizing saving and canalizing into productive investment.

9. The impact of globalization has also been very conducive on saving and investment in India, as reflected by Table 1.6.

Inferences

The Indian economy is showing effect of structural changes as the share of primary sector to real GDP has decreased to 17.0 percent in 2008–09 from 20.2 percent in 2004–05. The service sector recorded the rise to 64.5 percent in 2008–09 from 60.2 percent in 2004–05.

Savings and investments play a very decisive role in the Indian economy. Savings are contributed by the household sector and others, and so are the investments. For details, please refer to Table 1.7.

Table 1.7   Gross Domestic Saving and Investments Percent of GDP (At Current Market Price)

	2004–05	*2005–06*	*2006–07*	*2007–08*	*2008–09*
Gross Domestic Saving	32.2	33.1	34.4	36.4	32.5
Public Sector	2.3	2.4	3.6	5.0	1.4
Private Sector	29.9	30.7	30.9	31.4	31.1
Household Sector	23.3	23.2	22.9	22.6	22.6
Financial Saving	9.8	11.4	10.9	11.2	10.4
Saving in Physical Assets	13.5	11.8	11.9	11.5	12.2
Private Corporate Sector	6.6	7.5	8.0	8.7	8.4
Gross Capital Formation	32.7	34.3	35.5	37.7	34.9
Investment					
Public Sector	7.4	7.9	8.4	8.9	9.4
Private Sector	23.8	25.3	26.4	27.6	24.9
Corporate Sector	10.3	13.5	14.5	16.1	12.7
Saving-investment Gap					
Public Sector	–5.1	–5.5	–4.8	–3.9	–8.0
Private Sector	6.1	5.4	4.4	3.8	6.2

Source: CSO (2009).

Inferences:

Gross Domestic Saving as proportion of GDP at market price is now 32.5% in 2008–09 which is lower than 36.4% in 2007–08.

Household sector contributes 22.6% of Gross Capital Formation in 2008–09.

Private sector contributes 24.9% of Gross Capital Formation in 2008–09.

The saving of household sector is composed of financial assets and physical assets. The trends in financial assets are as depicted by the following Table 1.8.

Capital formation is essential to generate demand to generate further demand. Table 1.9 suggests trends in GDCF since 2000–01.

Table 1.8 Household Saving in Financial Assets

(Amount in Rs Crores)

Item	2005–06P	2006–07P	2007–08#	2008–09^
A. Financial Assets (Gross)	597,867	768,967	734,653	815,416
	(16.7)	(18.6)	(15.6)	(15.0)
1. Currency	53,071	66,323	80,342	97,673
	(1.5)	(1.6)	(1.7)	(1.8)
	[8.9]	[8.6]	[10.9]	[12.0]
2. Deposits @	280,772	425,050	415,199	473,327
	(7.8)	(10.3)	(8.8)	(8.7)
	[47.0]	[55.3]	[56.5]	[58.0]
3. Claims on Government	87,168	40,627	−27,042	12,365
	(2.4)	(1.0)	(−0.6)	(0.2)
	[14.6]	[5.3]	[−3.7]	[1.5]
4. Investment in Shares and Debentures+	30,735	51,086	77,073	15,000
	(0.9)	(1.2)	(1.6)	(0.3)
	[5.1]	[6.6]	[10.5]	[1.8]
5. Contractual Savings*	1,46,121	1,85,881	1,89,081	217,051
	(4.1)	(4.5)	(4.0)	(4.0)
	[24.4]	[24.2]	[25.7]	[26.6]
B. Financial Liabilities	183,424	282,697	208,666	217,051
	(5.1)	(6.8)	(4.4)	(4.0)
C. Saving in Financial Assets (Net) (A–B)	414,443	486,270	525,987	598,365
	(11.6)	(11.8)	(11.1)	(11.0)
GDP at Current Market Prices	3,586,743	4,129,174	4,723,400	5,426,277
				(14.9)

P: Provisional. #: Preliminary. ^: Projections by EPWRF. @: Comprise bank deposits, non-bank deposits and trade debt (net).+: Includes units of Specified Undertaking of the Unit Trust of India and other mutual funds.
*: Comprise life insurance funds and provident and pension funds.
Source: RBI Handbook of Statistics (2009).
Note: 1. Components may not add up to the total due to rounding off. 2. Figures in ( ) indicate % to GDP at current market prices and [ ] indicate % to financial assets (gross).
Inferences:
• Deposits (bank, non-bank, and trade debt) increased from 47 percent in 2005–06 to 58.0 percent in 2008–09 of financial assets and investment.

CONCEPT OF FINANCIAL SERVICES

Financial services are defined as a bundle of intangible utilities aimed at satisfying the needs of users. Financial services bridges the gap between savers (those who have got surplus amounts) and those who need funds (the fund borrowers). A financial service performs:

1. Identification of resources for efficient allocation.
2. Providing constant evaluation of allotted of resources.
3. Providing liquidity to investors.

Table 1.9 Trends in Gross Domestic Capital Formation

(Percent of GDP at Current Market Prices)

Item	2000–01	2001–02	2002–03	2003–04	2004–05P	2005–06#
1	2	3	4	5	6	7
1. Household Sector	10.8	10.9	12.4	12.4	11.4	10.7
2. Public Sector	6.9	6.9	6.1	6.3	7.1	7.4
3. Private Corporate Sector	5.7	5.4	5.9	6.9	9.9	12.9
4. Valuables+	0.7	0.6	0.6	0.9	1.3	1.2
5. Gross Domestic Capital Formation (GDCF)*	24.3	22.9	25.2	28.0	31.5	33.8

Source: CSO (2009).
Notes: P: Provisional.
#: Quick estimates.
+: "Valuables" covers the expenditures made on acquisition of valuables, excluding works of art and antiques.
*: As GDCF is adjusted for errors and omissions, the sector-wise capital formation figures do not add up to the GDCF.

Inferences:
- The GDFC rose by 2.3 percent in 2005–06 over 2004–05, which was contributed mainly by the private sector by financing ongoing long-term capital expenditure.
- Difference between gross fixed capital formation and changes in stock narrowed, indicating pick up in fresh investments for creating additional capacity through fixed capital formation, especially by private sector.

An efficient financial service provides efficient allocation and evaluation of resources and constant arbitrage between the risk and returns associated with financial services.

FINANCIAL SERVICES IN INDIA

Financial services in India have prevailed since time immemorial. Kautilya's *Arthashatra* can said to be the first organized literature on financial services where he has amply described the rules and regulation of money and mint management. The old instruments, like *hundi*, resemble the bill of exchange or promissory note or bearer cheque of contemporary financial markets. It can be said that there were well-developed financial markets, instruments, and intermediaries in ancient India. *Sahukari* could be an example of financial intermediation.

Banking is said to be an age-old financial service in India, which started in early 17th century with the incorporation of the East India Company. Banks are considered the face of financial services. They assume a significant place in socio-economic area. At times, banks were considered socio-economic change agents.

The planners have put stress on planned development in financial markets. Initially to serve the objectives of planned economy, setting of development financial institution was started in 1948.

The L.P.G. (Liberalization, Privatization, and Globalization) have further strengthened the financial services in India. The financial services in India can boast of multiple institutions, instruments, and intermediaries with cutting-edge technology.

Types of Financial Services

Financial services can be categorized into two groups, namely, fund-based activities, where there is involvement of funds, and non-fund based activities.

Fund based financial services are as follows:

1. Underwriting.
2. Portfolio management.
3. Venture capital.
4. Non-recourse factoring.
5. Private equity.
6. Structural finance.
7. Leasing and hire purchasing.
8. Foreign exchange.
9. Stock market operations.
10. Bill discounting.
11. Mortgages and reverse mortgages.
12. Securitization, especially asset-based securitization.
13. Micro credit.

Non-fund based financial services are those where intellectual property is used and advices are offered. A fee or commission is charged for rendering services. Some of non-fund based financial services are:

1. Merchant banking—issues management, pre- and post-issue activities.
2. Financing activities.
3. Project advisory services.
4. Custodian services.
5. Credit card services.
6. Discretionary portfolio management.
7. Capital restructuring, tie up, merger and acquisition (pre and post due diligence).
8. Forex services.
9. Financial research services, including credit authentication and verification services.
10. Credit rating services.
11. Services related to inbound and outbound financial documents called processing charges.

A couple of these services have already been profiled in this chapter elsewhere. The following is the description of some of the remaining services:

1. **Underwriting:** Underwriters are important intermediaries in the new issue market. They agree to take the securities which are not fully subscribed. They give commitments regarding full subscription of the issue either by others or by themselves. Underwriters are appointed by the companies in consultation with its merchant bankers.

2. **Portfolio Management:** Portfolio manager can manage the funds of his clients according to his own will called discretionary services or according to the instructions given by the client called non-discretionary service.
3. **Factoring and Forfaiting:** Factoring is a fund based financial service and is a method of financing whereby a company sells its trade debts at a discount to a financial institution. It is a continuous arrangement between a financial institution (factor) and a company (client) which sells goods and services to its customers on credit. The factor purchases the a/c receivables of the client and keeps the record of client's trade debts by charging a fee.

   Forfaiting is also a source of financing against a/c receivables and is mostly used to help an exporter for financing goods exported on a medium term. The exporter gives up his right to receive payment in future under an export bill for immediate cash payments by the forfaitor. The right to receive payment on due date passes to forfaitor since the exporter has given this right to forfaitor. Forfaiting is done without any recourse to the exporter, that is, in case the importer makes a default, the forfaitor cannot recover the amount from the exporter.
4. **Leasing and Hire Purchase:** A lease may be defined as a contractual arrangement in which the owner of the asset (lessor) gives a right to use the asset to the user (leesee) for a pre-specified period in consideration of periodic payment (lease rental). At the end of the lease period the asset reverts back to the lessor unless there is a renewal in contract.

   Hire purchase is a method of selling goods where the goods are let out on hire by a finance company (creditor) to the hire purchase customer (hirer). The buyer is required to pay an agreed amount in periodical installments during a given period. The ownership of the asset lies with the creditor and passes to the hirer on the payment of last installment.
5. **Bills Discounting:** It is an asset-based financial service being provided by the finance companies. The bill of exchange is an instrument in writing containing an unconditional order, signed by the maker, directing a certain person to pay a certain sum of money only to a certain person, or to the bearer of that instrument. The seller can get the bills discounted from his bankers before maturity to meet his financial requirements.
6. **Custodian:** A custodian is an agent, broker, or banker who keeps the safe custody of the client's valuables or investments of the public in securities, which are financial claims. They are intermediaries between companies and clients (security holders) and institutions (Foreign Institutional Investors and Mutual Funds).
7. **Credit Rating:** Credit rating is a fee-based financial service in which the organization providing credit rating services, called rating agency, provides the relative ranking of credit quality of debt instruments available in the market. It is a method of assessment and grading of the companies who borrow money from the market to make timely repayment of principal as well as interest on a particular type of debt instrument. It expresses the credit risk associated with specific debt instruments.

8. **Credit Cards:** A credit card is a card which enables its holder to purchase goods and make other payments without making immediate payment. The card is being issued to the holder (after examining his credit worthiness) to use it up to a specified limit. The customer gets credit for 45 days.

9. **Debit Card:** In this the payment of goods and services are immediately realized by the seller by debiting the bank account of the customer.

EMERGING ISSUES IN FINANCIAL SERVICES

The Indian financial sector is experiencing tremendous growth. There is presence of robust financial system, well-established institutions with a strong supervisory system. There is also progressive integration of financial markets—banking, insurance, mutual funds, securities, and commodities—with high technology absorption. The financial services market in India is experiencing innovation, integration, and customer-oriented focus so much that e-delivery channel as alternate is becoming popular with Indian customers and financial sector is bracing to meet life cycle and lifestyle needs of great Indian middle class by offering them customized and structured products.

The emerging issues are:

1. The customers are becoming highly demanding, creating unhealthy competition and putting excessive pressure on the service providers.
2. The growth has only been confined to cities and metros, while there is a large untapped market consisting of semi-urban and rural areas.
3. The competition is intense there while profitability of service providers is under pressure.
4. E-banking and e-solution has a risk of cyber misuse.
5. There is presence of non-monetized sector and parallel economy causing disturbance to organized growth process.
6. In the name of innovation there is often copy of products or services offered by the competitors and marketing efforts have become very costly and the burden is borne by customers.

2

Regulatory Framework of Financial Services in India

Learning Objectives

- To know the concept of regulation.
- To know how financial services are regulated in India.

THE CONCEPT

The word "Regulation" means to regulate, to direct or to move in a desired direction. A regulatory framework, therefore, consists of a set of guidelines and directions to be adhered to while performing functions by the organization. Regulation is one step forward from control which implies a set of don'ts, that is, a list of negative actions whereas regulation stands for absence of direct control. A fine comparison between control and regulation could be seen in the form of regulation of traffic on road. One way is to regulate the traffic by a traffic policeman and the other way is to control the traffic by automatic lights. Traffic controlled by a traffic policeman is an example of control, whereas, traffic control by lights is an example of regulation. When we look at traffic regulation by automatic traffic lights, it stands for fairness, accuracy, precision, and timeliness. A financial regulation is exactly an extension of a regulation of traffic by automatic lights. In fact, regulatory framework aims at

1. improving market efficiency,
2. curbing unfair trade practices,
3. improving transparency in operation, and
4. promoting fairness and accuracy.

There are multiple regulators for various financial services in India. The regulatory framework has come into being following enactment of respective Bills, Acts, and other legislative matters by Parliamentary and judicial precedents. The following Figure 2.1 reflects an overview of regulators for specific services.

Figure 2.1   Regulation of Financial Services: An Overview

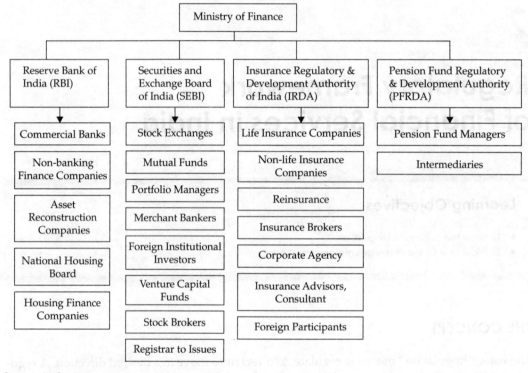

Source: Author.

We shall now examine regulatory framework as follows.

REGULATION OF BANKING AND NON-BANKING FINANCE COMPANIES (NBFCs)

It is important to note that, world over the banking sector is regulated more closely than any other sector. The rationale for such regulations may be

1. Banks hold a major portion of the public savings and they enjoy trust of public.
2. Banks intermediate between savings and investments and aid in channelizing funds to the economic sectors thereby ensuring efficient and productive use of funds.

3. Banks hold a large part of the money supply; hence they influence the monetary position of the economy thereby becoming the channel of the central bank for implementing monetary policy.
4. Banks administer the national payments and settlement system.

Thus, the efficiency with which the banks attract savings and transform them into investment will influence the performance of the economy. The two critical issues that need to be considered in this process are: first, the ability of the banks to control and manage the risks that arise while extending their functions and second, allocation of resources.

Approach to Regulation and Supervision of Banking and NBFCs

The approach prescribes broad parameters of banking operations within which the country's banking and financial system functions with the objectives of maintaining public confidence in the system, protecting depositors' interest, and providing cost-effective banking services to the public.

The regulation of banking and NBFCs in India started with two fundamental Acts:

1. Reserve Bank of India Act, 1934 governing the Reserve Bank, and
2. Banking Regulation Act, 1949 governing the banking sector.

Besides, there are other Acts regulating specific functions like

1. Public Debt Act, 1944/Government Securities Act, 2006 governing government debt market;
2. Securities Contract (Regulation) Act, 1956 regulating government securities market;
3. Indian Coinage Act, 1906 regulating currency and coins; and
4. Indian Companies Act, 1956 over-viewing banking companies, Banking Companies (Acquisition and Transfer of Undertakings) Act, 1970 and 1980 for nationalization of banks, Bankers' Books Evidence Act, Banking Secrecy Act, Negotiable Instruments Act, 1881.

It is interesting to note that some banking companies are governed by specific Acts like State Bank of India Act, 1954, The Industrial Development Bank (Transfer of Undertaking and Repeal) Act, 2003, The Industrial Finance Corporation (Transfer of Undertaking and Repeal) Act, 1993, National Bank for Agriculture and Rural Development Act, 1981, National Housing Bank Act, 1987, and Deposit Insurance and Credit Guarantee Corporation Act, 1961.

Origin of Regulation for Banking Companies

Earlier commercial banks were governed by the Company Law applicable to ordinary non-banking companies, and the permission of RBI was not required even for the floatation of a new bank. Analyzing the malpractices leading to the failure of banks, the Central Banking Enquiry Committee, in 1931, concluded that the provisions of the Indian Companies Act at the time were quite inadequate to deal effectively with banking malpractices and recommended comprehensive legislation to cover the organization, management, audit, and liquidation of banks in 1939. The central board of the RBI, submitted proposals for legislation in the form of a draft bill, which subsequently surfaced as the Banking Companies Act, 1949. This was changed to the Banking Regulation Act, 1949.

Regulatory Role of RBI: A Summarized Snapshot

As important as the promotional role is the regulatory role of the RBI. This is essential, as it has to control the overall credit and the price levels in the economy to maintain the value of the Indian rupee, ensure a sound and healthy banking system, effectively coordinate and control the credit through appropriate monetary and credit policies followed from time to time.

The RBI controls the activities of the commercial banks, NBFCs and financial institutions by virtue of the powers vested in it under the Reserve Bank of India Act, 1934. Given in the following are some of the most significant aspects of the regulatory role of the RBI conferred by the Reserve Bank of India Act, 1934:

1. Maintenance of the cash reserves by the scheduled commercial banks under Section 42.
2. Issues related to the collection and furnishing of credit information from the commercial banks under Sections 45A to 45F.
3. Chapters III B and III C relate to the provisions regarding non-banking finance companies receiving deposits and the prohibition of acceptance of deposits by unincorporated bodies, respectively. Apart from defining an NBFC and a financial institution, these chapters also relate to the following issues:
   a. Registration and net owned fund requirements.
   b. Assets, reserves funds, disclosure of information, and inspection.
   c. Powers of the auditors.
   d. Powers of the RBI to determine policy and issue directions, collect information regarding the deposits, prohibit acceptance of deposits, filing or winding up petitions, etc.

Apart from the various guidelines, the Act also empowers the RBI to control and supervise the activities of the commercial banks in India and no commercial bank can commence business without obtaining license from the RBI. This also applies to the opening of new branches. A bank, which satisfies the criteria laid down by RBI, is given the autonomy to open branches without prior approval of RBI. Some of the main provisions for regulating banks under RBI Act are:

1. Section 10BB—Power of RBI to appoint chairman of the BoDs on a whole-time basis or a managing director of a banking company.
2. Section 21—Power of RBI to control advances by banking companies.
3. Section 22—Licensing of banking companies.
4. Section 23—Restrictions on opening of new and transfer of existing places of business.

5. Section 35—Inspection.
6. Section 35A—Power of the RBI to give directions.
7. Section 36—Additional power and functions of the RBI.
8. Section 36AA—Powers of the RBI to remove managerial and other powers from office.
9. Section 36AB—Power of RBI to appoint additional directors.
10. Section 39—Reserve Bank to be the official liquidator.
11. Section 45—Power of the RBI to apply to central government for the suspension of business by a banking company and to prepare a scheme of reconstitution of amalgamation.
12. Section 47A—Power of RBI to impose penalty.

RBI has the power to prevent a commercial bank from undertaking certain types of transactions as well as control the advances made by the commercial banks. With this power to selective credit control, RBI is empowered to determine the policy in relation to advances to be made by banks generally or by any bank in particular. Under Section 21, the RBI is authorized to issue directions to banks as regards the purpose of the advances, the margins to be maintained in respect of the advances, the rate of interest and other terms and conditions on which advances may be made.

Apart from this, through the monetary policy measures, RBI controls the volume of credit in a quantitative way so as to influence the total volume of bank credit. Instruments used are bank rate, open market operations, and variable cash reserve ratio (CRR).

The Banking Regulation Act also confers on the RBI the general authority to inspect the books and accounts of the commercial banks. By virtue of this power, RBI can at any time have the books and accounts of any bank inspected.

Thus, both the Reserve Bank of India Act, 1934 and the Banking Regulation Act, 1949 provide the legal framework for the prudential regulation and supervision of banks, NBFCs and financial institutions by the RBI, which has employed periodic inspections as the prime and exclusive instrument of prudential supervision.

Supervision and Regulation of Banks and NBFCs

Banking supervision

In order to consolidate the supervision and financial system, the Board for Financial Supervision was set up under the aegis of Reserve Bank through Reserve Bank of India (Board for Financial Supervision) Regulations, 1994 with the objective of paying undivided attention to the supervision of the institutions in the financial sector. The Department of Supervision was carved out of the Department of Banking Operations & Development (DBOD) with the objective of segregating the supervisory role from the regulatory functions of RBI. Later, the Department of Supervision was split into Department of Banking Supervision (DBS) and Department of Non-Banking Supervision (DNBS) on July 29, 1997 with the latter being entrusted with the task of focused regulatory and supervisory attention toward the NBFCs segment.

Department of Banking Supervision (DBS)

The Department of Banking Supervision supervises commercial banks in the following forms:

1. Preparing independent inspection programs for different institutions.
2. Undertaking scheduled and special on-site inspections, off-site surveillance, and ensuring follow-up and compliance.
3. Determining the criteria for the appointment of statutory auditors and special auditors and assessing audit performance and disclosure standards.
4. Dealing with financial sector frauds.
5. Exercising supervisory intervention in the implementation of regulations which includes recommendation for removal of managerial and other persons, suspension of business, amalgamation, merger/winding up, issuance of directives, and imposition of penalties.

Department of Non-banking Supervision (DNBS)

The Department of Non-banking Supervision has the following responsibilities:

1. Administration of Chapter IIIB of the RBI Act, formulating regulatory framework and issuing directions to the NBFCs (including residuary non-banking companies, mutual benefit companies, chit fund companies).
2. Administration of Chapter IIIC of the RBI Act in respect of unincorporated bodies, Chit Funds Act in respect of chit fund companies, Prize Chits and Moneys Circulation Schemes (Banning) Act in respect of prize chits.
3. Identification and classification of NBFCs.
4. Registration of NBFCs under Section 45-IA of the RBI Act.
5. On-site inspection and follow-up.
6. Off-site surveillance and scrutiny of various returns.
7. Attending to complaints relating to NBFC sector.
8. Initiating deterrent action against the errant companies.

Considering the tremendous growth of NBFCs, a new regulatory framework was put in place in January 1998 to ensure that only financially sound and well-run NBFCs are allowed to access public deposits.

Supervisory jurisdiction

The supervision by Board of Financial Supervision (BFS) covers commercial banks, all-India development financial institutions, and NBFCs. The key elements of supervision include:

1. Setting up an off-site surveillance function, the major components of which include establishing a system for in-house monitoring of banks and other credit institutions,

based on a prudential supervisory reporting framework and setting up a market intelligence and surveillance unit (MISU).
2. Restructuring the system of bank inspections in terms of focus, process, reporting, and follow-up.
3. Strengthening the statutory audit of banks and enlarging the role of auditors in the supervisory process including using them as agents.

Strengthening the internal defenses within the supervised institutions, such as corporate governance, internal control and audit functions, and management information and risk control systems, are extension of the task of supervision.

The overall supervisory mechanism is divided into two parts:

1. On-site verification.
2. Off-site monitoring and surveillance.

The on-site verification involves examination of the books of accounts of the bank by the officials of the BFS or by external auditors.

Implications for banks

In terms of the new approach adopted for the on-site inspection of banks, the inspecting officers concentrate on core assessments based on the CAMELS model (Capital adequacy, Asset quality, Management, Earnings appraisal, Liquidity, and Systems and controls).

A rating system for domestic and foreign banks based on the international CAMELS model combining financial management and systems and control elements was introduced in July 1998 and it was further improved in April 2001. During the course of annual financial inspections "customer audit" is carried out to evaluate quality of customer service at branches of commercial banks. Old and new private banks displaying systemic weaknesses are also subject to quarterly monitoring.

Implication for all-India development financial institutions

Quarterly returns have been designed based on data on the liabilities and assets as well as data on sources and deployment of funds.

Implication for non-banking financial companies

Off-site surveillance of NBFCs involves scrutiny of various statutory returns (quarterly/half yearly/annual), balance sheets, profit and loss account, auditors' reports, and so on. A format for conducting the off-site surveillance of the companies with asset size of Rs 100 crore and above has also been devised.

Supervision of banks: Issues ahead

Consultative Process: One of the major changes brought about in the supervisory functioning is to introduce a consultative process with banks. The guidelines on asset-liability management (ALM) and comprehensive risk management systems were finalized on the basis of feedback received from banks and the banks advised to implement the guidelines. The supervisory focus in the coming years will be to monitor the progress of implementation of these systems and to ensure their full coverage.

Risk-based Supervision: The risk-based supervision would lead to prioritization of selection and determination of frequency and length of supervisory cycle, targeted appraisals, and allocation of supervisory resources in accordance with the risk perception of the supervised institutions. The risk-based approach will also facilitate the implementation of the supervisory review pillar of the proposed New Capital Accord, which requires that national supervisors set capital ratios for banks based on their risk profile.

Supervision of NBFCs plays a crucial role in broadening access to financial services, enhancing competition, and diversification of the financial sector. Based on the recommendations of the Internal Group and taking into consideration the feedback received thereon, it was decided to put in place a revised framework to address the issues pertaining to the overall regulation of systemically important NBFCs and the relationship between banks and NBFCs.

Bank have prudential regulations on various aspects such as income recognition, asset classification, and provisioning; capital adequacy; prudential exposure limits, accounting and disclosure requirements. However, the "non-deposit taking NBFCs" (NBFCs-ND) are subject to minimal regulation. The application of the prudential guidelines is thus not uniform across the banking and NBFC sectors and within the NBFC sector. There are distinct differences in the application of the prudential guidelines and norms between banks and NBFCs, as discussed in the following:

1. Banks are subject to income recognition, asset classification, and provisioning norms; capital adequacy norms; single and group borrower limits; prudential limits on capital market exposures; classification and valuation norms for the investment portfolio; CRR/statutory liquidity ratio (SLR) requirements; accounting and disclosure norms and supervisory reporting requirements.
2. NBFCs-D (NBFCs-D means deposit taking) are subject to similar norms as banks except CRR requirements and prudential limits on capital market exposures. Certain restrictions apply to the investments by NBFCs-D in land and buildings and unquoted shares.
3. Capital adequacy norms; CRR/SLR requirements; single and group borrower limits; prudential limits on capital market exposures; and the restrictions on investments in land and building and unquoted shares are not applicable to NBFCs-ND (Non-Deposit taking).
4. Unsecured borrowing by companies is regulated by the rules made under the Companies Act. Though NBFCs come under the purview of the Companies Act, they are exempted from the rules since they come under RBI regulation. While in the case of NBFCs-D, their borrowing capacity is limited to a certain extent by the capital adequacy norm; there are no restrictions on the extent to which NBFCs-ND may leverage, even though they are in the financial services sector.

5. Banks and NBFCs compete for some similar kinds of business on the asset side. NBFCs offer products and services which include leasing and hire-purchase, corporate loans, investment in non-convertible debentures, initial public offering (IPO) funding, margin funding, small ticket loans, and venture capital. However, NBFCs do not provide operating account facilities like savings and current deposits, cash credits, and overdrafts.

6. NBFCs avail of bank finance for their operations as advances or by way of banks' subscription to debentures and commercial paper issued by them.

7. Since both the banks and NBFCs are competing for increasingly similar types of some business, especially on the assets side, and since their regulatory and cost-incentive structures are not identical, the following restrictions have been placed on the activities of NBFCs which banks may finance:

   i. Bills discounted and rediscounted by NBFCs, except for rediscounting of bills discounted by NBFCs arising from the sale of

      a. commercial vehicles (including light commercial vehicles); and

      b. two-wheeler and three-wheeler vehicles, subject to certain conditions.

   ii. Investments of NBFCs both of current and long-term nature, in any company or entity by way of shares, debentures, and so on, with certain exemptions.

   iii. Unsecured loans or inter-corporate deposits by NBFCs to any company.

   iv. All types of loans/advances by NBFCs to their subsidiaries, group companies/entities.

   v. Finance to NBFCs for further lending to individuals for subscribing to IPOs.

   vi. Bridge loans of any nature, or interim finance against capital/debenture issues and/or in the form of loans of a bridging nature pending raising of long-term funds from the market by way of capital, deposits, etc. to all categories of NBFCs, that is, equipment leasing and hire-purchase finance companies, loan and investment companies.

   vii. Residuary non-banking companies (RNBCs) should not enter into lease agreements departmentally with equipment-leasing companies as well as other NBFCs engaged in equipment leasing.

8. Investment by a bank in a financial services company should not exceed 10 percent of the bank's paid-up share capital and reserves and the investments in all such companies, financial institutions, stock and other exchanges put together should not exceed 20 percent of the bank's paid-up share capital and reserves. Banks in India are required to obtain the prior approval of the Reserve Bank before being granted Certificate of Registration for establishing an NBFC and for making a strategic investment in an NBFC in India. However, foreign entities, including the head offices of foreign banks having branches in India may, under the automatic route for FDI, commence the business of NBFC after obtaining a Certificate of Registration from the Reserve Bank.

9. NBFCs can undertake activities that are not permitted to be undertaken by banks or which the banks are permitted to undertake in a restricted manner, for example, financing of acquisitions and mergers, capital market activities. The differences in the

level of regulation of the banks and NBFCs, which are undertaking some similar activities gives rise to considerable scope for regulatory arbitrage.

10. NBFCs-D may access public funds, either directly or indirectly through public deposits, CPs, debentures, inter-corporate deposits, bank finance, and NBFCs-ND may access public funds through all of the foregoing modes except through public deposits.

11. At present, there are no prudential norms or guidelines on the intra-group transactions and exposures (ITEs) between the NBFCs and their parent entities.

12. As per the provisions of the Banking Regulation Act, a bank is not allowed to set up a banking subsidiary. This eliminates the scope for more than one entity within a group competing for public deposits. However, this aspect is not well addressed under the existing framework where a bank operating in India may set up an NBFC-D as a subsidiary or where they acquire substantial holding in such an entity, that is, say more than 10 percent.

13. Foreign direct investment in NBFCs is permitted under the automatic route in 19 specified activities subject to compliance with the minimum capitalization norms. Once an NBFC is established with the requisite capital under Foreign Exchange Management Act (FEMA), subsequent diversification either through the existing company or through downstream NBFCs is undertaken without any further authorization.

14. Banks are not permitted to offer discretionary portfolio management scheme (PMS). As a corollary, the NBFCs sponsored by banks (namely, NBFCs which are subsidiaries of banks or where banks have a management control) are also not permitted to offer discretionary PMS, whereas other NBFCs are allowed to offer this product.

15. Where a foreign bank is holding between 10 and 50 percent (both included) of the issued and paid-up equity of an NBFC, it will be required to demonstrate that it does not have a management control in case the NBFC is to be kept outside the ambit of consolidated prudential regulations.

16. NBFCs which do not belong to any banking group are currently permitted to offer discretionary portfolio management as a product, as permitted by their respective regulators. Bank-sponsored NBFCs will also be allowed to offer discretionary Portfolio Management Services (PMS) to their clients, on a case-to-case basis.

17. Banks in India, including foreign banks operating in India, shall not hold more than 10 percent of the paid-up equity capital of an NBFC-D. This restriction would, however, not apply to investment in housing finance companies.

REGULATION OF INDIAN CAPITAL MARKET (STOCK MARKET)

1. In India, the capital market is regulated by the Capital Markets Division of the Department of Economic Affairs, Ministry of Finance. The division is responsible for formulating the policies related to the orderly growth and development of the securities markets (i.e., share, debt, and derivatives) as well as protecting the interest of the investors. In particular, it is responsible for (a) institutional reforms in the securities markets, (b) building regulatory and market institutions, (c) strengthening investor

protection mechanism, and (*d*) providing efficient legislative framework for securities markets, such as Securities and Exchange Board of India Act, 1992 (SEBI Act, 1992); Securities Contracts (Regulation) Act, 1956; and the Depositories Act, 1996. The division administers these legislations and the rules framed there under.

2. The five main legislations governing the Indian capital market are: (*a*) Capital Issues (Control) Act, 1947; (*b*) the Indian Companies Act, 1956, which sets out rules and regulations for the corporate sector in relation to issue, allotment and transfer of securities, and disclosures to be made in public issues; (*c*) the Securities Contracts (Regulation) Act, 1956, which provides for regulation of transactions in securities through control over stock exchange; (*d*) the SEBI Act, 1992, which established SEBI to protect investors and develop and regulate securities market; and (*e*) the Depositories Act, 1996, which provides for electronic maintenance and transfer of ownership of demat securities.

Legislations

Capital Issues (Control) Act, 1947

The Act was a means of controlling the raising of capital by companies and ensuring that national resources were channeled into proper lines, that is, for desirable purposes to serve goals and priorities of the government, and to protect the interests of investors. Under the Act, any firm wishing to issue securities had to obtain approval from the central government, which also determined the amount, type, and price of the issue. As a part of the liberalization process, the Act was repealed in 1992.

Companies Act, 1956

It deals with issue, allotment, and transfer of securities and various aspects relating to company management. The memorandum of association, articles of association and prospectus provide the ground work for public issues. It provides for standard of disclosure in public issues of capital, particularly in the fields of company management and projects, information about other listed companies under the same management, and management's perception of risk factors. It also regulates underwriting, the use of premium and discounts on issues, rights and bonus issues, payment of interest and dividends, supply of annual report and other information.

Securities Contracts (Regulation) Act, 1956

It provides for direct and indirect control of virtually all aspects of securities trading and the running of stock exchanges, and aims to prevent undesirable transactions in securities. It gives central government/SEBI regulatory jurisdiction over (*a*) stock exchanges through a process of recognition and continued supervision, (*b*) contracts in securities, and (*c*) listing of securities on stock exchanges. As a condition of recognition, a stock exchange complies with conditions prescribed by central government.

SEBI Act, 1992

It was enacted to empower SEBI with statutory powers for (a) protecting the interests of investors in securities, (b) promoting the development of the securities market, and (c) regulating the securities market. Its regulatory jurisdiction extends over corporates in the issuance of capital and transfer of securities, in addition to all intermediaries and persons associated with securities market. It can conduct enquiries, audits, and inspections of all concerned and adjudicate offences under the Act. It has powers to register and regulate all market intermediaries and also to penalize those in case of violations of the provisions of the Act, rules and regulations made there under. SEBI has full autonomy and authority to regulate and develop an orderly securities market.

The following departments of SEBI take care of the activities in the secondary market:

1. Market Intermediaries Registration and Supervision Department (MIRSD) is concerned with the registration, supervision, compliance monitoring, and inspection of all market intermediaries in respect of all segments of the markets, such as equity, equity derivatives, debt and debt-related derivatives.
2. Market Regulation Department (MRD) is concerned with formulation of new policies as well as supervising the functioning and operations (except relating to derivatives) of securities exchanges, their subsidiaries, and market institutions such as clearing and settlement organizations and depositories.
3. Derivatives and New Products Departments (DNPD) is concerned with supervising trading at derivatives segments of stock exchanges, introducing new products to be traded and consequent policy changes.

Depositories Act, 1996

The Depositories Act, 1996 provides for the establishment of depositories in securities with the objective of ensuring free transferability of securities with speed, accuracy, and security by (a) making securities of public limited companies freely transferable subject to certain exceptions; (b) dematerializing the securities in the depository mode; and (c) providing for maintenance of ownership records in a book entry form. In order to streamline the settlement process, the Act envisages transfer of ownership of securities electronically by book entry without making the securities move from person to person. The Act has made the securities of all public limited companies freely transferable, restricting the company's right to use discretion in effecting the transfer of securities, and the transfer deed and other procedural requirements under the Companies Act have been dispensed with.

Regulation of Capital Market by Reserve Bank of India (RBI)

Reserve Bank of India has regulatory involvement in the capital market but this has been limited to debt management through primary dealers, foreign exchange control, and liquidity support to market participants. It is RBI and not SEBI that regulates primary dealers in the government securities market. RBI instituted the primary dealership of government securities in March 1998. Securities transactions that involve foreign exchange transactions need the permission of RBI.

Rules and Regulations

The government has framed rules under the Securities Contracts Regulation Act (SCRA), SEBI Act, and the Depositories Act. SEBI has framed regulations under the SEBI Act and the Depositories Act for registration and regulation of all market intermediaries, and for prevention of unfair trade practices, insider trading, etc. Under these Acts, government and SEBI issue notifications, guidelines, and circulars, which need to be complied with by market participants.

Thus, the capital market is primarily regulated by SEBI which regulates 23 stock exchanges including two major stock exchanges (Bombay Stock Exchange and National Stock Exchange) and two depositories (National Securities Depositories Ltd and Central Depositories Services Ltd) along with a large number of intermediaries like merchant bankers, registrars to issue, mutual funds, printers, advertising agents, and FIIs.

Review of Regulatory Environment

The powers and functions of regulatory authorities for the securities market seem to be diverse in nature. SEBI is the primary body responsible for regulation of the securities market, deriving its powers of registration, and enforcement from the SEBI Act. There was an existing regulatory framework for the securities market provided by the Securities Contract Regulation (SCR) Act and the Companies Act, administered by the Ministry of Finance and the Department of Company Affairs (DCA) under the Ministry of Law, respectively. SEBI has been delegated most of the functions and powers under the SCR Act and shares the rest with the Ministry of Finance. It has also been delegated certain powers under the Companies Act. RBI also has regulatory involvement in the capital markets regarding foreign exchange control, liquidity support to market participants, and debt management through primary dealers.

The impact of regulation of stock market is that participants in the Indian capital market are required to register with SEBI to carry out their businesses. These include stockbrokers, sub brokers, share transfer agents, bankers to an issue, trustees of a trust deed, registrars to an issue, merchant bankers, underwriters, portfolio managers, and investment advisers. Stockbrokers are not allowed to buy, sell, or deal in securities, unless they hold a certificate granted by SEBI. Each stockbroker is subject to capital adequacy requirements consisting of two components: basic minimum capital and additional or optional capital relating to volume of business. The basic minimum capital requirements vary from one exchange to another. The additional or optional capital and the basic minimum capital combined have to be maintained at 8 percent or more of the gross outstanding business in the exchange (the gross outstanding business means the cumulative amount of sales and purchases by a stockbroker in all securities at any point during the settlement period). Sales and purchases on behalf of customers may not be netted but may be included to those of the broker.

SEBI Act of 1992 has introduced self-regulatory organizations (SROs) for regulating various participants in the securities market like Association of Mutual Funds in India (AMFI).

Issues relating to regulatory framework

Despite a plethora of disclosure requirements, there are still key areas where investors get little precious information of value like mergers and acquisitions, asset sell-off, intra-company, intra-group transactions, inter-corporate investments, and the disclosure levels are not up to the mark.

The wave of economic reforms initiated by the government has also influenced the functioning and governance of the capital market. The consistent reforms in Indian capital market, especially in the secondary market resulting in modern technology and online screen-based trading have revolutionized the stock exchanges. The debt market, however, is almost non-existent in India even though there has been a large volume of government bonds trading. Banks and financial institutions have been holding a substantial part of these bonds, as a statutory liquidity requirement. And a series of reforms were introduced to improve investor protection, automation of stock trading, integration of national markets, and efficiency of market operations.

Regulatory Framework in the Forex Market

With a view to facilitating external trade and promoting orderly development of foreign exchange market in India, a new Act called the Foreign Exchange Management Act, 1999 (FEMA) came into force from June 1, 2000, and the Foreign Exchange Regulation Act, 1973 stands repealed.

Under FEMA, foreign exchange transactions have been divided into two broad categories—current account transactions and capital account transactions. Transactions that alter the assets and liabilities of a person residing in India or a person residing outside India have been classified as capital account transactions. All other transactions would be current account transactions. Only the Government of India in consultation with the Reserve Bank would be empowered to impose reasonable restrictions on current account transactions. Accordingly, as per Government of India rules the current account transactions, remittances of only eight types of current account transactions are prohibited, 11 types of transactions need Government of India's prior approval whereas 17 transactions need prior permission from the Reserve Bank in case the amount of remittances exceeds prescribed limit for such remittances.

The Reserve Bank of India has notified comprehensive, simple and transparent regulations under the FEMA, 1999 governing various capital account transactions. The new regulations clearly indicate the types of permissible capital account transactions, that leave very few individual transactions to be dealt with by the Reserve Bank, simplify procedures, reduce the number of forms to a bare minimum, and grant more powers to authorized dealers.

Regulatory Framework for Insurance Industry

Insurance industry assumes a significant place in the economy. The industry has been regulated by Insurance Act, 1938, LIC Act, 1956, and GIC Act, 1972 before the setting up of Insurance Regulatory and Development Authority of India (IRDA), 2000.

Salient features of Insurance Act, 1938: It is an Act to consolidate and amend the law relating to the business of insurance. It extends to the whole of India. It shall come into force on such date as the central government may, by notification in the official gazette, appoint in this behalf. Important definitions are:

1. "Insurance company" means any insurer being a company, association, or partnership, which may be, would be under Indian Companies Act, 1913 (1 of 1913) or to which the Indian Partnership Act, 1932 (9 of 1932), applies.
2. "Insurer" means any individual or unincorporated body of individuals or body corporate incorporated under the law of any country, other than India, carrying on insurance business, not being a person specified in Clause (c) of this clause which
    i. carries on that business in India;
    ii. has his or its principal place of business or is domiciled in India; and
    iii. with the object of obtaining insurance business employs a representative, or maintains a place of business in India.
3. "Insurance agent" means an agent licensed under Section 42 who receives or agrees to receive payment by way of commission or other remuneration in consideration of his soliciting or procuring business including business related to continuance, renewal, or revival of policies of insurance.
4. "Life insurance business" means the business of effecting contracts of insurance upon human life, including any contract whereby the payment of money is assured on death (except death by accident only) or the happening of any contingency dependent on human life, and any contract which is subject to payment of premium for a definite term of the dependent's life and shall be deemed to include:
    i. the granting of disability and double or triple indemnity, accident benefits, if so provided in the contract of insurance;
    ii. the granting of amenities upon human life; and
    iii. the granting of superannuating allowances and annuities payable out of any fund applicable solely to the relief and maintenance of persons engaged or who have been engaged in any particular profession trade or employment or of the dependents of such person. "Actuary" means an actuary possessing such qualifications as may be prescribed by the authority.
5. "Policy holder" means a person to whom the whole of the interest of the policy holder in the policy is assigned once and for all, but does not include an assignee thereof whose interest in the policy is defensible or is for the time being subject to any condition. Part II of the Act consists of the provisions applicable to insurance like: It covers the rules related to the prohibition of transaction of insurance business by certain persons. Every insurer shall be subject to all the provisions of this Act in relation to any class of

insurance business so long as his liabilities in India in respect of business of that class remain unsatisfied.

Part II (A) of the Act covers Insurance Association of India, councils of the association of India, council of the association and committee thereof. It deals with provisions related to the incorporation of the Insurance Association of India, entry of names of members in the register, resignation and filling up of casual vacancies, powers of central government regarding the working of personnel in the life insurance companies. Part II (B) of the Act covers the rules related to the Tariff Advisory Committee and control of tariff rates. The Act also deals with licensing of surveyors and loss assessors. Part II (C) the Act reveals rules related to the solvency margin, methods of valuation of assets and liabilities, advance payment of premium, and restrictions on the opening of a new place of business. No insurers after the commencement of the Insurance Act, 1968, shall open a new place of business in India or change otherwise than within the same city, town or village, the location of an existing place of business situated in India without obtaining the prior permissions of the authority. Part III of the Act deals with provident societies, prohibition of transaction of insurance business by provident societies other than public companies or co-operative societies, working of provident societies and its registration. Part IV of the Act defines mutual insurance companies and co-operative life insurance societies.

6. "Mutual insurance company" means an insurer or a company incorporated under the Indian Companies Act, 1913 or 1882 or 1866, which has no share capital, and of which, by its constitution only, all policy holders are members.

7. "Co-operative life insurance society" means an insurer being a society registered under the Co-operative Societies Act, 1912 under an Act of state legislature governing the registration of co-operative societies which carries on business of life insurance and which has no share capital on which dividend or bonus is payable and of which by its constitution only original members on whose application the society is registered and policy holders are members. It also deals with reinsurance. Part V of the Act is miscellaneous and deals with various penalties related to the contravention of this Act. The Act also provides the format and regulations for the preparation of balance sheet, revenue accounts, profit and loss accounts, and for preparation of abstracts of actuary reports and requirement as applicable to such abstracts. The life insurance business has been regulated by LIC Act, 1956. Some salient provisions are:

This is an Act to provide for the nationalization of the life insurance business in India by transferring any such business to a corporation established for the purpose and to provide for the regulation and control of the business of the corporation and for matters connected therewith. The Act has seven chapters and three schedules.

Chapter 1 is the preliminary part mentioning various definitions related to the Life Insurance Corporation. Chapter 2 of the Act deals with the establishment of Life Insurance Corporation of India. The Act covers rules regarding constitution of the corporation and its capital. The corporation shall consist of such number of persons not exceeding 16 as the central government may think fit to appoint thereto and one of them shall be appointed by the central government to be the chairman thereof. The original capital of the corporation shall be 5 crores of rupees provided by the central government after due appropriation made by parliament by law, and the terms and conditions relating to the provisions of such capital shall be such as may be determined by the central government.

Chapter 3 of the Act mentions the functions of the corporation. It shall be the general duty of the corporation to carry on life insurance business whether inside or outside India, and the corporation shall so exercise its powers under this Act as to secure that life insurance business is developed to the best advantage of the community. Chapter 4 of the Act deals with the transfer of existing life insurance business to the corporation.

Chapter 5 of the Act deals with:

1. **Offices, branches, and agencies of the corporation:** The central office shall be at such place as the central government may notify in the official gazette.
2. **Committees of the corporation:** The corporation may entrust the general superintendence and direction of its affairs and business to an executive committee consisting of not more than five of its members, and the executive committee may exercise all powers and do all such acts and things as may be delegated by the corporation.
3. **Managing directors:** The corporation may appoint one or more persons to be the managing director or directors of the corporation and every managing director shall be the whole-time officer of the corporation, and shall exercise such powers and perform such duties as may be entrusted or delegated to him by the corporation. The chapter also contains the rules related to the working of corporation, zonal managers, and staff of the corporation.

Chapter 6 of the Act deals with the funds and their audit, actuarial valuations, and the utilization of profits from any business. The corporation shall have its own fund and all receipts of the corporation shall be credited thereto and all payments of the corporation shall be made there from. The accounts of the corporation shall be audited by auditors duly qualified to act as auditors of companies under the law for the time being in force relating to companies, and the auditors shall be appointed by the corporation with the previous approval of the central government and shall receive such remuneration from the corporation as the central government may fix. If for any financial year profits accrue from any business carried on by the corporation, then, after making provision for reserves and other matters for which provision is necessary or expedient the balance of such profits shall be paid to the central government.

Chapter 7 of the Act covers the miscellaneous rules like:

1. The exclusive privilege of corporation for carrying on life insurance business.
2. The exclusive privilege of corporation to cease.
3. Power of corporation to have official seal in certain cases.
4. Exception in case of insurance business in respect of persons residing outside India.
5. Requirement of foreign laws to be complied in certain cases.

6. Reverting of certain share in the administrator general.
7. Terminating contracts of chief agents and special agents.
8. Special provisions regarding winding up of certain insurers.
9. Deduction of income tax not to be made on interest or dividend.
10. The cases in which the Act does not apply.
11. Special provisions regarding transfer of controlled business of certain composite insurers.
12. The power of corporation to make rules and regulations.

In order to streamline insurance business (life and non-life) in India, the IRDA has been established under IRDA Act, 1999.

The Insurance Regulatory and Development Authority Act, 1999

It is an Act (Act no. 41 of 1999) to provide for the establishment of an authority to protect the interests of holders of insurance policies to regulate, promote, and ensure orderly growth of the insurance industry and for matters connected therewith or incidental thereto and further to amend the Insurance Act, 1938, the Life Insurance Corporation Act, 1956, and the General Insurance Business (Nationalization) Act, 1972.

The Act consists of six chapters and three schedules. Chapter I is the preliminary part which consist of some basic definitions related to the IRDA Act. The Act extends to the whole of India.

Chapter II deals with the IRDA. The authority shall be a body corporate by the name aforesaid having perpetual accession and a common seal with power, subject to the provisions of this Act, to acquire hold and dispose of property, both movable and immovable, and to contract and shall, by the said name, sue or be sued. The head office of the authority shall be at such place as the central government may decide from time to time.

The authority may establish offices at other places in India.

Composition of the authority:

1. a chairperson,
2. not more than five whole-time members, and
3. not more than four part-time members.

The members are to be appointed by the central government from among persons of ability, integrity, and standing who have knowledge or experience in life insurance, general insurance, actuarial science, finance, economics, law, accountancy, administration or any other discipline which would, in the opinion of central government, be useful to the authority.

The Act also covers rules related to the tenure of office, of the chairperson and other members, their removal from office, salary and allowances, future employment and vacancies, and so on. The chairperson shall have the powers of general superintendence and direction in respect of an administrative matter of the authority.

Chapter III of the Act deals with the transfer of assets, liabilities, etc., of Interim Insurance Regulatory Authority. The assets of the Interim Insurance Regulatory Authority shall be deemed to include all rights and powers, and all properties, whether movable or immovable, including, in particular, cash balance, deposits, and all other interests and rights in, or arising out of, such properties as may be in the possession of the Interim Insurance Regulatory Authority and all books of account and documents relating to the same; and liabilities shall be deemed to include debts, liabilities, and obligations of whatever kind.

Chapter IV of the Act mentions the duties, powers, and punitions of the authority. Subject to the provisions of this Act and any other law for the time being in force, the authority shall have the duty to regulate, promote, and ensure orderly growth of the insurance business and reinsurance business.

Chapter V of the Act deals with finance, accounts, and audit. The central government may, after the due appropriation made by the parliament by law in this behalf, make to the authority grants of such sums of money as the government may think fit for being utilized for the purpose of this Act. The authority shall maintain proper accounts and other relevant records and prepare an annual statement of accounts in such a form as may be prescribed by the central government in consultation with the comptroller and auditor general of India. The accounts of the authority shall be audited by the comptroller and auditor general of India at such intervals as may be specified by him and any expenditure incurred in connection with such audit shall be payable by the authority to the comptroller and auditor general.

Chapter VII of the Act is the miscellaneous part which covers rules related to following points:

1. Power of central government to issue directions.
2. Power of central government to supersede authority.
3. Furnishing of returns etc. to central government.
4. Chairperson, members, officers and other employees of authority to be public servants.
5. Protection of action taken in good faith.
6. Delegation of powers.
7. Power to make rules.
8. Establishment of Insurance Advisory Committee.
9. Power to make regulations.
10. Rules and regulations to be laid before parliament.
11. Application of other laws barred.
12. Power to remove difficulties.

Pension Fund Regulatory & Development Authority (PFRDA)

Pension Fund Regulatory & Development Authority (PFRDA) was set up on January 1, 2004. It is a regulator for pension fund on the lines of the insurance and capital market. It regulates pension funds, existing pension funds as well as new pension schemes announced by state governments. The employee provident fund, coal mines provident funds, etc., are not within its purview. PFRDA will also launch educational awareness role on the pattern of SEBI's investor's education program. The regulator's role is to evolve guidelines in consultation with the government with the opening up of the pension sector. A pension fund, subscriber education and protection fund, will also be set up in 2009. The PFRDA has issued license to six pension fund managers on February 19, 2009, namely, UTI Retirement Solution, SBI, ICICI Prudential AMC, Reliance Capital, IDFC AMC, and Kotak Mahindra AMC. It would decide on how many pension funds managers will be allowed initially to limit the schemes, the norms of selection of pension fund managers, norms for selection of central record keeping agencies (CRAs), capital requirements for these players, and investment norms for the pension funds. PFRDA has granted license to six pension fund managers mentioned earlier in 2009. In short, PFRDA has laid down all the operational guidelines w.e.f. February 2009 and new pension schemes will be available to all Indian citizens from May 1, 2009 for pension fund management and prescribe the level of investment by the pension fund managers in myriad instruments.

3

Risk and Return in Financial Services

Learning Objectives

- To understand the concept of risk and return.
- To apply risk and return in financial services.

CONCEPT OF RISK

The term "risk" usually refers to the probability of loss of a valued resource because of uncertainty. If the outcome, say dividend or expected market price is certain, then there is no uncertainty. For example, if we invest our money in the stock market then what is the likelihood that we will lose our money? We can refer to this "risk of loss" as R–, but "risk" is also about gain R+. Why do we "gamble" on the possibilities of a boom in the stock market? We do that in order to gain possible positive outcomes. R– and R+ are intertwined in a holistic fashion. One cannot have R– without R+, and vice versa, and as one changes, the other changes. However, both R– and R+ are chaotic in character and hence they may seem to be out of balance at times.

Risk is the chance that an outcome other than "expected outcome" will occur. In other words, risk can be defined as the chance that the actual outcome from an investment will differ from the expected outcome. This means that, the more variable the possible outcomes that can occur (that is, the broader the range of possible outcomes), the greater the risk.

We can therefore say that there are two elements that are crucial when defining risk. These are:

1. **Indeterminacy:** There are two possible outcomes (R+ and R–) and it is not known with certainty which outcome will result.
2. **Adversity:** One of the outcomes (R–) is undesirable but cannot be avoided altogether.

In order to further appreciate the concept of risk, let us consider the equity shares of two companies: A and B.

The shares of company A have a price that appears to be virtually fixed in place. It is a utility company (e.g., power supply company) issuing dividends regularly like a fixed income security. Naturally, the price of the utility stock will vary somewhat over time but it does not appear to deviate too much from its central level because of lesser uncertainty associated with returns.

On the contrary, the price of the shares of the second company B only moves in double digit percentage. There have been some frightening moves to the downside as well as healthy appreciations in price of company B shares in the recent past.

The question arises, which one of these two shares is riskier, A or B?

The answer depends on how you define risk.

If you think of risk using the simple concept that discusses the potential for price change, then we would pick B as being the riskier of the two assets, logically. Its daily price movement constitutes a greater percentage of its underlying price. However, we can look at risk on a number of different time scales. Now, if you are told that the price of company B shares, while moving around in double-digit percentage increments at a time, generally stays in a range between 70 and 90, what would you say when asked about the relative risky-ness of the two assets?

The answer is indeterminate from the information given to us. We know that A is a range-bound asset as well. However, we do not know the size of that range and nor do we know the underlying price. It could be that A stays in range, bracketed by 7 and 9 with similar percentage movements. In that case, A and B would appear to have equivalent risk.

The foregoing discussion of risk leads to the following conclusions:

- First, the concept of *risk is not subjective but a real-world concept*. When we want to invest in the stock market, we are interested in knowing the risk associated with that investment. For that matter, all investments carry risk. Will we gain or lose money? What are the odds of gaining money to losing money?
- Second, *risk can exist whether it is perceived or not*. Though investment in a firm like Infosys or Reliance can be considered an excellent investment, but we cannot say that it is not risky. Remember the decline in the share price of, say Infosys in April 2003 by Rs 2,000 in just two days.
- Finally, *risk can be imagined* where the possibility of loss is not there. Consider investing in Government of India paper. It is virtually risk-free, but we can imagine a possibility of civil war and government defaulting on payment.

TYPES OF RISK

There are various types of risks that a financial manager usually comes across in financial decision-making:

1. **Business Risk:** This refers to the risk of doing business in a particular industry or economic system. Once a firm is in a particular economic system (e.g., India or China or USA) or a particular industry (e.g., steel, cement, pharma) it is restrained by certain economy-wide or industry-wide factors which lead to variability of returns.
2. **Financial Risk:** Financial risk arises when companies resort to financial leverage or use debt financing. The more the company resorts to debt financing, the greater is the financial risk. This risk is further discussed in the chapter on leverage.
3. **Liquidity Risk:** Liquidity risk arises when an asset cannot be liquidated easily in the secondary market. Real assets have a higher liquidity risk than financial assets which are traded in the secondary market. Among financial assets also, shares of blue chip companies and government bonds are more liquid.
4. **Interest Rate Risk:** Interest rate risk is the variability in a security's return resulting from changes in the level of interest rates. Other things being equal, security prices move inversely to interest rates. The reason for this is related to the valuation of securities which will be discussed in the next chapter. This risk affects bondholders more directly than equity investors.
5. **Market Risk:** Market risk refers to the variability of returns due to fluctuations in the securities market. All securities are exposed to market risk but equity shares get most affected. This risk includes a wide range of factors exogenous to securities themselves like depressions, wars, and politics.
6. **Inflation Risk:** With rise in inflation there is reduction of purchasing power, hence this is also referred to as purchasing power risk and affects all securities. This risk is also directly related to interest rate risk, as interest rates generally go up with inflation.

MEASURING RISK

It is stated that risk is the chance that an outcome other than "expected outcome" will occur. But the question is how do we measure this "chance?" Is it possible to measure risk? How do we measure risk in practice? Are there any tools available for measuring risk? See Box 3.1.

Fortunately, experts have devised some very useful measures for risk measurement. Let us have a look at the most commonly used risk-measurement tools.

As we know risk is associated with the dispersion in the likely outcomes. Dispersion refers to variability. If an asset's return has no variability, it has no risk. Dispersion can be measured in many ways:

1. **Range of Returns**
   The difference between the highest possible rate of return and the lowest possible rate of return is called the range. It is one of the crudest measures of risk. However, as it is

Box 3.1   Risk's New Dimension

The attack on the World Trade Centre has changed, perhaps lastingly, perceptions of risk. It was the worst terrorist assault on American soil, producing the biggest insurance losses in history and the highest death toll in any insured event. The odds of terrorist attacks may not necessarily be any higher. But the fear of them certainly is. So, too, is the demand for insurance cover. Good news for insurers? But war risks, or the risk of nuclear attack, find no takers. In most countries, governments are supposed to pay for the costs of war.

Immediately after the attacks on America, cover against terrorist acts became the risk that nobody wanted. Insurers immediately increased airlines' premiums and cut their cover for third-party war and terrorism liabilities to a maximum of $50 million per airline, per "event." Under pressure from airlines threatening to ground their fleets, European Union governments agreed to provide temporary cover for a month, including liability for damage on the ground. The American government, too, has become the insurer of last resort. On September 21st Congress passed an emergency Act promising to repay American airlines for the added insurance cost over the next 180 days, as well as to cover, for the same period, airlines' war and terrorist liabilities when they exceed $100 million.

A few insurers now say they will be prepared to offer the necessary insurance for airlines. American International Group (AIG), the country's biggest insurer, said on September 25th that it hopes to be able to offer coverage for war and terrorism, for up to $1 billion per airline. Yet any coverage will come at a high price. Michael Frinquelli at Renaissance Fund Advisors, a hedge fund in New York that invests in insurance companies, says that, without government involvement, airline premiums would by now have risen up to tenfold. Even with the government's relief package, they will probably triple.

European governments, as well as Israel, are far more experienced in reinsuring man-made as well as natural catastrophes. In 1993, after a series of bombings on mainland Britain by the Irish Republican Army, a government-backed, mutually owned company, Pool Re, was set up. Insurers collect premiums for terrorist insurance, and the government chips in if claims for terrorist attacks exceed the pool's premiums plus reserves. France has a state-guaranteed reinsurer, the *Caisse Centrale de Réassurance*. It kicks in when private insurers' losses from policies for natural disaster exceed 150 percent of premiums. The Israeli government covers direct losses from terrorist attacks, although not for business interruption.

Do insurers need the American government as the ultimate guarantor for terrorist risk? They might prefer it to be the ultimate guarantor of the stock market. The fall in equity markets since September 11 has knocked more than twice as much off insurers' world stock market capitalization as the estimated $30 billion insurance cost of the terrorist attacks.

Source: *The Economist*, September 27, 2001.

based only on two extreme values it may not always convey meaningful information about risk.

2. **Width of the Probability Distribution**

   The width of a probability distribution of rates of return is another crude measure of dispersion. The wider the probability distribution, the greater is the risk or greater the variability of return. This variability can be appraised visually. A look at the probability distribution of company X in comparison with the probability distribution of company Y indicates that the firm X which has a narrower probability distribution is less risky as compared to firm Y which has a wider probability distribution (see Figure 3.1).

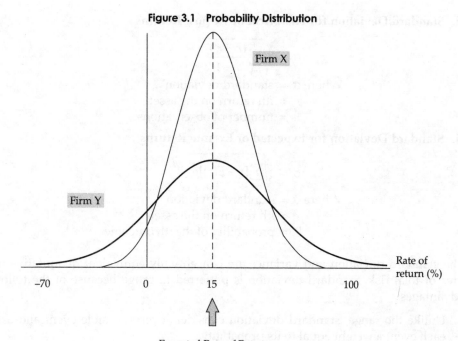

Figure 3.1 Probability Distribution

Source: Kothari and Dutta (2005).

3. **Variance of Returns**

This is the quantitative measure of dispersion and is also the most reliable measure of risk. It measures the variability in the rates of returns. The variance of an asset's rate of return can be found as the sum of the squared deviation of each possible rate of return from the expected rate of return multiplied by the probability that the rate of return occurs.

$$\text{VAR (k)} = \sum_{i=1}^{n} P_i(k_i - \bar{k})^2$$

Where VAR (k) = variance of returns

P_i = probability associated with the ith possible outcome

k_i = rate of return from the ith possible outcome

k = expected rate of return

n = number of years.

4. **Standard Deviation of Returns**

The most popular way of measuring variability of returns is standard deviation. The standard deviation denoted by σ is simply the square root of the variance of the rates of return explained earlier.

i. Standard Deviation for Historical or Ex-post Returns

$$\sigma = \sqrt{\sum_{i=1}^{n} \frac{(r_i - r')}{n-1}}$$

Where σ = standard deviation
r_i = ith return on the asset
n = number of observations.

ii. Standard Deviation for Expected or Ex-ante Returns

$$\sigma = \sqrt{\sum_{i=1}^{n} [r_i - E(r)]p_i}$$

Where σ = standard deviation
r_i = ith return on the asset
P_i = probability of the ith outcome.

The standard deviation and variance are conceptually equivalent quantitative measures of total risk. Standard deviation is preferred to range because of the following advantages:

1. Unlike the range, standard deviation considers every possible event and assigns each event a weight equal to its probability.
2. Standard deviation is a very familiar concept and many calculators and computers are programmed to calculate it.
3. Standard deviation is a measure of dispersion around the expected (or average) value. This is in absolute consensus with the definition of risk as "variability of returns."
4. Standard deviation is obtained as the square root of the sum of squared differences multiplied by their probabilities. This facilitates comparison of risk as measured by standard deviation and expected returns as both are measured in the same costs. This is why standard deviation is preferred to variance as a measure of risk.

5. **Coefficient of Variation**
Coefficient of variation is the standardized measure of dispersion about the expected value. It indicates the variability per unit of average return (see Figure 3.2). Symbolically,

$$CV = \frac{\sigma}{r'}$$

6. **Semi-deviation**
This is a new approach of risk measurement. The proponents of this approach argue that since an investor will be more concerned about the risk of loss or the chance of market price going below the purchase price while calculating risk we should consider only the negative deviations or downside deviations. Since we ignore the positive deviations (which are favorable) and consider only the negative deviations, hence the name "semi-deviation."

Figure 3.2   Coefficient of Variation

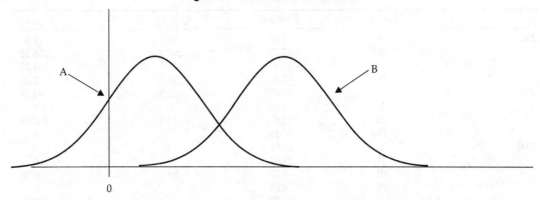

$\sigma_A = \sigma_B$, but A is riskier because there is a larger probability of losses.

$$\frac{\sigma}{\hat{k}} = CV_A > CV_B.$$

Source: Kothari and Dutta (2005).

The quarterly returns for the Alliance Growth Fund are as follows (see Table 3.1):

Table 3.1   Returns for the Alliance Growth Fund

Year	Quarter	Return
2005	I	−1.08
	II	−27.35
	III	−13.81
	IV	−1.87
2006	I	−19.67
	II	1.65
	III	−13.97
	IV	16.18
2007	I	22.08
	II	25.92
	III	−9.75
	IV	8.25
		−13.42

Source: Kothari and Dutta (2005).

Determine the variability in the fund's returns using downside deviations (semi-deviation) as a measure of risk.

Solution: The variability in the funds return using semi-deviation as a measure of risk can be calculated as follows (see Table 3.2):

Table 3.2 Variability in the Funds Return

Year	Quarter	Return	$(x_4 - \bar{x}_4)$	$(x_4 - \bar{x}_4)^2$
2005	I	−1.08	0.03	0.00
	II	−27.35	−26.23	688.10
	III	−13.81	−12.69	161.07
	IV	−1.87	0.75	0.56
2006	I	−19.67	−18.55	344.16
	II	1.65	–	0
	III	−13.97	−12.85	165.16
	IV	16.18	–	0
2007	I	22.08	–	0
	II	25.92	–	0
	III	−9.75	−8.63	74.50
	IV	8.25	–	0
		−13.42		1,433.58

Source: Kothari and Dutta (2005).

Inference: $x_4 = -1.11833$ Semi-deviation = $\sqrt{\dfrac{(x_4 - \bar{x}_4)^2}{11}}$ 1433.58 = 11.416%

DIVERSIFIABLE AND NON-DIVERSIFIABLE RISK

The fact that returns on stocks do not move in perfect tandem means that risk can be reduced by diversification. But the fact that there is some positive correlation means that in practice, risk can never be reduced to zero. So, there is a limit on the amount of risk that can be reduced through diversification. This is due to two major reasons:

1. **Degree of Correlation**
   The extent of risk reduction through diversification depends on the degree of positive correlation between stocks. The lower the correlation, the greater is the amount of risk reduction that is possible.

2. **Number of Stocks in the Portfolio**
   Risk reduction achieved by diversification also depends on the number of stocks in the portfolio. As the number of stocks increases (up to a certain extent), the diversifying effect of each additional stock diminishes as shown in Figure 3.3.

As Figure 3.3 indicates, the major benefits of diversification are obtained with the first 10 to 12 stocks, provided they belong to industries that are not closely related. Additions to the portfolio beyond this point continue to reduce total risk but at a decreasing rate.

From the figure it is also apparent that only one component of total risk is being reduced and the other component remains constant, whatever the number of stocks in your portfolio is.

The fixed component is that part of total risk (from various sources like interest rate risk, inflation risk, financial risk) which is related to the macro economy or the stock market as

Figure 3.3   Risk Reduction through Diversification

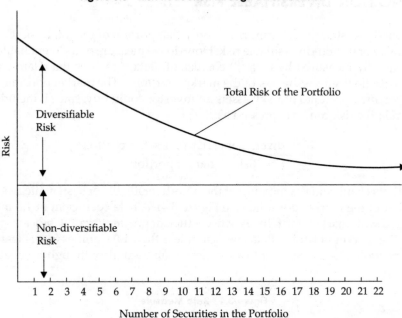

Source: Kothari and Dutta (2005).

a whole and hence cannot be eliminated by diversification is called non-diversifiable risk. Non-diversifiable risk is also referred to as market risk or systematic risk.

Some of the factors that may give rise to non-diversifiable risk are:

1. Change in tax rates
2. War and other calamities
3. Change in inflation rates
4. Change in economic policy
5. Industrial recession
6. Change in international oil prices, etc.

That part of total risk which reduces due to diversification is the risk specific to the company or industry and hence can be eliminated by diversification is called diversifiable risk. Diversifiable risk is also called unsystematic risk or specific risk.

Some of the factors that may give rise to diversifiable risk are:

1. Strikes in the company
2. Bankruptcy of a major supplier
3. Exit/death of a key company officer
4. Unexpected entry of new competitor into the market, etc.

MEASURING NON-DIVERSIFIABLE RISK

For a diversified investor, the relevant risk is only that portion of the total risk that cannot be diversified away or its non-diversifiable risk. How do we measure non-diversifiable or market risk? It is generally measured by beta (β) coefficient. Beta measures the relative risk of any individual portfolio vis-à-vis the risk of the market portfolio. The market portfolio represents the most diversified portfolio of risky assets an investor could buy, since it includes all risky assets. This relative risk can be expressed as:

$$\beta_j = \frac{\text{Non-diversifiable risk of asset or portfolio j}}{\text{Risk of market portfolio}}$$

Thus, the beta coefficient is a measure of the non-diversifiable or systematic risk of an asset relative to that of the market portfolio (see Figure 3.4). A beta coefficient of 1.0 indicates the risk associated with market portfolio. A beta coefficient greater than 1.0 indicates risk greater than that of the market portfolio. Beta coefficient less than 1.0 signifies assets less risky than the market portfolio. Beta coefficient can be less than zero also, though a negative beta is highly unlikely.

Figure 3.4   Beta Measure

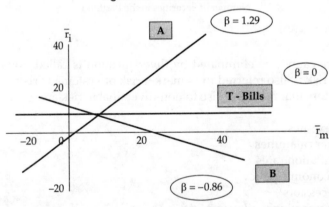

Source: Kothari and Dutta (2005).

Thus, beta coefficient measures a stock's market risk. It shows a stock's volatility relative to the market. In other words, beta coefficient shows how risky a stock is if the stock is held in a well-diversified portfolio.

Two important points need to be noted are:

1. The risk of the market portfolio is non-diversifiable which an investor cannot avoid because all the possible diversification has already been done.
2. As long as the asset's returns are not perfectly positively correlated with returns from other assets, there will be some way to diversify away its unsystematic risk. As a result, the beta coefficient depends only on those factors which lead to non-diversifiable risk.

Measuring Beta

To calculate beta coefficient we run a regression of past returns of stock i on returns from the market. The slope of the regression line so obtained, is nothing but the beta coefficient (see Figure 3.5).

Figure 3.5   Illustration of Beta Coefficient Calculation

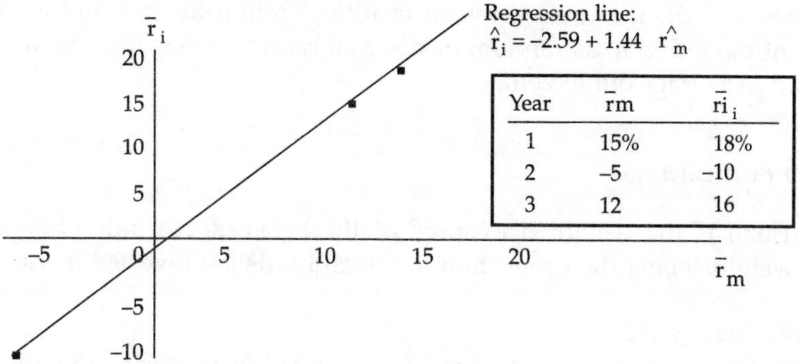

Year	$\bar{r}m$	$\bar{r}i_i$
1	15%	18%
2	–5	–10
3	12	16

Regression line:
$\hat{r}_i = -2.59 + 1.44 \ \hat{r}_m$

Source: Kothari and Dutta (2005).

The systematic relationship between the return on the security or a portfolio and the return on the market can be described using a simple linear regression, identifying the return on a security or portfolio as the dependent variable k_j and the return on market portfolio as the independent variable k_m, in the single-index model or market model developed by William Sharpe. This can be expressed as:

$$k_j = \alpha_j + \beta_j k_m + e_j$$

The beta coefficient parameter in the model represents the slope of the above regression relationship and as explained earlier, measures the responsiveness of the security or portfolio to the general market and indicates how extensively the return of the portfolio or security will vary with changes in the market return. The beta coefficient of a security is defined as the ratio of the security's covariance of return with the market to the variance of the market. This can be calculated as follows:

$$\bar{k}_j = 20$$

$$\bar{k}_m = 10$$

$$\beta_j = \frac{Cov(k_j k_m)}{Var(k_m)} = \frac{\sum P(k_j - \bar{k}_j)(k_m - \bar{k}_m)}{\sum P(k_m - \bar{k}_m)^2}$$

$$= \frac{740}{480} = 1.54$$

$$\alpha = \bar{k}_j - \beta_j \bar{k}_m$$

$$= 20 - (1.54 \times 10) = 4.6\%$$

The alpha parameter α is the intercept of the fitted line and indicates what the return of the security or portfolio will be when the market return is zero. For example, a security with an α of +2 percent would earn two percent even when the market return would be zero and would earn an additional two percent at all levels of market return. The converse is true, if a security has α of –2 percent. The positive α thus represents a sort of bonus return and would be a highly desirable aspect of a portfolio or security while a negative α represents a penalty to the investor.

The third term e_j is the unexpected return resulting from influences not identified by the model. Frequently referred to as random or residual return, it may take on any value but is generally found to average out to zero.

Beta (β) of a Portfolio

Beta of a portfolio is the weighted average of the betas of the individual assets in the portfolio, the weights being the proportion in which funds are invested in various assets in the portfolio.

Symbolically, $\beta p = \Sigma wi\, \beta I$.

For example, if the beta of a security A is 1.5 and that of security B is 0.8 with 40 percent of the funds being invested in security A and 60 percent in security B, the beta of our portfolio will be 1.08 ($1.5 \times 0.4 + 0.8 \times 0.6$).

CONCEPT OF RETURN

In simple terms, return means the reward that one gets by investing in a project. The Oxford English dictionary defines return as "Profit or income from investment of money or the expenditure of effort or skill." Whenever an investment is made in some asset, the objective is to earn some "profit" from it. However, the term "profit" itself is very ambiguous. Is it the periodic cash flow that is generated by the asset? For example, when a company declares a dividend of 30 percent, does that mean the investors have generated a return of 30 percent? Or is it the difference between the purchase price and selling price? For instance, if we purchase an equity share for Rs 100 and sell it for Rs 120, can we say that the profit or return is Rs 20?

In fact, the return is made up of two components:

1. **Periodic Cash Flows from the Asset:** These are the cash flows that you receive in the intervening time periods between when the investment is made and when the investment matures. For example, when you purchase the bonds issued by a company and you receive interest on these bonds periodically say after every 6 months. Or when you purchase some shares in a company listed on Bombay Stock Exchange and you receive dividends every year. Or when an investment is made by a company in a capital project which generates a cash flow every year for the life of the project.

So when a company declares a dividend of 30 percent, it is only one part of the return that is earned by the investors, that is, dividend yield. If shares of face value Rs 10 were issued at a premium of Rs 90, this translates into a dividend yield of 3 percent only as the dividends are always paid on the paid-up value. If a share is fully paid up, then it is face value on which dividend is paid.

2. **Capital Appreciation:** This represents an increase in the market price of the asset during the life of the investment. For example, the market price of the bonds purchased by you at Rs 100 per bond increases to Rs 120 per bond after 1 year or the market price of shares purchased by you at Rs 100 per share increases to Rs 150 per share after 6 months or the market value of the project having an initial investment of Rs 50 lakhs increases to Rs 75 lakh after 3 years. In all these cases, there is an appreciation or increase in the price of the asset. If the market price is less than the investment or acquisition price it means a negative return or loss (capital depreciation).

MEASURING THE RATE OF RETURN

Now we know what constitutes return, the next question that arises is how do we measure return? Measurement of return can be done in many ways. Depending on whether we want to measure returns over a single period of time or over multiple periods return can be classified as:

1. Single period return
2. Multiple period return

Similarly, depending upon whether we want to measure historical returns generated on an asset or the future expected return, the return can be classified as:

1. Ex-post return
2. Ex-ante return

It can be combination of the foregoing types like single period ex-post return, multiple period ex-post return, single period ex-ante return, or multiple period ex-ante return.

Single Period Ex-post Return

$$r_{it} = \frac{P_t - P_{t-1} + D_t}{P_{t-1}}$$

Where

r_{it} = return on the ith asset at time t

P_t = price of the ith asset at time t

P_{t-1} = price of the ith asset at time $t-1$
D_t = cash flow generated by the asset during the period.

The return that we calculate using the formula is known as the realized or historical or holding period return or ex-post return.

Let us use the formula for calculating the ex-post return on equity shares and bonds.

Suppose an investor Mr X purchased the shares of ITC Ltd at Rs 250 per share on April 1, 2003. The company paid a dividend of Rs 5 per share, during the financial year 2003–04 and the price of ITC Ltd as on March 31, 2004 is Rs 375. If Mr. X decides to sell the shares of ITC, the rate of return earned by him is

$$r = \frac{(375-250)+5}{250} = \frac{125+5}{250} = 0.52 \text{ or } 52\%$$

Suppose another investor Mr Y purchased the bonds issued by Premium Steel Ltd at Rs 1,000 per bond. The bond has a coupon rate of 10 percent payable annually. At the end of 1 year, the bonds are trading at Rs 1,200. If Mr Y decides to sell the bonds, the return earned by him would be

$$r = \frac{(1200-1000)+100}{1000} = 0.30 \text{ or } 30\%$$

Multi-period Ex-post Return

Suppose we want to calculate that over a period of 10 years, what has been the annual return on a security. How do we calculate this return? In order to understand, let us consider a security whose market prices for the last 2 years are as follows:

Time Period	Market Price (Rs)
t	195
t – 1	250
t – 2	160

(t represents the present time, $t-1$ means 1 year ago and $t-2$ implies 2 year ago)

The single period return over the 2-year period can be calculated as:

$$r_{0,2} = \frac{P_2 - P_0}{P_0} = \frac{195-160}{160} = 0.21875 \Rightarrow 21.875\%$$

What is the annual return on this security over the 2-year period?

Recall, the compounding formula, we relate the present value and future value.

$$FV_n = PV (1 + r)^n$$

Going two years back in time, the market price of the security was Rs 160. After two years it is Rs 195.

Therefore,

$$195 = 160 (1 + r)^2$$
$$\Rightarrow r = 0.10397 \Rightarrow 10.40\%$$

Alternatively, if we know the single period return, we can calculate the multi-period annual return using the following relationship:

$$(1 + r)^n = 1 + r_{0,n}$$

Where r = annual return over the period
$r_{0,n}$ = the single period return over the period.

Let us use this formula to determine the annual return using the single period return.

The single period return over the 2-year period is 21.875 percent.

$$(1 + r)^2 = 1.21875$$
$$r = \sqrt{1.21875} - 1 = 0.10397 \Rightarrow 10.40\%$$

As you can see the value is same as calculated earlier.

Single Period Ex-Ante Return

While calculating the historical return on a single asset, we faced no problem as precise data was available about the returns generated.

However, in reality an investor frequently has to decide whether or not to make an investment in a given asset on the basis of "expected returns." The returns as the name suggests are "expected" and hence will be generated in future. As future cannot be predicted with accuracy, so there is some amount of uncertainty associated with these returns. In other words, if we assume that there is an asset "A" and the expected return on that asset in future time period is 12 percent, we cannot say with certainty that a return of 12 percent will be generated on this asset. So, how can the investor find out the return on this asset that he expects to earn with some degree of certainty? In order to overcome this problem, we have to specify the "chance" of generating 12 percent return and what are the other possible returns on the asset "A." This "chance" is referred to as probability and when we specify all the possible returns with their respective probabilities, we get what we call a "probability distribution." See Boxes 3.2 and 3.3 for more details.

Box 3.2   Probability

The chance of an event taking place is called its probability. Probability can never be greater than 1 or less than 0. The sum total of all the probabilities of all mutually exclusive and collectively exhaustive events is always equal to 1.

Probability distribution is a listing of all possible outcomes with a probability assigned to each. A discrete probability distribution is one in which the number of possible outcomes is limited, or finite. On the other hand, in a continuous probability distribution the number of possible outcomes is unlimited, or infinite.

Box 3.3   Normal Probability Distribution

Normal distributions are a family of distributions that have the same general shape, that is, bell-shape. They are symmetric with scores more concentrated in the middle than in the tails. The graph never touches the x-axis. Example of normal distributions is shown in the following. Notice that they differ in how spread out they are. The area under each curve is the same, that is, 1. The height of a normal distribution can be specified mathematically in terms of two parameters: the mean (μ) and the standard deviation (σ).

The standard normal curve is a member of the family of normal curves with $m = 0.0$ and $d = 1.0$. The value of 0.0 was selected because the normal curve is symmetrical around m and the number system is symmetrical around 0.0. The value of 1.0 for d is simply a unit value. The x-axis on a standard normal curve is often relabeled and called Z scores.

There are three areas on a standard normal curve that all introductory statistics students should know. The first is that the total area below 0.0 is .50, as the standard normal curve is symmetrical like all normal curves. This result generalizes to all normal curves, in that the total area below the value of mu (μ) is .50 on any member of the family of normal curves.

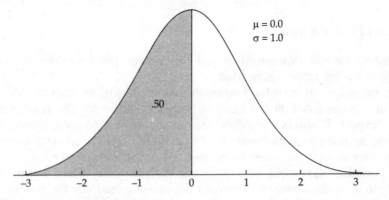

$$\mu = 0.0$$
$$\sigma = 1.0$$

.50

-3   -2   -1   0   1   2   3

This bell-shaped curve tells us that 99 percent of the values lie within ±3 standard deviations from the mean, 95 percent of the values lie within ±2 standard deviations from the mean, and 68 percent of the values lie within ±1 standard deviation from the mean.

So we have to specify what are the other possible returns expected from investing in asset "A" and what are the respective "chances" (i.e., probabilities). Suppose, an investor is told that the possible returns on asset A are 10, 12, and 14 percent with 20, 50, and 30 percent chance of occurrence, the probability distribution will look like this:

Possible Returns (%)	Probability
10	0.20
12	0.50
14	0.30

What does this convey? What is the expected return on the asset A now?

The expected return on asset A can be calculated as the weighted average of all possible returns (see Figure 3.6), the weights being the respective probabilities.

$$\text{Symbolically, } E\,(ri) \;=\; \sum_{i=1}^{n} r_i p_i$$

Where r_i = the ith expected return on the asset
P_i = the probability of ith return.

In other words, it implies that population mean is called the expected return (See Box 3.4). It is not what is expected, hoped, promised, or feared.

Box 3.4   Population Mean

The value to which the sample average tends in a very long time is called the population mean. Each sample average is an estimate, more or less accurate, of the population mean.

Figure 3.6   Probability Distribution of A's Rate of Return

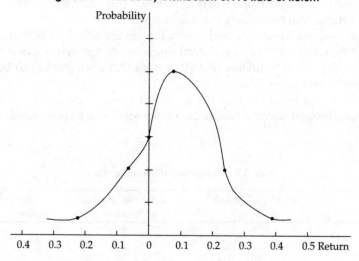

Source: Kothari and Dutta (2005).

CONCEPT OF DIVERSIFICATION

Generally, investing in a single security is riskier than investing in a "diversified group" of assets because in case of a single asset, the returns to the investor are based on the future of a single asset. Hence, it is often suggested that in order to reduce risk, investors should hold a "diversified group" of assets which might contain equity capital, bonds, real estate, savings account, bullion, collectibles, and various other assets. In other words, the investor is advised not to put all his eggs into one basket. This "diversified group" of assets is called a "portfolio." For example, if we have invested in equity shares, bonds, bullion, and real estate, we have created a portfolio of different assets class. However, we may create a portfolio within the same asset class also. For instance, if we are holding the equity shares of 10 companies, we have created an all equity portfolio. If we are holding the bonds/debentures of five companies, we have created a fixed income portfolio.

It is possible to construct a portfolio in such a way that the total risk of the portfolio is less than the sum of the risk of the individual assets taken together.

How does diversification help in risk reduction? Let us understand the concept of diversification through a very simple illustration.

Let us assume that "A" put his money equally into the stocks of two companies: Sunflame Limited, a manufacturer of room heating systems, and Duracool Limited, a manufacturer of air conditioners. If the temperatures soar high during summers in a particular year, the earnings of Duracool Limited would go up, leading to an increase in its share price and returns to shareholders. On the other hand, the earnings of Sunflame would be on the decline, leading to a corresponding decline in the share prices and investor's returns. On the other hand, if there is a prolonged and severe winter, the situation would be just the opposite.

While the return on each individual stock might vary quite a bit depending on the weather, the return on A's portfolio (50 percent Sunflame and 50 percent Duracool stocks) could be quite stable because the decline in one will be offset by the increase in the other. In fact, at least in theory, the offsetting could eliminate his risk entirely.

Assuming that low, moderate, and high temperatures are equally likely events (1/3 probability each), the expected return and standard deviation of the two stocks individually and of the portfolio of 50 percent Sunflame and 50 percent Duracool stocks can be calculated as follows (see Table 3.3 and Table 3.3a).

From the table, it can be noted that the portfolio earns 10 percent no matter what the weather is. Hence, through diversification, two risky stocks have been combined to make a risk-less portfolio.

Table 3.3   Illustration of Diversification

Temperature	Return on Sunflame Stock (%)	Return on Duracool Stock (%)	Return on Portfolio (50% Sunflame + 50% Duracool) (%)
Low	0	20	10
Moderate	10	10	10
High	20	0	10

Table 3.3a

Possible Outcomes	Probabilities	Return on Sunflame Stock (%)	Return on Duracool Stock (%)	Return on Portfolio
Low	1/3	0	20	10
Moderate	1/3	10	10	10
High	1/3	20	0	10
Expected Rate of Return $\bar{k}$		10%	10%	10%
σ		$\sqrt{66.67} = 8.16\%$	$\sqrt{66.67} = 8.16\%$	$\sqrt{0} = 0\%$

The returns on Sunflame and Duracool are said to be "perfectly negatively correlated" since they always move in exactly opposite directions. On the other hand, two stocks which go up or down together in the same manner are said to be "perfectly positively correlated." Both these situations rarely happen in practice. In general, all stocks have some degree of positive correlation because certain variables, like economic factors and political climate, tend to affect all stocks.

However, we do not need stocks which are perfectly negatively correlated in a portfolio in order to achieve the benefit of risk reduction through diversification. As long as the assets in a portfolio are not perfectly positively correlated, diversification does result in risk reduction.

Return on a Portfolio of Assets

The return on a portfolio of assets is the weighted average of the returns on individual assets, the weights being the proportion in which funds have been invested in various assets in the portfolio.

Symbolically,

$$E(r_{P1}) = \sum_{i=1}^{4} p_i r_i^{P1} = \sum_{i=1}^{4} p_i (w_1 r_i^A + w_2 r_i^B)$$

Risk on a Portfolio

The risk on a portfolio of two assets A and B is given by

$$\sigma^2 p = w_A^2 \sigma_A^2 + w_B^2 \sigma_B^2 + 2 \text{cov}(r_A, r_B)$$

Where

$\sigma^2 p$ = variance of the portfolio
w_A = proportion of funds invested in asset A
w_B = proportion of funds invested in asset B
σ^2_A = variance of returns on asset A
σ^2_B = variance of returns on asset B.

$cov(r_A, r_B)$ = covariance of returns on assets A and B, measures the amount by which the returns on the assets "move together" under the different events.

$$cov(r_A, r_B) = \sum_{i=1}^{4} p_i (r_A - E(r_A))(r_B - E(r_B))$$

From the equation it is clear, that the covariance between the two stocks must be counted twice. One more point that has to be noted is that as long as the correlation coefficient between two securities is less than 1.00, the standard deviation of the portfolio will be less than the weighted average of the two individual standard deviations. In other words, benefits of diversification will be realized when the coefficient of correlation is less than 1.00.

Minimum Variance Portfolio

The objective of diversification is to reduce risk. A portfolio that has the lowest level of risk is the optimal portfolio or the minimum variance portfolio.

The proportion of investment in an asset A of a two-asset portfolio (A and B) that will result into a minimum variance portfolio can be found using the following formula:

$$W_A^* = \frac{\sigma_B^2 - Cov_{A,B}}{\sigma_A^2 + \sigma_B^2 - 2Cov_{A,B}}, \text{ where symbols are in standard notation.}$$

The proportion to be invested in asset B = $1 - W_A^*$

CAPITAL ASSET PRICING MODEL (CAPM)

William F. Sharpe, John Lintner, and Jan Mossin developed the CAPM. It is one of the major developments in financial theory. The CAPM establishes a linear relationship between the required rate of return on a security and its systematic or un-diversifiable risk or beta.

The CAPM is represented mathematically by

$$R_i = R_f + \beta_i (R_m - R_f)$$

Where

R_i = expected or required rate of return on security j
R_f = risk-free rate of return
β_i = beta coefficient of security j
R_m = return on market portfolio.

Assumptions

The CAPM is based on some critical assumptions as follows.

1. Investors are risk-averse and use the expected rate of return and standard deviation of return as appropriate measures of risk and return for their portfolio. In other words, the greater the perceived risk of a portfolio, the higher return the risk-averse investors expect to compensate the risk.
2. Investors make their investment decisions based on a single-period horizon, that is, the next immediate time period.
3. Transaction costs in financial markets are low enough to ignore and assets can be bought and sold in any unit desired. The investor is limited only by his wealth and the price of the asset.
4. Taxes do not affect the choice of buying assets.
5. All individuals assume that they can buy assets at the going market price and they all agree on the nature of the return and risk associated with each investment.

The assumptions listed earlier are somewhat limiting but the CAPM enables us to be much more precise about how trade-offs between risk and return are determined in financial markets.

In the CAPM, the expected rate of return can also be thought of as a required rate of return because the market is assumed to be in equilibrium. The expected return as we have explained earlier is the return from an asset that investors anticipate or expect to earn over some future period. The required rate of return for a security is defined as the minimum expected rate of return needed to induce an investor to purchase it.

What do investors require (expect) when they invest? First of all, investors can earn a risk-free rate of return by investing in risk-free assets like treasury bills. This risk-free rate of return is designated R_f and the minimum return expected by the investors. In addition to this, because investors are risk-averse, they will expect a risk premium to compensate them for the additional risk assumed in investing in a risky asset.

Required rate of return = risk-free rate + risk premium.

The CAPM provides an explicit measure of the risk premium. It is the product of the beta for a particular security j and the market risk premium $R_m - R_f$

$$\text{Risk premium} = \beta_j (k_m - R_f)$$

This beta coefficient "β_j" is the non-diversifiable risk of the asset relative to the risk of the market. If the risk of the asset is greater than the market risk, that is, β exceeds 1.0, the investor assigns a higher risk premium to asset j than to the market. For example, suppose a fertilizer company had a β_j of 1.5, that its required rate of return on the market (k_m) was 15 percent per year and that its risk-free interest rate (R_f) was 6 percent per annum, using the CAPM the required rate of return can be calculated as:

$$R_i = R_f + \beta_j (k_m - R_f)$$
$$= 0.06 + 1.5 (0.15 - 0.06)$$
$$= 0.195 \text{ or } 19.5\%$$

The preceding calculations show that the required rate of return on this stock would be 19.5 percent; the sum of 6 percent risk-free return and a 13.5 percent risk premium. This 19.5 percent is larger than the 15 percent required return on the market because the fertilizer stock is riskier than the market.

The Characteristic Line

Suppose we would like to compare the expected return on a particular stock with the expected return on the market portfolio. Since both would contain a premium for risk, it would be better to compare the excess returns. Excess return is the return on the security/portfolio over and above the market portfolio. These excess returns can be determined either from the historical data (ex-post) or estimates about the future returns.

After calculating the excess returns on the security and the market portfolio, we can either plot the results on a graph paper or run a regression using MS-Excel.

By doing so we would get a line of "best fit." This line describes the historical relationship between the excess returns for the stock and excess returns for the market portfolio. This line is known as the characteristic line and is used as a proxy for the expected relationship between the stock returns and the market returns.

In Figure 3.7, alpha (α) is the intercept of the characteristic line on the y-axis. It denotes the expected excess return on the security if the expected excess return on the market portfolio is zero. Theoretically, α should be zero. This is so because if it is negative investors would avoid the stock because they can earn better returns by investing in some other asset or a combination of assets. If it is positive, the demand for such a security would increase resulting into an increase in its market price and consequently a decline in its expected return.

The Security Market Line (SML)

The line that we get by plotting the relationship between the required rate of return (R_i) and non-diversifiable risk (beta) is called the security market line (see Figure 3.8). This line describes the relationship between systematic risk and expected return in financial markets.

As per the CAPM assumptions, any individual security's expected return and beta statistics should lie on the SML. The SML intersects the vertical axis at the risk-free rate of return R_f and $R_m - R_f$ is the slope of the SML.

Since all securities are expected to plot along the SML, the line provides a direct and convenient way of determining the expected/required return of a security if we know the beta of the security. The SML can also be used to classify securities. Those with betas greater than 1.00 and plotting on the upper part of the SML are classified as aggressive securities while

Figure 3.7 Calculation of Required Rate of Return

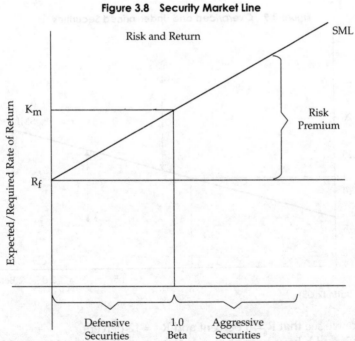

Source: Kothari and Dutta (2005).

Figure 3.8 Security Market Line

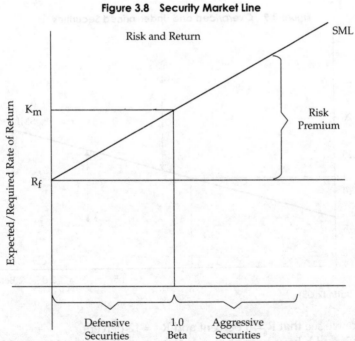

Source: Kothari and Dutta (2005).

those with betas less than 1.00 and plotting on the lower part of the SML can be classified as defensive securities, which earn below-average returns.

From the data given in the following Table 3.4, one may chart the SML and classify the securities.

Table 3.4 SML and Returns

	Expected Return	Risk-free Return	Beta	Market-risk Premium
Market	12.0	5	1.00	7
Security A	?	5	1.20	?
Security B	?	5	0.80	?

One of the major assumptions of the CAPM is that the market is in equilibrium and that the expected rate of return is equal to the required rate of return for a given level of market risk or beta. In other words, the SML provides a framework for evaluating whether high-risk stocks are offering returns more or less in proportion to their risk and vice versa. Let us see how we can appraise the value securities using CAPM and the SML.

Once a security's expected rate of return and beta have been computed, they may be plotted with reference to the SML. If the security's expected rate of return differs from the required rate of return, the security may be over- or under priced and may fall below or above the SML. Let us clarify with the help of the following figure (Figure 3.9).

Figure 3.9 Overpriced and Under-priced Securities

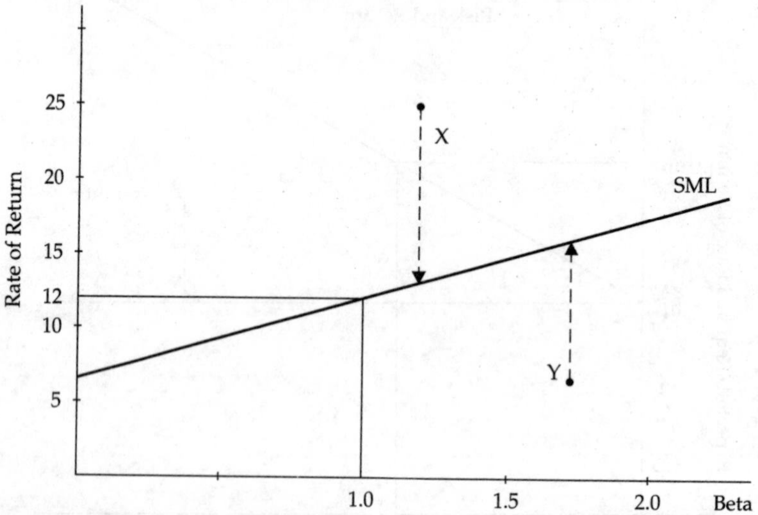

Source: Kothari and Dutta (2005).

From the figure we see that $R_f = 6$ percent and $R_m = 12$ percent.

Two securities X and Y have been shown in the figure. Both X and Y should have been on the SML but obviously they are not. Why? Let us take the case of X first. The expected rate of return of X is around 25 percent. But at a beta of around 1.2, using the SML, we see that the required rate of return is only around 13 percent. This tells us that security X is undervalued or priced too low because its average rate of return is inappropriately high for the level of risk it bears. On the other hand, security Y with a beta of around 1.7 requires a rate of return of around 16 percent but its expected return is only about 7 percent. This tells us that the asset is overvalued or overpriced and hence unattractive because it is expected to produce a return lower than stocks with similar betas. These two assets should move toward their equilibrium: required return positions on the SML (i.e., expected rate of return should be equal to required rate of return and correspond to their respective betas). The expected return as we know is computed as:

$$\text{Expected return, } \bar{k} = \frac{D_t + (P_t - P_{t-1})}{P_{t-1}}$$

$$= \frac{\text{Expected Income}}{\text{Market Purchase Price}}$$

While estimating the expected return a year hence, in the absence of historic data on returns and probabilities, the following formula which is derived from the basic formula given earlier may be used.

$$\text{Expected return } = \frac{D_0(1 + g)}{P_0} + g$$

$$\begin{aligned} \text{where } D_o &= \text{last paid dividend} \\ P_o &= \text{current purchase/market price} \\ g &= \text{growth rate.} \end{aligned}$$

To reach equilibrium and their required rate of return positions on the SML, both stocks have to go through a temporary price adjustment. In order to reach equilibrium, assuming betas remain the same, the expected return of X has to be brought down to be equal to the required rate of return and be plotted on the SML. To accomplish this, the denominator of the foregoing formula, namely the purchase price, has to be sufficiently increased. Similarly, for security Y, the purchase price has to be sufficiently reduced so that the expected return rises to be the same as the required rate of return.

Security X

$$R_f = 6\%, \beta_x = 1.5, R_m = 12\%$$
$$\begin{aligned} \text{Required rate of return} &= R_f + \beta_x (R_m - R_f) \\ &= 6 + 1.5\,(12 - 6) \\ &= 15\% \end{aligned}$$

Expected rate of return a year hence:

$$
\begin{aligned}
\text{Last paid dividend (Do)} &= \text{Rs } 2.50 \\
\text{Current purchase price (Po)} &= \text{Rs } 10 \\
\text{Growth rate} &= 5\% \\
\text{Expected rate of return} &= \frac{D_0(1 + g)}{P_0} + g \\
&= \frac{2.5(1.05)}{10} + 0.05 \\
&= 31.25\%
\end{aligned}
$$

By how much should the purchase price of X be increased so that it is at equilibrium? Since at equilibrium, the required rate is equal to the expected rate. This can be solved as follows:

$$
0.15 = \frac{2.5(1.05)}{P_0} + 0.05
$$

$$
\therefore P_0 = \text{Rs } 26.25
$$

In practice, how does the price of security X get pushed up to its equilibrium price? Investors will be interested in purchasing security X because it offers more than proportionate returns in comparison to the risk. This demand will push up the price of X as more of it is purchased and correspondingly bring down the returns. This process will continue till it reaches the equilibrium price and expected returns are the same as required returns.

Security Y

$$
R_f = 6\%, \beta_y = 1.25, R_m = 12\%
$$

$$
\begin{aligned}
\text{Required rate of return} &= R_f + \beta_y (R_m - R_f) \\
&= 6 + 1.25 (12 - 6) \\
&= 13.5\%
\end{aligned}
$$

Expected rate of return a year hence:

$$
\begin{aligned}
\text{Last paid dividend} &= \text{Rs } 2.00 \\
\text{Current purchase price} &= \text{Rs } 25 \\
\text{Growth rate} &= 3\% \\
\text{Expected rate of return} &= \frac{2(1.03)}{25} + 0.03 = 11.24\% \\
\text{Equilibrium price} &= 0.135 = \frac{2(1.03)}{P_0} + 0.04 \\
&= \text{Rs } 21.68
\end{aligned}
$$

Investors will be tempted to sell security Y because it offers less than the required rate of return. This increase in the supply of Y will drive down its price and correspondingly increase the return until the expected return rises enough to reach the SML and the security is once again in equilibrium.

Thus, the CAPM provides many useful insights to the finance manager to maximize the value of the firm. It shows the type of risk for which shareholders require compensation in the form of a higher risk premium, and hence, a higher return. Because finance managers also perform the investment function on behalf of shareholders, they must keep sight of the returns shareholders expect for taking risks.

Shifts in Security Market Line (SML)

The slope of the SML is given by the term $(R_m - R_f)$ and this is the risk premium that the investors demand for investing in a risky asset. Since the capital markets are dynamic and constantly in flux in response to the new information, the risk–return parameters change and consequently the security market line shifts in the risk–return space over a period of time.

Two important factors that affect the security market line are:

1. Inflation
2. Risk aversion

Shift due to Inflation

The risk-free interest rate is comprised of three components, namely, the real interest rate, expected inflation rate, and a liquidity premium.

Symbolically,

$$rf = r' + i^* + lp$$

Loosely speaking, we can say that the risk-free interest rate is composed of the real interest rate and the expected inflation rate. It implies that whenever the expectation of the financial markets about the expected inflation will change, the nominal rate will also accordingly change. Any change in the risk-free interest rate will correspondingly affect the SML also. If the inflation is expected to increase, the risk-free interest rate will accordingly increase and as it is the base rate for all the required rates of returns in the financial markets, the required rates of return will also change.

For example, suppose the risk-free rate is 5 percent and the real component is 3 percent and inflation component is 2 percent. Now if the expected inflation rate increases to 4 percent, with no change in the real interest rate, the risk-free rate increases to 7 percent, and consequently SML moves up, indicating an increase in the required rate of return. A decline in expected inflation rate would shift the SML downwards (see Figure 3.10).

Figure 3.10   Shift in SML Due to Inflation

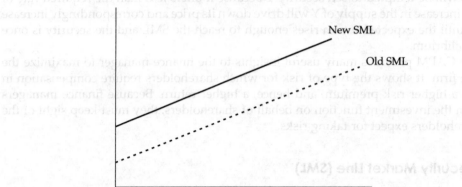

Source: Kothari and Dutta (2005).

Shift due to risk aversion

In the SML equation, the term $(R_m - R_f)$ represents the risk premium. The risk premium would depend on the degree of risk aversion in the investors. If the investors perceive too much uncertainty, they would demand a high risk premium for undertaking any risky investment otherwise they would demand a risk premium commensurate with the return. If the investors demand higher risk premium, the slope of SML would increase and it would shift upwards whereas if the investors demand lesser risk premium, the slope of SML would decrease and it would shift downwards (see Figure 3.11).

Figure 3.11   Shift in SML Due to Risk Aversion

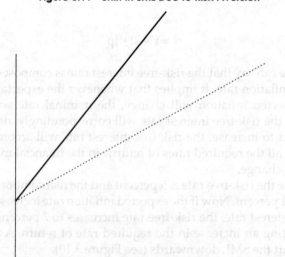

Source: Kothari and Dutta (2005).

APPLICATION OF RISK AND RETURN IN FINANCIAL SERVICES

The recent global crisis in the USA and its effect on world economy has clearly proved the failure of risk management techniques. It is a fact that risk is inevitable and cannot be avoided but needs to be managed. The failure of Lehman Brothers shows that they could not clearly assess the risk arising out of subprime loans and no doc credit given to inferior borrowers. The risk and return goes hand in hand. The recent crisis has broken the myth that high risk should invariably bring in high return. The very fact that subprime loans would provide high return did carry unimaginable risk resulted into collapse of Lehman Brothers. So much so, the U.S. government had to come to rescue these mighty institutions, be it AIG and others. The risks in financial services are mainly on account of two: (*a*) change in interest rate structure which disturbs cash flows and (*b*) market-oriented risk resulting into shift of consumers. Consumers in financial services do engage a number of service providers and instead of paying on time they keep changing the service provider. Credit card is one such example, so are the bank accounts and its products being enjoyed by consumers. On the other hand, the very presence of risk also suggests the presence of significant return embedded in investment program. All that is required is prudent financial norms and rigorous monitoring process on cash flows to detect the possibility of non-performing assets at its initial stage and to provide for possible contingent liabilities on slightly higher scale.

4

Banking Services in India

Learning Objectives

- To know about the concept, growth, and types of banks.
- To understand the impact of reforms on banking sector.
- To discuss the marketing strategies.

CONCEPT OF BANK

The word "bank" is said to have originated from the German word "bank" which means heap or mound or joint stock fund. Whereas the Italian word "Banco" means heap of money. There are different perceptions about banks, for example, The Banking Regulation Act, 1949 under Section 5 defines bank as, "the accepting for the purpose of lending or investment, of deposits of money from the public repayable on demand or otherwise and withdrawal by cheque, draft, order or otherwise." The *Oxford Dictionary* defines a bank as "An establishment for the custody of money, which pays out on customers order."

BANKS IN INDIA

There are different type of banks like commercial banks, investment banks, development banks, and specialized banks like EXIM Bank (for export and import), NBH (for housing), NABARD (for agriculture and rural development). However, the present chapter may confine to commercial banks. A commercial bank is one which deals with clients directly, provides services like deposit acceptance, lending, money remittances, collections, credit documents, cash credit, bank overdraft, public issue management with the sole objective of making and earning profit.

The growth of banking in India can be divided in to three phases:

1. **Phase I:** Early phase—1786 to 1969.
2. **Phase II:** Nationalization of Indian banks—1969 to 1991.
3. **Phase III:** Reforms in Indian banking system—1991 onwards.

Phase I

The General Bank of India was set up in the year 1786. Next came Bank of Hindustan and Bengal Bank. The East India Company established Bank of Bengal (1809), Bank of Bombay (1840), and Bank of Madras (1843) as independent units and called them Presidency Banks. These three banks were amalgamated in 1920 and the Imperial Bank of India was established which started as a private shareholders' bank, mostly Europeans shareholders. The then Imperial Bank of India is today's State Bank of India which is the largest bank with 10,000 plus branches.

In 1865 Allahabad Bank was established exclusively by Indians. Punjab National Bank Ltd in 1894, and Bank of India, Central Bank of India, Bank of Baroda, Canara Bank, Indian Bank, and Bank of Mysore were set up between 1906 and 1913. The Reserve Bank of India came into existence in 1935.

During the first phase, the growth was very slow and banks also experienced periodic failures between 1913 and 1948. There were approximately 1,100 banks, mostly small. To streamline the functioning and activities of commercial banks, the Government of India came up with The Banking Companies Act, 1949 which was later changed to Banking Regulation Act, 1949. Reserve Bank of India was vested with extensive powers for the supervision of banking in India as the Central Banking Authority. The important regulatory steps were:

1. 1949: Enactment of Banking Regulation Act.
2. 1955: Nationalization of State Bank of India.
3. 1959: Nationalization of SBI subsidiaries.
4. 1961: Insurance cover extended to deposits.

Phase II

The second phase has been accorded importance due to major steps in banking sector reform after independence. In 1955, the government nationalized Imperial Bank of India to be known as State Bank of India (SBI) with extensive banking facilities on a large scale, specially in rural and semi-urban areas. SBI acts as the principal agent of RBI and handles banking transactions of the union and state governments all over the country. Seven banks forming subsidiary of SBI was nationalized in 1960. Fourteen major commercial banks in the country were nationalized in 1969 followed by seven more banks in 1980.

Some of the major regulations of the second phase are the creation of credit guarantee corporation (1971) and creation of regional rural banks (1975).

Phase III

It is credited with financial sector reforms owing to M. Narsimhan's committee. The impact of financial sector reforms can be seen through:

1. Development in financial markets,
2. Regulatory role,
3. The expansion of banking system,
4. Growth and regulation of non-banking finance companies,
5. The capital market,
6. Mutual funds,
7. Insurance company,
8. Deregulation of banking system and customer-friendly approach, and
9. Overall approach to reforms.

The banks are primarily classified into scheduled banks and non-scheduled banks. Scheduled banks include nationalized banks, private sector banks, and foreign banks (see Table 4.1). Non-scheduled banks are those which are not included in the second schedule of the RBI Act. The following chart depicts structure of Indian banking industry.

Figure 4.1 Structure of Indian Banking Industry

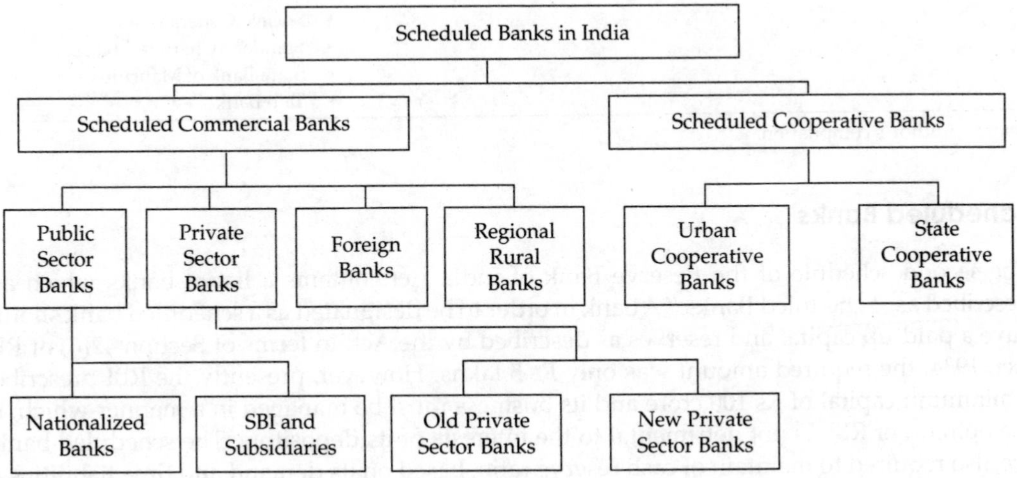

Source: Author.

Table 4.1 Major Banks—Public, Private, and Foreign Banks

Public	Private	Foreign
• Allahabad Bank	• Axis Bank (formerly UTI Bank)	• ABN AMRO
• Andhra Bank	• Bank of Rajasthan	• Abu Dhabi Commercial Bank Ltd
• Bank of Baroda	• Bassein Catholic Bank	• American Express Bank
• Bank of India	• Bharat Overseas Bank	• Antwerp Diamond Bank
• Bank of Maharashtra	• Catholic Syrian Bank	• Arab Bangladesh Bank
• Canara Bank	• City Union Bank	• Bank International Indonesia
• Central Bank of India	• Development Credit Bank	• Bank of America
• Corporation bank	• Dhanalakshmi Bank	• Bank of Bahrain & Kuwait
• Dena Bank	• Federal Bank	• Bank of Ceylon
• IDBI Bank	• Ganesh Bank of Kurundwad	• Bank of Nova Scotia
• Indian Bank	• HDFC Bank	• Bank of Tokyo Mitsubishi UFJ
• Indian Overseas Bank	• ICICI Bank	• Barclays Bank
• Oriental Bank of Commerce	• IndusInd Bank	• BNP Paribas
• Punjab & Sind Bank	• ING Vysya Bank	• Calyon Bank
• State Bank of Bikaner & Jaipur	• Jammu & Kashmir Bank	• ChinaTrust Commercial Bank
• State Bank of Hyderabad	• Karnataka Bank Limited	• Cho Hung Bank
• State Bank of India (SBI)	• Karur Vysya Bank	• Citibank India
• State Bank of Indore	• Kotak Mahindra Bank	• DBS Bank
• State Bank of Mysore		• Deutsche Bank
• State Bank of Patiala		• HSBC (Hongkong & Shanghai Banking Corporation)
• State Bank of Saurashtra	• Punjab National Bank	• JP Morgan Chase Bank
• State Bank of Travancore	• Saraswat Bank	• Krung Thai Bank
• Syndicate Bank	• South Indian Bank	• Mashreq Bank
• UCO Bank	• Yes Bank	• Mizuho Corporate Bank
• Union Bank of India		• Oman International Bank
• United Bank of India		• Royal Bank of Scotland
• Vijaya Bank		• Scotia
		• Societe Generale
		• Standard Chartered Bank
		• State Bank of Mauritius
		• Taib Bank

Source: Author's compilation.

Scheduled Banks

The second schedule of the Reserve Bank of India Act contains a list of banks which are described as "Scheduled Banks." A bank in order to be designated as a scheduled bank should have a paid-up capital and reserves as described by the Act. In terms of Section 42(6) of RBI Act, 1934, the required amount was only Rs 5 lakhs. However, presently the RBI prescribes a minimum capital of Rs 100 crore and its business must be managed in a manner which, in the opinion of RBI, is not detrimental to the interests of its depositors. The scheduled banks are also required to maintain of cash reserve ratio, based on its demand and time liabilities at prescribed rate. They are also known as public sector banks. A nationalized bank is one where control, management, and ownership vest in the government.

Non-scheduled Banks

The commercial banks not included in the second schedule of the RBI Act are known as non-scheduled banks. They are not entitled to get facilities like refinance and rediscounting of bills from RBI. They are mainly engaged in lending money, discounting and collecting bills, and agency services. RBI does not encourage the opening of non-scheduled banks.

Foreign Banks in India

Foreign banks have brought latest technology and banking practices in India. They have made Indian banking system more competitive and efficient. The government has come up with a road map for expansion of foreign banks in India.

The road map has two phases. During the first phase between March 2005 and March 2009, foreign banks may establish a presence by way of setting up a wholly owned subsidiary (WOS) or conversion of existing branches into a WOS. The second phase would commence in April 2009 after a review of the experience gained after due consultation with all the stake-holders in the banking sector.

Private Banks in India

All the banks in India were earlier private banks. Private sector banking in India received a fillip in 1994 when RBI encouraged setting up of private banks as part of its policy of liberalization of the Indian banking industry. Housing Development Finance Corporation Limited (HDFC) was among the first to receive an "in principle" approval from the RBI to set up a bank in the private sector. Private banks play a major role in the development of Indian banking industry. These banks have introduced innovative products and aggressive marketing strategies.

FUNCTIONS OF COMMERCIAL BANKS

A commercial bank performs following functions:

Primary Functions

It includes

Acceptance of deposits

Time deposits:

They are the deposits re-payable after a certain fixed period. It includes the following:

1. Fixed Deposits (FD): The deposits can be withdrawn only after expiry of certain period say 90 days, one year, three years, 10 years, etc. A fixed deposit gets higher rate of interest depending on amount and period. A depositor can take loan up to 75 percent of fixed deposit amount by paying 1.1 higher rate of interest than the rate of interest on deposit. An FDR can be used as collateral.
2. Recurring Deposits (RD) or Cumulative Term Deposits (CTD): In recurring deposits or cumulative term deposits a customer deposits a certain amount every month for a definitive period, one year, two years or so. Recurring bank account provides the element of compulsion to save as RD accounts get higher rates of interest than saving bank account. There is great flexibility in period of deposit with maturity ranging from 6 months to 120 months. The minimum monthly deposit varies from bank to bank. In most of the public sector banks, one can start a recurring deposit account with a monthly installment of Rs 100 only. Loan/overdraft facility is also available against recurring bank deposits.
3. Cash Certificates: Cash certificates are issued to the public for a longer period of time. It attracts the people because its maturity value is in multiples of the sum invested.

Demand deposits

These are the deposits which may be withdrawn by the depositor at any time without any prior notice. It includes the following:

1. Savings Account Deposits: The savings deposit promotes thrift among people and can only be held by individuals and non-profit institutions. The rate of interest paid on saving deposits is lower than that of time deposits. The savings account holder gets the advantages of liquidity (as in current account) and a small income in the form of interests. A cheque facility, automated teller machine (ATM) facility, and money-transfer facility is also available; interest is calculated on deposit lying between 10th day of the month to 30th day of the month.

   Savings bank account can be opened in the name of an individual or in joint names of the depositors. Savings bank accounts can also be opened and operated by the minors provided they have completed 10 years of age. Accounts by Hindu undivided families (HUF) not engaged in any trading or business activity can be opened in the name of the *Karta* (head of the family) of the HUF.

   The minimum balance to be maintained is less in case of public sector banks and relatively higher in case of private banks. In most of the public sector banks, minimum balance to be maintained is Rs 500. In case of private bank minimum balance varies between Rs 1,000 and 5,000. For pension savings account, minimum balance to be maintained is Rs 5 without cheque facility and Rs 250 with cheque facility.

2. Current Account Deposits: Current account offers high liquidity. No interest is paid on current deposits and there is no restriction on withdrawals from the current account generally by business firms and institutions. In a current account, a customer can deposit any amount of money any number of times. He can also withdraw any amount as many times as he wants, as long as he has funds to his credit.

A current account can be opened by:

- an individual who has attained majority;
- two or more individuals in their joint names;
- sole proprietorship concerns;
- partnership concerns;
- HUF;
- limited companies;
- clubs, societies;
- trusts, executors, and administrators; and
- others—government and semi-government bodies, local authorities, etc.

3. Demat Account: Demat refers to a dematerialized account. Demat account is just like a bank account where shares and securities (physical) are replaced by book entry or electronic form. A demat account is required to buy or sell stocks.

4. Deposit Scheme for Retiring Government and Public Sector Undertaking (PSU) Employees: This scheme is open to retired central and state governments' employees. The account can be opened at designated branches of public sector banks throughout the country. Minimum deposit limit to open the account is Rs 1,000, while the maximum limit equals total retirement benefits in multiple of Rs 1,000. Retirement benefits means:

- balance at the credit of employee in any of the government provident funds;
- retirement/superannuation gratuity;
- commuted value of pension;
- cash equivalent of leave; or
- savings element of government insurance scheme payable to the employee on retirement.

The account can be opened individually or jointly with his/her spouse. The account matures for closure after three years. Premature withdrawal is permissible after completion of 1 year and before completion of 3 years on reduced interest rate. Interest, at the rate notified by the central government from time to time, is credited and payable on half yearly basis. Present rate of interest is 7 percent per annum. Interest accrued, credited, or paid is fully tax-free and amount deposited under the scheme is free from wealth tax.

5. Internet Banking: Online banking (or Internet banking) allows customers to conduct financial transactions on a secure website operated by their retail or virtual bank and credit union.

It offers transactional (e.g., performing a financial transaction such as an account-to-account transfer, paying a bill, wire transfer and applications apply for a loan, new account) facilities like:

- electronic bill presentment and payment (EBPP);
- funds transfer between a customer's own checking and savings account, or to another customer's account;
- investment purchase or sale; and
- loan applications and transactions, such as repayments.

Advance of loans

A commercial bank provides loans and advances in various forms:

1. Overdraft: This facility is given to current account holders. A customer is allowed to draw money over and above the balance in the account up to a certain limit. It is a short-term temporary fund facility from bank against interest on overdrawn amount.
2. Cash Credit: Cash credit is a form of working capital. Under this arrangement sanctioned amount is credited to customers' accounts against the security of goods, personal surety, etc.
3. Discounting of Bills: Discounting of bills is another form of credit facility offered by bank. The bank may purchase inland and foreign bills from the drawers (normally seller of goods and services) against the production of essential documents like invoice, goods receipt, and bill of lading. The seller of goods gets instant discounts payment from the bank on the production of these documents against the acceptance by buyer (called documents against acceptance, D/A). Discounted payment is less than the full value of the bill. On maturity, these bills are presented to buyers (acceptor of bills). The ultimate responsibility is of seller as far as realization is concerned. The banker's discount is generally the interest on the full amount for the period of the bill till maturity.
4. Loans and Advances: It includes both demand and term loans, direct loans and advances given to customers, businessmen, and investors against personal security or goods of movable or immovable nature. The loan amount is credited to customer's account. A customer can withdraw at any time. The interest is charged for the full amount whether he withdraws the money from his account or not.
5. Housing Finance: In order to promote housing, a commercial bank provides housing loan directly or through its subsidiary like BOB Housing (a subsidiary of Bank of Baroda). Practically, every commercial bank has a housing subsidiary.
6. Educational Loan Scheme: A new educational loan scheme for students of full-time graduate/post-graduate professional courses has been introduced since August 1999. Under the scheme all public sector banks have been directed to provide educational loan up to Rs 15,000 for free seat and Rs 50,000 for the payment seat at interest not more than 12 percent per annum. This loan is available only for students whose annual

family income does not exceed Rs 1,00,000. The loan has to be repaid along with interest within 5 years from the date of completion of the course.

7. Loans against Shares Securities: A commercial bank provides loans against the security of shares/debentures of reputed companies up to 50 percent of market value of the shares.
8. Loan against Savings Certificates: A commercial bank is also providing loans up to 75 percent value of savings certificates like National Savings Certificate, Fixed Deposit Receipt, and Indira Vikas Patra.
9. Consumer Loans and Advances: One of the important areas for bank financing in recent years is consumer loans for purchase of durables like TV sets, washing machines, and microwave oven.
10. Securitization of Loans: Banks are recently trying to securitize a part of their loan portfolio and sell it to another investor. Under this method, banks will convert their business loans into a security or a document and sell it to some investment or fund manager for cash to enhance their liquidity position.

Credit creation

Credit creation is one of the primary functions of commercial banks. When a bank sanctions a loan to the customer, it does not give cash to him. A deposit account is opened in his name and the amount is credited to his account. Customer can withdraw the money whenever he needs. Credit is created with multiple effects.

Secondary Functions

Agency functions

A commercial function renders agency services, often fee based. Some of them are:

1. As an agent, the bank collects cheques, drafts, promissory notes, interest, dividends, etc., on behalf of its customers. Within the same city, it is free of cost. Outstation cheques will be collected by banks against commission.
2. The bank makes the payments such as rent, insurance premiums, and loan installment as per standing instructions.
3. The commercial bank purchases and sells foreign exchange after obtaining license from RBI.
4. Commercial bank may undertake the purchase, sale, collection of different securities such as shares, debentures, and bonds.
5. The bank may act as executors of will and trustees.
6. Commercial bank provides portfolio management, advisory services, project consultancy, and financial restructuring services.

General utility services

The general utility services are:

1. Custodian services like safekeeping of documents, valuables like jewels and jewelry.
2. Banks issue travelers cheques to help carry money safely while travelling within India or abroad though travelers cheque has now become out of fashion.
3. Facility of letter of credit is offered on behalf of buyer (importer) in favor of seller in the country of seller (exporter). The seller (exporter) gets immediate payment on the production of documents.
4. The banks act as referees and supply information about the business transaction and financial standing of their customers on enquiries made by third party.
5. The commercial banks collect information on business and financial conditions, etc., and make it available to their customers to help to plan their strategy. It is useful for those customers going for cross-border business.
6. The banks today have ATM facilities. Under this system the customer can withdraw amount any time, anywhere.
7. Banks provide credit cards, debit card (local and international both).
8. Commercial banks provide factoring services, corporate restructuring services, etc.

Banking products (for corporate sector)

Fund based services (products)

Fund based services are those where a bank has to make investment. There is a cost and risk of these services and return is expected from them. The difference between the cost and return is called spread.

Some funds based services are:

1. Working capital finance
2. Short-term finance
3. Bill discounting
4. Export credit
5. Structured cash flow financing
6. Channel/vendor financing

Non-fund based services (products)

These services are in nature of advisory. A bank charges commission or fee for rendering these services. Some of the non-fund based products are:

1. Letters of credit
2. Guarantees
3. Collection of documents

4. Bills collection
5. Cash management services
6. Loan syndication
7. Supply chain management
8. Payment gateway services

Banking Products (for Retail Customers)

These products are available to individuals. Banks provide these through creation of retailers' network (distributors—direct marketing associates (DMA) and direct sales associates (DSA)). Some of the assets and liability products are:

1. **Assets**
   i. Auto loans
   ii. Housing loans
   iii. Credit card and debit card
   iv. Wealth management
   v. Insurance
   vi. Education loan
   vii. Mutual funds
   viii. Personal loan
   ix. Loan against securities
   x. Mortgage products

2. **Liabilities**
   i. Retail deposits
   ii. Fixed deposits
   iii. Recurring deposits

REFORMS IN FINANCIAL AND BANKING SECTOR: OVERALL APPROACH TO REFORMS

The last 19 years have seen major improvements in the working of various financial market participants. The government and the regulatory authorities have followed a step-by-step approach, not a big bang one (See Table 4.3). The entry of foreign players has assisted in the introduction of international practices and systems. Technology developments have improved customer service. Some gaps however remain (e.g., lack of an inter-bank interest rate benchmark, an active corporate debt market, and a developed derivatives market). On the whole, the cumulative effect of the developments since 1991 has been quite encouraging. An indication of the strength of the reformed Indian financial system can be seen from the fact that India has not been affected by recent global meltdown.

The overall reforms in financial sector can be summarized as follows (Table 4.2).

Table 4.2   Financial Sector Reforms—Summarized View

Requirements	Fulfillments
➢ Banking Regulations	• Deregulated interest rate • Greater freedom to banks • Significant steps toward full capital account convertibility
➢ Credit and Recovery	• Securitization and Reconstruction of Financial Assets and Enforcement of Security Interests (SARFAESI) Act, 2002 • Debt Recovery Tribunal (DRT)
➢ Payment Systems	• Real Time Gross Settlements (RTGS) • Electronic Clearing System (ECS) • Electronic Fund Transfer (EFT) • Cheque Truncation—in the pipeline
➢ Communications and Infrastructure	• Internet Banking, e-Banking • Tax payment/utility payments • ATM, mobile banking

Source: Author's compilation.

Table 4.3   Significant Steps for Improvement as Undertaken by the Banking Industry (Indian Banks)

Area	Status
➢ Capital Norms	• Minimum capital at 9 percent as against 8 percent by Bank for International Settlements • Indian banks are ahead in Basel II readiness—implementation of road-map targets by March 2009 • Minimum capital requirement for entry set at Rs 3 billion for all banks in private sector
➢ Credit Information	• Credit Information Bureau of India Ltd • List of defaulters on RBI website
➢ Financial Track Record	• No financial crisis—escaped contagion effect of South East Asian meltdown
➢ Other Regulatory Initiatives	• Strong regulatory practice and prudence in place for "Managing Affluence" • Regulatory provisions to bring non-banking finance companies (NBFCs) and Commercial Banks under uniform prudential norms

Source: Author's compilation.

There are public sector, private sector, and foreign banks operational in the economy. Public sector banks (PSUs) dominate the banking industry as reflected by following table (Table 4.4):

Table 4.4   The Share of Banking Business in India: Public Sector, Private Sector, and Foreign Banks

	Public Sector Banks (%)	Private Sector Banks (%)	Foreign Banks (%)
Branches	88.4	11.3	0.3
Staff	87.2	10.8	2.0
Deposits	75.2	19.4	5.4
Advances	73.3	20.2	6.5
Net Profit	73.6	17.0	9.4

Source: Various Data from CSO.

MARKETING OF BANKING PRODUCTS AND SERVICES IN INDIA

India is one of the fastest growing economies in the world. It provides excellent marketing opportunity of bank products in view of following facts:

Saving rate (Gross Domestic Saving) was 30.7 percent 2009.

i. Less than 40 percent of Indian household has a bank account meaning thereby 60 percent of population is yet to be tapped, that is, vast untapped market exists.

ii. Growing middle class to the size of 350 million, that is, a market of 35 crore Indians who are willing to experiment new products and services.

iii. Number of high net worth individuals (HNI) is to be doubled to 4 lakhs by 2010 and India is one of 10 fastest growing population of HNI globally.

iv. Consumer finance stands only at about 2 to 3 percent of gross domestic product (GDP) as compared to 25 percent in European market. Thus, there exists a vast ready market for consumer finance products. The Table 4.5 reflects the trends in consumption boom in India and other Asian countries.

Table 4.5 Consumption Boom in India in 2008–09

	Consumer Loans/ GDP (%)	Mortgages/ GDP (%)	Credit Cards/ GDP (%)	Other Retail Loans/ GDP (%)
India	2	2	1.75	6
Thailand	13	9	2.5	8
Malaysia	26	13	9.8	16
Taiwan	36	17	82.4	17
Korea	58	37	121.9	41

Source: Author's compilation.

The table shows the presence of vast scope of growth.

1. Penetration level of wealth management services in India is 10 percent against overall 60 percent in European market.

2. It is estimated 5.2 million Indians make use of online banking. Indians paying bills online is expected to increase from the current 0.3 million in 2005–06 to 1.9 million in 2007–08.

3. E-commerce transitions will cross over Rs 3,000 crores mark in 2007–08 from Rs 2,000 crores in 2006–07.

4. A free and open banking sector where most businesses are now conducted at market determined rates.

5. Net non-performing assets (NPAs) have decreased to 2 percent at the end of March 2006 from 8 percent at the end of March 1997.

6. Capital adequacy ratio has increased to 12.8 percent in March 2006 from 10.4 percent in March 1997.

7. Operating expenses of scheduled commercial banks (SCBs) have declined to 1.4 percent in 2007 from 2.1 percent in 1992 of total assets. Similarly intermediation cost of SCBs has decrease to 1.9 percent in 2006–07 from 2.9 percent in 1995–96.

8. RBI has strengthened prudential norms regarding assets classification, disclosures, income recognition, and capital adequacy. This has resulted into the following:

   i. There is efficiency, improvement, and reduction in NPAs.
   ii. India complies with BIS 26 norms of best practices of supervisory criteria, country risk, and convertibility.
   iii. Indian banks are well on road toward Basel II compliance.
   iv. Credit deposit ratio is increasing—public sector banks (PSU banks), 66.2 percent; private banks, 76.3 percent.
   v. Bank credit is growing by about 30 percent of GDP in March 2000 to 48 percent at the end of March 2006.
   vi. Non-food credit by SCBs increased by an average of 26 percent in 2002–06 against the average of 17.8 percent in 1970–2006.
   vii. Indian banking sector grew by six times in the last decade—from Rs 5,984 billion in 1995 to Rs 36,105 billion.
   viii. Know Your Customer (KYC) norms and anti money laundering regulations are in force.
   ix. Indian banks are serving the "Two Faces" of India—the underprivileged, but progressive and the opulent—with equal focus.
   x. Deployment of credit is quite broad based with increasing flow to infrastructure, Small and Medium Enterprises (SME), agri-business, housing finance, and retail business.

9. It is a fact that Indian banks are one of the best in the league of Asian peers as indicated by Moody's investors services analysis in 2008:

   i. Indian lenders have highest return on equity (ROE) in Asia (20.38 percent), followed by Indonesia (20.19 percent), New Zealand (18.83 percent), and Japan (–6.42 percent).
   ii. Average gross bad loans as share of total loans—India (8.18 percent), Philippines (15.05 percent), Thailand (13.08 percent), China (11.80 percent), and Malaysia (9.73 percent).
   iii. Cost to income ratio in India at 44.56 percent is in line with the best regulated Asian countries like Singapore (44.15 percent), Taiwan (42.61 percent), and Hong Kong (40.05 percent).

10. Today Indian banking industry is in good health with wide area coverage as reflected by Table 4.6.

11. To sum up, Indian banks are on high growth track as reflected by

   i. Overall banking sector is growing by 18 percent
   ii. Retail sector (compound average growth rate, 5 years) in various segments are (2002–07):

Table 4.6   Branch Network: Contribution of Public Sector Banks (PSBs) and Private Banks (2007–08)

• About 70,000 strong branch network—more than 60% presence in rural areas	PSBs: 72% Private banks: 19% Foreign banks: 7% Others include UCBs, regional rural banks (RRBs), Local Area Banks, and NBFCs
• Consistent growth in profitability—spread is getting healthier—from 3.1% in 2004–05 to 3.2% in 2005–06	Spread: 3.2 percent Capital Adequacy Ratio: 12.0% Return on total asset (ROA): 1.0 %+
• NPA ratios compare favorably with global trends	Gross NPA: 3.34% Net NPA: 2.00%
• Consistently out-performing stock indices—total return to shareholders continues to be attractive	PSU banks: 61.2% India banking: 51.3% Old private: 40.0% New private: 33.9%

Source: RBI (2006) [Annual Reports].

1. Housing loan   : 50%
2. Consumer durables   : 16%
3. Credit card   : 45%
4. Two wheeler loan   : 31%
5. Car loans   : 26%
6. Other personal loans : 38%

   iii. Number of ATMs is 30,000 in 2007 up from 24,500 in 2006

12. It is interesting to note that PSU banks and private banks are performing very well as suggested by indicators of soundness, cost, return funds profitability and, operational efficiency. The following table endorses the foregoing (Table 4.7):

Table 4.7   Comparison of Performance between Public Sector Banks and New Private Sector Banks (March 2007)

Banks		Public Sector Banks	New Private
i)	Capital adequacy ratio	12.4	12.00
ii)	Asset quality:		
	Net NPA ratio	1.1	1.0
	Gross NPA ratio	2.7	1.9
iii)	Cumulative provision to gross NPAs	56.8 %	49.1 %
iv)	Cost of funds	4.4 %	4.5 %
v)	Return on funds	7.6 %	7.7 %
vi)	Return on funds–Cost of funds	3.2 %	3.2 %
vii)	Operating profit to assets ratio	1.73 %	1.88 %
viii)	Net profit to assets ratio	0.93 %	0.91 %
ix)	Total operating expenses to assets	1.77 %	2.11 %
x)	Wage bill to assets	1.14 %	0.61 %

Source: Author's compilation.

Inferences

1. Capital to Risk-Weighted Ratio (CRAR): The CRAR of scheduled commercial banks (SCBs), a measure of the capacity of the banking system to absorb losses, was at 12.3 percent at end March 2007.
2. Return on Assets: The return on total assets (ROA) of banks, the ratio of net profits to total assets, is one of the most widely used indicators of profitability. A higher ROA indicates the commercial soundness of the banking system.
3. Non-Performing Loans: The quality of assets of banks is a crucial indicator of the financial health of the banking system and hence, financial stability. A lower non-performing loan (NPL) ratio indicates prudent business strategy followed by a bank. The NPL ratio for Indian banks at 2.5 percent is higher from ratios in seven out of the 10 select countries compared in the report.
4. Capital Adequacy Ratio: A bank's capital is used as an indicator of bank soundness because of its role as the final buffer against losses that it may suffer. The report claims that the capital adequacy ratio of Indian SCBs at 12.3 percent is comparable with most emerging markets and developed economies.

Table 4.8   Comparison of Various Indicators with Select Countries

Countries	Return on Asset Ratio	Gross Non-performing Loans to Gross Advances Ratio	Provisions to Non-performing Loans Ratio	Capital Adequacy Ratio	Capital to Asset Ratio
India	0.9	25	56.1	12.3	6.3
Emerging Markets					
Argentina	2.1	3.2	132.3	–	13.7
Brazil	2.1	4.0	153.0	18.5	9.4
Mexico	3.2	2.2	194.7	16.1	13.2
Korea	1.1	0.8	177.0	13.0	9.5
South Africa	1.4	1.1	64.3	12.7	7.8
Developed Countries					
USA	1.2	0.8	129.9	13.0	10.6
UK	0.5	0.9	56.1	12.9	8.9
Japan	0.4	2.5	30.3	13.1	5.3
Canada	1.0	0.4	55.3	12.4	5.6
Australia	1.8	0.2	204.5	10.4	4.9

Source: RBI Report (2007) and various issues.

MARKETING OF BANKING PRODUCTS: CONTEMPORARY PRACTICES

1. Banks have redefined their focuses by suitably devising their punch line and value statement reflecting vision and approach. Consider the Bank of Baroda's punch line "India's International Bank" underlining the large presence of the bank abroad as well, HSBC's punch line "World's local Bank" adopting local customers, practices, and

banking habit and bringing them to international standard in order to create value to clients, PNB's "You can Bank Upon" suggesting the trust factor wherein a client can do hassles-free banking. Following are the punch lines of some of the banks:

- Allahabad Bank: A Tradition of Trust
- Andhra Bank: Much More to do, with You in Focus
- Bank of Baroda: India's International Bank
- Bank of India: Relationship Beyond Banking
- Bank of Maharastra: One Family One Bank
- Canara Bank: We are Changing for You
- Central Bank of India: Build a Better Life Around Us
- Dena Bank: Trusted Family Bank
- Indian Bank: Taking Banking Technology to The Common Man
- Indian Overseas Bank: Good people to Grow with...
- Oriental Bank of Commerce: Where Every Individual is Committed
- Punjab & Sind Bank: Where Service is a Way of Life...
- Punjab National Bank: The Name you can Bank Upon
- Syndicate Bank: Your Faithful and Friendly Financial Partner
- UCO Bank: Honours Your Trust
- Union Bank of India: Good People to Bank With
- United Bank of India: The Bank That Begins with U
- Vijaya Bank: A Friend You Can Bank Upon
- State Bank of India: The Nation Banks on us
- Bank of Rajasthan : Together We Prosper
- Catholic Syrian Bank: Support All the Way
- Dhanalakshmi Bank: Relationship Forever Since 1927
- Development Credit Bank: Feel the Difference
- Federal Bank: Your Perfect Banking Partner
- ICICI Bank: *Hum Hai Na*
- IDBI Bank: *Aao Sochain Bada*
- IndusInd Bank: We care dil se
- Karnataka Bank: Your Family Bank Across India

2. The banks have set up direct marketing associates (DMA) and direct sales associates (DSA) to reach the customers. These DMA and DSA market bank products for commission.
3. Services Turned into products- Banks provide services. These services are redefined into category of products through intangibles like saving products, loan products, assets products, liability products. Even these products are referred to as a brand, for example, premium saving bank account is "orange" with ING bank.
4. Customer acquisition and customer care has become the prime vehicle of growth. These ready-made products are converted into customized products, to suit the needs of customers. Privilege cards, loyalty cards, good wishes on birthday, marriage anniversary, free gift, donor cards, free entry to banks-sponsored social, cultural, and musical programs are some of the marketing strategies to woo and retain customers.

5. In the competitive market, product innovation and cutting-edge technology are import-ant factors for growth. Banks are busy with product innovations which are often copied by competitors with cosmetic changes.

6. All banking products are now made available under one roof. For a company, a bank provides working capital finances along with term lending consortium finance, tie-up with foreign partners, line of credit, forex and treasury management, etc. The buzz word is to give them (customers) what they want, so that they will give us (banks) what we want. So gone are the days that a corporate has to go to, say, IDBI, for term loan and PNB for working capital and cash credit. In case of individual and retail customers, these services are made available at the door steps of clients like free cash pick and delivery by Kotak Mahindra Bank.

7. Enhancing convenience at no extra cost, the marketing of banking products have emphasized that convenience, connectivity, and comfort with latest technology should be within the reach of customers. For example, an ATM card can be used as a debit and credit card.

8. Banks are changing their logo and positioning to meet the expectation of customers—four banks have done this, namely, Axis Bank (former UTI Bank), Canara Bank (new logo and style), Bank of Baroda, and Union Bank of India. They have repositioned in the market. The changes have been beneficial to these organizations as reflected by increased volume and increased profits.

9. There is synergy between banks and insurance companies. Banks tie up with insurance companies and banks sell insurance products called Banca insurance to their clients.

MARKETING OF BANKING SERVICES: EMERGING ISSUES

Indian Banking industry has following emerging issues like implementation of BASLE-II recommendation, consolidation, merger, and acquisitions.

Capital Adequacy and BASLE II

Basle II requires 8 percent of minimum capital adequacy ratio. Basel II aims at creating a better linkage between the minimum regulatory capital and risk, enhancing market discipline, supporting a level playing field in an increasingly integrated global financial system, establishing and maintaining a minimum capital cushion sufficient to foster financial stability in periods of adversity and uncertainty, and grounding risk measurement and management in actual data and formal quantitative techniques.

BASLE II prescribes three pillars. These are:

i. Pillar 1—the minimum capital adequacy ratio at 8 percent.
ii. Pillar 2—the supervisory review process—it requires the banks to establish an Internal Capital Adequacy Assessment Process (ICAAP) to capture all the material risks,

including those that are partly covered or not covered under the other two pillars. The ICAAP of the banks is also required to be subject to a supervisory review by the supervisors.

iii. Pillar 3—the market discipline—it prescribes public disclosures of information on the affairs of the banks to enable effective market discipline on the banks' operations.

RBI has already issued the guidelines for the new capital adequacy framework in regard to Pillar 1 and Pillar 3 on April 27, 2007. With regard to Pillar 2, the banks have been advised to put in place an ICAAP with the approval of the board. The foreign banks operating in India and the Indian banks having operational presence outside India are required to adopt Standardized Approach for credit risk and the Basic Indicator Approach for operational risk with effect from March 31, 2008. All other SCBs are encouraged to migrate to these approaches under Basel II in alignment with them, not later than March 31, 2009.

Consolidation

With the easy entry of strong foreign banks in India, the process of consolidation along with merger and acquisition (M&A) will take place. In the past, there were a number of merger and acquisitions in the Indian banking industry like ICICI took over Gujarat Lease, New India Bank was merged with PNB, Global Trust Bank was merged with Oriental Bank of Commerce, and Western Union Bank was merged with IDBI. These mergers were of distress nature.

The world over M&A and take-over of banks and banking services are now craftly designed to overcome competition, to sustain the advantages of synergy, to enjoy wider reach, and to make presence in unrepresentative territory for achieving pan India presence. However, the M&A activity during the last two decades leaves the Indian banking structure nowhere near the international size. Just look at Table 4.9.

Table 4.9   Asset Base (USD billion)

Bank	Asset Base	Bank	Asset Base
Barclays Bank	1,591.52	State Bank of India	155.72
USS	1,567.56	ICICI Bank	61.90
Mitsubishi UFJ Financial Group	1,508.54	Punjab National Bank	33.16
HSBC	1,501.97	Canara Bank	29.92
Citigroup	1,493.99	Bank of Baroda	26.07
BNP Paribas	1,484.11	Bank of India	25.12
Credit Agricole	1,380.62	IDBI	20.27

Source: *Business Today*, February 26, 2006.

It suggests that SBI's (the biggest public sector Indian bank) total asset are USD 155.72 billion against Citigroup's USD 1.5 trillion. SBI's Tier I capital is one-tenth that of Citigroup's. SBI's global position is 72 (not even in first ten of Asian banks).

ICICI Bank's (the biggest private sector Indian bank) asset base is USD 61.9 billion compared to that of Citigroup's USD 1.5 trillion.

Financial Inclusion

Financial inclusion refers to delivery of banking services at an affordable cost to the vast sections of disadvantaged and low-income groups who tend to be excluded from the formal banking channel. The Reserve Bank has undertaken a number of measures in recent years. Introduction of "Zero Balance" or "No frills" accounts has enabled the common person to open bank account.

As per the report of the Committee on Financial Inclusion (Rangarajan Committee), at least 250 million hitherto excluded rural households should be provided access to credit by each bank product innovation. For this Financial Inclusion Technology Fund (FITF) would be set up for developing user-friendly technology. And Rs 200 crore each in next 5 years will be provided with initial corpus of Rs 25 crore.

Thus, the marketing of banking products (from concept to delivery of banking services) is a focused strategy with banks. Multi-products, multi-location, universal banking, everywhere banking, wholesome banking, online and e-banking, world class products and technology are some of manifestations of growing banking industry where customers are demanding and discerning. External factors like lifestyle changes, technology, emergence of new customer base, demographic changes, knowledge, innovation, conversion and diversion, and financial inclusion and inclusive growth will determine the shape of banking industry.

The marketing of banking products and services, however, is subject to several limiting factors like government regulation, overall monetary and fiscal management, inflationary pressure, investment, peer group, availability and affordability of technology, and above all customers education and development of the economy.

With nearly 261 million mobile phone subscribers and a growth rate of about 8 million new subscribers each month, the opportunities for mobile banking seem infinite. Mobile banking has rendered a new meaning to the concept of any time, any where banking (*Economic Times*, August 21, 2008).

5

Insurance Services In India

Learning Objectives

- To know the concept, growth, essentials, and types of insurance.
- To know the products.
- To capture emerging issues in insurance industry.

CONCEPT

Insurance is a contract between two parties whereby one party called insurer undertakes, in exchange for a fixed sum called premium, to pay the other party called insured, a fixed amount of money on the happening of a certain event.

Insurance is a measure of social security by which contingent losses are to be protected against the premium. Over a period of time insurance is beneficial as it increases savings, provides tax relief under Section 88. Insurance policies are accepted as collateral and above all they provide great psychological relief from the ill effects of possible happenings.

TYPES OF INSURANCE

The following Figure 5.1 describes the types of insurance.

Figure 5.1 Types of Insurance

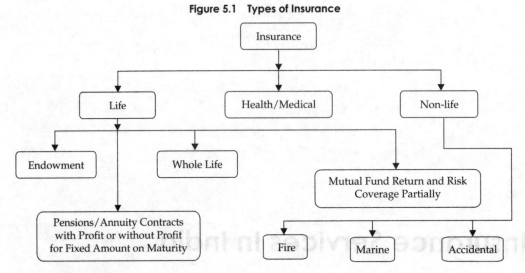

Source: Author's creation.

The distinction between life and general insurance is that with regard to the former, the claim is fixed and certain, but in the case of the latter, the claim is uncertain, that is, the amount of claim is variable and it is ascertained only some time after the event.

Thus, there are two types of insurance: life and non-life. The "Law of large Numbers" applies to both the classes of insurance: life and non-life. Non-life is commonly known as general insurance. The types of insurances covered under general insurance are vehicle insurance, building insurance, crop insurance, marine insurance, fire insurance, medi-claim, and so on.

GENESIS AND GROWTH OF INSURANCE INDUSTRY IN INDIA

The story of insurance is probably as old as the story of mankind. The same instinct that prompts modern businessmen today to secure themselves against loss and disaster existed in primitive men also. They too sought to avert the evil consequences of fire, flood, and loss of life and were willing to make some sort of sacrifice in order to achieve security. The concept of insurance dates back almost 6,000 years.

INSURANCE INDUSTRY IN INDIA

Life insurance in its modern form came to India from England, in the year 1818. Oriental Life Insurance Company started by Europeans in Calcutta was the first life insurance company on Indian soil. All the insurance companies established during that period were brought up with the purpose of looking after the needs of European community. Indian natives were not being insured by these companies. However, later with the efforts of eminent people like Babu Muttylal Seal, the foreign life insurance companies started insuring Indian lives. But Indian lives were being treated as sub-standard lives and heavy extra premiums were being charged on them. Bombay Mutual Life Assurance Society heralded the birth of first Indian life insurance company in the year 1870, and covered Indian lives at normal rates. Bharat Insurance Company (1896) was also one of such companies inspired by nationalism. The Swadeshi movement of 1905–07 gave rise to more insurance companies. The United India in Madras, National Indian and National Insurance in Calcutta, and the Co-operative Assurance at Lahore were established in 1906. In 1907, Hindustan Co-operative Insurance Company took its birth in one of the rooms of the Jorasanko, house of the great poet Rabindranath Tagore, in Calcutta. The Indian Mercantile, General Assurance, and Swadeshi Life (later Bombay Life) were some of the companies established during the same period.

Prior to 1912 India had no legislation to regulate insurance business. In the year 1912, the Life Insurance Companies Act, and the Provident Fund Act were passed. The Life Insurance Companies Act, 1912 made it necessary that the premium rate tables and periodical valuations of companies should be certified by an actuary. But the Act discriminated between foreign and Indian companies on many accounts, putting the Indian companies at a disadvantage.

The first two decades of the 20th century saw lot of growth in insurance business. From 44 companies with total business-in-force as Rs 22.44 crore, it rose to 176 companies with total business-in-force as Rs 298 crore in 1938. During the mushrooming of insurance companies many financially unsound entities were also floated which failed miserably. The Insurance Act, 1938 was the first legislation governing not only life insurance but also non-life insurance to provide strict state control over insurance business. The demand for nationalization of life insurance industry was made repeatedly in the past but it gathered momentum in 1944 when a bill to amend the Life Insurance Act, 1938 was introduced in the Legislative Assembly. However, it was much later on January 19, 1956, that life insurance in India was nationalized. About 154 Indian insurance companies, 16 non-Indian companies, and 75 provident societies were operating in India at the time of nationalization. Nationalization was accomplished in two stages: initially the management of the companies was taken over by means of an ordinance, later, the ownership too by means of a comprehensive bill. The Parliament of India passed the Life Insurance Corporation Act on June 19, 1956, and the Life Insurance Corporation of India was created on September 1, 1956, with the objective of spreading life insurance much more widely and in particular to the rural areas with a view to reach all insurable persons in the country, provide them adequate financial cover at a reasonable cost.

LIFE INSURANCE BUSINESS IN INDIA: MILESTONES RECALLED

The following are important landmarks in the genesis life insurance business in the country:

1. 1818: Oriental Life Insurance Company, the first life insurance company on Indian soil started functioning.

2. 1870: Bombay Mutual Life Assurance Society, the first Indian life insurance company started its business.
3. 1912: The Indian Life Assurance Companies Act enacted as the first statute to regulate the life insurance business.
4. 1928: The Indian Insurance Companies Act enacted to enable the government to collect statistical information about both life and non-life insurance businesses.
5. 1938: Earlier legislation consolidated and amended by the Insurance Act with the objective of protecting the interests of the insuring public.
6. 1956: The central government took over and nationalized 245 Indian and foreign insurers and provident societies. LIC was formed by an Act of Parliament, namely, LIC Act, 1956, with a capital contribution of Rs 5 crore from the Government of India. The capital of LIC is now Rs 100 crores.

GENERAL INSURANCE BUSINESS IN INDIA: MILESTONES RECALLED

General insurance business though not as old as life insurance in India yet it has existed for almost 100 years in India. The important milestones are:

1. 1907: The Indian Mercantile Insurance Ltd, the first company to transact all classes of general insurance business, was set up.
2. 1957: General Insurance Council, a wing of the Insurance Association of India, framed a code of conduct for ensuring fair conduct and sound business practices.
3. 1968: The Insurance Act was amended to regulate investments and set minimum solvency margins and the Tariff Advisory Committee set up.
4. 1972: The General Insurance Business (Nationalization) Act, 1972 nationalized the general insurance business in India with effect from January 1, 1973. Hundred and seven insurers amalgamated and grouped into four companies, namely, the National Insurance Company Ltd, the New India Assurance Company Ltd, the Oriental Insurance Company Ltd, and the United India Insurance Company Ltd GIC was incorporated as a corporation.

ESSENTIALS OF LIFE INSURANCE CONTRACT

Life insurance contract is one in which one party agrees to pay a given sum upon the happening of a particular event contingent upon the duration of life in exchange of the payment of consideration. The person who guarantees the payment is called insurer, the amount given is called the policy amount, and the person on whose life payment is guaranteed is called insured or assured. The particular event on which payment is to be given, may be death or survival on completion of term of policy. The consideration is called premium. The document evidencing the contract is called policy.

1. **Nature of Insurance Contract:** Unilateral contract is that where only one party to the contract makes legally enforceable promises. Generally, contracts are bilateral, that is, each party to the contract makes enforceable promises to the other party. But, the life insurance contract is unilateral in nature because the insurer makes an enforceable promise. The insured cannot be forced to pay the subsequent premium, the insured can only repudiate the contract of payment of full policy amount but he shall be liable to pay the part of the policy amount according to term and conditions of the contract. On the other hand, if the insured continues to pay the periodic premiums, the insurer will be obliged to accept the premiums and can be compelled to continue the contract.

2. **Conditional Contract:** Life insurance contract is subject to the conditions and privileges printed on the back of the policy. The schedule and endorsement placed on the policy shall be a part of the contract to fulfill certain conditions before the proof of death or of disability are the parts of the contract. It is also conditioned on the timely payment of premiums. If this condition is not fulfilled, the insurer is relieved of his basic promise of paying the sum assured but is bound to honor other subsidiary conditions, namely, payment of surrender values, etc. The conditions whether precedent or subsequent of the legal right must be fulfilled in order to complete the contract.

3. **An Aleatory Contract:** Under this contract, no mutual exchange of equivalent monetary value is done. This causes a contingency of the happening of which payment is made. The happening is a matter of chance, which may occur, or not. If death occurs only after payment of a few premiums, full policy amount is paid.

4. **Contract of Adhesion:** This contract means where the terms of contract are not arrived at by mutual negotiation between the parties as in case of ordinary contracts. It is contrary to the bargaining contract. In life insurance, the insurer decides upon the contract. It has two options, that is, either to accept or reject the contract.

5. **Contract of Certain Amount:** In case of non-life insurance, no amount is paid unless a particular event has taken place.

6. **Essentials of General Contract:** In this life insurance, all the essentials of the general contract like offer and acceptance, consideration, competence of the parties, legality of object, and free consent of parties as prescribed by the Indian Contract Act, 1872, for the formation of a valid contract, are present.

7. **Insurable Interest:** All policies of life insurance are void unless there is an insurable interest in the life assured. Insurable interest arises out of the pecuniary relationship that exists between the policy holder and the life assured so that the policy holder stands to lose by death of the assured and/or continues to gain by his continued existence. When such a relationship exists, there is an insurable interest in the life of assured. Insurable interest is thus a financial or other unlawful interest in the preservation of life to be insured.

   The insurable interest exists where the following conditions are fulfilled:

   i. An insurable interest must have pecuniary basis.
   ii. In life insurance it must exist at the time the policy is affected contrary to the indemnity insurance where insurable interest must exist at the time of loss.

iii. The happening of the event assured against would either cause a complete or partial loss of a legal or equitable right to involve him in any legal or equitable liability.

Parties having insurable interest in life insurance are:

i. Own life and
ii. Other's life like
   a. Business relationship:
   - A creditor in the life of his debtor
   - A partner in partnership firm in the lives of his partners
   - An insurer in the life of assured
   - An employee in the life of his employer
   - An employer in the life of his key employee
   b. Family relation:
   - Wife in the life of her husband
   - Husband in the life of his wife
   - Mere ties of blood and affection

8. **Utmost Good Faith (*Uberrima fides*):** Principle of utmost good faith is of the greatest importance in the assurance and follows closely upon the necessity for the parties to the contract to be of the same kind. It is different from the ordinary commercial practice. The legal term used in this case is *caveat emptor* (let the buyer beware). It is not the duty of the seller of goods to disclose all information regarding their quality. However, the seller should not mislead the purchaser by false description. It is the duty of the purchaser to satisfy himself that the quality is according to his requirements. But in life insurance, both parties must observe utmost good faith toward each other. The following conditions shall also be complied with:

   i. **Duty of Both Parties:** It is the duty of both the parties to disclose all material facts until the completion of the contract.
   ii. **Material Facts:** A material fact is that fact which would affect the judgment of a prudent insurer in fixing the premium or in considering whether he would enter into the contract at all.
   iii. **Full and True Disclosure:** The utmost good faith requires that there should be no concealment, misrepresentation, or misstatement as to the material facts. The proposer must disclose all material facts truly and fully. There should not be any false statements or half-truths or any silence on a material fact.
   iv. **Extent of the Duty:** If the proposer has answered all the questions of proposal forms fully and correctly to the best of his knowledge and belief he has done his duty unless he has knowledge of some other facts which are material to the contract. It is assumed that the facts on which no questions are asked or the insurer waives the information thereon are considered by him to be immaterial. In defense of a non-disclosure the proposer cannot say that he had omitted to disclose it by carelessness

or mistake or that he did not regard the matter as material. The ordinary man is not expected to display the skill of a medical specialist. He is expected to inform all the relevant facts concerning the contents of the policy.

9. **Representation and Warranties:**

   i. **Representation:** Every information given by a proposer for insurance to the insurer during the negotiation is a representation. A representation may be an expectation, matter of fact, or belief. Representations include either written or verbal statements made by the proposer in connection with the proposal or the medical examination. The proposer's answers to the various questions in the proposal and personal statement are all representations on the strength of which the insurer may be induced to enter into the contract.

   ii. **Warranty:** The answers to the questions in the proposal form are constructed as representation unless it is clear that both parties intent to treat them as warranties. Section 33 of the Marine Insurance Act, 1906, defines warranty as a statement by which the assured undertakes that some particular thing shall or shall not be done or that some condition shall be fulfilled, or whereby he affirms or negates the existence of a particular state of facts. The warranties are incorporated in the policy either expressly or by reference. The warranties must be literally true and must be exactly complied with whether it is material to the risk or not.

ESSENTIALS OF GENERAL INSURANCE CONTRACT

The following are essentials of general insurance contract.

Every asset has a value and the business of general insurance is related to the protection of economic value of assets. Assets would have been created through the efforts of owner, which can be in the form of building, vehicles, machinery, and other tangible properties. Since tangible property has a physical shape and consistency, it is subject to many risks ranging from fire, allied perils to theft and robbery.

Now insurance covers the risk of losses due to sudden changes in currency exchange rates, political disturbance, negligence and liability for the damages can also be covered.

Life Insurance Products

Life insurance products are varied and many (see Figure 5.2). These products are customized. Some popular products are:

1. Endowment policy.
2. Whole life policy.
3. Term life policy.
4. Money-back policy.

5. Joint life policy.
6. Group insurance policy.
7. Loan cover term assurance policy.
8. Pension plan or annuities.
9. Unit linked insurance plan.

Figure 5.2   Insurance Products

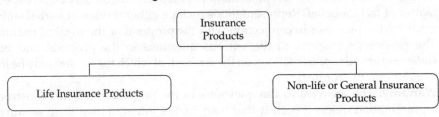

Source: Author's creation.

Endowment policy

An endowment policy covers risk for a specified period, at the end of which the sum assured is paid back to the policy holder, along with the bonus accumulated during the term of the policy. An endowment life insurance policy is designed primarily to provide a living benefit. Endowment life insurance pays the face value of the policy either at the insured's death or at a certain age or after a number of years of premium payment. Endowment policy is an instrument of accumulating capital for a specific purpose and protecting this savings program against the saver's premature death. Therefore, it is more of an investment than a whole life policy.

Whole life insurance policy

A whole life policy runs as long as the policy holder is alive. As risk is covered for the entire life of the policy holder, therefore, such policies are known as whole life policies. A simple whole life policy requires the insurer to pay regular premiums throughout the life. In a whole life policy, the insured amount and the bonus is payable only to the nominee of the beneficiary upon the death of the policy holder. There is no survival benefit as the policy holder is not entitled to any money during his lifetime.

Term life insurance policy

Term life insurance policy covers risk only during the selected term period. If the policy holder survives the term, the risk cover comes to an end. Term life policies are primarily designed to meet the needs of those people who are initially unable to pay the larger premium required for a whole life or an endowment assurance policy. No surrender, loan, or paid-up values are granted under term life policies because reserves are not accumulated. If the premium is not paid within the grace period, the policy lapses without acquiring any paid-up value.

Money-back policy

Money-back policy provides for periodic payments of partial survival benefits during the term of the policy, as long as the policy holder is alive. An important feature of money-back policies is that in the event of death at any time within the policy term, the death claim comprises full sum assured without deducting any of the survival benefit amounts, which may have already been paid as money-back components. The bonus is also calculated on the full sum assured.

Joint life insurance policy

Joint life insurance policies are similar to endowment policies as they too offer maturity benefits to the policy holders, apart from covering risks like all life insurance policies. But joint life policies are categorized separately, as they cover two lives simultaneously, thus offering a unique advantage in some cases, notably, for a married couple or for partners in a business firm.

Under a joint life policy the sum assured is payable on the first death and again on the death of the survivor during the term of the policy. Vested bonuses would also be paid besides the sum assured after the death of the survivor. If one or both the lives survive to the maturity date, the sum assured as well as the vested bonuses are payable on the maturity date. The premiums payable cease on the first death or on the expiry of the selected term, whichever is earlier.

Group insurance

Group insurance offers life insurance protection under group policies to various groups such as employers–employees, professionals, co-operatives, and weaker sections of society. It also provides insurance coverage for people in certain approved occupations at the lowest possible premium cost.

Group insurance plans have low premiums. Such plans are particularly beneficial to those for whom other regular policies are a costlier proposition. Group insurance plans cover large segments of the population including those who cannot afford individual insurance. A number of group insurance schemes have been designed for various groups. These include employer–employee groups, associations of professionals (such as doctors, lawyers, and chartered accountants), members of cooperative banks, welfare funds, credit societies, and weaker sections of society.

Loan cover term assurance policy

Loan cover term assurance policy is an insurance policy which covers a home loan. Such a policy covers the individual's home loan amount in case of an eventuality. The cover on such a policy keeps reducing with the passage of time as individuals keep paying their equated monthly installments (EMIs) regularly, which reduces the loan amount. This plan provides a lump sum in case of death of the life assured during the term of the plan. The lump sum will be a decreasing percentage of the initial sum assured as per the policy schedule. Since this is a non-participating (without profits) pure risk cover plan, no benefits are payable on survival to the end of the term of the policy.

Pension plan

A pension plan or an annuity is an investment that is made either in a single lump sum payment or through installments paid over a certain number of years, in return for a specific sum that is received every year, every half-year, or every month, either for life or for a fixed number of years. Annuities differ from all the other forms of life insurance in that an annuity does not provide any life insurance cover but, instead, offers a guaranteed income either for life or a certain period. Typically annuities are bought to generate income during one's retired life, which is why they are also called pension plans. By buying an annuity or a pension plan the annuitant receives guaranteed income throughout his life. He also receives lump sum benefits for the annuitant's estate in addition to the payments during the annuitant's lifetime.

Unit linked insurance plans (ULIP)

Unit linked insurance plan (ULIP) is life insurance solution that provides for the benefits of protection and flexibility in investment. The investment is denoted as units and is represented by the value that it has attained called as net asset value (NAV). The policy value at any time varies according to the value of the underlying assets at the time. ULIP provides multiple benefits to the consumer. The benefits include:

1. Life protection.
2. Investment and savings.
3. Flexibility.
4. Adjustable life cover.
5. Investment options.
6. Transparency.
7. Options to take additional cover against.
8. Death due to accident.
9. Disability.
10. Critical illness.
11. Surgeries.
12. Liquidity.
13. Tax planning.

General Insurance Products

General insurance provides much-needed protection against unforeseen events such as accidents, illness, fire, and burglary. Unlike life insurance, general insurance is not meant to offer returns but is a protection against contingencies. Almost everything that has a financial value in life and has a probability of getting lost, stolen, or damaged, can be covered through general insurance policy.

Property (both movable and immovable), vehicle, cash, household goods, health, and also one's liability toward others can be covered under general insurance policy.

Major insurance policies that are covered under general insurance are:

1. Home insurance.
2. Health insurance.
3. Motor insurance.
4. Travel insurance.
5. Marine insurance.

Home insurance

A home insurance policy protects against hazards like gas cylinder explosion, fire due to electric short circuit as well as man-made disasters like burglary, natural calamities like earthquakes, floods, landslides, and rains.

Home insurance policy covers broadly two things:

1. Building structure.
2. Contents inside the home.

Insurance covers for a building structure include:

1. **The Fire and Special Perils Cover:** This is a comprehensive package cover for protecting from damages to the structure of home due to fire, storm, flood, riot, strike and malicious damage, lightning, explosion and implosion, aircraft damage, damage due to impact by vehicles, subsidence, landslides and rockslides, bursting and/or overflowing of water tanks, apparatus and pipes, missile-testing operation, leakage from automatic sprinkler installations, bush fire.
2. **Earthquake Cover:** Covers damages to the structure of house due to earthquake.
3. **Terrorism Cover:** Covers damages to the structure of house due to acts of terrorism.

Home insurance does not cover the market value of the home. The price of the home includes the cost of the land and the cost of constructing the building structure on the land and the land cannot be insured. The insurance cover is only for the cost of constructing the building.

Insurance cover for contents inside the home covers only damages or loss of the contents inside the home—electronic and electrical goods, furniture and fixtures, clothing, jewelry and any other contents inside the home.

The covers that can be taken for the contents are the fire and special perils cover, earthquake cover, burglary, loss/damage to contents due to burglary or an attempted burglary, loss of jewelry, gold ornaments, silver articles, and precious stones kept under lock and key.

All the contents are covered on the market value of the items. This means that if there is a loss, the claim would be paid on the value of purchasing a similar new item minus depreciation.

Health insurance

Health insurance policy not only covers expenses incurred during hospitalization but also during the pre as well as post hospitalization stages like money spent for conducting medical tests and buying medicines. The cover will be to the extent of the sum insured. Also, mediclaim policies attract tax benefits under Section 80D. The maximum amount of deduction available under this section is Rs 15,000 and additional Rs 15,000 for medical insurance for parents and in case of senior citizens, the maximum limit of deduction is Rs 15,000 as per Union Budget 2008–09.

Individuals also have the option of covering themselves for medical expenses by opting for the "Critical Illness (CI)" rider available with life insurance policies, for example, ICICI Prudential Company. Life insurance companies have their own list of critical illnesses as defined by them.

Health insurance companies are offering innovative products to their customers these days. The latest product in this line is "cashless hospitalization." Here individuals do not have to pay for their hospital bills in case of hospitalization; the insurance company settles the bill directly. But certain conditions like the hospital should have a tie-up with the insurance company are required.

Motor insurance

Legally, no motor vehicle is allowed to be driven on the road without valid insurance. Hence, it is obligatory to get the vehicle insured. Motor insurance policies cover against any loss or damage caused to the vehicle or its accessories due to the natural and man-made calamities.

Motor insurance provides compulsory personal accident cover for individual owners of the vehicle while driving. One can also opt for a personal accident cover for passengers and third-party legal liability. Third-party legal liability protects against legal liability arising due to accidental damages. It includes any permanent injury or death of a person and damage caused to the property.

Travel insurance

Travel and tourism is a fast growing sector around the world. Travel insurance policy takes care of all travel worries. It secures the insured in their sojourn abroad. Travel insurance plans offer host of benefits such as medical expenses, loss or delay of baggage or passport, personal accident, financial emergency assistance, and hijack distress allowance.

Travel insurance plans cover expenses incurred due to delayed flight, cancellation of trip, and also take care of valued assets left at home.

Marine insurance

There are following terms which have to be clarified while taking the marine insurance policy:

1. **FOB (Free on Board):** Under FOB contract, the seller undertakes to deliver the goods over the ship's rail, at which point the risks pass from the seller to the buyer. The seller's responsibility is to pay all expenses until this point. He is to arrange for insurance up to the point. The buyer is also responsible for insurance from the time he assumes the risks.

2. **C&F (Cost and Freight):** Under this term the exporter bears the cost of carriage (freight). Risk passes from the exporter to the buyer at the port of shipment. The seller gives the notice of shipment to the buyer to enable him to arrange insurance. Until shipment, the risks however remain with the shipper.

3. **CIF (Cost, Insurance and Freight):** The seller is responsible for insurance from his own warehouse to that of the buyer at the destination point. This policy is called "warehouse to warehouse" marine policy. The policy is taken in the sellers' name and the claim is negotiated by the buyer, generally through a claims settling agent, at the destination place in his own country.

4. **ExW (Ex Works):** Title and risks pass to the buyer including payment of all transaction and insurance costs from the seller's door irrespective of mode of transportation. The buyer (importer) arranges insurance for consignment. The buyer has to bear all costs and risks involved in shipment transaction. Seller provides the goods for collection by the buyer on the seller's promise. Seller's responsibility is to put the goods in a good package, which is acceptable and disposable by the transporter.

5. **FCP (Free Carrier Point):** The seller's responsibility is to deliver the goods into the custody of the transporter at the named points or load the goods on the buyer's vehicle.

6. **FAS (Free Alongside Ship):** Title and risks including payment of transportation costs and insurance pass to the buyer once the goods are delivered alongside ship by the seller whether used for sea or inland waterways transport.

7. **CPT (Carriage Paid To):** This term is used for transport by rail, road, and inland water-ways. The seller and exporter are responsible for the carriage of goods to the nominated destination and to pay freight for the first carrier.

8. **CIP (Carriage & Insurance Paid):** This term is almost similar to CPT except that the seller has to arrange and pay for the insurance against the risks of loss or damage of the goods during shipment. The seller has to take the insurance and pay the freight.

9. **DAF (Delivered at Frontier):** Title, risk of damage/loss, and liability for import custom clearance pass to the buyer when cargo is delivered to the named border point by the seller using any mode of transportation. The term is used mainly for delivery of goods by rail or road.

10. **DES (Delivered Ex-Ship):** Title, risks of loss/damage or responsibility for discharge from vessel, and import customs clearance pass to the buyer when the seller delivers

goods on board the ship to destination port either for sea or inland waterways transportation.

11. **DEQ (Delivered Ex-Quay):** Title and risks pass to the buyer when delivered on board the ship at the destination point by the seller who delivers goods on dock at destination point cleared for import.

12. **DDU (Delivered Duty Unpaid):** Seller is responsible to make the goods available at the named place in the country of importation. The seller is responsible for all transportation cost and accepts the custom duty and taxes as per custom procedure.

13. **DDP (Delivered Duty Paid):** Title and risks pass to buyer when seller delivers goods to the named destination point cleared for import. The seller is responsible to make the goods available to the buyer at his risk and cost as promised by the buyer.

14. **Stock Throughput Policy (STP):** STP is popularly known as "Cradle to Grave" coverage. This policy was introduced in mid 1970s mainly for the following reasons: to have a single policy as against multiple marine and property policies; to avoid property tariff; to expand marine premium during soft marine market; and to obtain broader coverage for static risks under marine portfolio. In case of marine STP, it is the process of insuring both stock and transit/inventory exposures under a "Single Policy" to ensure seamless protection to the assured on a worldwide basis. STP is perfect for organizations that source raw materials or semi-finished goods for further value addition. These organizations then store and distribute finished goods across the world.

REFORMS IN INSURANCE INDUSTRY IN INDIA

Prior to year 2000 the insurance industry was monopolized with the presence of LIC in life insurance sector and GIC in the non-life insurance sector. The reform in insurance sector was initiated with the constitution of R.N. Malhotra Committee in 1993. The committee was formed to evaluate the Indian insurance industry and to recommend future direction. The major recommendations are:

1. **Structure**
   i. Government stake in the insurance companies to be brought down to 50 percent.
   ii. Government should take over the holdings of GIC and its subsidiaries so that these subsidiaries can act as independent corporations.
   iii. All the insurance companies should be given greater freedom to operate.

2. **Competition**
   i. Private companies with a minimum paid-up capital of Rs 1 billion should be allowed to enter the industry.
   ii. No company should deal in both life and general insurance through a single entity.
   iii. Foreign companies may be allowed to enter the industry in collaboration with the domestic companies.

iv. Postal life insurance should be allowed to operate in the rural market.

v. Only one state level life insurance company should be allowed to operate in each state.

3. **Regulatory Body**

i. The Insurance Act should be changed.

ii. An insurance regulatory body should be set up.

iii. Controller of insurance should be made independent.

4. **Investments**

i. Mandatory investments of LIC life fund in government securities to be reduced from 75 to 50 percent.

ii. GIC and its subsidiaries are not to hold more than five percent in any company.

5. **Customer Service**

i. LIC should pay interest on delays in payments beyond 30 days.

ii. Insurance companies must be encouraged to set up unit linked pension plans.

iii. Computerization of operations and updating of technology to be carried out in the insurance industry.

Following the recommendations of the committee the government passed the Insurance Regulatory and Development Authority (IRDA) Bill in December 1999 and IRDA was set up in April 2000. The reforms also lifted all entry restrictions for private players and allowed foreign players to enter the market with some limits on direct foreign ownership. Though the existing rule says that a foreign partner can hold 26 percent equity in an insurance company, a proposal to increase this limit to 49 percent has now been cleared by the government.

REVIEW OF PERFORMANCE OF INSURANCE INDUSTRY

Table 5.1 captures the growth of number of players in insurance industry since opening of insurance industry.

Table 5.1   Number of Players

	2000	2010		
	Public Sector	*Private Sector*	*Public Sector*	*Total*
Life Insurance	1	22	1	23
General Insurance	4	17	4	21
Special Insurance	1	–	2	2
Total	5	39	7	46

Source: www.irda.gov.in

Since the opening up of the insurance sector in 1999, foreign investments of Rs 8.7 billion have poured into the Indian market.

Performance of Insurance Industry in India

The fiscal 2008–09 witnessed global financial meltdown. Despite it, the Indian insurance industry, which has big opportunities to expand given the large population and untapped potential, grew satisfactorily. While life insurance business registered a growth of 10.15 percent, general insurance business recorded a growth of 9.09 percent in 2008–09. With this, insurance penetration (premium volume as a ratio of GDP) in rupee terms for the year 2008–09 stood at 4.74 percent; 4.17 percent for life insurance and 0.57 percent for non-life insurance. The level of penetration, particularly in life insurance, tends to rise as income levels increase. India, with its huge middle class households, has exhibited growth potential for the insurance industry. Saturation of markets in many developed economies has made the Indian market even more attractive for global insurance majors. The insurance market in India has witnessed dynamic changes including entry of a number of global insurers. Most of the private insurance companies are joint ventures with recognized foreign institutions across the globe.

Life insurance

The total capital of the life insurers at end March 2009 stood at Rs 18253.04 crore, with additional infusion of capital to the extent of Rs 5956.62 crore. There had been no infusion of capital in the case of LIC, which continued to be Rs 5 crore. The infusion of additional capital of Rs 5956.62 crore comprised of Rs 987.05 crore from new companies and remaining Rs 4969.57 crore from existing private insurers.

New policies

New policies underwritten by the life insurers were 509.23 lakh in 2008–09 as against 508.74 lakh during 2007–08 showing a marginal increase of 0.10 percent. The private insurers exhibited a growth of 13.19 percent, which is much lower than 67.40 percent recorded in the previous year. LIC, showed a negative growth for the second consecutive year at 4.52 percent as against its previous year negative growth of 1.61 percent. See Table 5.2 for more details.

Table 5.2 New Policies Issued: Life Insurers

Insurer	2007–08	2008–09
LIC	37,612,599	35,912,667
	(–1.61)	(–4.52)
Private Sector	13,261,558	15,010,710
	(67.40)	(13.19)
Total	**50,874,157**	**50,923,377**
	(10.23)	**(0.10)**

Source: IRDA (2009) Annual Report 2008–09.
Note: Figure in brackets indicates growth over previous year (in percent).

In terms of number of policies underwritten, private insurers have increased their market share from 26.07 percent in 2007–08 to 29.48 percent in 2008–09. To that extent, LIC has lost its market share.

Premium

Life insurance industry recorded a premium income of Rs 221791.26 crore during 2008–09 as against Rs 201351.41 crore in the previous financial year, recording a growth of 10.15 percent. Out of Rs 221791.26 crore, premium from unit-linked products, stood at Rs 90645.78 crore. This resulted in a fall in the share of unit linked premium to the total premium to 40.87 percent in 2008–09 from 46.14 percent in 2007–08. The decline was observed both in the case of LIC and private insurers. This decline can be attributed to subdued Indian equity market. The share of ULIP premium to total premium fell to 22.06 percent in LIC from 31.61 percent in 2007–08. The private insurers registered a marginal slowdown in ULIP products, as the composition of ULIP premium to the total premium for them was 86.74 percent in 2008–09, as against 88.34 percent in 2007–08. Regular premium, single premium, and renewal premium in 2008–09 were Rs 49370.56 crore (22.26 percent); Rs 37635.67 crore (16.97 percent); and Rs 134785.03 crore (60.77 percent), respectively. It may be recalled that in 2000–01, when the industry was opened up, the life insurance premium was Rs 34898.48 crore which comprised of Rs 6966.95 crore (19.96 percent) of regular premium, Rs 2740.45 crore (7.86 percent) of single premium and Rs 25191.07 crore (72.18 percent) of renewal premium. See Table 5.3 for more details.

The size of life insurance market, although recording positive growth witnessed retardation in the growth. The LIC could grow further its life business by 5.01 percent in 2008–09 as against an increase of 17.19 percent in 2007–08. The private insurers increased their premium by 25.10 percent in 2008–09 as against a higher rise of 82.50 percent in 2007–08. In terms of premium underwritten, the market share of private life insurance companies continued to rise in 2008–09, which surged to 29.08 percent from 25.61 percent in 2007–08. The market share of private insurers in first year premium increased to 38.88 percent in 2008–09 from 35.98 percent in the previous year. While, there has been an increase in the market share in the regular premium, market share of private insurers in single premium has declined. In the case of regular premium, the market share of private insurers went up further to 61.23 percent in 2008–09 from 52.23 percent in 2007–08. In contrast, the share of single premium of private life insurers fell to 9.56 percent from its previous year's level of 13.01 percent. On the other hand, the market share of LIC in single premium has increased to 90.44 percent in 2008–09 as against 86.99 percent in 2007–08.

Performance in the First Quarter of 2009–10

(i) Life insurance

During the first quarter of the current financial year life insurers underwrote a premium of Rs 14,456.34 crore, marginally higher than Rs 14320.20 crore in the comparable period of last year. LIC accounted for Rs 9028.68 crore and the private insurers accounted for Rs 5427.66 crore. While the premium underwritten by LIC increased by 19.99 percent, premium of the private insurers declined by 20.13 percent, over the corresponding period of the previous year. The number of policies written by life insurers grew by 12.06 percent. While the number of policies written by LIC increased by 22.59 percent, there has been a decline of 6.57 percent

Table 5.3   Premium Underwritten by Life Insurers

(Rs. Crore)

Insurer	2007–08	2008–09
Regular Premium		
LIC	26,222.00	19,140.61
	(–12.26)	(–27.01)
Private Sector	28,666.15	30,229.95
	(85.24)	(5.46)
Total	54,888.16	49,370.56
	(21.00)	(–10.05)
Single Premium		
LIC	33,774.56	34,038.47
	(28.24)	(0.78)
Private Sector	5,049.80	3,597.20
	(27.82)	(–28.77)
Total	38,824.36	37,635.67
	(28.18)	(–3.06)
First Year Premium		
LIC	59,996.57	53,179.08
	(6.71)	(–11.36)
Private Sector	33,715.95	33,827.15
	(73.56)	(0.33)
Total	93,712.52	87,006.23
	(23.88)	(–7.16)
Renewal Premium		
LIC	89,793.42	104,108.96
	(25.41)	(15.94)
Private Sector	17,845.47	30,676.07
	(102.16)	(71.90)
Total	107,638.89	134,786.61
	(33.83)	(25.22)
Total Premium		
LIC	1,49,789.99	157,288.04
	(17.19)	(5.01)
Private Sector	51,561.42	64,503.22
	(82.50)	(25.10)
Total	201,351.41	221,791.26
	(29.01)	(10.15)

Source: IRDA (2009) *Annual Report 2008–09*.
Note: Figure in brackets indicates the growth (in percent) over previous year.

in the case of private insurers. Of the total premium underwritten, individual premium accounted for Rs 10308.40 crore and the remaining Rs 4147.93 crore came from the group business. In respect of LIC, individual business was Rs 5963.64 crore and group business was Rs 3065.04 crore. The corresponding figures for private insurers were Rs 4344.75 crore and Rs 1082.90 crore respectively. Table 5.4 provides more details on the same.

Table 5.4   Life Policies Issued

Insurer	April–June 2008	April–June 2009
Public	4,819,546	5,908,412
	(–23.36)	(22.59)
Private	2,725,468	2,546,339
	(43.99)	(–6.57)
Total	7,545,014	8,454,751
	(–7.78)	(12.05)

Source: IRDA (2009) *Annual Report 2008–09.*
Note: Figure in brackets indicates the growth (in percent) over previous year.

The number of lives covered by life insurers under the group scheme was 89.90 lakh recording a growth of 60.16 percent over the previous period. Of the total lives covered under the group scheme, LIC accounted for 33.18 lakh and private insurers 56.72 lakh. The life insurers covered 37.86 lakh lives in the social sector with a premium of Rs 34.13 crore. In the rural sector, the insurers underwrote 21.89 lakh policies with a premium of Rs 1455.71 crore.

(ii) Non-life insurance

Non-life insurers underwrote a premium of Rs 8819.68 crore during the first quarter of the current financial year recording an increase of 4.57 percent over Rs 8434.00 crore underwritten in the same period of the last year. The private non-life insurers underwrote a premium Rs 3584.64 crore as against Rs 3541.78 crore in the corresponding period of the previous year (a growth of 1.21 percent). Public sector non-life insurers underwrote a premium of Rs 5235.04 crore higher by 7.01 percent over Rs 4892.22 crore in the first quarter of 2008–09. ECGC underwrote credit insurance of Rs 189.71 crore as against Rs 164.70 crore in the previous year. AIC underwrote agriculture insurance of Rs 131.70 crore as against Rs 53.70 crore in the previous year stand alone. Health Insurers (Star Health and Apollo DKV) underwrote premium of Rs 245.75 crore as against Rs 131.70 crore in the previous year. Premium underwritten in the Fire, Marine, Motor, Health, and Miscellaneous segments were Rs 1305.72 crore, Rs 579.91 crore, Rs 3460.16 crore, Rs 1826.74 crore and Rs 1653.62 crore recording a growth of 7.66 percent, 1.58 percent, 5.47 percent, 2.66 percent, and 3.90 percent, respectively over the corresponding period of the previous year. See Table 5.5 for more details.

Table 5.5   Non-Life Policies Issued

Insurer	April–June 2008	April–June 2009
Public	9,600,458	8,887,123
	(8.52)	(–7.43)
Private	4,971,011	5,318,470
	(27.93)	(6.99)
Total	14,571,469	14,205,593
	(14.44)	(–2.51)

Source: IRDA (2009) *Annual Report 2008–09.*
Note: Figure in brackets indicates the growth (in percent) over previous year.

The total number of policies issued by the non-life insurers for the first quarter of 2009–10 was 142.06 lakh as against 145.71 lakh in 2008–09 recording a decline of 2.51 percent in 2009–10. Of this, the public insurers issued 88.87 lakhs policies and private insurers 53.18 lakh policies, compared to 96.0 lakh and 49.71 lakh respectively in the previous year. The private insurers registered a growth of 6.99 percent while public insurers witnessed a negative growth of 7.43 percent.

Performance in the First Half of 2009–10

The insurance industry has registered a growth of 11.35 percent in premium collections in the first six months of this financial year at Rs 55,866.54 crore as compared to Rs 50,171.09 crore during the corresponding period of last year. The life insurance sector has grown by around 13 percent while the non-life segment witnessed a growth of around 8 percent in the first-half of 2009–10. First year premium income of life insurance players stood at Rs 39,046.59 crore in the April-September period as against Rs 34,599.37 crore in the corresponding period of last year. The total premium underwritten by the general insurance companies in the same period was Rs 16,819.95 crore as compared to Rs 15,571.72 crore in the year-ago period. With a change in the Insurance market due to the entry of new players and opening of the Insurance sector, there is a perceptible change in the market share of LIC and private insurance firms, during the last two years—as reflected by Table 5.6.

Table 5.6   Market Share of Life Insurance

Insurer	2007–08	2008–09
Regular Premium		
LIC	47.77	38.77
Private Sector	52.23	61.23
Total	100.00	100.00
Single Premium		
LIC	86.99	90.44
Private Sector	13.01	9.56
Total	100.00	100.00
First Year Premium		
LIC	64.02	61.12
Private Sector	35.98	38.88
Total	100.00	100.00
Renewal Premium		
LIC	83.42	77.24
Private Sector	16.58	22.76
Total	100.00	100.00
Total Premium		
LIC	74.39	70.92
Private Sector	25.61	29.08
Total	100.00	100.00

Source: IRDA (2009).

It is clear that the share of the LIC is decreasing in all types of premium in the year 2008–09, when compared with 2007–08, except in case of single premium, where it has registered positive growth in 2008–09 over 2007–08. See Table 5.7 for an overall analysis of the market share of companies.

Table 5.7 Market Share of Companies

Name of the Company	Market Share in %
LIC	48.1
ICICI Prudential	13.7
Allianz Bajaj	10.3
SBI Life	6.2
HDFC Standard Life	4.1
Birla Sun Life	3.4
Reliance Life	3.4
Max New York	2.4
Om Kotak	1.9
Aviva	1.8
Tata AIG	1.5
Met Life	1.4
ING	1.2
Shriram Life	0.3
Bharati Hexa Life	0.2

Source: IRDA (2009).

As per the data available it is clear that Bajaj Allianz had collected maximum first year premium (Rs 878.28 crore) up to January 2007 in individual single premium. Way ahead of any of its competitor in private sector, Bajaj Allianz was followed by SBI Life.

In case of individual non-single premium, it was ICICI Prudential having mobilized first year premium of Rs 2,658 crore up to January 2007 followed by Bajaj Allianz at Rs 1,649.25 crore. The performance of private insurance companies up to January 2008 suggested that SBI Life recorded maximum premium in first year premium of Rs 916.89 crore in case of individual single premium followed by Bajaj Allianz. When we look at the performance of private insurers, in case of individual non-single premium ICICI Prudential mobilized maximum first year premium at Rs 4,800 crore followed by Bajaj Allianz at Rs 3,903 crore. It can be argued that ICICI Prudential, Bajaj Allianz, and SBI Life are way ahead of their competitors as far as individual single and non-single premium is concerned. The share of Bajaj Allianz was 20.1 percent and SBI Life 36.15 percent in case of individual single premium up to January 2008. Thus, these three companies mobilized 67.87 percent of total first year premium in case of individual single premium covered by private insurers. In the category of non-single premium, ICICI Prudential contributed 26.67 percent, Bajaj Allianz's share was 21.6 percent, and HDFC Standard Life's share was 8.8 percent. Thus, it is clear that one insurance company may perform better in one segment whereas another may perform better in other. The total insurance premium collected by all 16 private insurance companies was Rs 22,503 crore up to January 2008 against Rs 12,360 crore up to January 2007, that is, a growth of 82 percent. In case of LIC the performance in case of individual single premium and non-single premium is almost identical up to January 2007 and January 2008. The LIC collected Rs 24,350 crore up to January 2008 as first year premium.

It is inferred that LIC has lost its commanding position and rightly so as private insurers are more technology savvy, aggressive, and have customer-centric insurance products and large number of innovative products. However, it should be remembered that size of market for life insurance products have also increased manifolds. Therefore, the LIC has been able to maintain its lead in absolute number but it is trailing behind private insurers in relative numbers.

Innovative products, smart marketing, and aggressive distribution have enabled fledgling private insurance companies to sign up Indian customers faster than anyone expected. Indians, who had always seen life insurance as a tax-saving device, are now suddenly turning to the private sector and snapping up the new innovative products on offer. Still with a large population and untapped market, insurance business happens to be a big opportunity in India, as insurance penetration in the country is poor. Insurance penetration or premium volume as a share of a country's GDP, for the year 2004–05, was at 2.53 percent for life insurance and 0.65 percent for non-life insurance. The level of penetration tends to rise as income increases, particularly in life insurance. India with about 350 million middle class households shows a potential for insurance industry. Saturation of markets in many developed economies has made the Indian market even more attractive for global insurance majors. The insurance sector was opened up for private participation 4 years ago and the private players are active in the liberalized environment. The insurance market has witnessed dynamic changes which include presence of a fair number of insurers, both life and non-life segment. Most of the private insurance companies have formed joint venture partnering well with recognized foreign players across the globe. The Indian insurance market accounts for only 0.59 percent of USD 2,627 billion global insurance market. Consumer awareness has improved. Competition has brought more products and better customer servicing. It has had a positive impact on the economy in terms of income generation and employment growth.

There are 23 players in life insurance and 23 players in general insurance industry in India as on January 1, 2008. Tables 5.8 and 5.9 profile the insurance players.

EMERGING ISSUES IN INSURANCE INDUSTRY

Emergence of Third Party Administrator

Third party administrators (TPAs) are the new intermediaries in the insurance sector. TPA is beneficial to the insured for better service; insurers are benefited by reduction in their administrative costs. TPAs are remunerated by the insurers. Once the policy has been issued, all the records will be passed on to the TPA and all the correspondence of the insured will be with the TPA.

Table 5.8   Life Insurance Companies

S. No.	Name of the Company
1.	Bajaj Allianz Life Insurance Company Limited
2.	Birla Sun Life Insurance Co. Ltd
3.	HDFC Standard Life Insurance Co. Ltd
4.	ICICI Prudential Life Insurance Co. Ltd
5.	ING Vysya Life Insurance Company Ltd
6.	Life Insurance Corporation of India
7.	Max New York Life Insurance Co. Ltd
8.	MetLife India Insurance Company Ltd
9.	Kotak Mahindra Old Mutual Life Insurance Limited
10.	SBI Life Insurance Co. Ltd
11.	Tata AIG Life Insurance Company Limited
12.	Reliance Life Insurance Company Limited
13.	Aviva Life Insurance Co. India Ltd
14.	Sahara India Life Insurance Co. Ltd
15.	Shriram Life Insurance Co. Ltd
16.	Bharti AXA Life Insurance Company Ltd
17.	Future Generali Life Insurance Company Ltd
18.	IDBI Fortis Life Insurance Company Ltd
19.	Canara HSBC Oriental Bank of Commerce Life Insurance Co. Ltd
20.	AEGON Religare Life Insurance Company Limited
21.	DLF Pramerica Life Insurance Co. Ltd
22.	Star Union Dai-ichi Life Insurance Comp. Ltd

Source: IRDA (2009).

Table 5.9   General Insurance and Special Insurance Companies in India

S. No.	Name of the Company
1.	Royal Sundaram Alliance Insurance
2.	Reliance General Insurance Co.
3.	IFFCO-TOKIO General Insurance Co.
4.	TATA AIG General Insurance Co. Ltd
5.	Bajaj Allianz General Insurance Co.
6.	Cholamandalam MS General Insurance Co.
7.	ICICI Lombard General Insurance Co.
8.	HDFC ERGO General Insurance Co. (earlier HDFC General Insurance Co. from September 27, 2000 to April 5, 2008)
9.	Star Health & Allied Insurance Company Limited
10.	Apollo DKV Insurance Company Ltd
11.	Future Generali India Assurance Company Ltd
12.	Universal Sompo General Insurance Company Ltd
13.	Shriram General Insurance Company Ltd
14.	Bharti AXA General Insurance Company Ltd
15.	Raheja QBE General Insurance Company Ltd
16.	New India Assurance Co. Ltd
17.	National Insurance Co. Ltd
18.	The Oriental Insurance Co. Ltd
19.	United India Insurance Co. Ltd
20.	Export Credit Guarantee Corporation Ltd
21.	Agriculture Insurance Co. of India Ltd

Source: IRDA (2009).

The job of the TPA is to maintain databases of policy holders and issue them identity cards with unique identification numbers and handle all the post-policy issues including claim settlements. In terms of infrastructure, the TPAs run a 24-hour toll-free number, which can be accessed from anywhere in the country. And they will have full-time medical practitioners under their employment who will immediately take a decision on whether the ailment is covered under the policy.

TPA license can be granted to any company registered under the Companies Act, 1956. IRDA, which licenses and regulates these TPAs, has specified stiff entry norms which include a minimum capital requirement of 1 crore, capping the foreign equity at 26 percent. License is usually granted for a period of 3 years.

In view of increased competition and pressure on revenue, insurance companies should keep their administrative and overhead cost under control for as long as possible. Therefore, intermediary like TPA will be required to outsource the following services:

1. Documentation and policy issuing.
2. Legal services and claims recovery services under subrogation rights.
3. Record verification under adjustment policies.
4. Medical examination services for life insurance policies and overseas medi-claim policies.
5. Co-insurance recovery services for both premiums and claims.
6. Follow-up of recoveries from reinsurance companies.
7. Servicing of motor policies.
8. Inspection and assessment of risk prior to issuance of policy.
9. Arbitration services.

Insurance penetration is very low in India both in case of life and non-life insurance as suggested by Table 5.10.

Insurance penetration is very low as measured by premium/GDP (%). Table 5.11 reflects insurance penetration life premium/GDP (%).

Low penetration means that a large scope for growth is there. It augurs well for life insurance players. Only 20 percent of insurable population is under life insurance cover.

In case of non-life, the penetration in India is the lowest as endorsed by following figure (Figure 5.3).

Insurance Density (Premium per Capita in US$)

Insurance density in India suggests that there is a vast scope of growth in the Insurance business, when compared with developed countries like UK, USA, Japan, etc.

It is clear that both insurance penetration and density are very low in India, thus providing very vast opportunities for growth of business.

**Table 5.10   Insurance Penetration—International Comparison–2006
(Select European and Asian Countries)**

Countries	Insurance Penetration # (Percent)		
	Life	Non-life	Total
1	2	3	4
European Countries			
UK	13.1	3.4	16.5
Switzerland	6.2	4.9	11.1
France	7.9	3.1	11.0
Ireland	7.9	2.5	10.4
The Netherlands	5.1	4.3	9.4
Belgium	6.5	2.7	9.2
Portugal	6.1	2.9	9.0
Germany	3.1	3.6	6.7
Asian Countries			
Taiwan	11.6	2.9	14.5
South Korea	7.9	3.2	11.1
Japan	8.3	2.2	10.5
Hong Kong	9.2	1.2	10.4
Singapore	5.4	1.1	6.5
Malaysia	3.2	1.7	4.9
PR China	1.7	1.0	2.7
India	**4.1**	**0.7**	**4.8**
World	**4.5**	**3.0**	**7.5**
USA	4.0	4.8	8.8
Canada	3.1	3.9	7.0

Source: Swiss Re.

Notes: # Insurance penetration is measured by the ratio of insurance premium to GDP (in percent).
The table is self-explanatory suggesting the poor position of India.

Table 5.11   Insurance Penetration Life Premium/GDP (%)

Country	Life Premium/GDP (%)
UK	8.9
Japan	8.32
South Korea	7.27
France	7.08
USA	4.14
Malaysia	3.6
Australia	3.51
India	2.53
China	1.78
Indonesia	0.82

Source: IRDA (2009).

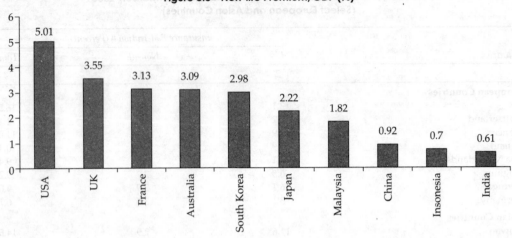

Figure 5.3 Non-life Premium/GDP (%)

Source: Author.

Table 5.12 Insurance Density (US$ Premiums Per Capita)

Country	Life	Non-life
UK	3,287	1,311
Japan	2,954	790
France	2,474	1,093
USA	1,753	2,122
Australia	1,366	1,203
South Korea	1,211	495
Malaysia	188	95
India	18	4.5
China	13	16
Indonesia	10	10

Source: IRDA (2009).

Meeting Competition: New Strategies

Insurance industry is very competitive. The clients in the industry are, by and large, passive, that is, need for insurance product is not a primary need and insurance products are for fairly long period of time. As such to create awareness, generate interest, and convert it into action is very tedious. Since the clients do not have good experience with insurers before liberalization as such they turned indifferent to the call of new products and investment solutions. Thanks to private players and aggressive marketing strategies, the investors have started looking at insurance as one of the sound investment opportunities.

Therefore, the industry has devised some new strategies to woo and create new customers. Some of them are:

1. **Banca Insurance:** It is a process of intermediation between client and insurer. An insurance company ties up with a bank preferably local dominating bank to use the network of the bank. For example, the tie up with Bank of Rajasthan and AVIVA, SBI Life with SBI Bank, ICICI Prudential with ICICI Bank, Kotak Mahindra with Cooperative Bank, Hongkong and Shanghai Banking Corporation (HSBC) with TATA, City Bank with Birla Sun Life. Thus, bank assurance is a venture between an insurance company and the bank having a vast network of branches. Products of insurance company are marketed by bank and its branches. It provides ready market to the insurance company. It depends on the bank and how many calls are converted into business. For banks, it is source of additional revenue as they get commission appropriate for corporate agency. For customers, the bank is known to them as they already deal with it. Thus, Banca Assurance provides win-win situation for insurer, bank, and clients.

2. **Products Innovation:** The industry is geared to tap the opportunities made available by emerging market, for example, the stock market was buoyant till recently. To take the advantages of bullish phase, all insurance companies floated:

   i. Systematic Investment Plan (SIP): In SIP a premium could be paid monthly. A part of monthly premium would go to contribute to premium for insurance and another part of the premium amount would be utilized for investment in stocks (shares).

      Investors have a choice to exercise their contribution toward stock market to be used for a regular income (investment in debt instruments), growth funds (investment in equity market), and balanced funds (investment in equity and bond both). Rupee cost average method is the other name of systematic investment plan. The technique emphasizes that a fixed amount must invested regularly irrespective of market level.

   ii. Product for each Category: Product innovation is reflected when an insurer brings out products for each category of clients with a number of options for "Switch, Swap and Surrender." In fact, insurance products are now seen as an investment avenue not as more risk coverage. There are perceptible changes in the mindset of investor like the removal of big mis-concept that advantages of life insurance are for dependents only. Insured may not gain till he is alive.

   iii. Technology Adds to Comfort: Insurer provides access from any location. Take an example of LIC. Insured can pay premium at any branch since there is online and WAN and LAN installation. It saves time and cost.

   iv. Electronic Clearing System (ECS) Facility: Some of the insurance companies collect premium through ECS where insured has to advise his banker for the same and the account of insured is debited without issue of cheque.

    v. Self-addressed and free Pick-up of Premium Amount: In order to provide better service to clients, insurance companies do send notice for premium reminder along with self-addressed envelope to clients. The clients have to keep the and post it. Postage will be borne by insurer.

3. **Micro Insurance:** It is for usual people in which a small premium of Rs 100 will provide life covers of Rs 10,000–20,000. Bajaj Allianz is the major player in this segment.

4. **Value Statement Endorsing the Vision:** All insurance companies have chosen their value statement reflected by the punch line. Consider the following:

    i. Bajaj Allianz Life Insurance Co. Ltd: *Jaisi Jaroorat Waisa Insurance*
    ii. Birla Sun Life Insurance Co. Ltd: Your Dreams Our Commitment
    iii. HDFC Standard Life Insurance Co. Ltd: *Sar Utha Ke Jiyo*
    iv. ICICI Prudential Life Insurance Co. Ltd: *Jeete Raho*
    v. ING Vysya Life Insurance Co. Pvt. Ltd: *Mera Farz*
    vi. Life Insurance Corporation of India: *Zindagi Ke Sath Bhi Zindagi Ke Bad Bhi*
    vii. Max New York Life Insurance Co. Ltd: Your Partner for Life
    viii. MetLife India Insurance Co. Pvt. Ltd: Peace of Mind...Guaranteed
    ix. SBI Life Insurance Co. Ltd: With Us...You are Sure
    x. New India Assurance Co. Ltd: Born to Lead
    xi. Oriental Insurance Co. Ltd: *Prithvi Agni Jal Aakash...sab ki suraksha hamare paas*

Take Oriental Insurance company endorsing insurance for basic elements like *"Prithivi, Agni, Jal, Aakash... Sab ki Suraksha Hamare Pass"*, ING Vysya says, Mera Ferz, HDFC Standard Life put premium on human dignity—"Sar Utha Ke Jiyo." These value statements meet the expectation of clients.

5. **International Best Practice at Local Level:** In order to regain clients, insurance companies having joint venture with world-class players provide international best practices to local clients. These practices aim at transparency, good governance, and full disclosures. A client is rest assured about treatment of his investment. Thus, insurance industry provides ample opportunity for growth. It has vast potentials. The need of the hour is to take a call, customize products and services, and deliver value to clients.

There are tremendous opportunities available in the industry.The current premium paying capacity is Rs 1,300 per person in India. The same is expected to touch Rs 4,100 by 2012. The insurance sector contributes 4 percent of GDP and it will grow to touch 6.2 percent of GDP by 2012. All that required is investor's education, good governance, and transparencies with best practices.

6

Capital Market Services

A corporate requires two types of financial resources. One is for short-term and other is for long-term. Short-term resources are those resources which are required for the time being and the money market normally caters to the short-term requirements.

Long-term resources are those resources required to meet capital expenditures like purchase of plant, machinery, new premises, acquiring of new businesses, merger and acquisition, long-term working capital, project finances, paying long-term debts, or capital restructuring. Capital market fulfills the requirements for long-term resources.

A capital market is a subsystem of financial market. It includes institutions (like development and investment institutions, banks, and corporates), instruments (like shares, debentures, and other corporate securities), intermediaries (like merchant bankers, mutual funds, bankers, registrar and share transfer agents, printers), and regulators (like SEBI, RBI, Department of Company Affairs). The network of institutions, instruments, and intermediaries connect two important players:

1. who have surplus savings and are willing to invest and
2. who require these savings for growth, expansion, capital expenditures, etc.

Stock market, a part of capital market, gives the way for union between savers and corporates. A stock market, though a part of capital market, is often used as a synonymous of capital market.

CAPITAL MARKET IN INDIA: A HISTORIC VIEW

The first stock exchange in the world was set up at Anthrop, Belgium in 1531 and first authorized stock exchange in the world was started in 1602 at Amsterdam (Holland). Stock market in India exists since 1830s where trading in shares of corporate, banks, and cotton presses had taken place. During 1840 and 1850 only half a dozen brokers were recognized by banks and merchants. 1850s witnessed a rapid development of commercial enterprises thus increasing broking business and number of brokers touched 60 by 1860. 1860–65 is a landmark in the history of the stock market. This period is referred to as Roy Chand Prem Chand's era, a legendary entrepreneur and businessman. He is said to have floated banks and companies by dozens. The American Civil War began in 1860 resulting into closure of export of cotton from the USA to Europe. This provided a unique opportunity to Indian cotton exporters and share mania began. Number of brokers increased to 250. Share price of Back Bay Reclamation Ltd touched Rs 5,000. However, with the end of the American Civil War in 1865, the boom disappeared from the capital market. Share prices crashed drastically, for example, the share of Bank of Bombay came down to Rs 87 from the high Rs 2,850. The first stock brokers' association was then established in Mumbai in 1887.

The growth of stock exchange in the country was situational, for example, civil war in America led to major spurt in commodities trading like jute (Calcutta Stock Exchange), cotton (Ahmedabad and Mumbai stock exchanges), and plantation (Madras Stock Exchange). There were 23 stock exchanges in the country till 2004, namely:

1. Bombay Stock Exchange
2. National Stock Exchange
3. Ahmedabad Stock Exchange
4. Banglore Stock Exchange
5. Bhubaneshwar Stock Exchange
6. Calcutta Stock Exchange
7. Cochin Stock Exchange
8. Coimbatore Stock Exchange
9. Delhi Stock Exchange
10. Guwahati Stock Exchange
11. Hyderabad Stock Exchange
12. Jaipur Stock Exchange
13. Ludhiana Stock Exchange
14. Madhya Pradesh Stock Exchange
15. Madras Stock Exchange
16. Magadh Stock Exchange
17. Manglore Stock Exchange
18. Meerut Stock Exchange
19. OTC (over the counter) Exchange of India (OTCEI)
20. Pune Stock Exchange

21. Saurashtra Kutch Stock Exchange
22. Uttar Pradesh Stock Exchange
23. Vadodara Stock Exchange

The Manglore Stock Exchange was de-recognized by SEBI in 2004, thus leaving 22 stock exchanges in the country. National Stock Exchange (NSE) and OTCEI have been set up by the government through development financial institutions (IDBI, LIC, UTI, and so on.) and public sector banks (PNB, SBI, etc.); remaining 20 stock exchanges have been set up by private initiatives. Except NSE and Bombay Stock Exchange (BSE), remaining 20 regional stock exchanges are struggling for survival. They have neither volumes, nor clients, and nor are listed companies. In order to survive, these stock exchanges have become members of national level exchanges through the formation of subsidiaries and acquired corporate membership.

INDIAN CAPITAL MARKET: A SUMMARIZED VIEW

The Indian capital market has passed through various phases since consolidation of economic reform in 1998. Table 6.1 gives the consolidated view of the market, brokers, intermediaries, and others in similar fields.

TYPES OF CAPITAL MARKET

Capital market is of two types:

New Issues Market (Also Known As Primary Market)

It is the market which provides opportunity to corporate sector to raise funds from public, corporates, high net worth individuals, trust, and others. Merchant bankers, mutual funds, financial institution, foreign institutional investors, body-corporate, and retail investors are main participants in new issues market.

New issue market is further divided into two parts:

1. Initial Public Offering (IPO): A maiden public issue by the company.
2. Follow-on Public Offering (FPO): FPO is also known as further issues market, that is, subsequent public issues including rights issues and bonus issues by existing public limited company.

Table 6.1   Various Registered Intermediaries with SEBI: A Comprehensive View

Market Intermediaries	As on March 31															
	1993	1994	1995	1996	1997	1998	1999	2000	2001	2002	2003	2004	2005	2006	2007	2008
1	2	3	4	5	6	7	8	9	10	11	12	13	14	15	16	17
Stock Exchanges (Cash Market)	21	22	22	22	22	22	23	23	23	23	23	23	22	22	21	19
Stock Exchanges (Derivatives Market)	–	–	–	–	–	–	–	2	2	2	2	2	2	2	2	2
Brokers (Cash Segment)	5,290	6,413	6,711	8,476	8,867	9,005	9,069	9,192	9,782	9,687	9,519	9,368	9,128	9,335	9,443	9,487
Corporate Brokers (Cash Segment)	–	143	616	1,917	2,360	2,976	3,173	3,316	3,808	3,862	3,835	3,787	3,773	3,961	4,110	4,190
Sub brokers (Cash Segment)	–	202	876	–	1,798	3,760	4,589	5,675	9,957	12,208	13,291	12,815	13,684	23,479	27,541	44,074
Brokers (Derivative)	–	–	–	–	–	–	–	–	519	705	795	829	994	1,120	1,258	1,442
Foreign Institutional Investors	18	158	308	367	439	496	450	506	527	490	502	540	685	882	997	1,319
Custodians	–	–	–	–	–	–	–	15	14	12	11	11	11	11	11	15
Depositories	–	–	–	–	1	1	2	2	2	2	2	2	2	2	2	2
Depository Participants	–	–	–	–	28	52	96	191	335	380	438	431	477	526	593	654
Merchant Bankers	74	422	790	1,012	1,163	802	415	186	233	145	124	123	128	130	152	155
Bankers to an Issue	–	–	70	77	80	72	66	68	69	68	67	55	59	60	47	50
Underwriters	–	–	36	40	38	43	17	42	57	54	43	47	59	57	45	35
Debenture Trustees	–	–	20	23	27	32	34	38	37	40	35	34	35	32	30	28
Credit Rating Agencies	–	–	–	–	–	–	–	4	4	4	4	4	4	4	4	5
Venture Capital Funds	–	–	–	–	–	–	–	–	35	34	43	45	50	80	90	106

Intermediaries in New Issue Market

Merchant banker

'Merchant Banker' means any person who is engaged in the business of issue management either by making arrangements regarding selling, buying, or subscribing to securities or rendering corporate advisory service in relation to such issue management. A merchant banker cannot carry on any activity of issue management unless he holds a certificate of registration and other conditions relating to the net worth, financial soundness, liability, and infrastructure and to act as adviser, consultant, manager, underwriter and portfolio manager. Categories I to IV are recognised: Category II to act as underwriter, adviser, and consultant to an issue, or Category IV to act only as adviser or consultant to an issue. A merchant banker should have a minimum net worth as in the following Table 8.2:

Table 8.2 Number of Merchant Bankers Required

Category	Minimum Net worth
1. Category I	Rs 5 crore
2. To act as lead merchant banker	—
3. To carry on the profile as an underwriter	—
4. To act as adviser and consultant	—
5. Amount which can be raised by the issue	Two lakh

Source: SEBI (2008).

All public issues should be managed at least by one merchant banker.

Appointment of lead and co-managers. All issues should be managed by at least one merchant banker functioning as the lead merchant banker. Further, in an issue of offer or rights to the existing members with or without the reservation... the amount of issue of the body corporate shall not exceed Rs 50 lakh the appointment of a lead merchant banker shall not be essential.

Every lead merchant banker shall, before taking up the assignment relating to an issue, enter into an agreement with such body corporate setting out their mutual rights, liabilities, and obligations relating to such issue and in particular to disclosures, allotment, and refund. Further, neither a merchant banker nor a bank or a financial institution who has been granted a certificate of registration under these regulations shall after June 30, 1998 carry on any business other than that in the securities market.

The number of lead merchant bankers may not exceed, in case of any issue as per Table 8.3.

Registrar

Registrar to an issue means the person appointed by a body corporate or any person or group of persons to carry out...

Intermediaries (number)

Intermediary													
Foreign Venture Capital Investors	–	–	–	–	–	–	1	2	6	9	14	39	78	97
Registrars to an Issue & Share Transfer Agents	100	264	386	334	251	242	186	161	143	78	83	83	82	76
Portfolio Managers	28	40	61	13	16	16	18	23	39	39	47	54	60	84	132	158	205
Mutual Funds	12	22	27	37	41	38	38	39	39	38	37	38	38	40	40
Collective Investment Schemes	–	–	–	–	0	0	0	0	0	0	0	0	0	0
Approved Intermediaries (Stock Lending Schemes)	1	1	4	6	10	8	4	3	3	3	3	3	3	2
STP (Centralised Hub)	1	1	3
STP Service Providers	4	2

Source: RBI (2009).

Note: The Magadh, Mangalore, Hyderabad, and Saurashtra Kutch stock exchanges have been derecognised by the SEBI. The data on intermediaries includes that of Magadh, Mangalore, Hyderabad, and Saurashtra Kutch stock exchanges.

Intermediaries in New Issue Market

Merchant banker

"Merchant Banker" means any person who is engaged in the business of issue management either by making arrangements regarding selling, buying, or subscribing to securities as manager, consultant, adviser, or rendering corporate advisory service in relation to such issue management. A merchant banker may be: Category I, to carry on any activity of the issue management, which will inter alia consist of preparation of prospectus and other information relating to the issue, determining financial structure, tie up of financiers, and final allotment and refund of the subscription; and to act as adviser, consultant, manager, underwriter, and portfolio manager; Category II, to act as adviser, consultant, co-manager, underwriter, and portfolio manager; Category III, to act as underwriter, adviser, and consultant to an issue; or Category IV, to act only as adviser or consultant to an issue. A merchant banker should fulfill capital adequacy as in the following (Table 6.2).

Table 6.2   Number of Merchant Bankers Required

Size of Issue	Number of Merchant Bankers
1. Less than Rs 50 crores	Two
2. Rs 50 crores but less than Rs 100 crores	Three
3. Rs 100 crores but less than Rs 200 crores	Four
4. Rs 200 crores but less than Rs 400 crores	Five
5. Above Rs 400 crores five or more	Five or as may be agreed by the board

Source: SEBI (2008).

All public issues should have at least one lead merchant banker to issue.

Appointment of lead merchant bankers: All issues should be managed by at least one merchant banker functioning as the lead merchant banker. Provided that, in an issue of offer of rights to the existing members with or without the right of renunciation, the amount of the issue of the body corporate does not exceed Rs 50 lakhs, the appointment of a lead merchant banker shall not be essential.

Every lead merchant banker shall, before taking up the assignment relating to an issue, enter into an agreement with such body corporate setting out their mutual rights, liabilities, and obligations relating to such issue and in particular to disclosures, allotment, and refund.

No merchant banker, other than a bank or a public financial institution, who has been granted a certificate of registration under these regulations shall after June 30, 1998 carry on any business other than that in the securities market.

The number of lead merchant bankers may not exceed in case of any issue as per Table 6.3.

Registrar

"Registrar to an Issue" means the person appointed by a body corporate or any person or group of persons to carry on the following:

Table 6.3 Capital Adequacy Requirement for Merchant Bankers

Category	Minimum Amount
Category I	Rs 50,000,000
Category II	Rs 5,000,000
Category III	Rs 2,000,000
Category IV	Nil

Source: SEBI (2008).

1. collecting applications from investors in respect of an issue;
2. keeping a proper record of applications and monies received from investors or paid to the seller of the securities; and
3. assisting body corporate or person or group of persons in
   i. determining the basis of allotment of securities in consultation with the stock exchange;
   ii. finalizing of the list of persons entitled to allotment of securities; and
   iii. processing and despatching allotment letters, refund orders, or certificates and other related documents in respect of the issue.

Underwriter

Underwriter is one who guarantees to purchase shares from the company in case his assured commitment is falling short. An underwriter claims underwriting commission. Underwriting was compulsory; however, it was done away with the introduction of book building process. Regulators are thinking to reintroduce underwriting once again.

Banks

Banks are appointed by merchant bankers for collection of application money.

Printers and advertising agencies

Printers and advertising agencies are appointed by merchant banker.

Brokers

Brokers to issue are appointed by lead merchant bankers. Brokers act as distributors of share application and act as collection centers too. Brokers are very strong players in the market as they have the closest link to retail investors. They get commission.

All intermediaries have to be registered with SEBI.

Capital Market Reforms

With the process of economic reforms in 1992, the capital market reforms were in forefront. G.S. Patel Committee is credited to have initiated reforms. Some major reforms since 1992 are enlisted here:

1. Improving the investment climate by allowing foreign institutional investors to invest in equity and debt markets.
2. Expanding the product range offered by the stock exchanges.
3. Strengthening the role and scope of capital markets regulation.
4. Revival of commodities' futures markets.
5. Allowing Indian companies to issues ADRs and GDRs in international exchanges and enabling them to raise resources through Euro Commercial Borrowings.
6. Divestment of government ownership in state-owned companies and financial institutions.
7. Tax reforms in the form of introduction of transaction tax that streamlined the tax mobilization from securities markets operations and also facilitated investors a choice of tax options in the form of choosing either long-term gains tax or short-term tax whichever they prefer and subscribe to.
8. Strengthening of institutional framework in primary and secondary markets.
9. Reform and restructuring of the state-owned assets management companies.
10. Allowing Indian companies and individuals to invest abroad.
11. Allowing stronger banks to assume greater exposure in the securities markets.
12. Setting up a mechanism for promoting corporate bond trading in stock exchanges, etc.
13. Nation-wide network of trading terminals.
14. Electronic trading and abolition of open outcry systems.
15. Dematerialization of shares.
16. Foreign participation in domestic brokerage business.
17. Foreign institutional investment in Indian stocks.
18. Venture capital.
19. Book building process for IPOs.
20. Investor protection guidelines.
21. Dual fungibility of ADRs/GDRs.
22. Delisting guidelines.
23. Corporate governance and disclosure standards.
24. Takeover code.
25. Insider trading.
26. Value At Risk-based margining.
27. T+2 securities settlement.
28. Straight through processing.
29. Screen-based trading of government securities.
30. Introduction of equity derivatives.
31. Exchange traded market for corporate bonds.

32. Central Listing Authority.
33. Mutual funds in the private sector.
34. Mutual fund investments abroad.
35. Demutualization and corporatization of stock exchanges.
36. Margin trading.
37. Exchange traded funds.
38. Anti-money laundering guidelines.
39. Electronic Data Information Filing and Retrieval (EDIFAR).
40. Integrated market surveillance.
41. Rating of IPOs.
42. Securities Appellate Tribunal.
43. Unique Client Identification.

Primary Market: Policy Initiatives

There are several policy initiatives having far-reaching implications. Some of them are:

1. SEBI has notified the disclosures and other related requirements for companies desirous of issuing Indian depository receipts in India. It has been mandated that: (*a*) the issuer must be listed in its home country; (*b*) it must not have been barred by any regulatory body; and (*c*) it should have a good track record of compliance of securities market regulations.
2. As a condition of continuous listing, listed companies have to maintain a minimum level of public shareholding at 25 percent of the total shares issued. The exemptions include: (*a*) companies which are required to maintain more than 10 percent, but less than 25 percent, in accordance with the Securities Contracts (Regulation) Rules, 1957; and (*b*) companies that have two crore or more of listed shares and Rs 1,000 crore or more of market capitalization.
3. SEBI has specified that shareholding pattern will be indicated by listed companies under three categories, namely, "shares held by promoter and promoter group," "shares held by public," and "shares held by custodians and against which depository receipts have been issued."
4. In accordance with the guidelines issued by SEBI, the issuers are required to state on the cover page of the offer document whether they have opted for an IPO grading from the rating agencies. In case the issuers opt for a grading, they are required to disclose the grades including the unaccepted grades in the prospectus.
5. SEBI has facilitated a quick and cost-effective method of raising funds, termed as "Qualified Institutional Placement (QIP)," from the Indian securities market by way of private placement of securities or convertible bonds with the qualified institutional buyers.
6. SEBI has stipulated that the benefit of "no lock-in" on the pre-issue shares of an unlisted company making an IPO, currently available to the shares held by venture capital funds (VCFs)/foreign venture capital investors (FVCIs), shall be limited to: (*a*) the shares held

by VCFs or FVCIs registered with SEBI for a period of at least 1 year as on the date of filing draft prospectus with SEBI; and (*b*) the shares issued to SEBI-registered VCFs/FVCIs upon conversion of convertible instruments during the period of 1 year prior to the date of filing draft prospectus with SEBI.

7. In order to regulate pre-issue publicity by companies which are planning to make an issue of securities, SEBI has amended the "Disclosure and Investor Protection Guidelines" to introduce "Restrictions on Pre-issue Publicity." The restrictions, inter alia, require an issuer company to ensure that its publicity is consistent with its past practices, does not contain projections/estimates/any information extraneous to the offer document filed with SEBI.

Resource Mobilization

Capital market has been very dominant in mobilizing resources from public and it has ensured common public participation. Mobilization of resources by corporate through capital market has been cost-effective and free from much of the hassles. There is a detailed procedure for raising the resources like a company should be public limited with relevant provisions in Articles of Association, apply to SEBI, obtain vetting of prospectus by SEBI, arrange intermediaries, and issue red-herring prospectus (a prospectus containing all details except price. The price would be discovered by book building process). See Tables 6.4 and 6.4a for more details.

The Behavior of Capital Market During 2009–10

Capital market

The Indian equity markets, which had declined sharply during 2008, reflecting the volatility in international financial markets and foreign institutional investment outflows, began the year 2009 on a subdued note. The market remained range bound during April–March 2009 but exhibited signs of recovery from April 2009. With the revival of foreign institutional investors' (FIIs) interest in emerging market economies including India, the equity markets gained strength during May–July 2009. There was a fresh spell of bullish sentiment in September 2009, with the Bombay Stock Exchange (BSE) Sensex recording a high of 17,126.84 during the month. The movement in equity indices in the Indian capital market was in line with trends in major international equity markets, a sign of increasing integration. Against the backdrop of these trends in Indian equity markets, the regulatory measures initiated during the year were clearly in the direction of introducing greater transparency, protecting investors' interests and improving efficiency in the working of Indian equity markets, while also ensuring the soundness and stability of the Indian capital market.

Merchant bankers are required to market the issues. The number of merchant bankers to be appointed will be decided by the size of the public issue. For details, see Table 6.5.

Table 6.4 Amount Mobilized from Public Issues

		Debt Issues					Share (%) of Private Placement in		Share (%) of Debt in Total Resource Mobilization (5/6*100)
Year	Public Equity Issues (Rs mm)	Public Issues (Rs mm)	Private Placements* (Rs mm)	Total (3+4) (Rs mm)	Total Resource Mobilization (2+5) (Rs mm)	Total Resource Mobilization (USD mm)	Total Debt (4/5*100)	Total Resource Mobilization (4/6*100)	
1	2	3	4	5	6		7	8	9
1995-96	88,820	29,400	100,350	129,750	218,570	–	77.34	45.91	59.36
1996-97	46,710	69,770	183,910	253,680	300,390	–	72.50	61.22	84.45
1997-98	11,320	19,290	309,830	329,120	340,450	–	94.14	91.01	96.67
1998-99	5,040	74,070	387,480	461,550	466,580	10,996	83.95	83.05	98.92
1999–2000	29,750	46,980	547,010	593,990	623,740	14,299	92.09	87.70	95.23
2000–01	24,790	41,390	524,335	565,725	590,520	12,661	92.68	88.79	95.80
2001–02	10,820	53,410	462,200	515,610	526,430	10,788	89.64	87.80	97.94
2002–03	10,390	46,930	484,236	531,166	541,556	11,353	91.16	89.42	98.08
2003–04	178,210	43,240	484,279	527,519	705,729	16,265	91.80	68.62	74.75
2004–05	214,320	40,950	551,838	592,788	807,108	18,448	93.09	68.37	73.45
2005–06	236,760	0.00	818,466	818,466	1055,226	23,654	100.00	77.56	77.56
2006–07	249,930	0.00	923,552	923,552	1173,482	26,921	100.00	78.70	78.70

Source: SEBI (2007).

Note: *Data from 2000–01 onward include only issues with a tenor and put/call option of 1 year or more, while data for earlier years include all privately placed debt issues irrespective of tenor.

Table 6.4a   Resource Mobilization through Primary Market

(Rs Crores)

Sr. No.	Calendar Year	2006	2007	2008	2009(P)
1.	Debt	389	594	0	3,500
2.	Equity	32,672	58,722	49,485	23,098
	Of which IPO	24,779	33,912	18,393	19,296
	No. of IPO	75	100	35	20
3.	Private Placement	117,407	184,855	155,743	238,226
4.	Euro Issue (ADRs/GDRs)	11,301	33,136	6,271	15,266

Source: RBI (2007) Economic Survey 2009–10, pp. 108.
Note: P-Provisional.

Table 6.5   Resource Mobilization from Primary Market: Domestic and Overseas Issues

	Total Floatations	Domestic Floatations	Domestic Shares	Domestic Debt	Public	Rights	Private Placement	Overseas Floatations
April 2006–March 2007	131,868.99	121,300.16	77,734.27	43,565.89	29,763.99	2,672.49	88,863.68	10,568.83
April 2007–March 2008	208,086.73	176,417.14	128,923.69	46,188.50	51,805.76	26,201.98	98,409.40	31,669.58

Source: CMIE (2008).

Primary market

Though resource mobilization from the primary market through equity investments was sluggish in 2009, both in terms of number of issues and amount raised through public rights issues and follow-on public offerings, there was an increase in debt market activity and private placements. The total number of initial public offerings (IPOs) declined to 20 in 2009 from 37 in 2008. The total amount mobilized through equity issues in 2009 was lower at Rs 23,098 crore as compared to Rs 49,485 crore raised in 2008. The amount raised through IPOs, however, increased slightly in 2009 to Rs 19,296 crore from Rs 18,393 crore in 2008. There was no debt issue in 2008. The total amount mobilized through three debt issues during 2009 was Rs 3,500 crore. The total amount raised through private placement of debt in 2009 at Rs 2,38,226 crore was higher by 53.0 percent than its previous year's level of Rs 1,55,743 crore. Total resources mobilized through the primary market at Rs 280,090 crore recorded an increase of 32.4 percent in 2009.

Secondary market

Indian equity markets witnessed a revival in the secondary market segment, which had recorded a sharp decline in the wake of the global financial crisis during the later half of 2008. The secondary market staged a handsome recovery in 2009 following stimulus measures implemented by the Government and resurgence of foreign portfolio flows displaying renewed interest by foreign investors. Furthermore, election results announced in May 2009 removed uncertainty on economic policies and as such boosted Indian equity markets and both benchmark and sectoral indices rallied. Market sentiments improved during November– December 2009, leading to gains in equity prices and an uptrend in equity market indices.

Amongst the National Stock Exchange (NSE) indices, both Nifty and Nifty Junior recorded positive annual equity returns (current year-end index divided by previous year-end index multiplied by 100) of 75.8 percent and 128.6 percent in 2009 as against negative annual equity returns of 51.8 percent and 63.5 percent respectively during the calendar year 2008. In terms of month-to-month movement, the NSE S&P CNX Nifty index showed improvements during March–May, July–September and November–December 2009. The S&P CNX Nifty index moved up from its previous year's closing level of 2,959 to 5,201 on December 31, 2009, recording an increase of 75.8 percent over the year. Nifty junior was on an uptrend in terms of month-end values from March to December 2009, except a marginal decline in its value in end-October 2009. The rise in the Nifty Junior index, on a point-to-point basis, was 128.6 percent in end-December 2009. The movement in the BSE Sensex and BSE 500 indices was more or less in the same direction as in the case of Nifty indices during the year 2009. During 2009, the Asian stock markets were on a recovery path. The cumulative change in global indices in end-December 2009 over the end-December 2003 level revealed a significant rise in these indices across countries. The Jakarta Composite index (Indonesia) registered a rise of 264.1 percent to 2,510 at end-December 2009, while the BSE Sensex was up by 199.1 percent to 17,465 in end-December 2009. Nikkei 225, Japan, however remained lower than its end-December 2003 level. Notwithstanding an improvement in global stock indices during the year, they were still lower than the levels reached in 2007.

STOCK EXCHANGE

Stock exchange is a place where buyers and sellers would meet and exchange financial assets for a price. The Securities Control Regulation Act, 1956 defines stock exchange as a body of individuals, whether incorporated or not, constituted for the purpose of regulating or controlling the business of buying, selling, or dealing in securities which include shares, scrips, stocks, bonds, debentures stock, or other marketable securities of a like nature in corporated company or other body corporate, government securities, and rights or interest in securities. It is pertinent to note that with the advancement and adaptation of technology, the stock exchange would be redefined as it is a facility to facilitate the exchange to tradable, negotiable, and transferable corporate securities. The "place" has become meaningless now, that is, in order to purchase or an investor is not required to visit Dalal Street in Mumbai or Delhi Stock Exchange at Asaf Ali Road in Delhi. He can very well buy and sell while sitting in his drawing room through the technology which has made BSE and NSE a pan India presence. Products of these exchanges are available online through very small aperture terminals (VSATs).

Structure of the Stock Exchanges

In terms of legal structure, the stock exchanges in India could be segregated into two broad groups—19 stock exchanges which were set up as companies, either limited by guarantees or by shares, and the three stock exchanges which were associations of persons (AOP), namely, BSE, Ahmedabad Stock Exchange (ASE), and Madhya Pradesh Stock Exchange. The 19 stock exchanges which have been functioning as companies include the stock exchanges of Bangalore, Bhubaneswar, Calcutta, Cochin, Coimbatore, Delhi, Gauhati, Hyderabad, Interconnected SE, Jaipur, Ludhiana, Madras, Magadh, NSE, Pune, OTCEI, Saurashtra-Kutch, Uttar Pradesh, and Vadodara. Apart from NSE, all stock exchanges whether established as corporate bodies or Association of Persons (AOPs), were non-profit making organizations.

Members of Stock Exchange

Stock market is one of few trades where intermediation in the form of brokers is a must. It is a fact that no purchase or sale is possible without members of the stock exchange. A broker (member) may be an individual or may be a corporate. An individual member should process: (*a*) contractual ability, (*b*) should be a major, (*c*) should not have been punished by any penal law, (*d*) should possess 2 years' experience, and (*e*) should be at least 12th pass. It is interesting to note that members of stock exchanges are elected by existing members in Annual General Meeting (AGM) of the exchanges. One can also become the member by purchasing membership card (known as ticket at BSE) in auction of membership.

A broker may be a corporate entity. To be a corporate member, a company (public or private limited) has to be formed in accordance with Section 322 of Companies Act, 1956 where one of the directors will assume unlimited liability. Whether a member is individual or corporate the requirement of capital adequacy and eligibility criteria as depicted in the following should have to be met.

Capital adequacy for members

Since ultimately buying and selling is done only through members of stock exchange, a member should have adequate capital and eligibility as revealed by Table 6.6.

The vibrant capital market and economic policy of the country has resulted in resource mobilization from domestic investors, as well as, foreign investors, as is evident by Table 6.7.

Regulation of Secondary Market

Secondary market: SEBI intervention

The following departments of SEBI regulate the activities in the secondary market (see Table 6.8).

Table 6.6 Financial Requirements for the Members of Stock Exchange in Different Market Segments

Requirement	Members of			Professional Clearing Members of	
	CM and F&O Segment	CM and WDM Segment	CM, WDM and F&O Segment	CM Segment	CM and F&O Segment
Net Worth	Rs 100 lakh	Rs 200 lakh	Rs 200 lakh	Rs 300 lakh	Rs 300 lakh
Interest Free Security Deposit (IFSD)	Rs 125 lakh	Rs 250 lakh	Rs 275 lakh	Rs 25 lakh	Rs 34 lakh
Collateral Security Deposit (CSD)	Rs 25 lakh	Rs 25 lakh	Rs 25 lakh	Rs 25 lakh	Rs 50 lakh
Annual Subscription	Rs 1 lakh	Rs 2 lakh	Rs 2 lakh	Nil	Rs 2.5 lakh

Source: NSE (2008), Annual Report.
Note: CM = Cash Market, F&O = Future and Option, WDM = Whole Debt Market.

Table 6.7 Eligibility Criteria for Trading Membership on Cash Basis

(Amount in Rs. Lakh)

Particulars	CM Segment	CM and F&O Trading
Constitution	Individuals/Firms/Corporates	Individuals/Firms/Corporates
Paid-up capital (in case of corporates)	30	30
Net Worth	100	100*
Interest Free Security Deposit (IFSD)	100	125**
Collateral Security Deposit (CSD)	25	25**
Annual Subscription	1	1
Education	Individual trading member/two partners/two directors should be graduates. Dealers should also have passed SEBI approved certification test for Capital Market Module of NCFM.	Individual trading member/two partners/two directors should be graduates. Dealers should also have passed SEBI approved certification test for Derivatives and Capital Market Module of NCFM.
Experience	....Two years' experience in securities market..	
Track Recod	The Applicant/Partners/Directors should not be defaulters on any stock exchange. They must not be debarred by SEBI for being associated with capital market as intermediaries. They must be engaged solely in the business of securities and must not be engaged in any fund-based activity.	

Source: NSE (2008).

Notes: *Networth of Rs 100 lakh is required for self-clearing members in the F&O segment and a networth of Rs. 300 lakh is required for members clearing for self as well as for other trading members.

**Additional Rs 25 lakh is required for clearing membership (self-clearing member/members clearing for self as well as for others) in the F&O segment. In addition, a member clearing for others is required to bring in IFSD of Rs 2 Lakh and CSD of Rs 8 Lakh per trading member he undertakes to clear in the F&O segment.

Table 6.8 Regulation of Secondary Market by SEBI: An Overview

Sr. No.	Name of the Department	Major Activities
1.	Market Intermediaries Registration and Supervision Department (MIRSD)	Registration, supervision, compliance monitoring, and inspections of all market intermediaries in respect of all segments of the markets, namely, equity, equity derivatives, debt, and debt related derivatives.
2.	Market Regulation Department (MRD)	Formulating new policies and supervising the functioning and operations (except relating to derivatives) of securities exchanges, their subsidiaries, and market institutions such as clearing and settlement organizations and depositories (collectively referred to as "Market SROs").
3.	Derivatives and New Products Departments (DNPD)	Supervising trading at derivatives segments of stock exchanges, introducing new products to be traded, and consequent policy changes.

Source: NSE (2008).

Listing

Listing means admission of securities of an issuer to trading privileges on a stock exchange through a formal agreement. The prime objective of admission to dealings on the exchange is to provide liquidity and marketability to securities, as also to provide a mechanism for effective management of trading. An issuer has to take various steps prior to making an application for listing its securities on the stock exchange. These steps are essential to ensure the compliance of certain requirements by the issuer before listing its securities. The various steps to be taken include:

1. Approval of memorandum and Articles of Association.
2. Approval of draft prospectus.
3. Submission of application.
4. Listing conditions and requirements.

In case a company fulfills these criteria, then the following information are sent for further processing:

1. A brief note on the promoters and management.
2. Company profile.
3. Copies of the annual report for last 3 years.
4. Copies of the draft offer document.
5. Memorandum and Articles of Association.

The listing fees depend on the paid-up share capital of the company as reflected by Table 6.9.

Table 6.9 Details of Listing Fee

Particulars	Amount (Rs)
Initial Listing Fees	7,500
Annual Listing Fees Companies with paid-up share and/or debenture capital:	
Of Rs 1 crore	4,200
Above Rs 1 crore and up to Rs 5 crores	8,400
Above Rs 5 crores and up to Rs 10 crores	14,000
Above Rs 10 crores and up to Rs 20 crores	28,000
Above Rs 20 crores and up to Rs 50 crores	42,000
Above Rs 50 crores	70,000

Source: NSE (2008).

Companies which have a paid-up capital of more than Rs 50 crore will pay additional listing fees of Rs 1,400 for every increase of Rs 5 crore or part thereof in the paid-up share/debenture capital. The listing fee varies from exchange to exchange. The foregoing fee structure relates to NSE.

Eligibility Criteria for Listing of IPOs by Companies

Qualifications for listing IPO are:

1. **Paid-up Capital**
   The paid-up equity capital of the applicant shall not be less than Rs 10 crore and the capitalization of the applicant's equity shall not be less than Rs 25 crore.

2. **Conditions Precedent to Listing**
   The issuer shall have adhered to conditions precedent to listing as emerging from, inter alia, Securities Contracts (Regulations) Act, 1956, Companies Act, 1956, Securities and Exchange Board of India Act, 1992, any rules and/or regulations framed under foregoing statutes, as also any circular, clarifications, and guidelines issued by the appropriate authority under foregoing statutes.

3. **At least 3 Years Track Record of Either**
   (*a*) The applicant seeking listing or (*b*) the promoters (promoters mean one or more persons with a minimum 3 years of experience, each of them in the same line of business, and holding at least 20 percent of the post-issue equity share capital individually or severally)/promoting company, incorporated in or outside India or (*c*) partnership firm which subsequently converted into a company (not in existence as a company for 3 years) can approach the exchange for listing. The company subsequently formed would be considered for listing only on fulfillment of conditions stipulated by SEBI

in this regard. For this purpose, the applicant or the promoting company shall submit annual reports of three preceding financial years to NSE/BSE and also provide a certificate to the exchange in respect of the following:

i. The company has not been referred to the Board for Industrial and Financial Reconstruction (BIFR).
ii. The net worth of the company has not been wiped out by the accumulated losses resulting in a negative net worth.
iii. The company has not received any winding up petition admitted by a court.
      The applicant desirous of listing its securities should satisfy the exchange on the following:

   a. No disciplinary action by other stock exchanges and regulatory authorities in past 3 years.
   b. Redressal mechanism of investor grievance.

4. **Distribution of Shareholding**
   The shareholding pattern of applicants(s)/promoting company(ies) on March 31 of last three calendar years shows promoters and other groups' shareholding pattern separately, which should be as per the regulatory requirements.

5. **Details of Litigation**
   The applicant, promoters/promoting company(ies), group companies, companies promoted by the promoters/promoting company(ies) litigation record, the nature of litigation, status of litigation during the preceding 3 years period need to be clarified to the exchange.

6. **Track Record of Director(s) of the Company**
   In respect of the track record of the directors, relevant disclosures may be insisted upon in the offer document regarding the status of criminal cases filed or nature of the investigation being undertaken with regard to alleged commission of any offence by any of its directors and its effect on the business of the company, where all or any of the directors of issuer have or has been charge-sheeted with serious crimes like murder, rape, forgery, or economic offences.

Trading in Stock Exchanges

Stock trade is now scrip t-less, region-less, online, and anonymous call matching. Trading is quiet and it can be done from any where. In order to execute the trade, an investor should be conversant with the group. Accordingly, the BSE has classified all the listed scrips into group A, B1, B2, Z, S. Scrips in group A are known as specified shares. Specified shares are those shares in which, at a point of time, forward trading was allowed and scrips for index (Sensex, BSE, NSE, Nifty-Fifty) are taken from group A only. To be included in a Sensex, a company should be in first hundred m-cap and its market capitalization should be more than 0.5 percent of total market capitalization, shares of the company should be traded every day, and the company should have listed at least for a year.

B1 and B2 shares are in cash section, that is, delivery-based segment. Z shares in Z category are of those companies which failed to comply with listing requirements and are for the benefit of small cap investors and S shares are of small companies. An investor desirous of purchase and sale of securities is required to get registered with an authorized broker.

The momentum of reforms in secondary market continues. The following is a summary of reforms and policy initiatives in last 3 years.

1. Amendments to Disclosure and Investor Protection Guidelines.
2. Appointment of a sub-committee on disclosures and accounting for integrating initial and continuous disclosures of companies.
3. Stipulation that Permanent Account Number (PAN) would be the sole identification number for all participants in the security markets.
4. Successful completion of demutualization process by 16 stock exchanges.
5. SEBI permitted short selling by institutional investors and waived entry load by mutual funds for investors making applications for investment in mutual fund schemes direct.
6. In continuation of the comprehensive risk management system put in place since May 2005 in T+2 rolling settlement scenario for the cash market, the stock exchanges have been advised to update the applicable Value at Risk (VaR) margin at least five times in a day by taking the closing price of the previous day at the start of trading and the prices at 11:00 a.m., 12:30 p.m., 2:00 p.m., and at the end of the trading session. This has been done to align the risk management framework across the cash and derivative markets.
7. In order to strengthen the "Know Your Client" norms and to have sound audit trail of the transactions in the securities market, "Permanent Account Number (PAN)" has been made mandatory with effect from January 1, 2007 for operating a beneficiary owner account and for trading in the cash segment.
8. In order to implement the proposal on creation of a unified platform for trading of corporate bonds, SEBI has stipulated that the BSE Limited would set up and maintain the corporate bond reporting platform. The reporting shall be made for all trades in listed debt securities issued by all institutions such as banks, public sector undertakings, municipal corporations, corporate bodies, and companies.
9. In line with the Government of India's policy on foreign investments in infrastructure companies in the Indian securities market, the limits for foreign investment in stock exchanges, depositories, and clearing corporations have been specified as follows: (*a*) foreign investment up to 49 percent will be allowed in these companies with a separate foreign direct investment (FDI) cap of 26 percent and cap of 23 percent on foreign institutional investment (FII); (*b*) FDI will be allowed with specific prior approval of Foreign Investment Promotion Board (FIPB); (*c*) FII will be allowed only through purchases in the secondary market; and (*d*) FII shall not seek and will not get representation on the board of directors.
10. The application process of FII investment has been simplified and new categories of investment (insurance and reinsurance companies, foreign central banks, investment managers, international organizations) have been included under FII.

11. Mutual funds have been permitted to introduce Gold Exchange Traded Funds.
12. Foreign institutional investors have been allowed to invest in security receipts.
13. Providing minimum public shareholding of 25 percent in case of all listed companies barring a few exceptions.
14. Listed companies to comply with revised guidelines on corporate governance, including appointment of the independent directors (under Clause 49).
15. Separate window for execution of block deals.
16. Making PAN compulsory for all categories of investors for opening a demat account with effect from April 1, 2006.
17. In accordance with the International Organization of Securities Commission (IOSCO) recommendations, it has been made necessary to execute transactions on the stock exchanges through the clearing corporations/clearing house of the stock exchanges.
18. Guidelines issued for issue of electronic contract notes.
19. A committee was set up to study the future of the regional stock exchanges.
20. Introduction of Gold Exchange Traded Funds.
21. Introduction of unique client code for mutual fund schemes.
22. Mutual funds were allowed to invest in ADRs/GDRs and foreign securities within the overall limit of USD 4 billion.
23. Venture capital funds were allowed to invest in foreign securities.
24. Outstanding limit for FII investment in debt securities was raised from USD 1.75 billion to USD 2.0 billion and the same for the corporate debt was raised from USD 0.5 billion to USD 1.5 billion.
25. Grading of IPOs made mandatory.
26. PAN was made the sole identification number for all transactions in securities markets.
27. Amendment of Clause 32 of the Equity Listing Agreement allowing companies to send abridged balance sheet and profit and loss account/auditor's report in place of sending the full balance sheet and annual report.
28. Authorized BSE and NSE to set up and maintain corporate bond reporting platforms to capture all information relating to trading in corporate bonds and both exchanges permitted to begin order-driven trade matching platform for listed corporate debt securities with effect from July 1, 2007.
29. Exclusive email ID to be given by the primary market intermediaries such as merchant bankers, registrars to issues, and share transfer agents for registering investor complaints.
30. As of June 2007, there were over 4,800 companies listed on the BSE and over 1,200 companies listed on the NSE. India's NSE has emerged as the world's third fastest-growing bourse in terms of increase in listed companies—outpacing global names such as NYSE, Nasdaq, and London Stock Exchange. While NSE recorded a 15 percent jump in the number of listed firms to 1,244 during the 1-year period ended April 2007, BSE has consolidated its position as home to the maximum number of listed companies in the world. NSE's 15 percent growth is next only to 23.3 percent growth at Poland's Warsaw Stock Exchange and 15.4 percent for Malta Stock Exchange, as per data compiled by the World Federation of Exchanges (WFE).

NEW DEVELOPMENTS IN CAPITAL MARKET

Book Building

Book building is a process which is used by companies to launch an issue. There is a lot of difference between the way a book building issue works to what investors have been traditionally accustomed to which is investing through fixed price issues in IPO.

In the fixed price case, a price is decided upon for the issue and this is the (fixed) price at which investors could put in their applications. This means that the price is known upfront and hence investors can take a decision as to whether they want to put in their money or not.

Under book building, bids are collected from interested investors about the price and the quantity that they are willing to buy. Thus, the price of the issue is not fixed upfront. Instead the price is determined through the book building route.

This floor price is the indicative minimum bid price per share. Next is cut off price option. This can be used when investors want to subscribe to the issue but are not sure about the final closing price. What they can do is to indicate their willingness to opt for the cut off price which would mean that they agree to the final price decided whatever that might be. Finally there is the issue price. This is the price that is fixed after the issue closes and the various bids are aggregated. Thus, the issue will have its price fixed only after the whole process is completed.

Dematerialization

It means "Cancel the physical shape and convert it into electronic format." Demat has been successfully used in India where above 98/1 of corporates securities have been converted to paperless holding, that is, electronic form like a pass-book of bank account. Demat has benefited investors as investors are not worried about loss of shares in transit, loss due to theft, bad delivery, etc. National Security Dipository Ltd (NSDL) and CDSL are the only two depositories working in the country and there are many depository participants like Stock Holding Corporation of India Limited (SHCIL), and ICICI Securities Ltd.

Value Paid Investment

The Primary Market Advisory Committee (PMAC) of the market regulator SEBI is actively considering introducing a value-paid instrument that would be backed by an irrevocable lien. To put it simply, banks would block the full application amount—the total value of the shares applied for—in the investor's account till the shares are allotted. The amount would continue to remain in the client's account but would not be available for withdrawl or cheque payment. It would, therefore, continue to earn interest in the intervening period. On receipt of advisory from the registrar about the allotment of shares, the bank would release the amount equal to the cost of total number of shares the client has been allotted. The move would apply to both physical and electronic applications.

Corporatization of Stock Exchanges—Demutualization

Corporatization is the process of converting the organizational structure of the stock exchange from a non-corporate structure to a corporate structure.

Traditionally, some of the stock exchanges in India were established as "Association of persons," for example, the BSE, ASE, and Madhya Pradesh Stock Exchange (MPSE). Corporatization of such exchanges is the process of converting them into incorporated companies.

Some of the frequently used terms are explained:

Broker

A broker is a member of a recognized stock exchange, who is permitted to do trades on the screen-based trading system of different stock exchanges. He is enrolled as a member with the concerned exchange and is registered with SEBI. His registration number begins with INB. For derivatives section "INF" will be mentioned.

Sub broker

A sub broker is a person who is registered with SEBI (with INS) as such and is affiliated to a member of a recognized stock exchange. For derivatives segment, there is no sub broker.

Member–Client agreement form

This form is an agreement entered between client and broker in the presence of witness where the client agrees (is desirous) to trade/invest in the securities listed on the concerned exchange through the broker after being satisfied of broker's capabilities to deal in securities. The member, on the other hand, agrees to be satisfied by the genuineness and financial soundness of the client and makes the client aware of his (broker's) liability for the business to be conducted.

Details for client registration form

1. Name, date of birth, photograph, address, educational qualifications, occupation, residential status (resident Indian/NRI/others).
2. Unique Identification Number (wherever applicable).
3. Bank and depository account details.
4. Income tax number (PAN/GIR) which also serves as unique client code.
5. If you are registered with any other broker, then the name of broker and concerned stock exchange and client code number.
6. Proof of identity submitted either as MAPIN UID Card/Pan No./passport/voter ID/ driving license/photo identity card issued by employer registered under MAPIN.

For proof of address (any one of the following):

1. Passport
2. Voter ID
3. Driving license
4. Bank passbook
5. Rent agreement
6. Ration card
7. Flat maintenance bill
8. Telephone bill
9. Electricity bill
10. Certificate issued by employer registered under MAPIN
11. Insurance policy

Each client has to use one registration form. In case of joint names/family members, a separate form has to be submitted for each person. In case of corporate client, following additional information has to be provided:

1. Details of promoters/partners/key managerial personnel of the company/firm in specified format.
2. Bank and depository account details.
3. Copies of the balance sheet for the last two financial years (copies of annual balance sheet to be submitted every year).
4. Copy of latest shareholding pattern including list of all those holding more than 5 percent in the share capital of the company, duly certified by the company secretary/whole-time director/MD (copy of updated shareholding pattern to be submitted every year).
5. Copies of the Memorandum and Articles of Association in case of a company/body incorporate/partnership deed in case of a partnership firm.
6. Copy of the resolution of board of directors' approving participation in equity/ derivatives/debt trading and naming authorized persons for dealing in securities.
7. Photographs of partners/whole-time directors, individual promoters holding 5 percent or more, either directly or indirectly, in the shareholding of the company and of persons authorized to deal in securities.
8. If registered with any other broker, then the name of broker and concerned stock exchange and client code number.

Unique client code

In order to facilitate maintaining database of their clients, it is mandatory for all brokers to use unique client code which will act as an exclusive identification for the client. For this purpose, PAN number/passport number/driving license/voters ID number/ration card number coupled with the frequently used bank account number and the depository beneficiary account can be used for identification, in the given order, based on availability.

MAPIN

MAPIN is the Markets Participants and Investors Indentification Number. The SEBI (Central Database of Market Participants) Regulations, 2003 were notified on November 20, 2003. As per these regulations, all the participants in the Indian securities market, namely, SEBI-registered intermediaries, listed companies and their associates, and the investors would need to get registered and obtain a Unique Identification Number (UIN). The system for allotment of UIN involves the use of biometric impressions for natural persons.

The major objective is creation of a comprehensive database of market participants.

Order confirmation

The stock exchanges assign a Unique Order Code Number to each transaction, which is intimated by broker to his client and once the order is executed, this order code number is printed on the contract note. The broker member has also to maintain the record of time when the client has placed order and reflect the same in the contract note along with the time of execution of the order.

Documents to be obtained from broker on execution of trade

The following documents are to be obtained for any trade executed:

1. Contract note in Form A to be given within stipulated time.
2. In the case of electronic issuance of contract notes by the brokers, the clients shall ensure that the same is digitally signed and in case of inability to view the same, shall communicate the same to the broker, upon which the broker shall ensure that the physical contract note reaches the client within the stipulated time.

Maximum brokerage rate

The maximum brokerage that can be charged by a broker has been specified in the Stock Exchange Regulations and hence, it may differ from across various exchanges. As per the BSE & NSE Bye Laws, a broker cannot charge more than 2.5 percent brokerage from his clients. This maximum brokerage is inclusive of the brokerage charged by the sub broker. Further, SEBI (Stockbrokers and Sub brokers) Regulations, 1992 stipulates that sub broker cannot charge from his clients, a commission which is more than 1.5 percent of the value mentioned in the respective purchase or sale note.

Securities transaction tax (STT)

STT is a tax being levied on all transactions done on the stock exchanges at rates prescribed by the central government from time to time.

Account period settlement

An account period settlement is a settlement where the trades pertaining to a period stretching over more than one day are settled. For example, trades for the period Monday to Friday are settled together. The obligations for the account period are settled on a net basis. Account period settlement has been discontinued since January 1, 2002, pursuant to SEBI directives.

Rolling settlement

In a rolling settlement trades executed during the day are settled based on the net obligations for the day. Presently the trades pertaining to the rolling settlement are settled on a T+2 day basis where T stands for the trade day. Hence, trades executed on a Monday are typically settled on the following Wednesday (considering two working days from the trade day).

Pay-in day and pay-out day

Pay-in day is the day when the brokers shall make payment or delivery of securities to the exchange. Pay-out day is the day when the exchange makes payment or delivery of securities to the broker. The prescribed pay-in and pay-out days for funds and securities for normal settlement are as follows.

The pay-in and pay-out days for funds and securities are prescribed as per the settlement cycle. A typical settlement cycle of normal settlement is given in Table 6.10.

Table 6.10 An Overview of the Normal Settlement Cycle at BSE

	Activity	Day
Trading	Rolling settlement trading	T
Clearing	Custodial confirmation	T+1 working days
	Delivery generation	T+1 working days
Settlement	Securities and funds pay in	T+2 working days
	Securities and funds pay out	T+2 working days
Post Settlement	Valuation debit	T+2 working days
	Auction	T+3 working days
	Bad delivery reporting	T+4 working days
	Auction settlement	T+5 working days
	Close out	T+5 working days
	Rectified bad delivery pay in and pay out	T+6 working days
	Re-bad delivery reporting and pick-up	T+8 working days
	Close out of re-bad delivery	T+9 working days

Source: BSE (2007).

Auction

The exchange purchases the requisite quantity in the auction market and gives them to the buying trading member. The shortages are met through auction process and the difference in price indicated in contract note and price received through auction is paid by member to the exchange, which is then liable to be recovered from the client.

Margin trading facility

Margin trading is trading with borrowed funds/securities. It is essentially a leveraging mechanism which enables investors to take exposure in the market over and above what is possible with their own resources. SEBI has been prescribing eligibility conditions and procedural details for allowing the margin trading facility from time to time.

Corporate brokers with net worth of at least Rs 3 crore are eligible for providing margin trading facility to their clients subject to their entering into an agreement to that effect. Before providing margin trading facility to a client, the member and the client have been mandated to sign an agreement for this purpose in the format specified by SEBI. It has also been specified that the client shall not avail the facility from more than one broker at any time.

The facility of margin trading is available for Group 1 securities and those securities which are offered in the initial public offers and meet the conditions for inclusion in the derivatives segment of the stock exchanges.

For providing the margin trading facility, a broker may use his own funds or borrow from scheduled commercial banks or non-banking finance companies (NBFCs) regulated by the RBI. A broker is not allowed to borrow funds from any other source.

The "total exposure" of the broker toward the margin trading facility should not exceed the borrowed funds and 50 percent of his "net worth." While providing the margin trading facility, the broker has to ensure that the exposure to a single client does not exceed 10 percent of the "total exposure" of the broker. Initial margin has been prescribed as 50 percent and the maintenance margin has been prescribed as 40 percent.

SEBI's risk management system

1. Categorization of securities into groups 1, 2, and 3 for imposition of margins based on their liquidity and volatility.
2. VaR-based margining system.
3. Specification of mark to market margins.
4. Specification of intra-day trading limits and gross exposure limits.
5. Real-time monitoring of the intra-day trading limits and gross exposure limits by the stock exchanges.
6. Specification of time limits of payment of margins.
7. Collection of margins on T+1 basis.
8. Index-based market-wide circuit breakers.
9. Automatic de-activation of trading terminals in case of breach of exposure limits.
10. VaR-based margining system has been put in place based on the categorization of stocks based on the liquidity of stocks depending on its impact cost and volatility. It addresses 99 percent of the risks in the market.
11. Additional margins have also been specified to address the balance 1 percent cases.

Securities lending scheme

Securities lending and borrowing is a scheme which enables lending of idle securities by the investors to the clearing corporation and earning a return through the same. For securities borrowing and lending system, clearing corporations of the stock exchange would be the nodal agency and be registered as the "Approved Intermediaries" (AIs). The clearing corporation can borrow, on behalf of the members, securities for the purpose of meeting shortfalls. The defaulter selling broker may make the delivery within the period specified by the clearing corporation. In the event of the defaulted selling broker failing to make the delivery within the specified period, the clearing corporation has to buy the securities from the open market and return the same to the lender within seven trading days. In case of an inability to purchase the securities from the market, the transaction shall be closed out.

Arbitration

Arbitration is an alternative dispute resolution mechanism provided by a stock exchange for resolving disputes between the trading members and their clients in respect of trades done on the exchange.

Investor protection fund (IPF)/customer protection fund (CPF) at stock exchanges

Investor protection fund is the fund set up by the stock exchanges to meet the legitimate investment claims of the clients of the defaulting members that are not of speculative nature. SEBI has prescribed guidelines for utilization of IPF at the stock exchanges. The stock exchanges have been permitted to fix suitable compensation limits, in consultation with the IPF/CPF Trust. It has been provided that the amount of compensation available against a single claim of an investor arising out of default by a member broker of a stock exchange shall not be less than Rs 1 lakh in case of major stock exchanges, namely, BSE and NSE, and Rs 50,000 in case of other stock exchanges.

BSE IndoNext

Regional stock exchanges (RSEs) have registered negligible business during the last few years and thus small and medium-sized enterprises (SMEs) listed there find it difficult to raise fresh resources in the absence of price discovery of their securities in the secondary market. As a result, investors also do not find exit opportunity in case of such companies.

BSE Indo*Next* has been formed to benefit such SMEs, the investors in these companies and capital markets at large. It has been set up as a separate trading platform under the present Bombay Online Trading (BOLT) system of the BSE. It is a joint initiative of BSE and the Federation of Indian Stock Exchanges (FISE) of which 18 RSEs are members.

MARKETING OF CAPITAL MARKET SERVICES

Marketing of capital market services has assumed significant changes and it has become more organized and corporatized. All the big corporates, commercial, and investment banks have floated their broking arms and finance companies through which they market the public issue. These finance companies become the member of stock exchange and acquire the status of corporate members. It is interesting to note that capital market products are made available only through intermediaries. No one can buy directly from others unless the deal is routed through stockbroker who should be a member of stock exchange. These corporates and banks have captive clients making available products at lesser cost.

Thus, the capital market plays a vital role in fostering economic growth of the country as it augments the quantities of real savings, increases the net capital inflow from abroad, raises the productivity of investments by improving allocation of invest able funds, and reduces the cost of capital in the economy.

7

Mutual Fund

Learning Objectives

- To know the concept, growth, and regulation of mutual funds in India.
- To analyze recent trends in mutual fund.

An investor desires safety, liquidity, and appreciation of his investment. He wants to be compensated adequately for having sacrificed his income today for gain tomorrow. This gain may be in terms of dividend (a regular stream) or in the form of capital appreciation. He keeps looking out for instruments, institutions, and intermediaries to serve the purpose. A mutual fund may meet requirements of investors who desire to take the advantages of booming market while keeping risk within the manageable limit or to directly ward off risk while saving the time.

A mutual fund is a collective investment scheme (CIS) in which all members contribute according to their capacity, pool the funds so that it becomes a big corpus. A big corpus is in better position to enter exchange as there is no room for small investors, small fund, and small time. If one does want to play in the market then size, capacity, and scale do matter a lot. A mutual fund is therefore primarily to help small investors to pool their savings, make investment, and sustain the advantages of market participation also. A mutual fund is a trust that pools the savings of a number of investors who share a common financial goal. The money thus collected is then invested in capital market instruments such as shares, debentures, and other securities. The income earned through these investments and the capital appreciation realized are shared by its unit holders in proportion to the number of units owned by them. Thus, a mutual fund is the most suitable investment for the common man as it offers an opportunity to invest in a diversified, professionally managed basket of securities at a relatively low cost.

EMERGENCE OF MUTUAL FUNDS

The origin of mutual funds goes back to the times of the Egyptians and Phoenicians when they sold shares in caravans and vessels to spread the risk of the ventures. The foreign and colonial government Trust of London of 1868 is the first organized mutual fund in the world. The USA is considered to be the Mecca of modern mutual funds. Much later in 1954, the committee on finance for the private sector in USA recommended mobilization of savings of the middle class investors through unit trusts.

EMERGENCE OF MUTUAL FUNDS IN INDIA

A mutual fund is set up in the form of a trust, which has a sponsor, trustees, an asset management company (AMC), and a custodian. The trust is established by a sponsor or more than one sponsors who are the promoters of a company. The trustees of the mutual fund hold its property for the benefit of the unit holders. AMC approved by Securities and Exchange Board of India (SEBI) manages the funds by making investments in various types of securities. Custodian, who is registered with SEBI, holds the securities of various schemes of the fund in its custody. The trustees are vested with the general power of superintendence and direction over AMC. They monitor the performance and compliance of SEBI regulations by the mutual fund.

SEBI regulations require that at least two-thirds of the directors of trustee company or board of trustees must be independent, that is, they should not be associated with the sponsors. Also, 50 percent of the directors of AMC must be independent. All mutual funds are required to be registered with SEBI before they launch any scheme.

The mutual fund has grown in India systematically.

1. Unit Trust of India (UTI) is the first and foremost mutual fund in the country. It was established on 1963 by an Act of Parliament and was set up by the Reserve Bank of India (RBI) and functioned under the regulatory and administrative control of the RBI till 1978 when the Industrial Development Bank of India (IDBI) took over the regulatory and administrative control of UTI. The first scheme launched by UTI was Unit Scheme 1964. In 2003, UTI underwent a major restructuring; UTI was bifurcated into two separate entities. One is the Specified Undertaking of the Unit Trust of India with Assets under Management (AUM) of Rs 29,835 crores (as on January 2003). The Specified Undertaking of Unit Trust of India functions under an administrator and under the rules framed by Government of India and does not come under the purview of the Mutual Fund Regulations. The second is the UTI Mutual Fund Ltd, sponsored by State Bank of India (SBI), Punjab National Bank (PNB), Bank of Baroda (BOB), and Life Insurance Corporation (LIC). It is registered with SEBI and functions under the Mutual Fund Regulations.

2. The mutual fund industry got momentum in the country with the setting up of mutual funds by public sector banks. SBI was the pioneer in this respect. All public sector banks set up their mutual funds.

3. There is emergence of private sector mutual funds in the country, so much so that world's leading financial players like Morgan Stanley, Allianz, and Prudential have started in the country.

MAJOR MUTUAL FUND COMPANIES IN INDIA

Besides UTI and PSU bank-sponsored mutual funds, some the other prominent mutual funds are:

ABN AMRO Mutual Fund

ABN AMRO Mutual Fund was set up on April 15, 2004 with ABN AMRO Trustee (India) Pvt. Ltd as the Trustee Company. The AMC, ABN AMRO Asset Management (India) Ltd, was incorporated on November 4, 2003. Deutsche Bank A G is the custodian of ABN AMRO Mutual Fund.

Birla Sun Life Mutual Fund

Birla Sun Life Mutual Fund is the joint venture of Aditya Birla Group and Sun Life Financial. Sun Life Financial is a global organization evolved in 1871 and is being represented in Canada, the USA, the Philippines, Japan, Indonesia, and Bermuda apart from India. Birla Sun Life Mutual Fund follows a conservative long-term approach to investment. Recently it crossed AUM of Rs 10,000 crores.

HDFC Mutual Fund

HDFC Mutual Fund was set up on June 30, 2000 with two sponsors, namely, Housing Development Finance Corporation Limited and Standard Life Investments Limited.

HSBC Mutual Fund

HSBC Mutual Fund was set up on May 27, 2002 with HSBC Securities and Capital Markets (India) Private Limited as the sponsor.

ING Vysya Mutual Fund

ING Vysya Mutual Fund was set up on February 11, 1999 with the same named Trustee Company. It is a joint venture of Vysya and ING. The AMC, ING Investment Management (India) Pvt Ltd, was incorporated on April 6, 1998.

Prudential ICICI Mutual Fund

The mutual fund of ICICI is a joint venture with Prudential Plc. of America, one of the largest life insurance companies in the USA. Prudential ICICI Mutual Fund was set up on October 13, 1993 with two sponsors, Prudential Plc. and ICICI Ltd. The Trustee Company formed is Prudential ICICI Trust Ltd and the AMC is Prudential ICICI Asset Management Company Limited incorporated on June 22, 1993.

Sahara Mutual Fund

Sahara Mutual Fund was set up on July 18, 1996 with Sahara India Financial Corporation Ltd as the sponsor. Sahara Asset Management Company Private Limited, incorporated on August 31, 1995, works as the AMC of Sahara Mutual Fund. The paid-up capital of the AMC stands at Rs 25.8 crore.

Tata Mutual Fund

Tata Mutual Fund (TMF) is a trust under the Indian Trust Act, 1882. The sponsors for Tata Mutual Fund are Tata Sons Ltd and Tata Investment Corporation Ltd. The investment manager is Tata Asset Management Limited and its Tata Trustee Company Pvt. Limited. Tata Asset Management Limited is one of the fastest growing in the country with more than Rs 7,703 crores (as on April 30, 2005) of AUM.

Kotak Mahindra Mutual Fund

Kotak Mahindra Asset Management Company (KMAMC) is a subsidiary of Kotak Mahindra Bank Ltd (KMBL). It is presently having more than 199,818 investors in its various schemes. KMAMC started its operations in December 1998. Kotak Mahindra Mutual Fund offers schemes catering to investors with varying risk–return profiles. It was the first company to launch dedicated gilt scheme investing only in government securities.

Reliance Mutual Fund

Reliance Mutual Fund (RMF) was established as a trust under Indian Trusts Act, 1882. The sponsor of RMF is Reliance Capital Limited, and Reliance Capital Trustee Co. Limited is the trustee. It was registered on June 30, 1995 as Reliance Capital Mutual Fund which was changed on March 11, 2004. Reliance Mutual Fund was formed for launching of various schemes under which units are issued to the public with a view to contribute to the capital market and to provide investors the opportunities to make investments in diversified securities.

Standard Chartered Mutual Fund

Standard Chartered Mutual Fund was set up on March 13, 2000, sponsored by Standard Chartered Bank. The trustee is Standard Chartered Trustee Company Pvt. Ltd. Standard Chartered Asset Management Company Pvt. Ltd is the AMC which was incorporated with SEBI on December 20, 1999.

Franklin Templeton India Mutual Fund

The group, Franklin Templeton Investments, is a California (USA)-based company with a global AUM of over USD 500 billion. It is one of the largest financial services groups in the world.

Morgan Stanley Mutual Fund India

Morgan Stanley is a worldwide financial services company and it is leading in the market in securities, investment management, and credit services. Morgan Stanley Investment Management (MSIM) was established in the year 1975. It provides customized asset management services and products to governments, corporations, pension funds, and non-profit organizations. Its services are also extended to high net worth individuals and retail investors. In India it is known as Morgan Stanley Investment Management Private Limited (MSIM India) and its AMC is Morgan Stanley Mutual Fund (MSMF).

Alliance Capital Mutual Fund

Alliance Capital Mutual Fund was set up on December 30, 1994 with Alliance Capital Management Corp. of Delaware (USA) as sponsor. The trustee is ACAM Trust Company Pvt. Ltd, and the AMC, the Alliance Capital Asset Management India (Pvt.) Ltd, has its corporate office in Mumbai.

Benchmark Mutual Fund

Benchmark Mutual Fund was set up on June 12, 2001 with Niche Financial Services Pvt. Ltd as the sponsor and Benchmark Trustee Company Pvt. Ltd as the Trustee Company. Incorporated on October 16, 2000 and headquartered in Mumbai, Benchmark Asset Management Company Pvt. Ltd is the AMC.

Chola Mutual Fund

Chola Mutual Fund under the sponsorship of Cholamandalam Investment & Finance Company Ltd was set up on January 3, 1997. Cholamandalam Trustee Co. Ltd is the Trustee Company and AMC is Cholamandalam AMC Limited.

The growth in Mutual Funds as reflected by Assets under management suggests that there is a wide acceptance of mutual funds in India, as reflected by Table 7.1.

Table 7.1   Mutual Funds and Assets under Management in India: A Summarized View

Mutual Fund Name	No. of Schemes*	As on	Corpus (Rs in Crores)
AIG Global Investment Group Mutual Fund	52	August 31, 2009	1,571.48
Baroda Pioneer Mutual Fund	33	May 29, 2009	3,874.76
Benchmark Mutual Fund	13	February 29, 2008	4,954.72
Bharti AXA Mutual Fund	40	August 31, 2009	319.02
Birla Sun Life Mutual Fund	271	February 28, 2009	49,983.17
Canara Robeco Mutual Fund	84	August 31, 2009	8,477.97
DBS Chola Mutual Fund	58	August 31, 2009	2,816.92
Deutsche Mutual Fund	117	August 31, 2009	14,603.07
DSP Blackrock Mutual Fund	101	August 31, 2009	15,403.54
Edelweiss Mutual Fund	49	July 31, 2009	75.90
Escorts Mutual Fund	30	March 31, 2008	173.42
Fidelity Mutual Fund	51	August 31, 2009	9,375.56
Fortis Mutual Fund	166	August 31, 2009	11,024.24
Franklin Templeton Mutual Fund	181	March 31, 2008	25,621.97
HDFC Mutual Fund	189	February 29, 2008	46,291.97
HSBC Mutual Fund	94	August 31, 2009	7,782.38
ICICI Prudential Mutual Fund	320	May 29, 2009	68,324.06
IDFC Mutual Fund	160	August 31, 2009	24,002.59
ING Mutual Fund	113	April 30, 2008	57,575.02
JM Financial Mutual Fund	104	August 31, 2009	9,252.85
JPMorgan Mutual Fund	30	August 31, 2009	4,637.98
Kotak Mahindra Mutual Fund	116	August 31, 2009	37,274.00
LIC Mutual Fund	66	August 31, 2009	41,920.68
Mirae Asset Mutual Fund	47	April 30, 2009	175.96
Morgan Stanley Mutual Fund	13	August 31, 2009	2,293.62
PRINCIPAL Mutual Fund	93	August 31, 2009	9,505.45
Quantum Mutual Fund	11	August 31, 2009	72.23
Reliance Mutual Fund	265	August 31, 2009	121,327.89
Religare Mutual Fund	93	April 30, 2009	8,618.52
Sahara Mutual Fund	44	August 31, 2009	220.35
SBI Mutual Fund	126	February 29, 2008	29,492.97
Shinsei Mutual Fund	17	August 31, 2009	158.36
Sundaram BNP Paribas Mutual Fund	160	August 31, 2009	14,794.08
Tata Mutual Fund	183	August 31, 2009	21,996.67
Taurus Mutual Fund	41	December 31, 2008	209.23
UTI Mutual Fund	205	March 31, 2008	48,347.60

Source: http://www.mutualfundsindia.com/corpus.asp

Note: *indicates currently in operation.

The mutual fund industry indicates that there are players like banks, institutions and foreign mutual funds have also gained the grounds in the Mutual Funds industry. For details see Table 7.2.

Table 7.2 Mutual Fund Data for the Month Ended, August 31, 2009

(Amount in Rs Crores)

Category	No. of New Schemes Launched during the Month	Sales			Redemption	Asset Under Management		Inflow/ Outflow
		New Schemes	Existing Schemes	Total	Total	As on August 31, 2009	As on July 31, 2009	
B Bank Sponsored	0	0	122,750	122,750	115,940	121,288	113,281	8,007
C Institutions	0	0	89,927	89,927	87,144	42,646	35,094	7,552
D Private Sector & Joint Venture:								
Indian	4	297	341,756	342,053	330,418	243,163	222,328	20,835
Predominantly Foreign	1	53	26,956	27,009	26,851	26,378	26,767	–389
Grand Total (B + C + D)	5	350	581,389	581,739	560,353	433,475	397,470	36,005

Source: http://www.mutualfundsindia.com/corpus.asp

During 2009, total net resources mobilized by MFs increased to Rs 1,43,775 crore as compared to net redemptions amounting to Rs 624 crore in 2008. Private-sector mutual funds, which had witnessed heavy redemption pressure in 2008, recorded a turnaround with total net resource mobilization of Rs 114,095 crore in 2009 as against a net redemption of Rs 12,506 crore in 2008. Total funds mobilized by public-sector mutual funds were marginally higher at Rs 17,624 crore in 2009 (Rs 14,587 crore in 2008). The Unit Trust of India (UTI), which had recorded net redemptions of Rs 2,704 crore in 2008, mobilized Rs 12,056 crore in 2009 (see Table 7.2a).

Table 7.2a Trends in Resource Mobilization (Net) by MFs

(Rs Crores)

		Calendar Year			
S. No.	Sector	2006	2007	2008	2009
1.	UTI	6,426	9,245	–2,704	12,056
2.	Public Sector	12,229	8,259	14,587	17,624
3.	Private Sector	86,295	120,766	–12,506	114,095
4.	**Total (1 to 3)**	104,950	138,270	–624	143,775

Source: SEBI, as appeared in RBI (2001, p. 108).

REGULATIONS OF MUTUAL FUNDS IN INDIA

Mutual funds have been a significant source of investment in both government and corporate securities. SEBI regulates the functioning of mutual funds and it requires that all mutual funds should be established as trusts under the Indian Trusts Act. The actual fund management activity shall be conducted from a separate AMC. The minimum net worth of an AMC or its affiliate must be Rs 50 million to act as a manager in any other fund. Mutual funds can be penalized for defaults including non-registration and failure to observe rules set by their AMCs. Mutual funds dealing exclusively with money market instruments have to be registered with RBI. All other schemes floated by mutual funds are required to be registered with SEBI. In 1995, the RBI permitted private sector institutions to set up Money Market Mutual Funds (MMMFs). They can invest in treasury bills, call and notice money, commercial paper, commercial bills accepted/co-accepted by banks, certificates of deposit, and dated government securities having unexpired maturity up to 1 year. The mutual funds are now regulated by Association of Mutual Funds in India (AMFI) which is a self-regulatory organization (SRO).

As far as mutual funds are concerned, SEBI formulates policies and regulates the mutual funds to protect the interest of the investors. SEBI notified regulations for the mutual funds in 1993. Thereafter, mutual funds sponsored by private sector entities were allowed to enter the capital market. The regulations were fully revised in 1996 and have been amended thereafter from time to time. SEBI has also issued guidelines to the mutual funds from time to time to protect the interests of investors.

All mutual funds whether promoted by public sector or private sector entities including those promoted by foreign entities are governed by the same set of regulations. There is no distinction in regulatory requirements for these mutual funds and all are subject to monitoring and inspections by SEBI. The risks associated with the schemes launched by the mutual funds sponsored by these entities are of similar type.

REGISTERING OF A MUTUAL FUND IN INDIA

An applicant proposing to sponsor a mutual fund in India must submit an application in Form A along with a fee of Rs 25,000. The application is examined and once the sponsor satisfies certain conditions such as being in the financial services business and possessing positive net worth for the last 5 years, having net profit in three out of the last five years and possessing the general reputation of fairness and integrity in all business transactions, it is required to complete the remaining formalities for setting up a mutual fund. These include, inter alia, executing the trust deed and investment management agreement, setting up a trustee company/board of trustees comprising two-thirds independent trustees, incorporating the AMC, contributing to at least 40 percent of the net worth of the AMC, and appointing a custodian. Upon satisfying these conditions, the registration certificate is issued subject to the payment of registration fees of Rs 25 lakhs.

TYPES OF SCHEME

A mutual fund may provide open-end and closed-end funds. Open-end fund is one in which buy and sell is available all days. There is no last date and no lock-in period.

An open-end mutual fund is a fund that does not have a set number of shares. It continues to sell shares to investors and will buy back shares when investors wish to sell. Units are bought and sold at their current net asset value. Open-end funds keep some portion of their assets in short-term and money market securities to provide available funds for redemptions. A large portion of most open mutual funds is invested in highly liquid securities, which enables the fund to raise money by selling securities at prices very close to those used for valuations.

A closed-end fund is one where there is a last date for making investment. There is usually lock-in period, that is, duration during which redemption is not permitted. A closed-end mutual fund has a set number of shares issued to the public through an initial public offering. These funds have a stipulated maturity period generally ranging from 3 to 15 years. The fund is open for subscription only during a specified period. Investors can invest in the scheme at the time of the initial public issue and thereafter they can buy or sell the units of the scheme on the stock exchanges where they are listed. Once underwritten, closed-end funds trade on stock exchanges like stocks or bonds. The market price of closed-end funds is determined by supply and demand and not by net asset value (NAV), as is the case in open-end funds. Usually closed-end mutual funds trade at discounts to their underlying asset value.

COSTS ASSOCIATED WITH MUTUAL FUND

The costs may be divided into entry, exit, and swap fee. The cost may include:

1. Ongoing yearly fees to keep invested in the fund, namely, the expense ratio.
   The ongoing expenses of a mutual fund are represented by the expense ratio. This is sometimes also referred to as the management expense ratio (MER) which is composed of:

   i. The cost of hiring the fund manager(s): Also known as the management fee, this cost is between 0.5 and 1 percent of assets on average.
   ii. Administrative costs: These include necessities such as postage, record keeping, and customer care service.
   On the whole, expense ratios range from as low as 0.2 percent (usually for index funds) to as high as 2 percent. The average equity mutual fund charges around 1.3–1.5 percent.

2. Transaction fees/loads
   Loads are just fees that a fund uses to compensate brokers or other salespeople for selling the mutual fund. The following are loads to be considered:

   i. Front-end loads: It is incurred at the time of purchase of fund.
   ii. Back-end loads (also known as deferred sales charges): It is applied when securities are sold.
   A no-load fund sells its shares without a commission or sales charge.

SCHEMES OF MUTUAL FUNDS

Primarily there are three schemes:

1. Income fund—where investment is made in debt.
2. Growth fund—where investment is made in shares and marketable securities.
3. Balanced fund—mean where investment is made in equity and debt funds.

Bond/Income Funds

The terms "fixed-income," "bond," and "income" are synonymous. These terms denote funds that invest primarily in government and corporate debt. While fund holdings may appreciate in value, the primary objective of these funds is to provide a steady cash flow to investors.

Bond funds are likely to pay higher returns than certificates of deposit and money market investments but bond funds are not without risk.

Income fund also known as Fixed Income Fund suggests that these types of funds are increasing their popularity with the investors, as more and more amounts are mobilized through this type of funds. For details see Table 7.3.

Table 7.3 Trends in Income Fund (Both Open-end and Closed-end) under all Schemes

(Rs in Crores)

March, 31	Amount	%
2008	220,762	44
2007	119,322	26
2006	60,278	26
2005	47,605	32
2004	160,134	29.5
2003	3,172	82.57

Source: http://www.mutualfundsindia.com

Equity Funds or Growth Funds

Funds that invest in stocks represent the largest category of mutual funds. Generally, the investment objective of this class of funds is long-term capital growth with some income.

Growth funds are those mutual funds that aim at achieving capital appreciation by investing in growth stocks. They focus on those companies which are experiencing significant earnings or revenue growth, rather than companies that pay out dividends.

Growth funds tend to look for the fastest-growing companies in the market. Growth fund managers are willing to take more risk and pay a premium for their stocks in an effort to build a portfolio of companies with above-average earnings momentum or price appreciation.

In general, growth funds are more volatile than other types of funds, rising more than other funds in bull markets and falling more in bear markets. Only aggressive investors, or those with enough time to make up for short-term market losses, should buy these funds.

Growth funds are volatile, however, they are sought after despite their volatility because they tend to pay more return to the aggressive investor, if amounts mobilized under this is any indication. See Table 7.4 for more details.

Table 7.4 Trends in Growth Fund

(Rs in Crores)

March, 31	Amount	%
2008	156,722	31
2007	113,386	37
2006	92,867	40
2005	36,771	25
2004	18,958	3.5
2003	411	10.7

Source: http://www.mutualfundsindia.com

Balanced Funds

The objective of these funds is to provide a balanced mixture of safety, income, and capital appreciation. The strategy of balanced funds is to invest in a combination of fixed income and equities. A similar type of fund is known as an asset allocation fund. Objectives are similar to those of a balanced fund, but these kinds of funds typically do not have to hold a specified percentage of any asset class. Balanced fund is also known as hybrid fund. It is a type of mutual fund that buys a combination of common stock, preferred stock, bonds, and short-term bonds, to provide both income and capital appreciation while avoiding excessive risk. Balanced funds provide investor with an option of single mutual fund that combines both growth and income objectives, by investing in both stocks (for growth) and bonds (for income). Such diversified holdings ensure that these funds will manage downturns in the stock market without too much of a loss. But on the flip side, balanced funds will usually increase less than an all-stock fund during a bull market.

Balance funds have also been appreciated by investors. However, these funds present a mixed picture of ups and downs. For more details see Table 7.5

Table 7.5 Trends in Liquid/Money Market Fund

(Rs in Crores)

March, 31	Amount	%
2008	89,402	17
2007	72,006	30
2006	61,500	27
2005	54,068	27
2004	351,069	64
2003	257	6.68

Source: http://www.mutualfundsindia.com

Besides the foregoing funds, there are other funds also.

Money Market Funds

The money market consists of short-term debt instruments, mostly treasury bills. This is a safe place to park money. A typical return is twice the amount one would earn in a regular savings account and a little less than the average certificate of deposit (CD).

A money market fund is a mutual fund that invests solely in money market instruments. Money market instruments are the forms of debt that mature in less than 1 year and are very liquid. Treasury bills make up the bulk of the money market instruments. Securities in the money market are relatively risk-free.

Money market funds are generally the safest and most secure mutual fund investments. The goal of a money market fund is to preserve principal while yielding a modest return. Money market mutual fund is akin to a high-yield bank account but is not entirely risk free.

International Funds

An international fund (or foreign fund) invests only outside home country. Global funds invest anywhere in world. They do tend to be more volatile and have unique country and/or political risks. But, on the flip side, they can, as part of a well-balanced portfolio, actually reduce risk by increasing diversification.

Sector-specific Funds

Sector funds are targeted at specific sectors of the economy such as financial, technology, or health. Sector funds are extremely volatile.

Regional funds make it easier to focus on a specific area of the world. An advantage of these funds is that they make it easier to buy stock in foreign countries, which is otherwise difficult and expensive.

Socially responsible funds (or ethical funds) invest only in companies that meet the criteria of certain guidelines or beliefs. Most socially responsible funds don't invest in industries such as tobacco, alcoholic beverages, weapons, or nuclear power.

These are the funds which invest in the securities of only those sectors or industries as specified in the offer documents, for example, pharmaceuticals, software, fast moving consumer goods (FMCGs), and petroleum stocks. The returns in these funds are dependent on the performance of the respective sectors/industries. While these funds may give higher returns, they are more risky compared to diversified funds.

Tax Saving Schemes

These schemes offer tax rebates to the investors under specific provisions of the Income Tax Act, 1961 as the government offers tax incentives for investment in specified avenues, for example, Equity Linked Savings Schemes (ELSS). Pension schemes launched by the mutual funds also offer tax benefits. These schemes are growth oriented and invest predominantly in equities. Their growth opportunities and risks associated are like any equity-oriented scheme.

Index Funds

This type of mutual fund replicates the performance of a broad market index.

An index fund is a type of mutual fund that builds its portfolio by buying stock in all the companies of a particular index and thereby reproducing the performance of an entire section of the market. The most popular index of stock index funds is the Standard & Poor's 500. An S&P 500 stock index fund owns 500 stocks—all the companies that are included in the index.

Investing in an index fund is a form of passive investing. Passive investing has two big advantages over active investing. First, a passive stock market mutual fund is much cheaper to run than an active fund. Second, a majority of mutual funds fail to beat broad indexes such as the S&P 500.

Large Cap Funds

Large cap funds are those mutual funds which seek capital appreciation by investing primarily in stocks of large blue chip companies with above-average prospects for earnings growth. Different mutual funds have different criteria for classifying companies as large cap. Generally, companies with a market capitalization in excess of Rs 1,000 crore are known large cap companies.

Mid Cap Funds

Mid cap funds are those mutual funds which invest in small- and medium-sized companies. Generally, companies with a market capitalization of up to Rs 500 crore are classified as small. Those companies that have a market capitalization between Rs 500 crore and Rs 1,000 crore are classified as medium sized.

Equity Mutual Funds

Equity mutual funds are also known as stock mutual funds. Equity mutual funds invest pooled amounts of money in the stocks of public companies. Equity fund managers employ different styles of stock picking when they make investment decisions for their portfolios. Some fund managers use a value approach to stocks, searching for stocks that are undervalued when compared to other, similar companies. Another approach to picking is to look primarily at growth, trying to find stocks that are growing faster than their competitors, or the market as a whole. Some managers buy both kinds of stocks, building a portfolio of both growth and value stocks.

No-Load Mutual Funds

Mutual funds can be classified into two types: load mutual funds and no-load mutual funds. Load funds are those funds that charge commission at the time of purchase or redemption. They can be further subdivided into: (*a*) front-end load funds and (*b*) back-end load funds. Front-end load funds charge commission at the time of purchase and back-end load funds charge commission at the time of redemption.

On the other hand, no-load funds are those funds that can be purchased without commission. No-load funds have several advantages over load funds. First, funds with loads, on an average, consistently under perform no-load funds when the load is taken into consideration in performance calculations. Second, loads understate the real commission charged because they reduce the total amount being invested. Finally, when a load fund is held over a long time period, the effect of the load, if paid up front, is not diminished because if the money paid for the load had invested, as in a no-load fund, it would have been compounding over the whole time period.

Exchange Traded Funds

Exchange traded funds (ETFs) represent a basket of securities that are traded on an exchange. An exchange traded fund is similar to an index fund in that it will primarily invest in the securities of companies that are included in a selected market index. An ETF will invest in either all of the securities or a representative sample of the securities included in the index.

Value Funds

Value funds are those mutual funds that tend to focus on safety rather than growth and often choose investments providing dividends as well as capital appreciation. They invest in companies that the market has overlooked, and stocks that have fallen out of favor with mainstream investors, either due to changing investor preferences, a poor quarterly earnings report, or hard times in a particular industry.

Value stocks are often mature companies that have stopped growing and that use their earnings to pay dividends. Thus, value funds produce current income (from the dividends) as well as long-term growth (from capital appreciation once the stocks become popular again). They tend to have more conservative and less volatile returns than growth funds.

International Mutual Funds

International mutual funds are those funds that invest in non-domestic securities markets throughout the world. Investing in international markets provides greater portfolio diversification and capitalizes on some of the world's best opportunities. If investments are chosen carefully, international mutual fund may be profitable when some markets are rising and others are declining.

However, fund managers need to keep close watch on foreign currencies and world markets as profitable investments in a rising market can lose money if the foreign currency rises against the dollar.

Fund of Funds

A fund of funds is a type of mutual fund that invests in other mutual funds. Just as a mutual fund invests in a number of different securities, a fund of funds holds shares of many different mutual funds.

Fund of funds is designed to achieve greater diversification than traditional mutual funds. But on the flip side, expense fees on fund of funds are typically higher than those on regular funds because they include part of the expense fees charged by the underlying funds. Also, since a fund of funds buys many different funds which themselves invest in many different stocks, it is possible for the fund of funds to own the same stock through several different funds and it can be difficult to keep track of the overall holdings.

PERFORMANCE OF MUTUAL FUNDS IN INDIA

The mutual funds performance is assessed by the total number of assets under management. There is a continuous increase in the number of assets under management, suggesting that mutual funds have been accepted as a vehicle of effective investment for small investors. See Table 7.6 for more details.

Table 7.6 Mutual Fund: Total Net Assets under Management

As on March, 31	Rs in Crores
2008	505,152
2007	326,388
2006	231,862
2005	149,554
2004	139,616
2003	79,464

Source: Various publication of AMFI.

Table 7.6 suggests increasing popularity of investment through mutual funds. In last 6 years, the total net assets under management has increased by seven times, that is, from Rs 79,464 crore in March 2003. Compared with the data of 1998, the growth is about eight times as Rs 68,984 crore of total net assets was under management. Not only there has been sharp increase in assets under management but also category-wise trends reflect the growing importance of mutual fund.

The growth is spectacular. Amount mobilized has increased from Rs 314,673 crores in March 2003 to Rs 44,64,376 crores in March 2008. The figure of March 2003 does exclude amount mobilized by UTI mutual fund (Rs 7,062 crores). See Table 7.7 for more details.

It is known that a mutual fund offer income, growth, and balanced fund. Tables 7.8–7.13 provide the trends in income, growth, and other funds.

It is evident that the share of income and growth fund accounts for over 65 percent of total assets under various schemes. Added with the money market, over 90 percent of the share belongs to these three schemes.

Table 7.7 Amount Mobilized Categories Wise

(Rs in Crores)

Participants (as on March, 31)	2008	2007	2006	2005	2004	2003
A. Bank-sponsored Joint Ventures						
1. Predominantly Indian	143,324	52,512	48167	30,995	46,661	11,090
2. Others	346,270	161,501	89,059	59,451	–	–
Total	**489,594**	**214,013**	**137,226**	**90,446**	**46,661**	**11,090**
B. Institutions	194,030	124,607	46,220	12,800	21,897	17,535
C. Private Sector						
1. Indian	1,369,180	479,754	256,761	242,428	143,050	83,351
2. Foreign	182,305	N.A.	N.A.	N.A.	21,089	N.A.
3. Joint ventures, predominantly Indian	1,392,729	621,899	346,518	156,879	140,545	71,513
4. Joint ventures, foreign	836,538	498,319	311,433	337,109	216,948	124,122
Total (1 + 2 + 3 + 4)	3,780,752	1,599,972	914,712	736,416	521,632	278,986
Grand Total (A + B + C)	**4,464,376**	**1,938,592**	**1,098,158**	**839,662**	**590,190**	**314,673**

Source: Compilation of various AMFI publications.

Table 7.8   Assets under Management as on March 31, 2008

(Rs in Crores)

Type	Open End	Close End	Total	Percent to Total
Income	123,898	96,864	220,762	44
Growth	123,058	33,664	156,722	31
Balanced	13,591	2,692	16,283	3
Liquid/Money Market	89,402	–	89,402	17
GILT	2,833	–	2,833	1
ELSS	13,327	2,693	16,020	3
Gold ETFs	483	–	483	<1.1
Other ETFs	2,647	–	2,647	1
	369,239	**135,913**	**505,152**	**100**

Table 7.9   Assets under Management as on March 31, 2007

Type	Open End	Close End	Total	Percent to Total
Income	30,894	88,428	119,322	26
Growth	93,657	17,029	113,386	37
Balanced	7,409	1,701	9,110	3
Liquid/Money Market	72,006	–	72,006	30
GILT	2,257	–	2,257	1
ELSS	8,398	1,713	10,211	3
Gold ETFs	96	–	93	<1.1
Other ETFs	–	–	–	–
	217,417	**108,971**	**326,388**	**100**

Table 7.10   Assets under Management as on March 31, 2006

Type	Open End	Close End	Total	Percent to Total
Income	30,879	29,399	60,278	26
Growth	86,401	6,460	92,867	40
Balanced	6,701	792	7,493	3
Liquid/Money Market	61,500	–	61,500	27
GILT	3,135	–	3,135	1
ELSS	5,091	1,498	6,589	3
Gold ETFs	–	–	–	–
Other ETFs	–	–	–	–
	193,713	**38149**	**231,862**	**100**

Table 7.11   Assets under Management as on March 31, 2005

Type	Open End	Close End	Total	Percent to Total
Income	39,408	9,197	47,605	32
Growth	35,060	1,651	36,771	25
Balanced	4,163	704	4,867	3
Liquid/Money Market	54,068	–	54,068	36
GILT	4,576	–	4,576	3
ELSS	708	1,019	1,727	1
Gold ETFs	–	–	–	–
Other ETFs	–	–	–	–
	137,983	11,571	149,534	100

Table 7.12   Assets under Management as on March 31, 2004

Type	Open End	Close End	Total	Percent to Total
Income	158,636	1,498	160,134	29.5
Growth	18,879	79	18,958	3.5
Balanced	2,504	32	2,536	<1
Liquid/Money Market	351,069	–	351,069	64.6
GILT	10,155	–	10,155	1.8
ELSS	203	316	519	.6
Gold ETFs	–	–	–	–
Other ETFs	–	–	–	–
	541,446	1,925	543,371	100

Table 7.13   Assets under Management as on March 31, 2003

Type	Open End	Close End	Total	Percent to Total
Income	3,061	114	3,175	82.57
Growth	411	17	411	10.70
Balanced	–	–	–	–
Liquid/Money Market	257	–	257	6.68
GILT	2	–	2	.05
ELSS	–	–	–	–
Gold ETFs	–	–	–	–
Other ETFs	–	–	–	–
	3,731	131	3,845	100

ADVANTAGES OF MUTUAL FUNDS

1. **Professional Management:** A mutual fund is a relatively inexpensive way for a small investor to get a full-time professional to make and monitor investments.
2. **Diversification:** By owning shares in a mutual fund instead of owning individual stocks or bonds, the risk is spread out. The idea behind diversification is to invest in a large number of assets so that a loss in any particular investment is minimized by gains in others.
3. **Economies of Scale:** Because a mutual fund buys and sells large amounts of securities at a time, its transaction costs are lower than what an individual would pay for securities transactions.
4. **Liquidity:** Just like an individual stock, a mutual fund allows shares to be converted into cash at any time.

Major disadvantages of a mutual fund are cost, hidden costs, and complicated process of redemption.

EMERGING ISSUES IN INDIAN MUTUAL FUNDS INDUSTRY

Real Estate Funds in India: A New Beginning

One sector that has assumed growing importance owing to liberalization in economy in India is its real estate sector. The consequent increase in business opportunities has escalated demands for commercial and residential space. Real estate in India is currently in a nascent stage with unlimited growth options. Proactive measures taken by the government has encouraged liquidity flow into the real estate sector from the organized sectors in India as well as foreign lands. Real estate investment in India lures heavy-weight investors with its lucrative returns. It is estimated that a similar investment in developed countries would fetch a return of 3 to 4 percent, whereas it fetches 12 to 15 percent in India.

Some of the prominent companies promoting real estate funds in India are HDFC Property Fund, DHFL Venture Capital Fund, Kotak Mahindra Realty Fund, Kshitij Venture Capital Fund (a group venture of Pantaloon Retail India Ltd), and ICICI's Real Estate Fund, India Advantage Fund. Regulated under SEBI's Venture Capital Funds, these are closed-end schemes with initial public offers (IPOs) contributing to a discount on NAVs.

Moreover, there is also a long list of international investors pumping in foreign funds in India like US-based Warburg Pincus, Blackstone Group, Broadstreet, Morgan Stanley (Morgan Stanley Real Estate Fund, MSREF), Columbia Endowment Fund, Hines, Tishman Speyer, Sam Zell's Equity International, and JP Morgan Partners. The 10th Five-Year Plan ending in 2007 proposed that SEBI should regulate the real estate mutual funds in India. These can invest in real estate in India directly or indirectly. SEBI would introduce the real estate mutual funds (REMFs) as closed-end units and list in stock markets. Globally, REMFs are also known as real estate investment trusts (REITs). The essential difference between a REIT and a mutual fund is that investments made in REIT are traded in real estate stocks and not invested in stock of companies. It provides a heavier liquidity than mutual funds.

Launching Global Funds

Indian fund houses are set to launch global funds as RBI and SEBI ease norms for overseas investments. With RBI raising the cap on mutual funds' overseas investment from USD 4 billion to USD 5 billion, fund houses like SBI, ABN Amro, Fidelity, Deutsche, and HSBC plan to launch global funds soon. They say these funds will invest across various assets abroad.

While RBI has raised the overall cap, SEBI has enhanced the limit on overseas investment for individual fund houses from USD 200 million to USD 300 million. Though fund houses may not have reached their existing foreign investment limit, they say the increased cap will lead to a launch of more global funds which will play international markets with better volumes. SEBI has enhanced rules for overseas investments of mutual funds. It has raised the limit from USD 200 million to USD 300 million. It has said that mutual fund can invest in ADRs and GDRs of foreign companies. Mutual funds can now invest in IPOs, FPOs to be listed on foreign bourses. It can invest in money market instruments not below investment grade. Mutual funds can now invest in G-secs not below investment grade. SEBI has allowed that mutual funds can invest in derivatives listed on recognized bourses. They can now invest in short-term deposits in foreign banks. Mutual funds can invest in REITs listed on foreign bourses now. SEBI has said that the overall cap for foreign ETF investment has been put at USD 1 billion.

"Know Your Customer" (KYC)

It is guideline to understand the customers.

The objective of KYC guidelines is to prevent banks from being used for money laundering activities. KYC procedures also enable banks to know/understand their customers and their financial dealings better which in turn help them manage their risks prudently. Banks should frame their KYC policies incorporating the following four key elements:

1. Customer acceptance policy
2. Customer identification procedures
3. Monitoring of transactions
4. Risk management

For the purpose of KYC policy, a "Customer" may be defined as:

1. a person or entity that maintains an account and/or has a business relationship with the bank;
2. one on whose behalf the account is maintained (i.e., the beneficial owner);

3. beneficiaries of transactions conducted by professional intermediaries, such as stock-brokers, chartered accountants, or solicitors, as permitted under the law; and

4. any person or entity connected with a financial transaction which can pose significant reputational or other risks to the bank, say, a wire transfer or issue of a high value demand draft as a single transaction.

Prevention of Money Laundering

In terms of the Prevention of Money Laundering Act, 2002, the rules issued there under, and the guidelines/circulars issued by SEBI regarding the anti-money laundering (AML) laws, all intermediaries, including mutual funds, have to formulate and implement a client identification program, verify and maintain the record of identity and address(es) of investors.

Technologies in Mutual Funds: Areas to be Affected by Changing Technologies

Three areas of the mutual fund industry are expected to see the maximum change in the near future as a result of technological improvement. They are:

1. Distribution of mutual fund products
2. Information on schemes
3. Customer care

This in turn will allow efficient management of the industry that can provide a wider array of products and services to consumers. Further, this development will also clear the way for mutual funds, banks, stock brokerage firms, and insurance companies to move increasingly into each other's territory, thereby forcing each player to become more efficient, more creative, and more customer-focused than ever before.

Online Investing in Mutual Funds: Poised to Take Off

Online investments in the primary market, mutual funds, and other financial assets are likely to grow manifold in the next few years. Such services will make financial tasks like checking balances, paying application amount, and transferring funds cheap and hassle-free. Large number of issuers of equity, debt, and mutual funds have already started offering their products online. The structure of the mutual fund industry explains to some extent why such a large number of funds are using new technologies to provide information to investors. Investment advisers, Registrar and Transfer Agents (RTAs), broker-dealers, and other members of the industry typically create a website that is shared by all of the funds in the group. A single website may therefore provide information about several different funds, allowing investors to reach large numbers of competing products.

Mutual fund industry in India is yet to make significant commitments in technology which are exclusively industry oriented. Formulating and executing appropriate strategies that reflect the changing industry landscape in addition to the widespread application of electronic commerce are major challenges. Finding opportunities to quickly exploit unique strengths in new ways in a new competitive environment will be a parallel challenge for the mutual fund industry. However, in the near future, while online service functions in the mutual fund industry will expand quickly, online sales functions will not. In the near term, there will be limited success of the Internet as a direct sales tool, and more use as an information source for unit holders and prospective investors.

TERMINOLOGY

Some of the terms frequently used in mutual funds industry are:

1. **Sale Price:** The price one pays when he invests in a scheme. Also called offer price. It may include a sales load.
2. **Repurchase Price:** The price at which a close-ended scheme repurchases its units and it may include a back-end load. This is also called bid price.
3. **Redemption Price:** The price at which open-ended schemes repurchase their units and close-ended schemes redeem their units on maturity. Such prices are NAV related.
4. **Sales Load:** A charge collected by a scheme when it sells the units. Also called, "front-end" load. Schemes that do not charge a load are called "no load" schemes.
5. **Repurchase or "Back-end" Load:** A charge collected by a scheme when it buys back the units from the unit holders.
6. **Net Assets Value (NAV):** Net asset value is the market value of the assets of the scheme minus its liabilities. The per unit NAV is the net asset value of the scheme divided by the number of units outstanding on the valuation date. The performance of a scheme is reflected in its net asset value (NAV) which is disclosed on daily basis in case of open-ended schemes and on weekly basis in case of close-ended schemes. The NAVs of mutual funds are required to be published in newspapers. The NAVs are also available on the websites of mutual funds. All mutual funds are also required to put their NAVs on the website of Association of Mutual Funds in India (AMFI) www. amfiindia.com and thus the investors can access NAVs of all mutual funds at one place.

The mutual funds are also required to publish their performance in the form of half-yearly results which also include their returns/yields over a period of time, that is, last 6 months, 1 year, 3 years, 5 years, and since the inception of schemes. Investors can also look into other details like percentage of expenses of total assets as these have an effect on the yield and other useful information in the same half-yearly format.

The mutual funds are also required to send annual report or abridged annual report to the unit holders at the end of the year.

Various studies on mutual fund schemes including yields of different schemes are being published by the financial newspapers on a weekly basis. Apart from these, many research agencies also publish research reports on performance of mutual funds including the ranking of various schemes in terms of their performance. Investors should study these reports and keep themselves informed about the performance of various schemes of different mutual funds.

Investors can compare the performance of their schemes with those of other mutual funds under the same category. They can also compare the performance of equity-oriented schemes with the benchmarks like BSE Sensitive Index, S&P CNX Nifty.

The recent crisis in global economy has also ill-affected the performance of mutual funds in India. There is nearly 80 percent erosion in value of funds between January–October 2008.

On the basis of performance of the mutual funds, the investors should decide when to enter or exit from a mutual fund scheme.

8

Leasing and Hire-purchase

Learning Objectives

- To know the concept and types of leasing.
- To be familiar with hire purchase.

INTRODUCTION

Leasing is a contract for exclusive possession of property (usually but, not necessarily land or building) for a determinate period or at will. The person making the grant is called the lessor and the person receiving the grant is called the lessee. Two important requirements for a lease are that the lessee has exclusive possession and the lessor's terms of interest in property be longer than the term or the lease.

Dictionary of Business and Management (2nd edition) defined lease as a form of contract transferring the use of occupancy of land, space, structure, or equipment in consideration of a payment, usually in the form of a rent.

Equipment Leasing Association (ELA), UK, has defined the term lease as follows:

A lease is a contract between a lessor and a lessee for the hire of a specific asset selected from a manufacturer or vendor of such assets by the lessee. The lessor retains the ownership of the asset. The lessee has the possession and use of the asset on payment of specified rentals over a period.

The Institute of Chartered Accountant of India (ICAI) has defined the term lease in the following way:

"Lease is an agreement whereby the lessor conveys to the lessee, in return for rent, the right to use an asset for an agreed period of time."

TYPES OF LEASES

Primarily there are two types of leases—finance lease and operating lease.

Finance Lease

There are many views about finance lease. Some of them are as follows.

A financial lease is a contract under which a lessee agrees to make a series of payments to a lessor which, in total, exceeds the purchase price of the equipment acquired. Typically, payments under a financial lease are spread over a period of time equal to the major portion of the useful life of the equipment.

IAS-17 classifies finance lease as a lease under which "The lessor transfers to the lessee substantially all risks and rewards incident to ownership of an assets, Title may or may not eventually be transferred."

The Guidance Note on Accounting for Leases Institute of Chartered Accountants of India defined finance lease as "a lease under which the present value of minimum lease payments at the inception of the lease exceeds or is equal to substantially the whole of the fair value of the lease asset. The finance lease is often called as capital lease."

A finance lease, as the word finance connotes, is a way of equipment financing whereby the lessor extends credit to the lessee and transfers to the lessee all responsibilities of ownership such as maintenance and insurance taxes for a period of time equal to the economic life of the asset. At the termination of lease contract, the lessee may either purchase the asset or return the asset to the lessor. The lease rentals in a financial lease are generally set so that the lessor may recover the purchase price and achieve a rate of return approximately equal to the lessee's marginal cost of debt financing over the period of the lease. Most of the financial leases are full pay out, that is, the return to the lessor is sufficient to cover the asset cost, the cost of financing the lessor overhead, and a rate of return acceptable to the lessor. Financial leases are similar to mortgage type loans wherein fixed payments are scheduled for a fixed period of time and consist of interest and principal repayments. Financial leases are non-cancelable.

Characteristics of a Financial Lease

1. The equipment and supplier are selected by the lessee. A lessee decides to use the services or the specific equipment after an evaluation of the related benefits and costs. In some cases the lessor may involve in deciding what equipment is required or lessor may recommend that lessee may consider alternative equipment from a supplier with a sound reputation.

2. The lessee uses the equipment for business purposes. The major goal of leasing is financing the use of the capital equipment for commercial, industrial, and professional purposes. Installment sale, consumer finance, and hire-purchase activities are normally excluded from the business of equipment leasing.
3. The lessor purchases the equipment. The substance of the lease contract is separation of ownership and use of equipment.
4. The lessor retains title to the equipment throughout the lease term. The parties to the lease agreement enter into an agreement with the intention that the term should run its full course. A lessee is not entitled to ownership benefits because the lessor is the owner of the asset during the currency of the lease.
5. The lessee has the exclusive right to use the equipment. A finance lease agreement by its very nature entitles the lessee the exclusive use and possession of the leased equipment.
6. The lease is non-cancelable. The lessor normally has the right to compensation in the event of termination of lease period to the expiry of the agreed term, whether termination is voluntary or by default. The lessor and lessee may, however, agree to substitute the existing lease with a new lease of different equipment(s).
7. The risks inherent in the equipment and occasioned by its use fall primarily on the lessee. The lessor has no obligation to replace the obsolete or the faulty leased equipment during the lease term. The burden of the obsolescence falls on the lessee in the same way as for any other equipment financing arrangement is concerned.

The finance lease can be sub-divided into: (*a*) leveraged lease, (*b*) sale and lease back, (*c*) cross-border (international) lease, and (*d*) foreign-to-foreign lease.

1. In a leveraged lease, the equipment is generally purchased by a leasing company/ companies by providing 20–40 percent of the cost of the equipment. The remaining amount is borrowed from institutional investors such as banks, financial institutions, or any other finance/investment companies. Therefore, leveraged lease contract, involve three parties, that is, lessor (leasing company), lessee (user company), and lender (financier). The leveraged lease represents a very complex transaction involving several parties and a number of agreements for financing large capital equipment. The basic documents found in leveraged lease transactions are the participation agreement (which is signed by all parties), the trust agreement, indenture trust, lease agreement for the tax shields associated with the ownership of the asset and to residual value of the asset at the end of its economic life.
2. In a sale and lease back agreement, a company owning a particular asset/block of assets sells to a leasing company and the company gets back the same on lease from the leasing company. By this type of lease transactions, the company is able to free its investments blocked in these assets.
3. In a cross-border (international) lease, the parties involved in the leasing transactions are located in two different nations, that is, the manufacturer/supplier is in one country and the lessor and lessee in another country.

4. In the case of foreign-to-foreign lease, the three parties, namely, the manufacture/ supplier, lessor, and lessee, are located in three different countries. No two parties are located in the same nation. These types of leases are taken up by the leasing companies in the USA and the UK.

Operating Lease

An operating lease (or service or maintenance lease) is viewed somewhat differently by the tax, accounting, and legal authorities. Generally, the leasing community views an operating lease as one having the following characteristics:

1. The lease does not involve an extension of credit or a long-term fixed commitment.
2. The lessor may provide special services such as maintenance, repairs, and insurance.
3. The lease is of short length of time compared with the economic life of the asset.
4. The lease is cancelable.
5. The lease is treated as an off-balance sheet financial reporting purposes of the lessee.

The following are major differences between a finance lease and an operating lease:

1. Financial lease is like an installment sale and it is a legal obligation to pay for the total cost of the equipment plus interest portion over a period of time. Lessee commits to a series of payments which in total lease rentals exceeds the original cost of the equipment.

   Operating lease is a rental contract in which the lessee is not obliged and committed to pay more than the cost of equipment during contractual period.
2. In financial lease, lessor provides a pure financial function. The repairs and maintenance, taxes, insurance, etc., are borne by the lessee and lessee assumes the risk of obsolescent and underutilization.

   In operating lease, lessor provides service function. Operating lease usually includes provision for repairs and maintenance, taxes and insurance are borne by the lessor. In most of the cases, the lessor (leasing company) assumes the risk of obsolescence and underutilization. The operating leases are generally for a short period as compared to the life of the equipment.
3. Financial lease creates a financial commitment on the part of the lessee similar to that of a loan whereas operating lease does not create any financial commitment to the total cost of the equipment on the part of the lessee.
4. Financial lease is evaluated, whether the equipment is taken on lease or one is borrowing funds to acquire equipments from the perspective of the lessee. Whereas operating lease is evaluated in terms of lease the equipment or buy the equipment.
5. Financial lease is non-cancelable for a specified period, usually referred to as the primary period. The financial lease is fully amortized over the primary lease period.

   On the other hand, operating lease is cancelable and the lease term ranges from one hour to three years. The lease rentals required to be paid in operating lease are not sufficient to cover fully the investment in the lease asset plus the rate of return required on the investment.

6. In financial lease, aircrafts, satellites, heavy machinery, chemical plants, earth moving machines, etc., are provided by the lessors, and computers, office equipment, data processing machines, Xerox machines, and vehicles are provided in the operating lease.

VARIOUS TYPES OF LEASING

1. **Direct Lease:** The direct lease is essentially a hybrid of the operating and financial lease. Direct leases are usually full pay out and provide for renewal or purchase option but do not include lessor service such as repairs, maintenance, and taxes.

   Direct lease may be characterized by the following attributes:

   (i) They have a duration of three or more years.
   (ii) The lessor holds the title.
   (iii) The lessee may renew or purchase at the expiration of lease term.
   (iv) They may include a mid-stream of trade in option (primarily with vendor lessor).
   (v) They are usually full pay out.

2. **Master Lease:** It's a blanket leasing covering numerous pieces of assets that establishes an open-ended contract with rates and terms for both equipment needed at present and equipment needed in the near future. It places responsibility upon the lessor to provide up-to-date equipment throughout the lease period. The master lease is similar to a blanket purchase order and in effect also establishes a line of credit between lessee and lessor.

3. **Percentage Lease:** Under the percentage lease, the lessee pays a flat minimum rental and additional rentals based on a percentage of gross revenue during the period. Generally, the additional percentage rent is calculated as a percentage of revenue received above a minimum base amount; such lease arrangements help compensate lessee in part for the effect of inflation since percentage leases are generally structured for the long-term use of commercial equipment.

4. **Wet and Dry Leases:** A dry lease provides finances as well as fuel and servicing for aircraft. The provisions of a wet lease are similar to those of an operating lease.

5. **Net, Net, Net and Triple Net Leases:** The term triple net and net, net, net are sometimes applied to financial leases. The lessee agrees to make lease payments, bears the cost of maintenance, insurance, taxes, and the like, and assumes the risk of ownership. Frequently, net, net, net is used to refer to maintenance, taxes, and insurance.

6. **Closed- and Open-ended Leases:** Closed ended or walk away leases are usually arranged on a net lease basis and at the end of the lease, the equipment is returned to the lessor. The full risk of residual value loss rests with the lessor. Ownership rights are closed to the lessee.

   Open-ended leases are generally net leases, where title to the equipment passes to the lessee upon exercising of a purchase option or payment of guaranteed residual.

7. **Swap Lease:** Swap lease allows the lessee to exchange the equipment in need of major repair with properly working replacement equipment to avoid costly maintenance and repair delays.

8. **Full Pay-out Lease:** The full pay-out lease is a lease in which the lessor aims not only to recover the whole of the initial capital investment out of rentals payable under the contractual agreement with the lessee but also to achieve a predetermined yield on the funds employed to finance the investment. The counterpart to a full pay-out lease is the part pay-out non-pay out lease.

9. **True Lease:** If a lease in a particular country conforms to the local rules and regulations, it may be considered to be a true lease. A true lease in one country may not necessarily constitute a true lease in another country.

10. **Wash Lease:** In wash lease, the lessor-investor is considered the owner of the equipment for tax purposes but the lessee-user of the equipment is the legal owner. This lease is called "wash lease" since the subsequent lease payments to the lessor exactly equal or "wash out" the subsequent loan payments to the lessee. The lessor acts as if he had purchased the equipment from the lessee.

11. **Upgrade Lease:** In upgrade lease, the leasing company undertakes to replace out dated equipment with modern ones at specific rental terms. This helps the lessee to upgrade the production system so that lessee can take the advantage of latest technology.

12. **Capital Lease:** A lease is classified as a capital lease if it meets one of the following criteria:

    (i) Lease arrangement is so structured as to transfer the ownership of the equipment from the lessor to the lessee at the end of the lease term.

    (ii) The lessee has the option to purchase the equipment at a bargain price.

    (iii) The non-cancelable period of the lease is equal to 75 percent or more of the useful life of the equipment.

    (iv) The present value of minimum lease payments is equal to or more than 90 percent of the fair market value of the equipment.

13. **Employee Lease:** Employee leasing is a lease back arrangement under which an employer transfers all the workers or groups to a leasing company, which then assigns the same employees back to their original employer under a leasing arrangement.

LEASING IN INDIA

Starting in the 1970s with the first leasing company, incidentally also known as "First Leasing Company" in 1973, the industry has grown through several ups and downs. In the beginning, the boom was triggered due to limited number of players in the market, but with increasing number of players in the 1980s, competition intensified and growth slowed down. In the 1990s almost all banks, financial institutions, and financial companies had their own leasing and hire-purchase companies. At present there are about 600 leasing companies.

TAX ASPECTS OF LEASING: A SUMMARIZED VIEW

1. The tax aspects of leasing can be divided into two parts: the income tax aspects and the sales tax aspects.
2. The income tax aspects of leasing are primarily concerned with (*a*) lessee's claim for lease rentals and the operating costs of the leased assets being treated as tax-deductible expenses; and (*b*) tax liability on rental income in the hands of the lessor, and the tax shield on depreciation.
3. The rental income derived by the lessor is included under the head "Profit and Gains of Business or Profession" for the purpose of assessing the income tax liability.
4. From the lessee's angle, the rental expense can be treated as tax-deductible expense. The costs incurred in insuring and maintaining the leased asset are also tax deductible.
5. By virtue of a circular issued by the Central Board of Direct Taxes (CBDT) in 1943, the lease agreement must not provide for a transfer of ownership of the leased asset or a bargain purchase option to the lessee. Inclusion of either of these provisions will result in the lease transaction being treated as a hire-purchase transaction. The tax implications of a hire-purchase transaction are not the same as those of a lease transaction.
6. Leasing can be used as a tax planning device by (*a*) exploiting the flexibility in structuring lease rentals; (*b*) transferring the investment-related tax shields from a firm which has a low appetite for such tax shields to a lessor who can absorb them. The firm transferring the tax shields can benefit through a reduction in the lease rentals.
7. Sales tax affects a lease transaction at the following stages: (*a*) when the asset is purchased by the lessor for the purpose of leasing, (*b*) when the right to use the asset is transferred to the lessee for a valuable consideration, and (*c*) when the asset is sold by the lessor at the end of the lease period.
8. The validity of the provision to levy sales tax on lease transactions and the other related aspects have been challenged by the leasing companies and stay orders have been obtained from different state high courts. Consequently, the lessor's liability to pay sales tax on rental income remains as a contingent liability.

LAWS AND ACTS GOVERNING LEASING IN INDIA

Leasing involves compliance of relevant provisions of various Acts and legislations enumerated as under:

1. Indian Contract Act, 1872
2. Transfer of Property Act, 1882
3. Sale of Goods Act, 1930
4. Indian Easement Act, 1882
5. The Companies Act, 1956

6. Partnership Act, 1932
7. Income Tax Act, 1961
8. Urban Land (Ceiling and Regulation) Act, 1976
9. Limitation Act, 1930
10. Indian Stamp Act, 1899
11. Arbitration Act, 1940
12. Sales Tax Laws

DOCUMENTS REQUIRED FOR LEASING

Leasing requires a series of documentation which included both, commercial as well as legal documents. Commercial documents are purchase order, invoice, acknowledgement of delivery, insurance cover, import license, guarantees, and so on. Legal documents are:

1. lease agreement,
2. letter of guarantee and indemnity,
3. service agreement for leased asset, and
4. lease deed (for real estate).

NEW ACCOUNTING NORMS FOR LEASING

The Institute of Chartered Accountants of India (ICAI) has come out with a revised guidance note on accounting for leases. The two salient features of the guidelines are: (*a*) leasing companies to account for leased assets in the fixed assets column instead of as current assets; and (*b*) leasing companies do not account for the lease equalization charge and the lease adjustment account while preparing their profit and loss account for tax purpose.

Among the other recommendations of the ICAI, the lessees will have to include a footnote in the annual balance sheets, chartering out the future rental payable on the leased assets at present value. However, the lessees need not mention the nature of assets in the balance sheet. The recommendations of the new guidance note will apply to all assets leasing during accounting period beginning on or after April 1, 1996.

According to the Association of Leasing and Financial Service Companies (ALFSC), with uniformity, consistency, and matching of cost and revenues being the three basic tenets of accounting practices, the matching of cost and revenues for the leasing industry in particular needs a special treatment due to the nature of the activity. While Schedule 14 of the Companies Act allows depreciation to be written off over the life of the asset, the lessor and the owner of a leased asset can avail of the depreciation benefits for taxation purposes only during the life of the lease. This results in mismatch between the cost and revenue which is balanced by the lease equalization fund.

BUY OR LEASE

It is an important issue to weight buy or lease equipments.

Financial Considerations

1. In the case of outright purchase of equipment, the company will require the total amount of funds representing the cost of equipment at the time of acquisition, whereas in case of lease only the amount of lease installment is needed.
2. If the funds required for outright purchase are obtained through sales of shares or borrowings, then the dividend rate/interest rate payable on them is to be compared with the cost of leasing. For this total amount payable over the period of lease is to be considered.
3. For comparison of cost of equity capital or borrowed funds with the excess of lease amount over the cash purchase price, both the alternatives have to be reduced to a common time period. In case of lease, the company has to pay lease rents for a number of years. This requires consideration of risk involved in the two alternatives. The company has to carefully consider its ability to meet the periodical lease rental obligations on time. If it fails to meet its obligations on due date, the lessor may take back the equipment and the company's plans may be frustrated.
4. In case of purchase of equipment, the scrap value of the purchase equipment at the expiry of the period of lease is also to be considered but such a consideration may not arise if the equipment is taken on lease.
5. The tax implications of the two alternatives play a very important role in deciding the questions. In case of lease, total amount of lease rentals is a charge on profit whereas in the case of outright purchase, amount of depreciation and, if purchase is financed from borrowed funds, interest on such funds will be charged in computing taxable income. Further, the benefit of investment allowance is also available to the owner of the equipment.
6. It is easier to replace equipment taken on lease; hence, in case there is rapid change in technology, leasing is better than buying.
7. Financial decision in leasing requires a pay-off between leasing and borrowing. For deciding on lease, company has to determine present values of after-tax cash outflows for each year and then decide as under:
   (i) If present value of cash outflows under leasing alternative is more than present value of cash outflows as per buying alternative, company should buy the asset.
   (ii) If present value of cash outflows under leasing alternative is less than present value of cash outflows as per buying alternative, company should acquire the asset on lease terms.

Advantages of Leasing

A company opts for leasing because of its manifold advantages as enumerated in the following:

1. Leasing offers 100 percent financing. A manufacturing concern gets full cost of its equipment from a leasing company.
2. It shifts risk to technological obsolescence on the lessor.
3. It is a convenient source of financing assets as compared to borrowing from banks or institutions.
4. Liquidity: Lessee has the option of selling the owned assets and taking it back on lease, thus enhancing the liquidity.
5. Leasing conserves borrowing capacity through "off the balance sheet" financing. Leasing obligation does not appear on the balance sheet. This improves the financial position and does not affect financial ratios.
6. Burden of equipment maintenance is on lessor.
7. It has lower administrative costs.
8. Tax shield is available for lease rentals.
9. Inflationary impact is avoided.
10. Insolvency risks are avoided.

Disadvantages of Leasing

1. Leasing deprives the lessor to become owner of the asset.
2. Lessee is not allowed to make alterations or changes in the asset.
3. In case of assets having substantial terminal value or end use, leasing is not advantageous.
4. Depreciation is claimed by lessor.
5. Tax liability in subsequent years may increase for lessor as depreciation will be offset by lease rentals.
6. In case of leasing by consortium of companies, as per Income Tax Law, depreciation is not allowed to be shared. This discourages big leases or syndicate leases.
7. It has high interest cost.

HIRE-PURCHASE

Hire-purchase is a method of selling goods. In a hire-purchase transaction, the goods are let out on hire by a finance company (creditor) to the hire-purchase customer (hirer). The buyer is required to pay an agreed amount in periodical installment during a given period.

The ownership of the property remains with creditor and passes on to hirer on the payment of last installment.

Legal Position

Hire Purchase Act, 1972 defines a hire-purchase agreement as one where:

1. Payment is to be made in installments over a specified period.
2. The possession is delivered to the purchaser at the time of entering into a contract.
3. The property in the goods passes to the purchaser on payment of the last installment.
4. Each installment is treated as hire charge so that if default is made in payment of any one installment, the seller is entitled to take away the goods.
5. The hire purchaser is free to return the goods without being required to pay any further installments falling due after the return.

Features of Hire-Purchase Agreement

1. Under hire-purchase system, the buyer takes possession of goods immediately and agrees to pay the total hire-purchase price in installments.
2. Each installment is treated as hire charge.
3. The ownership of the goods shifts from buyer to seller on the payment of the installment.
4. In case the buyer makes any default in the payment of any installment the seller has right to repossess the goods from the buyer and forfeit the amount already received treating it as hire charge.
5. The hirer has the right to terminate the agreement any time before the property passes to him.

High-Purchase and Credit Sale

Hire-purchase transaction is different from credit sale. In case of actual sale, the title of property, that is, ownership and possession is transferred to the purchaser simultaneously. In hire-purchase, the ownership remains with the seller until last installment is paid. Further when the buyer stops payment of dues, the seller has no right to repossess the goods. He has the only right to sue the buyer for the non-payment by returning the goods but has the right of disposing the goods in any manner as he like.

Hire-Purchase and Leasing

Ownership

In a contract of lease, the ownership rests with the lessor throughout and the leasee (hirer) has no option to purchase the goods.

Depreciation

Leasing is a method in which depreciation and investment allowance cannot be claimed by the leasee. In hire-purchase, depreciations and investment allowances can be claimed by the hirer.

Tax Benefit

The entire lease rental is a tax-deductible expense; only the interest component of the hire-purchase installment is tax deductible.

Salvage Value

The lessee, not being the owner of the assets, does not enjoy the salvage value of the assets. The hirer, in purchase, being the owner of assets enjoys salvage value of the assets.

ILLUSTRATION

The following are the details regarding an equipment to be given on lease by A Ltd.

1. Cost of the equipment of the lessor, Rs 100,000, is financed 80 percent through debt and balance through equity. Cost of the debt amounts to 18 percent and equity 15 percent before tax.
2. The lessor is in 55 percent tax bracket. The equipment is used for three shifts. The rate of depreciation is normal, 15 percent and 7.5 percent for each additional shift. Depreciation is charged according to diminishing balance method.
3. The salvage value of the equipment is Rs 16,000.
4. The direct cost to the lessor is Rs 500 in the 1st year.
5. Estimated cost for maintenance and general administration in respect of the equipment to the lessor is Rs 1,500 annum.
6. The lessee agrees to pay the following:

    i. Annual rent of Rs 36,000 for 5 years. The payment is to be made at the end of each year.
    ii. A security deposit of Rs 3,000 which is refundable at the end of the lease term.
    iii. A sum of Rs 1,350 non-returnable management fees payable at the time of inception of the lease.

Suggest whether it is beneficial for the lessor to lease the equipment using Internal Rate of Return (IRR) technique.

(Adapted from Maheshwari 2009)

Solution:

(i)

Cost of Capital for Lessor

Source	Amount (Rs)	After Tax Cost	Total Cost (Rs)
Equity	20,000	15.0%	3,000
Long-term Debt	80,000	8.1%	6,480
*18 × 45/100 = 8.1%			9,480

Tax Adjusted Average Cost of Capital $= \dfrac{9,480}{1,00,000} \times 100 = 9.5\%$

(ii)

Computation of Annual Tax Liability

	Years				
	1 (Rs)	2 (Rs)	3 (Rs)	4 (Rs)	5 (Rs)
Lease Revenue	+36,000	+36,000	+36,000	+36,000	+36,000
Direct Cost	500	–	–	–	–
Maintenance & Administration					
Cost	–1,500	–1,500	–1,500	–1,500	–1,500
Depreciation	–30,000	–21,000	–14,700	–10,290	–7,203
Income Before Tax	+4,000	+13,500	+19,800	+24,210	+27,297
Income Tax @55%	–2,200	–7,425	–10,890	13,315	–15,013
Income After Tax	+1,800	+6,075	+8,910	+10,895	+12,284

(iii)

Computation of Annual Net Cash Inflows

	Years				
	1 (Rs)	2 (Rs)	3 (Rs)	4 (Rs)	5 (Rs)
Lease Revenue	+36,000	+36,000	+36,000	+36,000	+36,000
Sale of Equipment	–	–	–	–	+16,000
Direct Cost	–500	–	–	–	–
Administration Cost	–1,500	–1,500	–1,500	–1,500	–1,500
Refund of Deposit	–	–	–	–	–3,000
Tax Paid	–2,200	–7,425	–10,890	–13,315	–15,013
	31,800	27,075	23,610	21,185	32,487

(iv)

Cash Outflows at Year "O"

		Rs
Cost of Equipment		100,000
Less Maintenance Fees	1,350	
Security Deposit	3,000	4,350
Net Cash Outflow		95,650

(v)   Computation of International Rate of Return

Year	Cash Outflow (Rs)	Cash Inflow (Rs)	Discount Factor at 15% (Rs)	Present Value (Rs)	Discount Factor at 12% (Rs)	Present Value (Rs)
0	−95,650					
1		31,800	0.870	27,666	0.893	28,397
2		27,075	0.756	20,469	0.797	21,579
3		23,610	0.658	15,535	0.712	16,786
4		21,185	0.572	12,118	0.636	13,535
5		32,487	0.497	16,146	0.567	18,420
				91,934		98,717
		NPV		−3,716		+3,067

IRR = 13 +

$$IRR = 12 \left\{ \frac{3,067}{3,067 + 3,716} \right\} \times 3$$

$$= 12 + 1.36$$
$$= 13.36\%$$

The weighted average cost of capital is only 9.5 percent while the IRR from leasing out the asset is 13.36 percent. Hence, it is beneficial for A Ltd to lease out the equipment.

9

Securitization

CONCEPT

Securitization is the process of conversion of existing illiquid assets or future cash flows into marketable securities, that is, securitization deals with the conversion of assets which are not marketable into marketable ones. The conversion of existing non-performing assets (NPAs) or receivables into marketable securities is known as asset-backed securitization and the conversion of future cash flows into marketable securities is known as future-flows securitization. Securitization is a process by which the forecast future income (the money that's due to come in) of an entity is transformed and sold as debt instruments such as bonds with a fixed rate of return. This allows the company to get cash upfront which can be put to productive use in the business. Securitization is done by suitably "re-packaging" the cash flows or the free cash generated by the firm that is issuing these bonds.

Some of the assets that can be securitized are loans given by banks, institutions, or finance companies, like car loans and housing loans, and future cash flows like ticket sales, sale of oil in future, credit card payments, car rentals, or any other form of future receivables.

Suppose Mr X wants to open a multiplex and is in need of funds for the same. To raise funds, Mr X can sell his future cash flows (cash flows arising from sale of movie tickets and food items in the future) in the form of securities to raise money.

This will benefit investors as they will have a claim over the future cash flows generated from the multiplex. Mr X will also benefit as loan obligations will be met from cash flows generated from the multiplex itself. He will have cash in advance which can be used for construction and other purposes.

Similarly a bank in the traditional lending process makes a loan, maintaining it as an asset on its balance sheet, collecting principal and interest, and monitoring whether there is any deterioration in borrower's creditworthiness. This requires a bank to hold assets (loans given) till maturity. The funds of the bank are blocked in these loans and to meet its growing fund requirement a bank has to raise additional funds from the market. Securitization is a way of unlocking these blocked funds. The loans given out by bank are its assets. Thus, the bank has a pool of these assets on its balance sheet and so the funds of the bank are locked up in these loans.

Thus, securitization of debt, or asset securitization, is a process by which identified pools of receivables, which are usually illiquid on their own, are transformed into marketable securities through suitable repacking of cash flows that they generate. Securitization, in effect, is a credit arbitrage transaction that permits for more efficient management of risks by isolating a specific pool of assets from the originator's balance sheet. Further, unlike in the case of conventional debt financing, where the interest and principal obligations of a borrowing entity are serviced out of its own general cash flows, debt servicing with asset-backed securities (ABS) is from the cash flows originating from its underlying assets.

The entity that securitizes its assets is called the originator: the name signifies the fact that the entity is responsible for originating the claims that are to be securitized. Those who invest their money in the instrument are called investors.

The securitized assets could be either existing receivables to be known as assets-backed securitization, or receivables to arise in future to be known as future flows securitization.

In US markets, another distinction is common: between mortgage-backed securities and asset-backed securities. This is only to indicate the distinct application: the former relates to the market for securities based on mortgage receivables, which in the USA forms a substantial part of total securitization markets, and securitization of other receivables. Recent sub-prime prices in the USA may be related to mortgage-backed securities.

It is important for the entire exercise to be a case of transfer of receivables by the originator; there is a legal transfer of the receivables to a separate entity called assignment of receivables and the transfer of receivables has to be a "true sale" of the receivables, and not merely a financing against the security of the receivables.

Since securitization involves a transfer of receivables from the originator to investors, it is necessary to bring in an intermediary that would hold the receivables on behalf of the end investors. This entity is created solely for the purpose of the transaction: therefore, it is called a special purpose vehicle (SPV) or a special purpose entity (SPE) or special purpose company (SPC). The function of the SPV in a securitization transaction could stretch from being a pure conduit or intermediary vehicle, to a more active role in reinvesting or reshaping the cash flows arising from the assets transferred to it, which is something that would depend on the end objectives of the securitization exercise.

Therefore, the originator transfers the assets to the SPV, which holds the assets on behalf of the investors, and issues to the investors its own securities. Therefore, the SPV is also called the issuer.

There is no uniform name for the securities issued by the SPV, as such securities take different forms. These securities could represent a direct claim of the investors on all that the SPV collects from the receivables transferred to it: in this case, the securities are called pass-through certificates or beneficial interest certificates as they imply certificates of proportional beneficial interest in the assets held by the SPV. Pass-throughs represent direct ownership interest in the underlying assets, which are typically held in trust for the investors, so that payments on the assets are passed through to the investors directly from the assets (after payment of all fees and expenses, including excess servicing). Alternatively, the SPV might be re-configuring the cash flows by reinvesting it, so as to pay to the investors on fixed dates, not matching with the dates on which the transferred receivables are collected by the SPV. In this case, the securities held by the investors are called pay-through certificates. Pay-throughs are general obligations on preferred stock of the issuer (SPV). As the assets are owned by this entity (SPV), who would receive payments on a separate security backed by the general credit of the entity rather than an interest in the assets, payments on these assets are said to be paid rather than passed through to the investors. The securities issued by the SPV could also be named based on their risk or other features, such as senior notes or junior notes, floating rate notes.

The investors can be banks, mutual funds, other financial institutions, government, etc. In India only qualified institutional buyers (QIBs) who possess the expertise and the financial muscle to invest in securities market are allowed to invest in Pass Through Certificates (PTCs). High rated securitized instruments can offer low risk and higher yields to investors. The low risk of securitized instruments is attributable to their backing by financial assets and some credit-enhancement measures, like insurance/underwriting or guarantee, used by the originator.

The administrator or the servicer is appointed to collect the payments from the obligors. The servicer follows up with the defaulters and uses legal remedies against them. Another word commonly used in securitization exercises is "bankruptcy remote transfer." It means that the transfer of the assets by the originator to the SPV is such that even if the originator were to go bankrupt, or get into other financial difficulties, the rights of the investors on the assets held by the SPV is not affected. In other words, the investors would continue to have a paramount interest in the assets irrespective of the difficulties, distress, or bankruptcy of the originator. Normally the originator carries out this activity. Once assets are securitized, these assets are removed from the bank's books and the money generated through securitization can be used for other profitable uses like for giving new loans. For an originator, securitization is an alternative to corporate debt or equity for meeting its funding requirements. As the securitized instruments can have a better credit rating than the company, the originator can get funds from new investors and additional funds from existing investors at a lower cost than debt.

See Box 9.1 for details on the participants in the process of securitization.

NEED OF SECURITIZATION

Securitization is needed as:

1. **Funding alternative** well-structured ABS stands on its own credit rating and thus generates genuine incremental funding.

Box 9.1   Participants in Securitization

Parties in a securitization transaction is summed up

- The originator, also interchangeably referred to as the seller, is the entity whose receivable portfolio forms the basis for assets based securitization (ABS) issuance.
- Special purpose vehicle (SPV), as the issuer of the ABS, ensures adequate distancing of the instrument from the originator.
- The servicer bears all administrative responsibilities relating to the securitization transaction.
- The trustee or the investor representative acts in a fiduciary capacity safeguarding the interests of investors in the ABS.
- The credit rating agency provides an objective estimate of the credit risk in the securitization transaction by assigning a well-defined credit rating.
- The regulators' principal concerns are related to capital adequacy, liquidity, and credit quality of the ABS, and balance sheet treatment of the transaction.
- Service providers include credit enhancers and liquidity providers.
- Specialist functionaries include legal and tax counsels, accounting firms, and pool auditors.

2. **Balance sheet management:** securitization can also generate matched funding for balance sheet assets. Further, it may also enable the disposal of non-core assets through suitable structuring.
3. **Re-allocation of risks:** securitization transfers much of the credit risk in the portfolio to the ABS investors and helps to quantify the residual credit risk that the originator is exposed to. Securitization also transfers the originator's market risks, that is, liquidity, interest rate, and prepayment risks, to ABS investors and reduces risk capital requirement. This can lead to more competitive pricing of the underlying asset products.
4. **Securitization:** improves operating leverage.

FEATURES OF SECURITIZATION

A securitized instrument generally has the following features:

1. **Marketability:** The very purpose of securitization is to ensure marketability to financial claims. The concept of marketability involves two issues: (*a*) the legal and systemic possibility of marketing the instrument; (*b*) the existence of a market for the instrument.
2. **Wide Distribution:** The basic purpose of securitization is to distribute the product. The extent of distribution which the originator would like to achieve is based on a comparative analysis of the costs and the benefits achieved thereby. Wider distribution leads to a cost-benefit in the sense that the issuer is able to market the product with lower return, and hence, lower financial cost to himself.
3. **Homogeneity:** To serve as a marketable instrument, the instrument should be packaged into homogenous lots. Most securitized instruments are broken into lots affordable to

the marginal investor, and hence, the minimum denomination becomes relative to the needs of the smallest investor.

4. **Securitization Improves Disintermediation:** Securitization is employed to dis-intermediate. It is, however, important to understand that it merely redefines the intermediary's role. Securitization seeks to eliminate funds-based financial inter-mediaries by fee-based distributors.

5. **Securitization Endorses Structured Finance:** Securitization is a "structured financial instrument." It is a financial instrument structured or tailored to the risk–return and maturity needs of the investor rather than a simple claim against an entity or asset.

6. **Securitization is a Tool of Risk Management:** It is an important tool of risk man-agement for banks as they acquire securitized assets with potential diversification benefits. When assets are removed from a bank's balance sheet or without recourse basis, all the risks associated with the asset are eliminated, save the risks retained by the bank.

SECURITIZATION PROCESS

The essential features of a securitization process comprise of the following (see Figures 9.1 and 9.2):

1. **Creation of Asset Pool and its Sale**: The originator/seller (of assets) creates a pool of assets and executes a legal true sale of the same to an SPV. An SPV in such cases is either a trust or a company, as may be appropriate under applicable law, set up to carry out a restricted set of activities, management of which would usually rest with an independent board of directors.

2. **Issuance of the Securitized Paper**: It is performed by the SPV. Design of the instrument, however, would be based on the nature of interest that investors would have on these asset pool. In the case of pass-through issuances, the investors will have a direct ownership interest in the underlying assets, while pay-through certificates are debt issued by the SPV secured by the assets and their cash flows.

3. **Credit Risk**: Interest, amortization, and redemption payments are entirely dependent on the performance of the pooled assets, and will have nothing to do with the credit of the originator.

4. **Pool Selection**: The process of selecting assets to build a securitization pool would take care of loan characteristics, cash flow, legal, and credit points such as type of asset, minimum and maximum loan size, rate, maturity, and concentration limits.

Securitization involves various participants like originator, SPV, Credit rating agency and so on. For more details, see Figure 9.1.

The securitization process involves the interplay of various participants. Figure 9.2 encompasses the securitization process for assets based securitization.

Figure 9.1 Securitization Process—Assets Based Securitization (ABS)

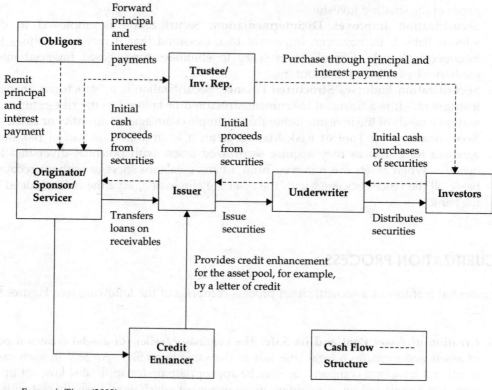

Source: Economic Times (2002).

Process of future receivables is explained as in the following: An oil monetization deal structured for Reliance Industries Ltd (RIL) by Industrial Credit and Investment Corporation of India (ICICI) is one such unique deal. Under the deal, the future flow of oil receivables accruing to RIL from the sale of oil produced from the Panna-Mukta oilfields is being securitized. In simple terms, ICICI is paying RIL cash upfront today which it will recover from proceeds of oil sales in the future, of course, at a cost.

Three parties are normally involved in such a deal: the originator, the obligor, and the investor. The originator (RIL here) sells his future stream of receivables (oil in this case), the obligor is the entity who buys a specified stream of goods from the originator and from whom future receivables are due (in this case it is one of the government-designated oil companies), and the pool of receivables in the form of securities.

RIL is one of the promoters of an oil exploration company with a 30 percent share in the venture. The other partners are Oil and Natural Gas Corporation (ONGC) and Enron.

The legal owner of the cash flows is an SPV, floated by the investor in this case in form of a trust. The SPV is the investor representative and its primary job is to protect the investor's interests and ensure a regular return.

Figure 9.2 Securitization of Future Receivables

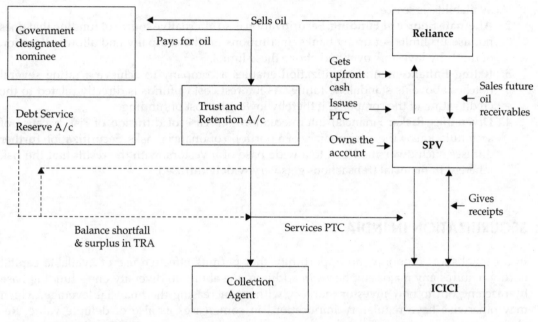

Source: *Economic Times* (2002).

As per the structure, the originator sells a pool of its future receivables from the obligator to the SPV. Against this sale, the originator gets a purchase consideration. As a result, the receivables from the obligor would be routed to the SPV through a trust and retention account (TRA) which is owned by the SPV.

The structure of the deal is based on three underlying factors:

1. The production sharing contract between the producers and the buyers of the oil/gas, which outlines the terms and conditions at which the output will be available.
2. The joint venture operating agreement, which outlines the ratio, at which the proceeds would be shared among the partners.
3. The mining agreement, which outlines the details of the term of lease of the oil field between the government and the promoters.

BENEFITS OF SECURITIZATION

Following are benefits of securitization:

1. **Efficient use of Capital:** When assets are securitized, they receive off balance sheet treatment. It releases a portion of the capital tied up by these assets. In effect, this allows

the company to continuously churn assets and expand business volumes when capital availability is scarce.

2. **Alternate Source of Funding:** Securitization is an alternative source of funding that does not use up limits set up by banks/institutions on the company and allows allocation of funds by investors over and above these limits.

3. **Rating Enhancement:** Securitization enables a company to achieve a rating several notches above its standalone rating. As interest cost of funds is directly related to the credit rating of the company, it thereby lowers its cost of funding.

4. **Diversifies Risks:** Financial intermediation is a case of diffusion of risk because of accumulation by the intermediary of a portfolio of financial risks. Securitization further diffuses such diversified risk to a wide base of investors, with the result that the risk inherent in financial transactions gets very widely diffused.

SECURITIZATION IN INDIA

In a capital-short economy, an opportunity that permits effective use of available capital hardly requires any major emphasis. In addition, the ability to diversify one's funding base by reaching out to new investor markets, without increasing the financial leverage, which may otherwise have regulatory implications in some cases, is also of definite value. Re-allocating risk in a planned and transparent manner helps in managing them better.

Understanding the needs of securitization, the Government of India has enacted Securisation and Reconstruction of Financial Assets and Enforcement of Security Interest Act, 2002, which mandates that only banks and financial institution can securitize their financial assets. As a requirement of the Act, Asset Reconstruction Company of India Limited (ARCIL) is the first SPV to commence business in India. ICICI Bank, Karur Vyasya Bank, Karnataka Bank, Citicorp (I) Finance, SBI, IDBI, PNB, HDFC, HDFC Bank, and some other banks have promoted ARCIL. A lot of banks have been selling off their NPAs to ARCIL.

10

Credit Rating

The origins of credit rating can be traced to the 1840s when Louis Tappan established the first mercantile credit agency in New York in 1841. The agency rated the ability of merchants to pay their financial obligations. It was subsequently acquired by Robert Dun and its first ratings guide was published in 1859. Another similar agency was set up by John Bradstreet in 1849 which published a rating book in 1857. These two agencies were merged together to form Dun & Bradstreet in 1933. In 1900 John Moody founded Moody's Investors Service. In 1916, Poor's Publishing Company Published its first ratings, followed by the Standard Statistics Company in 1922, and Fitch Publishing Company in 1924. The Standard Statistics Company and the Poor's Publishing Company merged in 1941 to form Standard and Poor's which was subsequently taken over by McGraw-Hill in 1966. In the 1970s, a number of credit rating agencies commenced operations all over the world. These include the Canadian Bond Rating Service (1972), Thomson Bankwatch (1974), Japanese Bond Rating Institute (1975), McCarthy Crisanti and Maffei (1975), acquired by Duff and Phelps (1991), Dominican Bond Rating Service (1977), IBCA Limited (1978), and Duff and Phelps Credit Rating Co. (1980).

In India, the Credit Rating and Information Services India Ltd (CRISIL) was set up as the first credit rating agency in 1987, followed by ICRA Ltd (previously known as Investment Information and Credit Rating Agency of India Ltd) in 1991, and Credit Analysis and Research Ltd (CARE) in 1994.

The credit rating is thus a symbolic indicator of the relative capability of a corporate entity to service its debt obligations with specific reference to the instrument being rated. A rating is neither a general purpose evaluation of a corporate entity, nor an overall assessment of the credit risk likely to be involved in all the debts contracted or to be contracted by such entity.

A rating is an opinion on the future ability and legal obligation of an issuer to make timely payments of principal and interest on a specific fixed income security. The rating measures the probability that the issuer will default on the security over its life which depending on the instrument, may be a matter of days to 30 years or more. In addition, long term ratings incorporate an assessment of the expected monetary loss should a default occur. (www.moodys.co.in)

Credit rating does not amount to a recommendation to buy, hold, or sell an instrument as it does not take into consideration factors such as market prices, personal risk preferences, and other considerations which may influence an investment decision. Rating does not create any fiduciary relationship between a rating agency and the user of a rating as there is no legal basis for such a relationship. A credit rating agency does not perform an audit. It has to rely on information provided by the issuer and collected by the analysts from different sources, including interactions with different entities during the rating process. The primary objective of rating is to provide guidance to investors and creditors in determining a credit risk associated with a debt instrument and credit obligation.

CREDIT RATINGS IN INDIA

Credit rating is mandatory for issuance of the following instruments:

1. Public issue of debentures and bonds convertible/redeemable beyond a period of 18 months needs credit rating.
2. Commercial paper must not have a rating below the P2 grade from CRISIL, or AZ grade from ICRA and PR2 from CARE.
3. Non-banking finance companies (NBFCs) must get their fixed deposit programs rated. The minimum rating required by the NBFCs to be eligible to raise fixed deposits are FA(-) from CRISIL, MA(-) from ICRA, and BBB from CARE.
4. Rating of fixed deposit programs of limited companies, in case of NBFCs, is mandatory.

ESSENTIAL FEATURES FOR RATING SYSTEM

1. Credible and independent structure and procedures
   To quote from Standard & Poor's:

Ratings are of value only as long as they are credible. Credibility arises primarily from the objectivity which results from the rater being independent of the issuer's business. The investor is willing to accept the rater's judgment only where such credibility exists. When enough investors are willing to accept the judgment of a particular rater, that rater gains recognition as a rating agency.

2. An investor would be willing to look at rating as an important input for his investment decision only when there is a perceived default risk.
3. Creation of active debt market is crucial for rating agencies to continue to provide their services.

TYPES OF CREDIT RATING

Credit rating is of different types, depending upon the requirements of the rater and the rated. The following are the common types of credit ratings:

i. **Bond Rating:** Rating the bonds or debt securities issued by a company, government, or quasi-government body is called bond rating. This occupies the major business of credit rating agencies.

   i. **Equity Rating:** The rating of equity of capital market is called equity rating.
   ii. **Commercial Paper Rating:** It is mandatory on the part of a corporate body to obtain the rating of an approved credit rating agency to issue commercial paper. In India P1 rating is prescribed for issue of commercial paper by corporate bodies.

CREDIT RATING METHODOLOGY

The rating methodology followed by CRISIL involves an analysis of the following:

Business Analysis

1. Industry risk including analysis of the structure of the industry, the demand–supply position, a study of the *key* success factors, the nature and basis of competition, the impact of government policies, cyclicality and seasonality of the industry.
2. Market position of the company within the industry including market shares, product and customer diversity, competitive advantages, and selling and distribution arrangements.
3. Operating efficiency of the company; this would include locational advantages, labor relationships, technology, manufacturing efficiency as compared to competitors, etc.
4. Legal position including the terms of the prospectus, trustees and their responsibilities, and systems for timely payment.

Financial Analysis

1. **Accounting Quality:** This is of particular importance in India where till recently reporting practices of companies varied substantially. Here CRISIL would look at any overstatement/understatement of profits, auditors' qualifications in their report, methods of valuation of inventory, depreciation policy, etc.
2. **Earning Protection:** This would include sources of future earnings growth for the company, and future profitability.
3. **Adequacy of Cash Flows:** Under this, CRISIL would take note of whether cash flows would be sufficient to meet debt servicing requirements in addition to fixed and working capital needs. An opinion would be formed regarding the sustainability of the cash flows in future and the working capital management of the company.
4. **Financial Flexibility:** This is a very important area which would be examined minutely by any rating agency. A company's ability to source funds from other sources (e.g., group companies), ability to defer capital expenditure, and alternative financing plans in times of stress are some of the main considerations here.

Management Evaluation

A rating exercise would obviously not be an analysis of the numbers alone. The quality and ability of the management would be judged on the basis of past track record, their goals, philosophies and strategies, and their ability to overcome difficult situations would be analyzed. In addition to ability to repay, an assessment would be made of the management's willingness to repay debt. This would involve an opinion of the integrity of the management.

Regulatory and Competitive Environment

Structure and regulatory framework of the financial system would be examined. Trends in regulation/deregulation would also be examined keeping in view their likely impact on the company.

Fundamental Analysis

1. **Capital Adequacy:** An assessment of the true net worth, including its adequacy as compared to the volume of business and the risk profile of assets.
2. **Asset Quality:** This would encompass the company's credit risk management, systems for monitoring credit, exposure to individual borrowers, management of problem credits, etc.
3. **Liquidity Management:** Capital structure, term matching of assets and liabilities, and policy on liquid assets in relation to financing commitments would be some of the areas examined.

4. **Profitability and Financial Position**: A great deal of weightage would be paid by the agency on past historical profits, the spreads on funds deployed, accretions to reserves, etc.

5. **Interest and Tax Sensitivity**: Exposure to interest rate changes, tax law changes, etc., would be examined.

The procedures of rating adopted by other rating agencies are almost identical.

RATING OF SOVEREIGNS

Typically, the rating of issuers in a country is always lower than the rating assigned to the sovereign. This is because sovereigns have the power to levy taxes to augment their revenues. In some cases, however, the issuer may have cross-border operations which are insulated from the creditworthiness of the sovereign. The factors which are considered while assigning sovereign ratings are political risks, social and economic indicators, external relations, and performance of the external sector among others.

RATING PROCESS

The key systems and procedures of ratings are as follow:

1. The rating process begins with the receipt of mandate letter from the issuer company.

   Credit rating agency shall enter into a written agreement with each client whose securities it proposes to rate, and every such agreement shall include the following provisions, namely:

   (i) The rights and liabilities of each party in respect of the rating of securities shall be defined. The fee to be charged by the credit rating agency shall be specified.

   (ii) The client shall agree to a periodic review of the rating by the credit rating agency during the tenure of the rated instrument.

   (iii) The client shall agree to co-operate with the credit rating agency in order to enable the latter to arrive at, and maintain, a true and accurate rating of the client's securities and shall in particular provide to the latter, true, adequate, and timely information for the purpose.

   (iv) The credit rating agency shall disclose to the client the rating assigned to the securities of the latter through regular methods of dissemination, irrespective of whether the rating is or is not accepted by the client.

(v) The client shall agree to disclose, in the offer document:

- the rating assigned to the client's listed securities by any credit rating agency during the last 3 years; and
- any rating given in respect of the client's securities by any other credit rating agency, which has not been accepted by the client.

(vi) The client shall agree to obtain a rating from at least two different rating agencies for any issue of debt securities whose size is equal to or exceeds Rs 100 crores.

Credit rating agency shall, during the lifetime of securities rated by it, continuously monitor the rating of such securities.

2. Analytical teams are formed so as to draw on analytical and sectoral skills within the organization.

3. Analysts obtain credit-related data, both statistical and qualitative, from sources like annual reports, prospectus, industry, sectoral or economic data, government reports, news reports, regulatory, and other knowledgeable sources.

4. Meetings with management: Meetings are held with key operating personnel of the company covering broadly the background, history, organizational structure, operating performance, financial management, and topics of special relevance to the company's future. The central focus of all discussions is the same with analysts looking for information that will help them to understand the issuer's ability to generate cash from operations to meet debt obligations over the next several years. It is the management's opportunity to explain the company's business and financial strategies. Finally, a meeting with top management is held, where apart from corporate strategy and philosophy, key issues relevant to the rating are discussed.

5. Report preparation: After a thorough analysis of all the information collected during the rating process, a detailed report setting out all the parameters in the rating and list of key issues is prepared.

6. Rating meetings: The report is presented initially at a preview meeting and then to the rating committee. The composition of the rating committee is such as to ensure objectivity and impartiality.

7. Confidentiality: The specific nature of the information provided by company is kept strictly confidential.

8. Completion time: For new ratings, it normally takes two to four weeks after the information flow comes in to arrive at a final rating opinion. The time taken is determined by the complexity and diversity of the issuer's operations.

9. Review: Once the rating is assigned, it is communicated to the issuer. The issuer is given an opportunity to make one request for a review only in case fresh facts or clarifications have to be presented.

10. Acceptance: In India, the issuer has the option of not accepting the assigned rating in which case the rating is not disclosed by the rating agency. Once the rating is accepted, it comes under the surveillance process of the rating agency.

11. Market reporting: Once the rating is accepted, it is communicated to the relevant credit markets through press releases and publications of the rating agency.

Credit rating agency shall disseminate information regarding newly assigned ratings, and changes in earlier rating promptly through press releases and websites, and in the case of securities issued by listed companies, such information shall also be provided simultaneously to the concerned regional stock exchange and to all the stock exchanges where the said securities are listed.

Credit rating agency shall carry out periodic reviews of all published ratings during the lifetime of the securities.

If the client does not co-operate with the credit rating agency so as to enable the credit rating agency to review the credit rating given previously, it shall carry out the review on the basis of the best available information.

12. Surveillance: Apart from an ongoing review of the rated entity's performance, a detailed annual surveillance exercise is done. This reviews the major developments in the company during the period and their impact on the rating of the debt obligation.

RATING SYMBOLS

Each agency has its own rating symbol. We shall review rating symbols of CRISIL, CARE, and ICRA in the following.

Credit Rating Agencies in India

In India, there are four rating agencies, namely, (*a*) Credit Rating and Information Services of India Ltd (CRISIL), (*b*) Investment Information and Credit Rating Agency of India Ltd (ICRA), (*c*) Credit Analysis & Research (CARE), and (*d*) Duff & Phelps Credit Rating India (DCR), now known as FITCH.

CRISIL

CRISIL was jointly promoted, in 1988, by India's leading financial institutions, ICICI and Unit Trust of India (UTI). Its other shareholders include LIC, SBI, HDFC, GIC, Standard Chartered Bank, Bank of Tokyo, Banque Indo shez, Sakura Bank, UCO Bank, Canara Bank, Central Bank of India, Indian Overseas Bank (IOB), Vysya Bank Ltd, and Bank of Madura Ltd. CRISIL went public in 1992 and to date is India's only listed credit rating agency. In 1995, CRISIL entered into a strategic alliance with Standard & Poor's to extend its credit rating services to borrowers from the overseas market. The services offered are broadly classified as rating, information services, infrastructure services, and consultancy. CRISIL provides:

1. Rating services for ratings of debt instruments, long, medium, and short term, securitized assets, and builders.
2. Information services offering corporate research report and the CRISIL 500 Index.
3. The infrastructure and consultancy division assisting specific sectors such as power, telecom, and infrastructure financing.

Different rating symbols by Credit Rating Agencies for debentures indicate different meanings. For more details see Table 10.1 for CRISIL's rating symbols.

Table 10.1   CRISIL Rating Symbol—Debenture Rating Symbols High Investment Grades

AAA (Triple A) Highest Safety	Debentures rated "AAA" are judged to offer highest safety of timely payment of interest and principal. Though the circumstances providing this degree of safety are likely to change, such changes can be envisaged and are most unlikely to affect adversely the fundamentally strong position of such issues.
AA (Double A) High Safety Investment Grades	Debentures rated "AA" are judged to offer adequate safety of timely payment of interest and principal. They differ in safety from "AAA" issues only marginally.
A Adequate Safety	Debentures rated "A" are judged to offer adequate safety of timely payment of interest and principal. However, changes in circumstances can adversely affect such issues.
BBB (Triple B) Moderate Safety	Debentures rated "BBB" are judged to offer sufficient safety of timely payment of interest and principal for the present. However, changing circumstances are more likely to lead to a weakened capacity to pay interest and repay principal than for debentures in higher rated categories.
BB (Double B) Inadequate Safety	Debentures rated "BB" are judged to carry inadequate safety of timely payment of interest and principal.
B High Risk	Debentures rated "B" are judged to have greater susceptibility to default; while currently interest and principal payments are met, adverse business or economic conditions would lead to lack of ability or willingness to pay interest or principal.
C Substantial Risk	Debentures rated "C" are judged to have factors present that make them vulnerable to default. Timely payment of interest and principal is possible only if favorable circumstances continue.
D Default	Debentures rated "D" are in default and in arrears of interest or principal payments or are expected to default on maturity. Such debentures are extremely speculative and returns from these debentures may be realized only on reorganization or liquidation.

Source: CRISIL research team (2009).
Notes: 1. CRISIL may apply "+" (plus) or "–" (minus) signs for ratings from AA to C to reflect comparative standing within the category.
2. Preference share rating symbols are identical to debenture rating symbols except that the letter "pf" are prefixed to the rating symbols, for example, "pf" are prefixed to the rating symbols, for example, pfAAA ("pf Triple A").

Table 10.2 discusses the rating symbol of CRISIL for fixed deposits.

Table 10.2 CRISIL Fixed Deposit Rating Symbols Investment Grades

FAAA (F Triple A) Highest Safety	This rating indicates that the degree of safety regarding timely payment of interest and principal is very strong.
FAA (F Double A) High Safety	This rating indicates that the degree of safety regarding timely payment of interest and principal is strong.
FA Adequate Safety	This rating indicates that the degree of safety regarding timely payment of interest and principal is satisfactory.
Speculative Grade	
FB Inadequate Safety	This rating indicates inadequate safety of timely payment of interest and principal.
FC High Risk	This rating indicates that the degree of safety regarding timely payment of interest and principal is doubtful.
FD Default	This rating indicates that the issue is either in default or is expected to be in default upon maturity.

Source: CRISIL research team (2009).
Note: CRISIL may apply "+" (plus) or "–" (minus) signs for ratings from FAA to FC to indicate the relative position within the rating category.

Table 10.3 shows the rating symbols for short-term instruments.

Table 10.3 CRISIL Ratings for Short-term Instruments

P-1	This rating indicates that the degree of safety regarding timely payment on the instrument is very strong.
P-2	This rating indicates that the degree of safety regarding timely payment on the instrument is strong.
P-3	This rating indicates that the degree of safety regarding timely payment on the instrument is adequate.
P-4	This rating indicates that the degree of safety regarding timely payment on the instrument is minimal and it is likely to be adversely affected by short-term adversity or less favorable conditions.
P-5	This rating indicates that the instrument is expected to be in default on maturity or is in default.

Source: CRISIL research team (2009).

ICRA

ICRA, set up in 1991, has been promoted by IFCI and 21 other shareholders comprising foreign and nationalized banks and Indian insurance companies. It is the second rating agency in India. Services offered by ICRA can be broadly classified as analytical services, advisory services, and investment services.

1. The analytical services comprise rating of debt instruments and credit assessment.
2. Advisory services include strategic counseling general assessment such as restructuring exercise and sector-specific services such as for power, telecom, ports, and municipal ratings.
3. The information or the research desk provides research reports on specific industry, sector, and corporate.
4. The information services also include equity-related services, namely, equity grading and equity assessment.

In 1996, ICRA entered into a strategic alliance with Financial Proforma Inc., a Moody's subsidiary to offer services on risk management training and software. Moody's and ICRA have entered into a memorandum of understanding to support these efforts.

Like CRISIL, another rating agency called ICRA also provides different rating symbols. See Table 10.4 for more details.

Table 10.4   ICRA Rating Scale

Long-Term instruments—including Debentures, Bonds, Preference Shares

LAAA	Highest safety. Indicates fundamentally strong position. Risk factors are negligible.
LAA+	High safety. Risk factors are modest and may vary slightly. The protective factors
LAA	are strong and the prospect of timely payment of principal and interest as per
LAA–	terms under adverse circumstances, as may be visualized, differs from LAAA only marginally.
LA+	Adequate safety. The risk factors are more variable and greater in periods of
LA	economic stress. The protective factors are average and any adverse change in
LA–	circumstances, as may be visualized, may alter the fundamental strength and affect the timely payment of principal and interest as per terms.
LBBB+	Moderate safety. Considerable variability in risk factors. The protective factors
LBBB	are below average.
LBBB–	
LBB+	Inadequate safety. The timely payment of interest and principal are more
LBB	likely to be affected by present or prospective changes in business/economic
LBB–	circumstances.
LB+	Risk prone. Risk factors indicate that obligations may not be met when due.
LB	
LB–	
LC+	Substantial risk. There are inherent elements of risk and timely servicing of
LC	debts/obligations could be possible only in case of continued existence of
LC–	favorable circumstances.
LD	Default. Extremely speculative. Either already in default in payment or interest and/or principal as per terms or expected to default. Recovery is likely only on liquidation or re-organization.

Source: CRISIL research team (2009).

CARE

CARE has been promoted, in 1992, by IDBI jointly with Canara Bank, UTI, private sector banks, and insurance companies. The services offered by CARE include credit rating of debt instruments, credit assessment of companies, advisory services, credit reports, and performance ratings.

1. CARE undertakes ratings of all types of debt instruments of all maturities, including short-term instruments like commercial paper and certificates of deposits not exceeding 12 months; and medium-and long-term instruments like term deposits, floating rate notes, bonds, and debentures.
2. CARE also undertakes rating of securitized paper and structured obligations.
3. CARE undertakes credit assessment of companies for use by banks and financial institutions. It is without reference to any particular instrument. CARE analyzes the overall debt; management of the company and its capacity to service its obligations.
4. CARE also undertakes "performance rating" of parallel marketers of liquefied petroleum gas (LPG) and superior kerosene oil (SKO), as per the scheme notified by Ministry of Petroleum and Natural Gas, Government of India.

CARE rating agency has also given its own rating symbols for long-term and medium-term instruments. See Table 10.5 for more details on the same.

Table 10.5 CARE Rating Symbols Long-term and Medium-term Instruments

CARE AAAC CARE AAA (FD)/(CD)/(SO)	Instruments carrying this rating are considered to be of the best quality, carrying negligible investment risk. Debt service payments are protected by stable cash flows. While the underlying assumptions may change, such changes as can (FD)/(CD)/(SO) be visualized and are most unlikely to impair the strong position of such instruments.
CARE AA CARE AA (FD)/(CD)/(SO)	Instruments carrying this rating are judged to be of high quality by all standards. They are also classified as high investment grade. CARE AA securities are rated lower than CARE AAA because of somewhat lower margins of protection. Changes in assumptions may have a greater impact or the long-term risks may be somewhat larger. Overall, the difference from CARE AAA rated securities is marginal.
CARE A CARE A (FD)/(CD)/(SO)	Instruments with this rating are considered upper medium grade instruments and have many favorable investment attributes. Safety for principal and interest are considered adequate in CARE A. Assumptions that do not materialize may have a greater impact as compared to the instruments rated higher.
CARE BBB CARE BBB (FD)/(CD)/(SO)	Such instruments are considered to be of investment grade. They indicate sufficient safety for payment of interest and principal, at the time of rating. However, adverse CARE BBB changes in assumptions are more likely to weaken the debt servicing capability compared to the higher rated instruments.
CARE BB CARE BB (FD)/(CD)/(SO)	Such instruments are considered to be speculative, with inadequate protection for interest and principal payments.
CARE B CARE B (FD)/(CD)/(SO)	Instruments with such rating are generally classified susceptible to default. While interest and principal payments are being met, adverse changes in business conditions are likely to lead to default.
CARE C CARE C (FD)/(CD)/(SO)	Such instruments carry high investment risk with likelihood of default in the payment of interest and principal.

Short-term Instruments

Grades	Commercial Paper
High Investment Grade	PR-1
Medium Investment Grade	PR-2
Investment Grade	PR-3
Speculative Grade	PR-3
Speculative Grade	PR-4
Poor Grade	PR-5

Source: CARE research team (2009).

Duff & Phelps Credit Rating India (DCR)

DCR is a joint venture between Duff & Phelps, USA and Alliance Capital Ltd, Calcutta. Its expertise is in the rating of structured obligations with international standards. It offers rating of all other short-term, medium-term, and long-term debt instruments.

11

Venture Capital

Learning Objectives

- To learn the concepts and mechanics of venture capital.
- To know about regulatory framework for venture capital in India.

VENTURE CAPITAL (VC)

Venture capital is a means of equity financing for rapidly growing private companies. Finance may be required for the start-up, development and expansion, or purchase of a company. Venture capital firms invest funds on a professional basis, often focusing on a limited sector of specialization, for example, IT, infrastructure, health/life sciences, or clean technology.

With venture capital financing, the venture capitalist acquires an agreed proportion of the equity of the company in return for the funding. Equity finance offers the significant advantage of having no interest charges. It is "patient" capital that seeks a return through long-term capital gain rather than immediate and regular interest payments, as in the case of debt financing. Given the nature of equity financing, venture capital investors are therefore exposed to the risk of the company failure. As a result the venture capitalist must look to invest in companies which have the ability to grow very successfully and provide higher than average returns to compensate for the risk.

Economics defines venture capital as providing seed, start-up and first stage financing, and also funding the expansion of companies that have already demonstrated their business potential but do not yet have access to the public securities market or to credit-oriented institutional funding sources.

The European Venture Capital Association describes it,

as risk finance for entrepreneurial growth oriented companies. It is investment for the medium to long term return for both parties. It is a partnership with the entrepreneur in which the investor can add value to the company because of his knowledge, experience and contact base.

International Finance Corporation, Washington DC defines "VC as an equity or equity featured capital seeking investment in view of ideas, new companies, new products, new processes or new services that offer the potential of high returns on investment. It may also include investment in turnaround situations."

Initially, Securities and Exchange Board of India (SEBI) defined venture capital as an equity support for projects launched by first generation entrepreneurs using commercially untested but sophisticated technologies. However, this definition has been subsequently relaxed and the restrictive features concerning "technology financing" were dispensed with.

Venture capital is thus a long-term investment that often requires the venture capitalist to wait for five or more years before realizing a significant return on the capital resource.

It would appear from the foregoing that venture capital investments would have one or more of the following characteristics:

1. equity or equity-featured instrument of investment;
2. young companies that do not have access to public sources of equity or other forms of capital;
3. industry, products, or services that hold potential of better than normal or average revenue growth rates;
4. companies with better than normal or average profitability;
5. products/services in the early stages of their life cycle;
6. higher than average risk levels that do not lend themselves to systematic quantification through conventional techniques and tools;
7. turnaround companies; or
8. long-term (more than three years) and active involvement with investors.

HISTORY AND EVOLUTION OF VENTURE CAPITAL

Since its humble beginnings in 1946 through the American Research and Development Corporation of General Detroit "the institutionalization of the venture investment process" has made significant strides. Venture capital in one form or the other has come to stay in over 35 countries including Japan, South Korea, Philippines, Singapore, Malaysia, Taiwan, and India in Asia, Kenya and Nigeria in Africa, and Argentina and Brazil in South America.

VENTURE CAPITAL INDUSTRY IN INDIA

In India, the venture capital industry had its formal introduction with the budget speech of the finance minister in 1988, though extremely focused in its technology development objective. Coincidentally around the same time, the Industrial Credit and Investment Corporation of India (ICICI) came forth with initiatives for addressing technology-intensive projects. One such initiative, the Venture Capital Division, was spun off into Technology Development and Information Company of India Limited (TDICI) which has since emerged as a significant player and pioneer in the industry.

There are more than 132 venture capital funds and 129 foreign venture capital funds that are operating in India. Broadly, there are three categories of VCFs/companies going by the agencies that have promoted them. They are: (*a*) funds promoted by all-India Development Finance Institutions (DFIs)/state level DFIs, (*b*) funds promoted by commercial banks, and (*c*) funds promoted by private sector financial services companies.

Venture Capital in India: Glimpses

1. Phase I: Formation of TDICI in the 1980s and regional funds such as Gujarat Venture Finance Ltd (GVFL) and Andhra Pradesh Industrial Development Corporation (APIDC) in the early 1990s.
2. Phase II: Entry of foreign VCFs between 1995 and 1999.
3. Phase III (2000 onwards): Emergence of successful India-centric VC firms.
4. Phase IV (current): Global venture capitalists and Private Equity (PE) firms actively investing in India.
5. 150 funds active in the last 3 years (government, overseas, corporate, domestic).

Financing Instruments

The Indian venture capital industry has innovative instruments for structuring the venture investment to meet following challenges:

1. constraints on pricing imposed by the securities pricing regulations;
2. Indian entrepreneurial ethos which lays considerable emphasis on ownership and control of the company; and
3. company law regulations under Section 43 (a), Section 370, etc.

Types of Venture Capital Funds

These could be classified into three broad categories:

1. Equity investments
2. Quasi equity forms of hybrid debt
3. Normal loan

THE VENTURE INVESTMENT PROCESS

Activities in a venture capital fund follow the following sequence:

1. Generating a deal
2. Due diligence
3. Investment valuation
4. Pricing and structuring the deal
5. Value addition and monitoring
6. Exit

Generating a Deal

In generating a deal, the venture capital investor creates a pipeline of "deals" or investment opportunities that he would consider for investing in. The VCFs focusing on early stage, technology-based deals would develop a network of R&D centers working in those areas.

Due Diligence

Due diligence is associated with evaluating an investment proposal. It includes carrying out reference checks on the proposal-related aspects such as management team, products, technology, and market. The important feature to note is that venture capital due diligence focuses on the qualitative aspects of an investment opportunity.

Investment Valuation

The investment valuation process is an exercise aiming to arrive at "an acceptable price" for the deal. An evaluation process may have following sequence:

1. Evaluate future revenue and profitability.
2. Forecast likely future value of the firm based on expected market capitalization or expected acquisition proceeds depending upon the anticipated exit from the investment.
3. Target on ownership position in the invested firm so as to achieve desired appreciation on the proposed investment. The appreciation desired should yield a hurdle rate of return on a discounted cash flow basis.
4. Symbolically the valuation exercise may be represented as follows:
   $NPV = (Cash)/(Post) \, I \times [(PAT \times PER)] \times k$; where,

   - NPV = net present value of the cash flows relating to the investment comprising outflow by way of investment and inflows by way of interest/dividends (if any) and realization on exit. The rate of return used for discounting is the hurdle rate of return set by the venture capital investor.
   - Post = Pre + Cash.

- Cash represents the amount of cash being brought into the particular round of financing by the venture capital investor.
- "Pre" is the pre-money valuation of the firm estimated by the investor. While technically it is measured by the intrinsic value of the firm at the time of raising capital, it is more often a matter of negotiation driven by the ownership of the company that the venture capital investor desire and the ownership that the founders/management team is prepared to giggle away for the required amount of capital. PAT is the forecast of profit after tax in a year and often agreed upon by the founders and the investors (as opposed to being arrived at unilaterally). It would also be net of preferred dividends, if any. PER is the price earning multiple that could be expected of a comparable firm in the industry. "k" is the present value interest factor corresponding to a discount rate "r" for the investment horizon. It is quite apparent that PER times PAT represents the value of the firm at that time and the complete expression really represents the investor's share of the value of the investor firm.

In reality the valuation of the firm is driven by a number of factors. The more significant among these are:

1. Overall economic conditions: A buoyant economy produces an optimistic long-term outlook for new products/services and, therefore, results in more liberal pre-money valuations.
2. Demand and supply of capital: When there is a surplus of venture capitalists chasing a relatively limited number of venture capital deals.
3. Specifics of the deals: The founder's management of team's track record, innovativeness/unique selling propositions (USPs), the service, potential size of product/market, etc., affects valuations in an obvious manner.
4. The degree of popularity of the industry/technology in question also influences the pre-money. Computer Aided Software Engineering (CASE) tools and artificial intelligence were onetime darlings of the venture capitalist community that have subsequently given place to biotech and retailing.
5. The standing of the individual venture capitalist: Well-established venture capitalists who are sought after by entrepreneurs, for a number of reasons, could get away with tighter valuation than their lesser known counterparts.
6. Investor's considerations could vary significantly. A study by an American venture capitalist, Venture One, showed that large corporations who invest for strategic advantages such as access to technologies, products, or markets pay twice as much as a professional venture capital investor for a given ownership position in a company but only half as much as to investors in a public offering.
7. Valuation offered on comparable deals around the time of investing in the deal.

Structuring the Deal

Venture capital investments require and permit innovativeness in financial engineering. While venture capital investments follow no set formula, they attempt to address the needs and concerns of the investor and the investee.

The investor tries to ensure the following:

 i. reasonable reward for the given level of risks;
 ii. sufficient influence on the management of the company through board representation;
 iii. minimization of taxes; and
 iv. ease in achieving future liquidity on the investment.

The entrepreneur at the same time seeks to enable:

 i. the creation of the business that he has conceptualized (operating and strategic control);
 ii. financial rewards for creating the business;
 iii. adequate resources needed to achieve their goal; and
 iv. voting control.

Common considerations for both sides include:

 i. flexibility of structure that will allow room to enable additional investments later, incentives for future management, and retention of stock if management leaves;
 ii. balance sheet attractiveness to suppliers and debt financiers; and
 iii. retention of key employees through adequate equity participation.

Value Addition and Monitoring

The venture capitalist continuously monitors the performance of the project and keeps on assessing the value addition to his investment. A venture capitalist may, therefore, require regular cash flow statement and operational performance statement to compare with projected cash flow and income statement. He also tries to read out the difficulties in the implementation of the project.

Exit

A venture capitalist may like to exit from his investment in a venture at an opportune time either through diluting his stake through capital market (public issue) or to any other strategic investor. Thus, by arresting the appreciation on the investment, the same investment is now available for other venture.

STAGES IN VENTURE CAPITAL FUNDING

"Start-up Financing" is provided to companies completing product development and initial marketing. Companies may be in the process of organizing or they may already be in business for 1 year or less but may have not sold their product commercially. Usually such firms will have made market studies, assembled the key management, developed a business plan, and are ready to do business.

"First Stage Financing" is provided to companies that have expended their initial capital (often in developing and market testing a prototype) and require funds to initiate full-scale manufacturing and sales.

"Second Stage Financing" is working capital for the initial expansion of a company that is producing and shipping and has growing accounts receivable and inventories. Although the company has made progress, it may not be showing profits yet.

"Third Stage or Mezzanine Financing" is provided for major expansion of a company when sales volume is increasing and that is breaking even or profitable. These funds are used for further plant expansion, marketing, working capital, or development of an improved product.

"Bridge Financing" is needed at times when a company plans to go public within 6 months to 1 year. Often, bridge financing is structured so that it can be repaid from the proceeds of a public underwriting. It can also involve restructuring of major stockholder positions through secondary transactions. Restructuring is undertaken if there are early investors who want to reduce or liquidate their positions or if management had changed and the stockholdings of the former management, their relatives and associates are being bought out to relieve a potential over-supply of stock when going public.

"Acquisition (Buyout) Financing" provides funds to finance an acquisition of another company. Management/leveraged buyout funds enable an operating management group to acquire a product line or business (which may be at any stage of development) from either a public or private company; often these companies are closely held or family owned. Management/LBOs usually involve revitalizing an operation with entrepreneurial management acquiring a significant equity interest.

REGULATORY ISSUES WITH VENTURE CAPITAL INDUSTRY IN INDIA

Venture capital industry was sought to be developed by the government by giving tax breaks and concessions on the income of venture capital company (VCC)/VCF. As per SEBI regulations, VCF/VCC are allowed to function irrespective of whether they want to claim the concession under tax laws or not. Under Section 10(23F) of the Income Tax Act, the income of VCF/VCC is totally exempt from income tax by way of dividend and long-term capital gain from equity investment provided they satisfy the following eligibility criteria:

1. It is registered with SEBI.
2. It invests an amount not less than 80 percent of its total money raised for investment by acquiring equity shares of venture capital undertakings in the following manner:
   i. Twenty percent or more of such monies shall be invested during or before the end of the previous year in which the application is made by way of acquiring equity shares of the venture capital undertakings.

   ii. Fifty percent or more such monies (including the investment referred earlier) shall be invested during or before the end of previous year immediately succeeding the previous year in which investment of 20 percent as referred in (i) in the foregoing has been made, by way of acquiring equity shares of the venture capital undertakings.

   iii. Eighty percent or more of such monies (including the investments referred earlier) shall be invested, during or before the end of the previous year immediately succeeding the investment, referred in (ii) has been made, by way of acquiring equity shares of the venture capital undertakings.

3. It invests an amount not less than 80 percent of its total paid-up capital by way of acquiring equity shares of the venture capital undertaking in the following manner, namely:

   i. Tewnty percent or more of such capital shall be invested during or before the end of the previous year in which the application is made by way of acquiring equity shares of the venture capital undertakings.

   ii. Fifty percent or more of such capital (including the investment in the foregoing) shall be invested during or before end of the previous year immediately succeeding the previous year in which investment of 20 percent as referred in the foregoing has been made, by way of acquiring equity shares of the venture capital undertakings.

   iii. Eighty percent or more of such capital (including investment in the foregoing) shall be invested during or before the end of the previous year immediately succeeding the previous year in which the 50 percent investment, referred earlier, by way of acquiring equity shares of the venture capital undertakings.

4. It shall not invest more than 5 percent of its total monies raised or total paid-up capital in one venture capital undertaking.

5. It shall not invest more than 40 percent in the equity capital of one venture capital undertaking.

6. It shall maintain books of accounts, get these audited by a chartered accountant and furnish to the Director of Income Tax (Exemption).

Other regulations concerning the venture capital industry are:

1. Section 372 of the Indian Companies Act, 1956 (Companies Act, henceforth) precludes all corporate, other than the recognized VCFs approved under the government guidelines from making significant venture capital investments.

2. Section 43(A) of the Companies Act acts as a deterrent. Consequently, investment by a public company venture capital investor beyond 25 percent of paid-up capital would entail loss of the legal status and accompanying privileges of a private company to the investee.

3. The government guidelines on venture capital companies are in itself a source of several restraints to even an approved venture capital investor. These include:

   i. regulation of portfolio composition;

   ii. technology/innovativeness requirement in qualifying projects;

   iii. volume of capital (minimum) to be raised, sources from which the capital may be raised, and capital structure of the venture capital company; and

   iv. composition of non-venture capital assets in the VCF portfolio.

4. Income from dividends and capital gains from equity investments is exempted for the venture capital companies, whereas it is taxable in the case of shareholders.

   As mentioned earlier, venture capital may be provided by the VCFs established as trusts or VCCs established under the Companies Act. SEBI rules permit establishment of venture capital institutions under either of the methods provided:

1. VCFs set up asset management companies (AMCs) that screen, make, and manage individual investments.

2. VCC established as a company satisfies the eligibility criteria drafted by SEBI for the purpose of registration, namely:

   i. Memorandum of association has its main activity of carrying out the business of venture capital fund.

   ii. Memorandum and articles of association explicitly prohibits invitation to the public to subscribe to its securities.

3. VCF established as a trust satisfies the eligibility criteria drafted by SEBI for the purpose of registration, namely:

   i. The instrument of trust is in the form of a deed and has been duly registered under the provisions of the Indian Registration Act, 1908.

   ii. The main objective of the trust is to carry on the activity of a VCF.

K.B. CHANDRASEKHAR COMMITTEE ON VENTURE CAPITAL

Recognizing the acute need for higher investment in venture capital activities to promote technology and knowledge-based enterprises, SEBI appointed a committee headed by Shri K. B. Chandrasekhar to identify the impediments in the growth of the venture capital industry in India and suggest suitable measures. The board considered the report of the committee and approved the recommendations in principle. The recommendations, inter alia, include harmonization of multiple regulatory requirements into a nodal regulatory system under SEBI, tax pass through for VCF, flexibility in investment and exit, facilitating mobilization of global and domestic resources through hassle-free entry of foreign venture capital investors on the pattern of foreign institutional investors (FIIs), and increase in the list of sophisticated institutional investors to invest in VCFs. The recommendations for incentives for employees by providing Employee Stock Option Plans (ESOPs) in foreign companies and global opportunities of investment for domestic funds and venture undertakings were also accepted. The matters directly related to SEBI such as relaxation of entry norms for initial public offerings (IPOs) of venture-funded companies to treat the funding by registered VCF for entry eligibility in the lines of banks/financial institutions and exemption from Takeover Code in certain situations were also approved in principle.

An entrepreneur has the choice of taking a loan or he may go for a buy out deal or also may approach venture capitalists for requirement of funds. He makes a comparison among the three options, that is, between venture capital, buy out deals and loan, for making a sound decision. Refer to Table 11.1 for more details.

Table 11.1   Comparing Venture Capital with Bought out Deals and Conventional Loan Financing

	Venture Capital	*Bought Out Deal*	*Conventional Loan Financing*
Participation in Management	High. As the VCF/VCC has an equity stake in the Venture Capital Unit (VCU), it is generally bound to follow the advice. Also, considering the expertise of VCC/VCF, participation is high in strategic planning.	Low. Though the equity in the company is held by the sponsor, there would not be any direct interference in the management except in exceptional cases.	Nil. The lender does not have the expertise or interest in promoting the company as long as the payments schedule is followed.
Returns to the Investor	Extremely high in most of the cases considering the high risk in such investment. Uncertainly is quite high.	High. The company is not into technologically intensive. Exit from the investment is reasonably certain.	Moderate. As the payment schedule is finalized before the investment, there is no uncertainty.
Time Period	Very long. Exit from investment takes 7–10 years on an average.	Not very long. Exit from investment is normally done immediately after the expiry of lock-in period.	May be set as per choice of the investor/lender.
Regulations	Not high as the venture capital is considered reasonably nascent for regulations to be in place. Also, with high risk being inherent in the investment process, regulations only oversee the process of such investment not the safety.	High. Bought out deals are reasonably well regulated as it concerns listing of security in the stock exchange where small investor's interest have to be protected.	Moderate. Regulations cover the safety of such investments/lending.

Source: Author's compilation.

Venture capital funds have various types of investments in various types of industries. Refer to Table 11.2 for more details.

THE OPPORTUNITY FOR VENTURE CAPITAL IN INDIA

The following points suggest tremendous opportunity for venture capital:

1. high growth in technology and knowledge-based industries (KBI);
2. KBI growing fast and mostly global, less affected by domestic issues;

Table 11.2   Venture Capital/PE Investments by Stage and Investment Profiles in Ventures by Types of Industry in 2007

Type of Industry	Number of Deals	Value USD Million in India	Share (%)
IT and ITES	48	876	15.51
Manufacturing	14	389	6.89
Health care and Life Science	13	126	2.23
Textile and Garments	6	160	2.83
BFSI	26	2,121	37.55
Hotels and Resorts	3	104	1.84
Media and Entertainment	9	413	7.31
Engineering and Construction	13	812	14.38
Shipping and Logistics	9	257	4.55
Energy	3	98	1.74
Telecom	2	50	0.89
Others	16	242	4.28
Total	162	5,648	

Source: TSJ (2007).

3. several emerging centers of innovation—biotech, wireless, IT, semiconductor, pharmaceutical;
4. ability to build market-leading companies in India which serve both global and domestic markets;
5. India moving beyond supplier of low-cost services to higher-value products; and
6. quality of entrepreneurship on ascending curve.

ADVANTAGES OF VENTURE CAPITAL

1. It injects long-term equity finance which provides a solid capital base for future growth.
2. The venture capitalist is a business partner, sharing both the risks and rewards. Venture capitalists are rewarded by business success and the capital gain. The venture capitalist is able to provide practical advice and assistance to the company based on past experience with other companies which were in similar situations.
3. The venture capitalist also has a network of contacts in many areas that can add value to the company, such as in recruiting key personnel, providing contacts in international markets, introducing to strategic partners, and if needed co-investing with other venture capital firms when additional rounds of financing are required.
4. The venture capitalist may be capable of providing additional rounds of funding should it be required to finance growth.

12

Factoring Services

Learning Objectives

- To learn the concept and types of factoring.
- To understand the mechanics of factoring.

MEANING AND CONCEPT

Factoring is a method of financing whereby a firm sells its trade debts at a discount to a financial institution. In other words, factoring is a continuous arrangement between a financial institution (namely the factor) and a firm (namely the client) which sells goods and services to trade customers on credit. As per the arrangement, the factor purchases the client's trade debts including accounts receivables either with or without recourse to the client, and thus, exercises control over the credit extended to the customers and administers the sale ledger of his client. Factoring is the financing of receivables. In the process, cash flow is accelerated, purchasing power increases, production moves up, and credit rating improves. In other words, the factor purchases the book debt of a supplier, releases the capital tied up in accounts receivables, and provides financial accommodation to the suppliers. The book debts of the supplier are assigned to the factor who collects them on maturity on payment of charges in terms of discount. To put it in a layman's language, a factor is an agent who collects the dues of his client for a certain fee.

Factoring services, thus simply stated, involve assignment of book debt or account receivable by clients in favor of the factoring company for a consideration. The origin of factoring dates back to the 19th century when in countries like the USA, UK, and France specialized financial institutions were established to assist the firms in meeting their working capital requirements by purchasing the receivables. The word factor is derived from Latin word *"facere,"* which means to make or do or to get things done. In other words, factor is an agent who does things for his principal, that is, the client, for a consideration called commission. The factoring services thus assume the form of financial agency, collection agency, and insurance cover against bad debts.

CONTRACT OF FACTORING

Factoring is an arrangement or contract between the factor and the supplier and is governed by the law of contract. The terms of the factoring contract are mutually settled and reduced in writing. The important aspects of the factoring contract are:

1. offer to sell book debts on terms and conditions mutually agreed;
2. acceptance of the offer by the factor with the right to enforce debts and rights of an unpaid seller vested in him;
3. power of attorney from supplier to the factor;
4. determination and payment of purchase price of debts;
5. conditions for recourse or non-recourse factoring;
6. notice of sale or assignment of debts to be endorsed on invoices to enable the factor to recover debts;
7. non-collection of dues directly by the supplier;
8. credit allowed to buyers to be advised to factor;
9. commission, fee, and charges, and payment thereof;
10. duration of agreement;
11. other warranties and covenants;
12. notice of termination; and
13. jurisdiction.

TYPES OF FACTORING SERVICES

The various services offered by factors for domestic sales are: (*a*) factoring, (*b*) resource factoring, (*c*) advanced factoring, (*d*) maturity factoring, and (*e*) undisclosed factoring. Some other factoring services may include:

1. **Notified Factoring:** In the case of notified factoring, the customer is intimated about the assignment of debt to the factor and also directed to make payments to the factor instead of the firm. This is invariably stated on the face of the invoice that the receivables arising out for the invoice has been assigned to the factor.
2. **Non-notified or Confidential Factoring:** This facility is one under which the supplier/ factor arrangement is not declared to the customer unless or until there is a breach of the agreement on the part of the supplier or, exceptionally, where the factor considers himself to be at risk.

3. **Factoring with Recourse/without Recourse:** Whether notified or not, factoring can be further classified as with recourse and without recourse factoring. Under with recourse arrangement, the supplier will carry the credit risk in respect of receivables he has sold to the factor. The factor will have recourse in the event of non-payment for whatever reason, including the financial inability of the customer to pay. Effectively, the factor has the option to sell back to the supplier any receivables not paid by a customer regardless of the reason for non-payment. In without recourse factoring the bad debts are borne by the factoring agent or factor. However, the factor commission would be higher in without recourse factoring. With recourse factoring is similar to bill discounting scheme.

4. **Credit Factoring:** The factor purchases book debts with recourse to the seller and provides finance; interest is charged until the bill amount is collected from the buyer of goods. All work connected with sales administration and collection of dues is to be done by the client himself.

5. **Debt Administration Factoring:** It involves no financing. The service provided is purely administrative. The factor will administer the sale ledger and forward the invoice to the buyer and collect debt on the due date.

6. **Bulk Factoring:** This is only a variation of invoice discounting in which finance is provided by the factor only after the assignment of debt is notified by the seller to the debtor with instructions to make payment to the factor.

7. **Bank Participation Factoring:** In bank participation factoring, the supplier creates a floating charge on the factoring reserves in favor of banks and borrow against these reserves. For instance, if factor reserve is 20 percent, the supplier firm can borrow to the extent of 80 percent, of this reserve from bank, thereby reducing its investments on receivable.

8. **International Factoring:** This deals with export sales. The factoring service may include completing legal and procedural formalities pertaining to export.

MODUS OPERANDI OF FACTORING

In the normal course of business transactions of credit sales generally the factoring business is involved. Realization of credit sales is the main function of a factoring firm. Once a sale transaction is completed and the invoice is raised on the buyer, the factor is approached by the seller to realize the bill amount from the buyer of goods or services.

The modus operandi includes:

The Sale of Goods and Services

i. Sells goods to the buyer as per the terms of agreement and invoices him in the usual way—only inscribing an instruction to the effect that the invoice is assigned to the factor and payment should be made to the factor.

ii. Hands over copies of invoices, deliver challan to the factor under cover of a schedule of offer, lorry receipts or railway receipts (the seller should not raise a bill of exchange on the buyer).

iii. The factor makes payment up to 80 percent of the value of the assigned invoice.
iv. The seller will receive balance payment from the factor after the deduction of factor's service charges, etc., after the buyer makes payment for the invoice, the factor.

Functions of Factor

Depending on the type of factoring, the main functions of a factor are:

i. Collection of receivables.
ii. Sale ledger management.
iii. Financing of trade debts.
iv. Credit investigation and undertaking of credit.

Accounting Procedure at Bank

All bills discounted or purchased should be entered in the bills discounted or purchased register in serial order and the serial number is changed annually. Particulars of documents, due date, and other relevant details to be recorded legibly.

i. In realization of the bill, it should be marked off with date of actual realization.
ii. The outstanding items in the bills discounted or purchased register should be reviewed at frequent intervals preferably every Friday, and reminders are to be sent for the pending bills for clearance. The dates of such reminders are also noted in the remarks column.
iii. The details of all the bills returned unpaid should be noted in the "bills returned unpaid register."
iv. These bills of customers are generally returned unrealized, therefore there is a need to realize the outstanding liability and to stop the discounting facility given to such customers.
v. Subsidiary ledger showing party-wise details should be maintained to watch that the bills purchased are within the limit sanctioned.
vi. At periodical intervals, the individual outstanding bills purchased or discounted should be extracted from the register of bills purchased or discounted and tallied with the outstanding in the general ledger.

THE RBI GUIDELINES

The Reserve Bank of India (RBI), in the light of the recommendations of the expert group headed by C.S. Kalyansunderam, issued the following guidelines in 1988 for banking companies to start factoring services:

1. Banks shall not undertake directly the factoring business. While banks may invest in shares of other factoring companies, they shall not act as promoters of such companies. Banks may set up separate subsidiaries or invest in factoring companies jointly with other banks with the approval of RBI.
2. A factoring company may undertake factoring business and such other activities as are incidental thereto.
3. Investment of a bank in the shares of factoring companies inclusive of its subsidiaries carrying factoring business should not in aggregate exceed 10 percent of the paid-up capital and reserves of the bank.
4. Banks or their subsidiaries undertaking factoring business are required to furnish the required information to RBI periodically.

RBI has preferred banks to operate in factoring business through separate subsidiaries and not through their merchant banking divisions because the nature of factoring business is different from merchant banking and its involves handling of voluminous paper work and large amount of money on an on-going basis.

In India the State Bank of India (SBI) has set up a subsidiary called SBI Factor Ltd.

FORFAITING

Forfaiting is a technique to help the exporter to sell his goods on credit and yet receive the cash well before the due date. The word "forfaiting" evolved from the French word "forfeit" which means, the exporter forfeits/surrenders his rights or claims to payment which he could have received in future in lieu of immediate cash payment. In other words, forfaiting involves en-cashing future trade receivables now, at a charge. Thus, the total cost of forfaiting comprises a commission and an interest if the firm draws an advance against receivables. Alternatively, it is also possible that the exporter may leave his funds after collection with the forfeiter to receive an interest from him.

Table 12.1 describes the comparison between international factoring and international forfaiting.

Benefits of International Forfaiting

i. . **Benefits to Exporters:**
   a. Flexibility in operation
   b. Assured payment
   c. Relief from maintaining records, etc.
ii. **Benefits to Importers:**
   a. 100 percent finance
   b. Flexible finance

Table 12.1 International Factoring versus International Forfaiting

Basis	International Factoring	International Forfaiting
Meaning	It is a method whereby the factor undertakes to collect the debts assigned by exporters.	It is a method whereby the exporter sells the export bills to the forfeiter and obtains cash.
Nature of Facility	Money comes to exporters only after collection of bills by the factor.	Money comes to the exporter even before the collection of exporter's debt.
Position of Agent	Factor acts as an agent of exporters to whom the accounts receivables are assigned by exporters.	Forfeiters, after having made payment to exporters, become sole owners to collect the debts.
Risk	The factor does not undertake the risk which lies with the exporter.	The forfeiters after buying the exporters' debts assume full risk.
Relationship	Relationship between the exporter and the factor continues even after the assignment of debts by exporters.	After the sale of debts on discount by exporters the relationship between the exporter and the forfeiter is served as far as that particular transaction is concerned.
Nature of Credit Covered	Factoring covers export of consumer goods for relatively short period.	Forfaiting covers export of capital goods by medium and large firms.

Source: Author's compilation.

ILLUSTRATION

A manufacturing firm has a total sale of Rs 180 lakhs and its average collection period is 90 days. The past experience indicates that bad-debt losses are around 2 percent of credit sales. The firm spends Rs 500,000 on administering its sales which includes salaries of one officer and three clerical personnel who handle credit checking, collection, etc., telephone and telex charges which are unavoidable costs. A factor is prepared to forward to buy the firm's receivables by charging 2 percent commission. A factor will pay advance receivables to a concern at an interest rate of 20 percent after withholding 10 percent as reserve.

WORKING NOTE

1. Average level of receivables:
    Credit sale = Rs 180,00,000
    Average collection period = 90 days
    Average level of receivables = $18,000,000 \times 90/360$ = Rs 4,500,000
2. Factoring commission and reserve is 2 and 10 percent respectively of cost of average receivables to 90 days.

    (a) Factoring commission = $4,500,000 \times 2/100$ = Rs 90,000
    (b) Reserve = $4,500,000 \times 10/100$ = Rs 4,50,000

3. Amount available for advance:
   Amount available = 4,500,000 – 90,000 – 4,50,000 = Rs 3,960,000

However, the factor will also deduct interest on his advance @ 20 percent p.a. before paying advance for 90 days.

Advance to be paid = (3,960,000 × 20 × 90)/(100 × 360) = Rs 198,000
$$= 3,960,000 - 198,000 = Rs \ 3,762,000$$

Evaluation of Factoring Decision

Actual cost of factoring to the firm		
Factoring commission (90,000 × 360/90)		360,000
Interest charges (198,000 × 360/90)		792,000
	(A)	1,152,000
Firm's savings on taking factoring services		
Cost of credit administration		500,000
Cost of bad debts (1,80,00,000 × 2/100)		360,000
	(B)	860,000
Net cost of factoring to the firm: (A) – (B)		292,000

13

Plastic Money

Learning Objectives

- To know the concept of plastic money.
- To understand the types, procedure, advantage, and disadvantage of plastic money.

PLASTIC MONEY

Plastic money represents currency and near currency. It is not the currency itself and cannot be converted into currency. It is the most convenient way to smoothen the exchange process of economic activity. The plastic money, since it is made of plastic, is the use of plastic card for the purpose of purchase, exchange, shop, withdrawal, payment, etc. The simplest and the easiest expression of plastic money is credit card and debit card. Often credit and debit cards and plastic money are used interchangeably. Credit cards are financial instruments, which can be used more than once to borrow money or buy products and services on credit. The credit card was first used in 1950 with the launch of charge cards in USA by Diners Club and American Express. Credit card however became more popular with use of magnetic strip in 1970.

TYPES OF PLASTIC CARDS

Debit card and credit card are basically two types of plastic cards which represent monetary transactions.

In-Store Card

1. They are issued by retailers or companies.
2. These cards have currency only at the issuer's outlet for purchasing products of the issuer company.
3. Payment can be on monthly or extended credit basis. For extended credit facility interest is charged.

Smart Card

1. Embedded in the smart card, a microchip stores the monetary value.
2. When a transaction is made using the card, the value is debited and the balance comes down automatically.
3. Once the monetary value comes down to nil, the balance is to be restored all over again for the card to become operational.
4. It is used for making purchases without necessarily requiring the authorization of personal identification number as in a debit card.

Credit Card

1. Holder is able to purchase without having to pay cash immediately.
2. Generally a limit is set to the amount of money a card holder can spend in a month.
3. At the end of month holder has to pay a percentage of outstanding along with interest (30 to 36 percent per annum).

Standard segregation of credit cards

A credit card may be of the following kinds:

1. Standard Card: It is a basic card (without frills).
2. Classic Card: Brand name for the standard card issued by Visa.
3. Gold Card/Executive Card: A credit card that offers a higher line of credit than a standard card. Income eligibility is also higher. In addition, issuers provide extra perks or incentives to card holders.
4. Platinum Card: A credit card with a higher limit and additional perks than a gold card.
5. Titanium Card: A card with an even higher limit than a platinum card.

Special features of credit card

A credit card offers the following features which result into savings:

1. Hotel discounts.
2. Travel fare discounts.
3. Free global calling card.
4. Lost baggage insurance.
5. Accident insurance.
6. Insurance on goods purchased.
7. Waiver of payment in case of accidental death.
8. Household insurance.

Precautions taken after receiving credit card

Following precautions must be observed:

1. Not to bend the card.
2. Not to expose to electronic devices and gadgets.
3. No direct exposure to sunlight.
4. Never put your account number on the outside of an envelope or on a postcard.
5. Draw a line through blank spaces on charge or debit slips above the total so the amount cannot be changed.
6. Don't sign a blank charge or debit slip.
7. Tear up carbons and save your receipts to check against your monthly statements.
8. Cut up old cards—cutting through the account number—before disposing of them.
9. Open monthly statements promptly and compare them with your receipts. Report mistakes or discrepancies as soon as possible to the special address listed on your statement for inquiries.
10. Keep a record—in a safe place separate from your cards—of your account numbers, expiration dates, and the telephone numbers of each card issuer so you can report a loss quickly.
11. Carry only those cards that you anticipate you'll need.

The credit card holder must:

1. Sign on the signature panel on the reverse of the card immediately with a non-erasable ball-point pen (preferably in black ink).
2. Keep the card safely.

A credit card may be rejected at retail outlet if:

1. The card is hot listed.
2. It has crossed its expiration date.
3. Non-receipt of dues of one-card blocks future transactions on any other card(s) held of the same card-issuing bank.

4. The magnetic stripe on the reverse of the card is damaged.
5. Systems or technology fails.

Debit Card

1. The purchase amount is automatically deducted or debited to the account of card holder electronically and would appear in the monthly statement of account.
2. The debit card program requires the customer to open an account with the bank which is not generally required.

It is issued to the customer by the bank in order to make cash withdrawals at automated teller machines (ATMs). Direct debit is a facility that allows bills to be paid automatically using savings account. The banks usually offer flexibility in this facility: total amount due and minimum amount due. In the former option, the credit card company may debit the entire outstanding bill amount from savings account. In the latter, a limit could be assigned on the monthly debit if credit card bill is more than the stipulated limit, the outstanding balance can be paid by another mode.

A debit card combines the functions of an ATM card and a cheque. When a debit card is used at a merchant establishment, the merchant swipes card through an electronic point of sale (EPOs) terminal which is directly linked up with the debit card issuing bank and the card holder's account immediately gets debited. There are two types—one is the personal identification number (PIN)-based card and the other the signature-based card. In India, MasterCard issues the PIN-based card in association with Citibank while Visa International issues the signature-based card in association with HDFC Bank. While the PIN-based card is thought more secure, the signature-based card is more widely accepted in India.

The user requires card number, card validity month/year, and a code called credit verification value (CVV) or card validation code (CVC) that is available on the card itself.

CVV is a three-digit code typically imprinted at the end of signature panel on the reverse of the card (or a four-digit code little above the end of card number on front side) and is meant to serve as authorizing code.

Features of debit card

1. Obtaining a debit card is easier than obtaining a credit card.
2. The use of debit card saves showing identification or giving out personal information at the time of the transaction.
3. Debit cards may be more readily accepted by merchants than cheques, especially in other states or countries.
4. Returning goods or canceling services purchased with a debit card is treated as if the purchase were made with cash or a cheque.

Precaution for use of debit card

1. If the card is lost or stolen, report the loss immediately to concerned financial institution.
2. Hold on to receipts from your debit card transactions.
3. If you have a PIN number, memorize it. Do not keep your PIN number with your card. Never give PIN number to anyone. Keep your receipts in one place for easy retrieval and better oversight of your bank account.

A customer has a choice, to either go for a debit or a credit card. He would have to take a decision by comparing the debit to the credit card. Table 13.1 gives a brief synopsis of the decision making process.

Table 13.1   Comparative Features of Debit and Credit Card

Variables	Debit Card (pay now product)	Credit Card (pay later product)
Bank a/c Requirements for Card Holder	Must	Optional
Nature of Financing	Own sources	Consumer loan
Lead Time for Cash Outflows	Nil	1 day to 45 days, may be even more
Membership Fees	Rs 50–250 (sometimes offered free)*	Rs 250–2,000 (sometimes offered free)**
Annual Fee	Rs 50–300 (many a time waived)	Rs 200–2,000 (many time waived)
Chance of Bed Debt for Bankers	Nil	Substantial
Recovery Cost of Bankers	Nil	Substantial
Expense for using the Money by the Customer	Nil	2% to 3% p.m. interest is charged if not paid in time
Chance of Overspending	Nil	Substantial

Source: Author's compilation.
Notes: *For 1st year it is free but from 2nd year onwards, Rs 150–250 p.a. may be charged depending on banks.
       **For 1st year it is free but from 2nd year onwards, Rs 750–1,000 p.a. may be charged depending on banks.

Cheque Cards

1. It enables the holder to withdraw cash by using cheques from any branch of the bank located within the country.
2. It enables the identification of the customer and provides a certain degree of guarantee against the cheque being dishonored.

Gift Card

1. It can be used more than once, till the value of the card has been spent.
2. Available in various denominations Rs 500 to Rs 20,000
3. Valid for a period of 1 year from the date of issue.

Charge Card

1. A convenient means of payment of goods purchased at member establishments.
2. This facility gives a consolidated bill for a specified period, usually one month (bills are paid in full on presentation).
3. No interest charged.
4. Useful during business trips and for entertainment expenses which are usually borne by the company.

A customer can also go for a charge card, in place of a credit card, but he would first compare the two, before taking a decision. Refer to Table 13.2 for more details on the same.

Table 13.2   Comparison of Credit Card with Charge Card

Parameters	Credit Card	Charge Card
Issuance	On the basis of financial evaluation and creditworthiness of card holder	On the basis of amount in the account designed for charge and by financial evaluation
Payment Period	Revolving credit payment—normally within 45 days of purchase	Normally within 30 days of purchase
Amount Payment	Revolving credit payment—minimum of 5% of the purchase	100% of the purchase
Interest Rate	2.5–3% per month depending on the type of card and issuing bank	No interest is charged as there is no extension of payment period Penalty may, however, be levied in case on default in both the cases
Annual Payment and Commission	Only annual payment—no commission is charged	Both annual payment and commission is charged
Maximum Amount of Purchase	Depending on the creditworthiness usually five times the net income of the individual	No preset spending limits

Source: Author's compilation.

International Credit Card

Banks and their subsidiaries have no restriction from the point of view of exchange control in issuing international credit cards (ICCs) to residents in India. Banks can issue a single credit card which is valid in India as well as in other countries. However, in such cases card-issuing organizations should keep accounts of rupee transactions segregated from foreign exchange transactions. Residents may be nominated as additional/add-on card holders by non-residents. In case where the cards have been arranged by non-resident Indians (NRIs) these liabilities may be met out of Non-resident (NR) and Foreign Currency Non-resident (FCNR) accounts in India also. No remittance is allowed from India to settle the claims against use of such additional/add-on cards. Residents have been permitted by Reserve Bank to accept ICCs issued abroad at the request of a non-resident/overseas organization provided that liabilities arising out of use of such card are met by the non-resident/organization arranging issue of the card. Credit cards issuing banks/organizations have been permitted by Reserve Bank to issue credit cards valid in India, Nepal, and Bhutan to non-resident of Indian nationality and/or origin. Claims arising from use of such cards may be settled by remittances from abroad or by debit to accounts maintained with authorized dealers in India. No remittance from India shall be permitted for settlement of dues if these cards are used in other countries. Residents' proceedings abroad are released foreign exchange in currency notes against ICC up to USD 500 or its equivalent. Rest of the entitlement of exchanges is released in the form of travelers' cheque denominated in foreign currency. The amount of unspent exchange held in form of currency notes is required to be surrendered to an authorized dealer or full-fledged money changer in India within 90 days of return to India. ICCs can be used only for those personal purposes for which release of exchange is permitted.

TERMS USED IN PLASTIC MONEY

1. **Card Issuers:** The reason for more and more banks diversifying into plastic money business lies in the high returns associated with this business. For instance, banks charge about 2 to 2.5 percent commission from member establishments (MEs) selling goods and services through credit cards. For the customers, banks offer a credit period of 30–45 days, but charge about 2.95 percent on all outstandings remaining unpaid on expiry of the credit period. Thus, a single purchase transaction through plastic money, assuming the customer does not pay within the stipulated credit period, will fetch a commission of about 5 percent per month to the bank which works out at as much as 60 percent per annum—miles ahead of the minimum lending rate of banks.

2. **Card Holders:** The card holders include both salaried individuals and business organizations. The eligibility criteria for individual to acquire plastic money are predicated on the gross and net annual incomes.

3. **Member Establishments (MEs):** Member establishments are establishments enlisted by the plastic money issuers who accept valid credit cards toward payment for the goods sold or services rendered by them in lieu of cash. While enlisting MEs, their reputation, integrity, standing, and popularity are taken into consideration. The volume of business they are likely to generate and the scope of use of card at the establishment are also considered. MEs include retail outlets, departmental stores, restaurants, hotels, hospitals, travel agencies, garages, petrol pumps, and co-operative societies. Based on the type of business, location, turnover, etc., floor limit for MEs is fixed. Normally, the ME transactions against an individual credit card should not exceed the floor limit. MEs will have to pay to the issuer of plastic money a certain percentage of discount on the plastic money transactions. However, MEs like Indian Airlines or Indian Railways do not pay discount to the issuer and in such cases the card issuer collects a transaction fee from the card holder.

4. **Member Affiliates (MAs):** The issuer may sometimes enter into a tie-up for issuance of credit card. In such cases, the organizations which have tie-ups also issue credit cards of the issuer to their clients. These organizations are called member affiliates (MAs). Credit cards issued by MAs are similar to those issued by the issuer, except that they contain the name and logo of the MA on the face of the card, besides the issuer's name and logo. This agreement enlarges the scope and operations of the plastic money. Also, the MA can issue card to its clients without actually having to invest on the elaborate infrastructure required for servicing credit cards.

5. **Charge Slip:** A charge slip is a voucher (debit) which is an evidence of the card holder using the card and consents for the indebtedness of the amount mentioned therein. Charge slip is prepared in triplicate by the ME and signed by the customer/card holder in token of acknowledgement of receipt of goods and/or services in the amount of total shown thereon and agrees to perform the obligations set forth in the card holder's agreement with the issuer.

6. **Floor Limit:** Member establishments are given a limit known as floor limit which implies that they can honor the card for the amount only on any day. In case the purchase exceeds that limit, they have to obtain an authorization from the bank. Floor limit is monetary limit within which ME can honor the card. MEs have to enter into an agreement with the card bank by which they are obliged to honor the credit cards when presented by the card holders.

7. **Validity Period:** Validity, may be 2 to 5 years, is printed on the card. Credit cards, for safety reasons, are not issued as life cards.

8. **Account Statement:** Account statement or bills are sent by banks to the card holders periodically, normally on a monthly basis. This statement of account is a statement containing the summary of transactions done by the card holder with a request to make the payment to the bank. If the payment indicated is not made in the stipulated time, a service charge (normally 2 to 3 percent of the outstanding amount) is levied by the bank and payable by the card holder. Payments are sought by local cheques/drafts/cash payable at the centers where the banks have facility of collection center. These amounts can also be debited to the card holder's accounts where current or saving bank accounts are maintained by the card holders.

9. **Grace/Interest Free Period:** The number of days given to the card before the card issuer starts charging interest is called grace period. Generally the grace period is the number of days between the statement date and the due date of payment. Grace periods on credit cards are usually 2 to 3 weeks.

10. **Cash Advance:** Cash advances on credit cards are convenient and the easiest facility to utilize. Majority of the banks in India charge a transaction fee as well as service fee/interest charge on cash advances. This service fee accrues from the date of the advance (as soon as you receive the cash) to the date of full payment. The charges vary from banks to banks. Cash advance facility is a part of the overall credit limit assigned to a card holder. The limit of cash advance is always less than the borrowing limit or the credit limit.

METHODOLOGY IN CREDIT CARD BUSINESS

Methodology of plastic money:

Issuance

A credit card is issued by the sponsor bank to the card holder after due evaluation of creditworthiness and financial status of the prospective card holder. Normally, there are different evaluation criteria for various types of credit cards. For example, a person drawing Rs 60,000 p.a. as gross pay is given a "Classic" card, whereas a person drawing at least Rs 90,000 p.a. is given an "Executive" card and a person drawing more than Rs 1,20,000 as gross annual pay is given a "Gold" card by Standard Chartered Bank. Similarly, Hong Kong Bank offers Gold and Classic cards for separate salary limits. For a non-salaried individual, the criteria of issuance of card may be on the basis of maintenance of bank account, filing of income tax returns, income derived from other sources, etc.

At the time of issuance of card, a credit limit is specified above which the card holder cannot purchase on the card within one billing cycle. The credit limit is determined at the discretion of the sponsoring bank say at five times the net monthly salary (or income) of the individual or 20 percent of gross annual income. If the payment schedule is followed satisfactorily by the card holder, then the bank may sometimes consider temporary increase in the credit limit on request. The enhancement of credit limit may be 10–50 percent of the previous limit for a period of around 3 months.

Once the card is issued by the bank by charging the entrance fee and annual fee in advance, for every subsequent year of renewal of the card, the card holder should pay annual fees to the sponsor. This fee is irrespective of the frequency of use of the card. It should also be noted that there is no stipulation on the minimum number of times a card has to be used in a year for the purpose of renewal of the card.

In case the credit card is lost, there is a maximum liability that has to be born by the card holder. In case of a photo-card, where the credit card has a photograph of the card holder embossed on it, then the liability of the lost card is zero.

Purchase

The credit card is operational immediately on receipt of the card. Purchases may be made once the card holder signs on the back of the card which will be used as a verification parameter by the ME. There is no limit on the amount of purchase as long as the purchase amount within a billing cycle does not exceed the credit limit. The billing cycle is generally for 45 days starting from the calendar month of subscribing to the card, where the payment is made 15 days after the calendar month ends. That is, if a purchase is made immediately after the start of the calendar month, credit equivalent to the amount of purchase will be available for 45 days. Billing period, however, may vary depending on the type and issuer in few cases.

Collection

After the purchase is transacted, the ME approaches the issuing bank or its clearing representative and claims the amount through the copy of the sales vouchers and purchases statement. The bank would discount the amount payable by 2–3 percent (varying from bank to bank) and pays it to the ME. The frequency of such transfer of money from bank to ME depends on the number of times the ME approaches the bank. Normally, ME approaches the bank within a day after the purchase is made.

To sum up:

1. Credit card bank advertises or approaches the prospective card holders.
2. Prospective card holders apply for credit card membership by filling the prescribed form which normally contains personal and financial particulars.
3. Issuer of credit card evaluates the form and issues the credit card and fixes the money limit for use of such card.
4. Card holder puts his signature on the prescribed place of the card before putting it to use and starts to use it.
5. ME prepares a charge slip (for cost to be recovered), gets it signed by the card holder, tallies the signature, and return one copy of the charge slip to the card holder. The second copy is sent to the card issuer for recovery of money and third copy is retained by him.
6. Card issuer receives the bill and charge slip and makes payment to the ME.
7. Card issuer prepares an account statement and sends it to card holder for payment to the bank directly or through its authorized collection centers.
8. Card holder makes the payment to the bank.

Credit card may be used for the following purposes:

1. Purchase of air, rail, and road tickets for traveling.
2. Settlement of hotel bills.
3. Cash withdrawals.
4. Settlement of club bills.
5. Payment of purchases bills.
6. Payment of insurance premium.
7. Refilling of fuel in vehicles.
8. Payment of phone, water, and electricity bills.
9. Payment of school/education expenses.
10. Subscribing to new issues and mutual funds (investments).
11. Medical expenses.
12. Substitute for cash, traveler's cheque, etc.
13. Used as an emergency cash.
14. Ideal source of consumer finance and short-term credit.

ECONOMICS OF CREDIT CARDS

The business of credit cards operate on a narrow profit margin. The main sources of revenue for credit card bank are initial fees, renewal fees, and fees charges for issuing duplicate cards. In addition, income is earned from interest on overdraft/delayed payment and commission from MEs.

Expenditure

Following are the various operating and administrative expenses in credit card business:

1. Credit card cost.
2. Advertisement and publicity.
3. Mailing cost.
4. Printing and stationery.
5. Interest cost for providing short-term credit to card holders where as MEs have to be paid on submission of bills.
6. Cost of imprinters provided to MEs.
7. Cost of recovery of money from card holders.
8. Administrative expenses—salary and wages, infrastructural costs, communication costs, postage, courier, etc.

Advantages of Credit Cards

1. Use of credit card is safe. Even if it is stolen, it cannot be used except in case of fraud.
2. It is as liquid as cash.
3. It is very convenient to handle and use.
4. It provides easy credit for short period between 20 and 45 days between the date of use of card and actual recovery.
5. It provides trade discounts, privileges and facilities like entertainments, reading material, medical and personal insurance.

Disadvantages of Credit Cards

1. Credit facilities are costly.
2. It has annual cost and recurring cost.
3. It encourages consumerism and extravagance.
4. It is acceptable only at select establishments.
5. It requires proper maintenance of personal account and proper checking of periodical statement.

Global Players in Credit Card Market

1. **MasterCard**: MasterCard is a product of MasterCard International and is distributed by financial institutions around the world. Card holders borrow money against a line of credit and pay it back with interest if the balance is carried over from month to month. Its products are issued by 23,000 financial institutions in 220 countries and territories.
2. **Visa Card**: Visa card is a product of Visa USA and is distributed by financial institutions around the world. A Visa card holder borrows money against a credit line and repays the money with interest if the balance is carried over from month to month in a revolving line of credit.
3. **American Express**: The world's favorite card is American Express Credit Card. More than 57 million cards are in circulation and it is still growing further.
4. **Diners Club International**: Diners Club is the world's No. 1 charge card and is all-time favorite for corporates. There are more than 8 million Diners Club card holders.
5. **JCB Cards**: The JCB card has a merchant network of 10.93 million in approximately 189 countries. It is supported by over 320 financial institutions worldwide and serves more than 48 million card holders in 18 countries worldwide. The JCB philosophy is "identify the customer's needs and please the customer with Service from the Heart."

Recent Innovations in Credit Card Business

Corporate cards

These cards are issued to corporate entities in their names along with the names of the executives. These cards are used in the normal courses of business by the executives, but the liability is that of the company to pay for the bills.

Photo credit cards

Standard Chartered Bank launched its photo card in India in July 1995 which is first of its kind in India having tamper-proof photograph and signature of the card holder on the face of the card.

Hot list

Hot list is a list issued and circulated by card-issuing bank periodically which contains numbers of lost and cancelled cards with the instructions to MEs to pick up/recover these cards. MEs are also advised not to honor the card if the card number embossed on the card is found listed in the hot list bulletin.

Insurance cover

In case of insurance covers under card holder's master policies, all card holders are covered under a personal accident insurance cover to the extent of a certain sum against risk of death due to accident. The cover is offered free and is automatic without any act on part of card holder. Holders of hot list cards or withdrawn cards are not covered under this.

Mail-order or Telephone-order

In mail-order or telephone-order transactions, the credit card number is quoted to the e-mail/telephone order company by an authorized person in exchange for goods, which are often delivered to a temporary address.

Service charges are calculated on the average daily balance method and if the overdues are more than 60 or 120 days old from the due date, a late fee is charged besides the service charge. If the total outstandings exceed credit limit, additional charges are levied on the excess amount and credit facility may be withdrawn.

The two leading credit cards in the world are Visa and MasterCard owned by international agencies providing a global network that allows authorization, clearing, and settlement of card transactions.

Credit Cards in India

The first card was issued in India by Visa in 1981. The country's first Gold Card was also issued by Visa in 1986.

The first international credit card was issued to a restricted number of customers by Andhra Bank in 1987 through the Visa program, after getting special permission from the RBI.

The credit cards have shape and size as specified by the ISO 7810 standard. It is generally of plastic quality. It is also sometimes known as plastic money.

The unprecedented growth in the number of credit card users has stimulated the Indian economy to a significant extent. The arrival of malls, multiplexes, online shopping stores, and shopping complexes have contributed to the growth of the use of plastic cards.

The number of credit card holders in India was close to 22 million as on January 2007. It has been also revealed that the increasing consumerism in the country has led to a two-fold increase in the number of credit card transactions from financial year (FY) 2003–04 to 2005–06. The trends were as favorable as ever in the FY 2006–07 and 2007–08 and the same is likely to continue in the coming financial years.

A year before economic reforms kicked off in 1991, Citibank stole a march ahead of its competitors and became the first bank to launch a credit card in India. Fifteen years later, the pioneer has been upstaged by a homegrown bank, ICICI Bank, which has raced to the top position in less than 4 years with more than 3 million cards.

With about 2.5 million card holders, Citibank is at second place. Standard Chartered Bank has issued about 1.78 million cards and is at third place. By issuing credit cards in 107 cities, ICICI Bank has established the largest reach. State Bank of India (SBI), the largest bank in the country with over 10,000 branches, has fanned out its credit card business in 45 cities. Citibank, which operates in 40 cities, is planning to scale it up to the 94 cities in which group company Citifinancial operates.

State Bank of India has crossed 1.5 million cards within 2 years of launching the card. HDFC Bank is at fifth place with a million cards on its books.

The following are various of credit cards in India:

- ANZ-Gold
- ANZ-Silver
- Bank of India-Indiacard
- Bank of India-Taj Premium
- BoI-Gold
- BoB-Exclusive
- BoB-Premium
- Canara Bank-Cancard
- Citibank-Gold
- Citibank-Silver
- Citibank WWF Card
- Citibank Visa Card for Women
- Citibank Cry Card
- Citibank Silver International Credit Card
- Citibank Women's International Credit Card
- Citibank Gold International Credit Card
- Citibank Electronic Credit Card
- Citibank Maruti International Credit Card
- Citibank Times Card
- Citibank Indian Oil International Credit Card
- Citibank Citi Diners Club Card
- HSBC-Gold
- HSBC-Classic
- ICICI Sterling Silver Credit Card
- ICICI Solid Gold Credit Card
- ICICI True Blue Credit Card
- SBI Card
- StanChart-Gold
- StanChart-Executive
- StanChart-Classic
- Thomas Cook Standard Chartered Global Credit Card

The Indian card market is at par with the best in the world.

Profitable usage

Credit cards can be used online with a separate security number to prevent misuse. This has increased profitability. An estimate by *Business Standard* in early 2004 reckoned that Citibank's profits on the card business were over USD 34 million and StanChart's was around

USD 23–34 million. Among the Indian banks, SBI cards was estimated to be the most profitable with over USD 11.6 million as operating profit.

Growing reach

Indian Railways runs one of the largest travel booking sites in Asia and offers door-delivery of train tickets if booked online using credit or debit cards. Credit cards are now increasingly being used to pay for even school fees and hospitalization expenses.

Safe and sound

Safety standards followed by players to prevent misuse match the best in the world. For example, any transaction above a particular sum is automatically referred to the issuing bank which calls up the card holder in a matter of seconds on the mobile phone to confirm the purchase.

Feature-driven

Product features too match the best anywhere in the world. Almost all credit cards come with standard frills such as free accident insurance, medical insurance at a heavy discount and much more. The card holder is offered the option of converting a big purchase made on credit card into a loan at a lower rate of interest spread over a long period. Banks now offer details of expenses incurred on credit cards under different heads—such as food, clothes, and jewelry—to enable easier tracking by the customer. E-mail alerts and mobile alerts on credit card details are commonplace.

Aggressive Marketing

Banks have not only raised the bar in quality and services but they have also devised aggressive growth strategies to notch up higher spends on cards. ICICI Bank, for example, launched three no-holds-barred campaigns simultaneously during the high festival season—a five percent cash back on all purchases over Rs 2,000; a lucky draw for a couple to the seven wonders of the world; and a chance to win a Mercedes E 240. Result: the bank saw spends shoot up by 36 percent during the last 3 months of 2004.

INNOVATION IN PLASTIC MONEY

The issuers of credit cards have begun to offer much more than just credit to the card holders.

1. **Personal Accident Insurance**: Some issuers provide a free insurance cover against loss of life due to accidents.

2. **Cash Withdrawal Facility**: Credit cards typically carry a pre-determined credit limit and a cash limit. Cash withdrawal may either be through ATMs of the designated bank branches or over-the-counter cash payment. The interest rate that is charged on cash withdrawal is much higher than in case of normally carry forwarding of credit in purchasing transaction.

3. **Temporary Increase in Credit Lines**: Card holders with a good credit record can seek a temporary increase in their credit limits. A Citi card holder, for instance, can increase his credit limit by 25 percent for 3 months.

4. **Add-on Facility**: The spouse or the parents or children (over 18 years) of the card holder is entitled to add-on cards on payment of an extra fee. The card holder assumes the responsibility of honoring the charges incurred on the additional card. In recent times, add-on facility is being given free of cost for initial subscription year as an incentive. Otherwise, an annual fee is payable for the purpose of issuing and servicing add-on credit card.

5. **Levered Investment Facility**: The card holders are often allowed to subscribe to designated equity or debentures issues in the primary market or subscribe to design schemes floated by mutual funds using their cards. Besides obviating the need to make a substantial initial investment, the card holders can liquidate the amount borrowed over a specified number of installments with interest.

6. **Rewards Points**: Most credit cards accumulate points on purchase which can be redeemed against gifts/discount coupons of shops/hotels.

7. **Affinity Cards**: These cards are issued by sponsor banks especially for a particular section of people who take pride in the vocation or alma mater making them periodically donate some amount to improve the cause they love.

8. **International Cards**: StanChart has pioneered the issue of globally accepted cards in India, the payment for which is done is rupee. Now every credit card issued in India by all the banks is internationally accepted.

FUTURE OF PLASTIC MONEY IN INDIA

With high and industry-favorable figures as in the foregoing, there is no doubt that the rise in number of credit card providers and users have come of age. The credit card industry is likely to soar more than any industry segment. To add to that, easy and continuous payment structures with each passing day and with every bank poised to expand its network, the Indian credit card user community is the biggest beneficiary. The intensifying competition prevalent in the present-day Indian credit card market has further fuelled the usage of credit card in the country like never before.

A thriving economy, substantial increase in disposable incomes and consequent rise in consumer expenditure, growing affluence levels and consumer sophistication have all led to a robust growth in credit cards, and each of the players mentioned earlier have posted an enviable annual growth rate of more than 100 percent over the last 2 years.

There is no doubt that more and more middle class Indians are letting plastic rule their day-to-day lives. Five years ago, there were 4.3 million credit cards being used in the country. That zoomed to 6.5 million in 2002. A year later that shot up once again to around 9 million credit cards. Today, even if debit cards are overtaking credit cards in popularity, the scorching pace of growth continues unabated.

Venture Infotek, a consumer payment processing company, estimates that the total spends in the credit card payment industry in 2003–04 was close to USD 5 billion at merchant establishments. This reflected a growth of 28 percent over the previous year. Projections for 2005 range from 10 to 14 million cards according to Electronic Payments International. According to another forecast put out by the Lafferty Group, India's credit card spending is estimated to grow at 34 percent in 2008.

HUGE MARKET REMAINS UNTAPPED

The most heartening part of the growth is that so much still remains to be covered. Consider this: only 2.4 percent of the working population in India owned a credit card in 2004. McKinsey predicts that 35 million credit cards will be issued by 2010 with an outstanding balance of over USD 7 billion. Compared to other Asian markets, Indian credit card market is still at a nascent stage. Credit cards per bankable population in India is 0.03 per person against 3 in South Korea, 2.66 in Taiwan, 2 in Hong Kong, 1.1 in Singapore, and 0.4 in Malaysia. As per an estimate of ICICI Bank, an average Indian credit card holder spends less than USD 500 on his card annually, compared to around USD 800 in Sri Lanka and over USD 3,000 in Hong Kong and Singapore. Outstanding dues on credit card (which are the money spinner for any card issuing bank) are the lowest in the region. The outstanding balance in India is at USD 1.5 billion, compared to USD 90 billion in Korea, USD 10 billion in Hong Kong, and USD 2.5 billion in Malaysia.

In value terms too the Indian market is a real cherry. The potential credit card market in India is estimated at USD 30 million while the debit card market is estimated at USD 130 million.

McKinsey expects India to improve its ranking from 10th in the credit card packing order in 2001 to 8th by 2010.

RBI MOOTS PLASTIC CURRENCY NOTES

The RBI has said it is considering use of plastic to make currency notes, replacing paper which has a shorter life. "The bank is deliberating upon the option of bringing in plastic currency which can be a mixture of paper, plastic and cotton."

Inspired by the success of the China UnionPay (the China UnionPay card was introduced in 2002; the card gives access to over 85,000 ATM counters of 40 major and other minor banks across the world), a similar card for common people in India will be launched with low interest rate and risk reduction facilities.

The National Payment Council of India (NPCI) is working on the registration process of the card. The NPCI authorities would decide on the type of the card—whether it would be a smart card or something else. If all plans and government procedures go well then this card will be available in the market by the end of 2009.

Plastic money use will be more intensified in days to come as:

1. India is going to be one of the premium visitor destinations attracting a large number of foreign tourists (say for terrorist attack on Mumbai in November 2008).
2. Indians going to different places within the country for holiday and leisure.
3. Liberalized economic environment bringing a lot of foreign industrialists, executives, and technicians into the country.
4. More frequent business travels undertaken by Indian entrepreneurs and executives.
5. Explosive rise in corporate citizens, with the formation of more and more joint stock companies.
6. The desire on the part of the middle classes and upper middle classes, to enhance their lifestyles by accessing more products and undertaking more leisure activities.

14

Mergers and Acquisitions

Learning Objectives

- To know the concept of merger and acquisition.
- To know various issues involved in merger and acquisition with reference to India.

CONCEPT—MERGER

It is a combination of two or more companies into one company. It can be classified into two kinds:

1. **Absorption:** When one company is loses its complete identity including assets and liabilities to another company. For example, fast moving consumer good (FMCG) company Balsara absorbed into Dabur.
2. **Consolidation:** When all participating companies lose their individual identities and form one new company. For example, consolidation of Interact Communication and Vision advertising into Interact Vision.

CONCEPT—ACQUISITION

When transfer of controlling interests of company(s) takes place from its own management to management of some other company(s) for fixed price of its shares, it is referred as "acquisition." For example, Spectramind was acquired by Wipro.

CONCEPT—JOINT VENTURE

Two or more companies join hands together for some specified purpose, for specified period, for specified market. For example, ICICI Bank and Prudential formed ICICI Prudential Asset Management Company.

TYPES OF MERGER

Horizontal Merger

It happens when companies interested in merger belong to same industry, for example, Daksh Services and IBM.

Reasons

1. Economies of scale in production capacities, distribution networks, advertising media, and R&D.
2. Economies of scope: Synergized benefit to produce broader range of products.
3. Minimize or eliminate competition.

Vertical Merger

It is forward or backward integration where all companies interested in mergers are part of stages of "sourcing raw material-manufacturing-distribution."

Reasons

1. Minimizing or eliminating uncertainty and transaction cost over input supply in case of backward integration.
2. Better management of inventory of intermediary and/or finished goods.

Conglomerate Merger

It is a combination of companies who are in unrelated business.
The different kinds of conglomeratemergers:

1. **Concentric:** Unrelated businesses but related sector. For example, one life insurance company and other is a bank.
2. **Pure Conglomerate:** Completely unrelated business in unrelated sectors.

A GLIMPSE OF MERGERS AND ACQUISITIONS

Mergers and Acquisitions in USA

The US merger and acquisition (M&A) activities can be classified into different stages (Gaughan, 2002). The first stage occurred between 1897 and 1904, the second between 1916 and 1929, the third between 1965 and 1969, the fourth between 1981 and 1989, and the fifth between 1993 and 2000. The third M&A stage is often referred to as the "conglomerate stage," because it was characterized by a large number of transactions that took place among companies with unrelated businesses operating in different industries. It coincided with a booming economy in the USA that provided companies with the necessary resources to acquire other companies.

Deregulation in certain industries gave rise to the fourth M&A stage. The top five industries in terms of M&A activity were oil and gas, textile, miscellaneous manufacturing, non-depository credit, and food (Andrade et al., 2001). The third M&A stage comprised of many more deals than the fourth merger stage. However, the dollar value of the transactions that occurred in the 1980s was much higher.

Overall the fourth stage is known for its billion-dollar mega-transactions. Many of the mega deals were financed with large amounts of debt. In contrast to previous stages, hostile takeovers played a significant role. Although the number of hostile transactions compared to the total number of transactions was relatively small, the dollar value of hostile deals was at times very high. In addition, international transactions accounted for a significant percentage of M&A activity (Gaughan, 2002).

The fifth M&A stage followed an economic recession. It was again characterized by many large mega transactions. Unlike the deals of the 1980s, these deals were financed through the increased use of equity. Those transactions were more strategic than hostile in nature and led to consolidation in many industries. The top five industries in terms of M&A activity were metal mining, media and telecommunications, banking, real estate, and hotels (Andrade et al., 2001). Moreover, it was strongly driven by globalization and the new economy. It came to an end with the burst of the "Internet-bubble" and the overall downshift of the global economy in the following years.

Another stage of mergers and acquisitions has been underway since 2004. The current transactions are driven by new economic growth and the recovery of stock markets. They are also driven by strategic choices of firms in light of this recent economic growth rather than by opportunistic factors. In addition to this, new investors such as private equity firms or hedge funds have emerged as a source for M&A activity (UNCTAD, 2006).

M&A Activities in Europe

Just like the USA, European M&A activity occurred in stages. Goergen and Renneboog (2003) identified five M&A stages in Europe. According to them the second industrial revolution triggered the first wave (1880–1904), which was characterized by the formation of monopolies.

Increasing business regulations led to the second stage (1919–29) with transactions aimed at vertical integration. The third stage was initiated in the 1950s and peaked in the 1960s. Similar to the USA, it brought about the creation of conglomerates.

The fourth stage (1983–89) was triggered by technological progress in the electronics and biochemistry industries. In addition, new financial instruments and markets were developed which facilitated the financing of such transactions. Similar to the USA, hostile takeovers played a significant role in the fourth European M&A stage (Goergen and Renneboog, 2003).

The 1990s experienced the fifth stage of mergers and acquisitions (1993–2000) until an abrupt reduction in transaction activity in 2001. The fifth stage happened during a period of economic boom and coincided with significant growth in the telecommunications and Internet industries. During this period the European M&A market grew significantly. While Europe accounted for 37 percent of the worldwide value of transactions in 1996, this proportion increased to 47 percent in 1999, making the European transaction market almost as large as the US market (Goergen and Renneboog, 2003). In terms of the number of transactions that occurred within the European Union between 1991 and 2000, the UK accounted for about one-third of the total M&A activity, followed by Germany which accounted for 16 percent.

Since 2003, European M&A activity has been increasing again. While in 2003 companies located in the European Union initiated 8,100 transactions, this number rose to 10,500 in 2006. Of those transactions in 2006, 66 percent took place in the service sector, in particular 27 percent in other services and 16 percent in the financial sector. The manufacturing sector accounted for 28 percent of targeted firms.

Mergers and Acquisitions in India

India is emerging as a global economic and political power in today's changing rules of business environment. According to research from Boston Consulting Group (BCG), India has contributed the second-largest number of emerging market players to BCG's 2008 top global challengers list. While China has added more companies to BCG's list, its international sale contribution is only 17 percent, compared to India's 45 percent. And although India is known for information technology (IT) services, it is also making a substantial contribution to the manufacturing sector and its manufacturing giants are generating greater shareholder returns than its major IT companies in changing business matrices in all corners of the world. Indian companies have made USD 22.3 billion worth of foreign acquisitions in 2007, according to data from Thomson Financial. The country's record year is 2006, which, led by Tata Steel's USD 12.9 billion takeover of Corus, reached USD 24 billion. Indian copper and aluminum producer Hindalco Industries paid USD 6 billion this year to acquire Novelis Inc., a Canadian manufacturer of semi-finished aluminum products. Indian automakers Tata Motors Ltd has bought British car brands Jaguar and Land Rover from Ford Motor Company. Other Indian companies that have expressed interest in acquisitions include petrochemical producer Reliance Industries and pharmaceuticals company Biocon Ltd.

It is worth noting that a significant portion of the Indian M&A activity is driven by the corporate sector, rather than by private equity investors. The global credit crunch continues to limit deals from highly-leveraged private equity firms, reducing competition for acquisition targets. The country's financial sector, which has seen a wave of M&A deals and initial public offerings, may expand further as anticipated banking reforms open the sector up to greater foreign participation.

In 2009, Tech Mahindra won an auction for control of Satyam Computer Services with a bid of USD 351 million for a 31 percent stake in the company. Its total outlay, including an offer to minority shareholders that is capped at 20 percent, is around USD 580 million. In a savvy legal move, Tech Mahindra made the deal through a wholly-owned subsidiary. This structure was designed to ensure that the buyer's liability was limited to its equity contribution. That is smart considering Satyam is currently facing litigation from customers and investors, especially in the USA, where the financial fallout is unclear.

Successful M&As which are not just portfolio acquisitions but which involve a degree of integration of two (or more) entities, in some cases even a full integration, put people as much as profits at the heart of the process. Traditional approaches to M&A—first financial and legal due diligence, moving quickly to sign the deal, and thinking of the integration consequences afterwards—are plainly inadequate. The new M&A must be comprehensive in all its aspects.

Recent Activities in M&A in India

Indian companies acquired by foreign companies:

1. Gujarat Gas by British Gas, UK
2. Hindustan Polymers by L G Polymers, Korea
3. ABS Industries by Bayer, Germany
4. Bombay Oxegen Goyal Gases by Gresheim, Germany
5. Hindustan Gases by Proxair, USA
6. Bharat Glass Tube by Schott Glass, Germany
7. Siel Compressors by Tecumesh Product
8. GEC Alshom by GE Electronics Distribution

Total deals in 2008 were 445 worth USD 30.72 billion compared with 676 deals worth USD 51.11 billion in 2007 as per global consultancy firm Grant Thompton.

Acquisition of Citigroup's captive business process outsourcing (BPO) arm Citigroup Global Services Limited (CGSL) for USD 505 million by India's leading IT services exporter Tata Consultancy Services.

ONGC Videsh Ltd, the overseas arm of the state-run Oil and Natural Gas Corp. Ltd, acquired Britain's Imperial Energy Plc with assets in Russia for USD 2.8 billion.

In 2008, 1,270 deals with Indian participation (national as well as cross boundary) for value of USD 50 billion had been announced. Indian M&A activity has slightly decreased in 2008 in terms of numbers (–6 percent). This decrease is smaller than the worldwide trend (–10 percent), but higher than the Asian one (–3.4 percent). The total known value of Indian deals has decreased by 18 percent, which is much smaller than the overall trend (World: –44 percent; Asia: –35 percent).

HDFC Bank Ltd acquired Centurion Bank of Punjab for USD 2.38 billion.

The share of Indian cross-border deals in the total value of deals got decreased, but was still high at 66 percent. Especially the number and value of foreign acquisitions in India had dropped in 2008.

With respect to the number of transactions, almost all sectors had experienced a decrease in 2008 with the notable exceptions of real estate retail, energy and power, and health care. The value of real estate, health care, energy and power, high technology, and consumer products, services and staples got increased.

Major companies who participated in M&A activities in India in 2008:

- AAA Project Ventures
- Asarco
- Centurion Bank of Punjab
- Daiichi Sankyo
- Etisalat
- General Chemical Industrial
- GMR Infrastructure
- Great Offshore
- HDFC Bank
- Idea Cellular
- InterGen
- Jaguar Cards
- NTT DoCoMo
- Phoenix Mills
- Ranbaxy Laboratories
- Reliance Energy
- Rui RE Development
- Seadragon Offshore
- Sterlite Industries
- Swan Telecom
- Tata Chemicals
- Tata Motors
- Tata Teleservices
- Telenor
- TM International
- Unitech Wireless

MOTIVES FOR MERGERS AND ACQUISITIONS

Management Related Motives

Personal gains

One theory argues that managers knowingly overpay in mergers and acquisitions (Seth et al., 2000). According to this hypothesis the driver behind transactions is executives' pursuit of personal gains. They try to build an empire in order to enhance their own power and prestige or try to reduce risk by engaging in diversification activities at the expense of shareholder value. Seth et al. (2000) find evidence that cross-border transactions which result in a total loss for the combined firm (measured by abnormal returns based on changes in the share price) are driven by the managerialism hypothesis, confirming the results of a previous study conducted by Berkovitch and Narayanan (1993) which was not limited to cross-border transactions only. In a follow-up study, Seth et al. (2002) find evidence that the source of value destruction for transactions motivated by managerialism is managers' efforts to reduce risk by diversification.

Hubris hypothesis

Another hypothesis, the hubris hypothesis, suggested that managers engage in mergers and acquisitions because they inadvertently overvalue target companies believing their evaluation is correct (Seth et al., 2000). The hubris hypothesis assumes irrational behavior on the managers' side, in contrast to the managerialism hypothesis that implies rational behavior (Wübben, 2007). Evidence regarding the hubris hypothesis is provided by Mukherjee et al. (2004). In their survey of Chief Financial Officers (CFOs) they find that CFOs who value a potential target company define merger cash flows as equity cash flows from the target. These cash flows are then discounted at the acquirer's weighted average cost of capital instead of the target's cost of equity, which is a bad practice and can lead to overpayment. In addition to this Seth et al. (2000) test the hubris hypothesis in the context of cross-border transactions and reveal that it can explain value creation instead of value destroying cross-border transactions as one would have expected.

Free cash flow theory

The theory of free cash flow is a third hypothesis that explains management related motives of mergers and acquisitions. Jensen (1986) defines free cash flow as "cash flow in excess of that required to fund all projects that have positive net present values". He argues that firms which generate significant levels of free cash flow experience a conflict of interest between managers and shareholders over payout policies, because any distribution to shareholders would reduce the resources that manager's control and therefore their power. This implies that managers have an incentive to minimize the distribution of free cash flows to shareholders. Accordingly, managers with free cash flows available also have an incentive to spend the free cash flow and are more likely to engage in value destroying or low benefit transactions.

Shareholder Value Related Motives

The synergy hypothesis

It suggests that mergers and acquisitions occur when the value of the combined firm after the transactions exceeds the sum of the values of the individual firms (Seth et al., 2000).

For example, synergies can arise from greater bargaining power with suppliers, economies of scale in production, avoidance of duplicate actions, pooling of management resources, or matching complementary resources and skills to enhance innovative capabilities (UNCTAD, 2000). The different sources of synergy are often classified as financial, operational, or managerial synergies (Trautwein, 1990). Results presented by Seth et al. (2000) suggest that gains in cross-border transactions are primarily explained by the synergy hypothesis. Also Berkovitch and Narayanan (1993) find that the synergy hypothesis is the reason behind the majority of mergers and acquisitions and results in positive gains. In their follow-up study, Seth et al. (2002) find evidence that the sources of value creation in cross-border transactions that are motivated by expected benefits from synergy are financial diversification, asset sharing, and reverse internalization of valuable intangible assets.

Trautwein (1990) describes two additional theories on mergers and acquisitions that are motivated by shareholder value creation: the monopoly theory and the valuation theory.

The monopoly theory

It argues that transactions are undertaken to attain market power which can be the motive behind horizontal or conglomerate mergers and acquisitions.

The valuation theory

It assumes that transactions occur because managers have an information advantage, that is, they have insider information about the target's value that is not available to the general public and which reveals that the target is undervalued. The valuation theory is based on the assumption that markets are not efficient.

Motives of Cross-border Transactions

All factors described earlier also hold for cross-border mergers and acquisitions. Following section will focus on motives that are particularly relevant to cross-border transactions and that might not have attracted attention so far.

External factors

According to the UNCTAD, changes of external factors such as the regulatory and economic environment particularly affect companies' cross-border acquisition behavior. Consequently, cross-border mergers and acquisitions are "strategic responses by companies in order to defend and expand their competitive positions in a changing [and globalizing] environment" (UNCTAD, 2000). For example, rapid technological changeshave increased the competitive pressure on companies.

Marketing variables

Companies have to keep up with new knowledge and shorter product life cycles while at the same time managing the costs and risks of innovation. Asset-seeking has been a rising driver over recent years for cross-border transactions as it provides companies with a possibility to quickly gain access to valuable intangible assets and skills that augment their innovative capabilities (UNCTAD, 2000).

Foreign direct investment policies

Policies that govern cross-border transactions underwent significant liberalization in the recent past. Today many countries try to draw foreign investment and thus remove restrictions on foreign direct investment and provide legal protection and guarantees. Cross-border transactions are also triggered by deregulation and privatization programs in various industries as well as changes in capital markets toward higher worldwide integration (UNCTAD, 2000).

Economic growth, tax rates, and exchange rates

Other factors that affect cross-border transactions are the potential of economic growth, tax rates, and exchange rates. Countries with greater potential for economic growth are more likely to attract foreign direct investment, as well as countries that impose relatively low tax rates on corporate earnings and countries where the local currency is expected to strengthen against the home currency of the investor (Madura, 2006). Another reason for companies to engage in cross-border mergers and acquisitions is to follow their clients abroad in order to continue and expand the business relationship (Weston et al., 2004).

On a more theoretical level there are three common theories which explain why companies expand their business internationally: the theory of comparative advantage, the imperfect markets theory, and the product cycle theory.

Theory of comparative advantage

According to the theory of comparative advantage "a country is said to have a comparative advantage in the production of a good […] if it can produce [that good] at a lower opportunity cost than another country" (Suranovic, 2008). It further suggests that both countries could benefit if each country specializes in the production of the good in which it has a comparative advantage.

The imperfect market theory

It argues that countries differ with respect to the resources available for the production of goods and that those resources are not freely transferable across countries. This implies that there are costs and restrictions related to transferring factors of production. If those factors were mobile and unrestricted, countries would not be able to benefit from comparative cost advantages and there would be no rationale for international business. However, as markets are imperfect companies have an incentive to seek out foreign opportunities (Madura, 2006).

The product cycle theory

It proposes that while a firm will initially create a product to satisfy home country demand, as time passes and the home market becomes mature with increasing competition, the firm might decide to enter foreign countries to expand its market and enhance its competitive position (Madura, 2006).

LEGAL FRAMEWORK OF M&A IN INDIA

1. Mergers and acquisitions in India are effected through a court process (multiple courts can be involved where the registered offices of the applicant companies are in different states) in accordance with Sections 391–394 of the Companies Act, 1956.
2. Publicly listed companies are required to tell relevant stock exchanges where they are listed at least 30 days before the filing of the application in the high court.
3. While the duration of the court process depends on various factors including the number of courts involved and level of public involvement, this could typically take between 5 months and 8 months.
4. Capital gains arising from a transfer by sale, exchange, extinguishment, or relinquishment of a right in a capital asset are subject to a capital gains tax.
5. Transfer of capital assets pursuant to a merger is, however, exempt from capital gains tax.

In the case of a merger, the conditions required to be fulfilled by the transferor company and the transferee companies are as follows:

Transferor Company

1. The transferor company is engaged in a business where loss was recurred in the past 3 years or more.
2. It holds three-fourths of the book value of fixed assets held by it 2 years before the date of amalgamation.
3. It owns an industrial undertaking, a ship or a hotel or is a banking company.

Transferee Company

1. The transferee company holds at least three-fourths of the book value of fixed assets acquired as a result of merger for at least 5 years after the merger.

2. It continues the business of transferor company for at least five years after the merger.
3. It achieves a level of production of at least 50 percent of installed capacity of the industrial undertaking within 4 years and continues to maintain it for 5 years from the date of the merger (installed capacity is capacity of production as on the date of merger).

Stamp Duty

Stamp duties are taxes on the instruments about the transactions. The power to legislate (except in certain cases where the union government prescribes) and collect stamp duty is with the respective state governments. The revenue from such duties forms a considerable part of the revenues of the state. Being a state subject, the stamp levies differ between various states and pose a problem in planning and avoiding duplicate levies in more than one state.

International M&A may often necessitate the transfer of shareholding interests of foreign holding companies in its Indian subsidiaries or joint venture companies. Capital gain on any such transfer is generally subject to capital gains tax. The IT Act however exempts such transfers out of international mergers subject to conditions.

Cross-border Merger

A cross-border merger is also permissible under the domestic laws of India provided the transferee company is an Indian company. In other words, a foreign company can merge into an Indian company but the vice versa would not be possible. The Andhra Pradesh High Court has upheld this position in the recent case of Moschip Semiconductor Technology Ltd (2004 120 COM CAS 108).

Capital Market Regulation—Takeover Code

1. A change of shareholding in publicly listed companies on account of these could trigger implications under the Takeover Code.
2. The Takeover Code (the more common name for the Substantial Acquisition of Shares and Takeovers Regulations) introduced by the Securities and Exchange Board of India (SEBI) in 1997 regulates the acquisitions of shares of publicly listed entities, and provides clarity in terms of triggers for a public offer, exemptions, price and size of the offer, disclosure norms, competitive bids, and penalties for non-compliance.
3. In general, the Takeover Code gets triggered when the acquirer purchases 15 percent or more of the voting capital of the target company, or where there has been a change in management control. In such a situation, the acquirer has to make an open offer to acquire a minimum of 20 percent of the voting capital from the public at a prescribed minimum offer price.
4. The Takeover Code does not apply in certain prescribed situations. One of the exceptions relevant to international mergers or demergers is the exception relating to acquisition/change of control pursuant to a scheme of arrangement or reconstruction including merger or demerger under any law or regulation, Indian or foreign.

IMPLICATIONS FOR M&A IN INDIA

As per the study done by Prashant Kale (2004), following interesting implications are there in M&A in emerging economies like India:

1. Acquisitions in emerging markets actually created positive value, on average, for both acquirer and acquired companies over entire study period. This result is different from that in developed market acquisitions, where acquisitions have generally created zero or negative value for the acquiring companies.
2. The value creation, in terms of abnormal stock returns following acquisitions, was significantly greater for acquired companies (8.79 percent) than for acquiring companies (1.71 percent).
3. Multinational acquirers, on average, created significantly greater value in their transactions than local acquirers did; but this difference in value creation reduced significantly over time. Overall, the greater value creation of multinational acquirers might be seen as a reflection of their greater acquisition experience and superior acquisition skills.
4. The impact of relatedness on acquisition value creation also varied over time. In the immediate few years after liberalization, there was little difference in the value creation patterns between related and unrelated acquisitions. But as liberalization progressed and conditions and practices in emerging markets like India began converging with those in developed countries, related acquisition clearly was viewed more favorably (average value creation of 3.75 percent) than unrelated acquisitions (average value creation of just 1.01 percent).

TERMINOLOGY USED IN M&A INDUSTRY

1. **Agglomeration:** A consolidation or merging.
2. **Any-and-all Bid:** A takeover bid in which the acquiring company sets a price that it is willing to purchase share at.
3. **Asset Stripper:** A corporate raider who acquires a target company with the intention of selling off some of the target's assets to repay outstanding debt, under the belief that the assets which remains after the stripping will be worth significantly more than the purchase price.
4. **Bear Hug:** A hostile takeover attempt predicated on making an offer at a premium large enough to ensure shareholder support even in the face of resistance from the target's board of directors.
5. **Bear Raid:** A trader's attempt to force down the price of a particular security by heavy selling or short selling.
6. **Black Night:** A company which makes hostile takeover bid on a target company.

7. **Blitzkrieg Tender Offer:** In a takeover, a tender offer that is so compelling that the offer is accepted very quickly.
8. **Cram-down Deal:** Colloquial term for a situation where shareholders are forced to accept undesirable terms in a merger or buyout, such as accepting junk bonds instead of cash or equity.
9. **Creeping Tender Offer:** A strategy in which a group of individuals gradually acquires target company's shares in the open market.
10. **Envy Ratio:** Price investor paid/percentage equity owned by investor.
11. **Godfather Offer:** A takeover technique where the acquiring company offers the target company an amount of money so large that management of the target company cannot refuge the proposal for the fear of shareholder retaliation.
12. **Hostile Takeover:** A takeover which goes against the wishes of target company's management and board of directors.
13. **Jonestown Defense:** An extreme kind of poison pill in which a company trying to avoid a hostile takeover will use tactics so extreme that they threaten the company's ability to survive.
14. **Rumortrage:** Trading based on a rumor of a takeover.
15. **Scorched-earthed Policy:** A reaction to a takeover attempt that involves liquidating valuable assets and assuming liabilities in an effort to make the proposed takeover unattractive to the acquiring company.
16. **Suicide Pill:** An extreme version of the poison pill defense in which a target company engages in an activity that might destroy the company in order to avoid a hostile takeover.
17. **Zombie:** A bankrupt or insolvent company which continues to operate while it awaits a closure or merger.

15

Miscellaneous

Learning Objectives

- To discuss real estate investment.
- To know consumer finance.
- To study investment banking.
- To understand bill financing.

REAL ESTATE INVESTMENT

Concept of Real Estate Investment Trust

The global real estate investment trust (REIT) industry is composed of the global industrial, office, residential, retail, diversified, and other REIT markets. The industrial REIT market covers companies or trusts engaged in the acquisition, development, ownership, leasing, management, and operation of industrial properties, including companies operating industrial warehouses and distribution properties.

Components of REIT

The office REIT market covers companies or trusts investing in office properties. The residential REIT market covers companies or trust with operations in residential properties. The retail REIT market covers companies or trusts with operations in retail properties. The diversified REIT market covers companies or trusts with significantly diversified operations across two or more property types, such as retail and office or retail and speciality.

The other REIT market covers companies or trusts that are involved in any other REIT activities such as servicing, originating, purchasing, and/or securitizing residential and/or commercial mortgage loans, including trusts that invest in mortgage-backed securities and other mortgage-related assets.

Growth of REIT

The global REITs industry was valued at a total capitalization of USD 799.2 billion at the end of 2008, representing a compound annual rate of change (CARC) of –5.8 percent for the period spanning 2004–08.

The retail REITs segment was the industry's most lucrative in 2008, with a value of USD 232.6 billion, equivalent to 29.1 percent of the industry's overall value. The performance of the industry is forecast to accelerate, with an anticipated compound annual growth rate (CAGR) of 7.8 percent for the 5-year period 2008–13, which is expected to drive the industry to a value of USD 1,165.5 billion by the end of 2013.

In comparison, the Americas and European industries reached respective values of USD 302.8 billion and USD 234.5 billion in 2008.

The retail REITs segment was the industry's most lucrative in 2008, with a value of USD 232.6 billion, equivalent to 29.1 percent of the industry's overall value. The office REITs segment had a value of USD 221.4 billion in 2008, equating to 27.7 percent of the industry's aggregate market capitalization.

The performance of the industry is forecast to accelerate, with an anticipated CAGR of 7.8 percent for the 5-year period 2008–13, which is expected to drive the industry to a value of USD 1,165.5 billion by the end of 2013.

In 2013, the global REITs industry is forecast to have a total capitalization of USD 1,165.5 billion, an increase of 45.8 percent since 2008. The compound annual growth rate of the industry in the period 2008–13 is predicted to be 7.8 percent.

Operations of REIT

Real estate investment trusts will be taken as market players. Buyers are those individuals and companies who make use of the properties owned and operated by REITs, and whose rents, leases, and similar payments form the main revenues of the trusts. Suppliers include companies involved in design, construction, and related activities required to develop real estate.

The legal requirements imposed on companies with REIT status have an impact on the competitive pressures they face, for example, by greatly restricting their ability to diversify in order to insulate themselves from variation in the real estate markets.

REITs are often viewed as offering stocks in themselves as investment "products," with investors as "buyers." In the present analysis, however, they will be considered as companies that develop and operate real estate, and which generate revenue through rental and similar income, but whose legal structure means that they experience somewhat different competitive pressures to non-REIT real estate companies. Their buyers are therefore the individuals and companies that rent or lease office, retail, residential, or other spaces owned by the REITs. Such buyers are of widely disparate size and financial strength. REIT companies can differentiate themselves considerably through the type and location of properties they offer, and switching costs can also be significant.

For example, a commercial client might have a long-term leasing contract on its office space, or it might be unwilling to incur the cost of moving staff and equipment to a different real estate company's premises. Such factors weaken buyer power. As a REIT must generate the majority of its revenues from real estate, it is unlikely to integrate forwards into its customers' business, which strengthens buyers. Overall, buyer power is moderate.

As part of qualification for REIT status, property companies must derive at least 75 percent of their profits from rental income and the value of assets involved in property rental must be at least 75 percent of the company's total assets. Thus, REITs need to acquire and maintain profitable real estate assets. They may do so by buying existing properties, or by building new ones. Thus, property owners, landowners, and companies able to design, construct, and renovate buildings are all significant suppliers. However, REITs are able to integrate vertically backwards into at least some of these functions. Westfield Group, for example, has its own team of designers, architects, and engineers that works on the development of new real estate ventures.

The ability of REITs either to buy existing properties or develop new ones weakens buyer power to an extent, since the two options can be seen as mutual substitutes for each other. Overall, supplier power is moderate.

The REIT industry contains a small number of large companies, but is still quite fragmented. The industry's top companies, Westfield Group, Mitsubishi Estate, Sun Hung Kai Properties, and Mitsui Fudosan, share only just under 10 percent of the total market capitalization value. Due to the restrictions of the activities of REITs, companies are dependent on the industry for revenues and diversity is only found in the type of property invested in, that is, office, retail, residential, and diversified REITs. It should also be considered that REITs are in direct competition with other players within the real estate industry including non-REIT property investment companies and private owners. Although REITs have a distinct competitive advantage in that they are exempt from corporation tax, significant restrictions on their operations mean that diversification potential is limited and therefore more diversified non-REIT property companies may have certain competitive advantages. Overall, rivalry with respect to the REITs industry is strong.

REIT in India: Present Scenario

The real estate sector in India is attracting huge investments. Private equity players are considering big investments, banks are giving loans to builders, and financial institutions are floating real estate funds. With 100 percent foreign direct investment (FDI) in real estate now being allowed, overseas developers are also closely looking at the market.

International investors like the US-based Warburg Pincus, Blackstone Group, Broadstreet, Morgan Stanley Real Estate Fund (MSREF), Columbia Endowment Fund, California Public

Employees' Retirement System (CalPERS), Hines, Tishman Speyer, Sam Zell's Equity International, JP Morgan Partners, and Amaranth Advisors have been found to show interest. A few funds belonging to Warren Buffet's Berkshire Hathway are also interested.

Indian institutions like Housing Development Finance Corporation Limited (HDFC), ICICI Venture, and Kotak Mahindra are launching funds to invest in real estate. HDFC, in association with State Bank of India (SBI) and ICICI Venture, has already launched a real estate fund, while ICICI Venture is also tying up with Tishman Speyer, one of the leading owner-developer-operator of up market properties in the world.

Most of these funds have been meeting investment bankers, banks, and housing finance companies in India to get a feel of the market. The developers are looking to tie up with Indian companies, while the private equity funds seek to test the market with small investments in big projects.

The developers are expected to bring in at least USD 100 million. The pure private equity players are expected to be passive players. They are likely to take a smaller stake in specific projects along with an Indian real estate developer. These investors would prefer board berths.

The combined investments by various groups into Indian real estate market could go up to USD 1.5 billion in near future. Funds are looking at returns of around 16–20 percent. The IT and outsourcing boom in the country has raised the need for quality commercial, residential, hospitality, and health care facilities as well

It is expected that the developers will bring in 10 percent of their own money, and raise the remaining money from overseas or in India. A group of non-resident Indians (NRIs) has raised USD 150 million under the Indian Real Estate Opportunities Fund and is scouting for projects in India.

HDFC, in association with SBI, has been raising Rs 750 crore with a green shoe option of Rs 250 crore for a real estate fund. It is likely to invest in residential, commercial, and IT properties. Kotak is also raising a real estate fund while ICICI Venture is in the process of raising Rs 750 crore real estate fund.

In the health care segment, Singapore-based Parkways Hospitals has shown interest. Gleneagles—a part of Parkway Hospitals—has a stake in the Apollo Gleneagles Hospital.

According to the new FDI policy, up to 100 percent investment will be allowed under automatic route in townships, housing, built-up infrastructure, and construction-development projects.

Construction projects would include hotels, resorts, hospitals, educational institutions, housing, and commercial premises. The government has also reduced the minimum mandatory area to allow FDI in real estate sector from 100 acres to 25 acres.

Leading Global Players in Real Estate Investment Trusts

Westfield group (Australia)

Westfield Group is an internally managed, vertically integrated, shopping center group undertaking ownership, development, design, construction, funds/asset management, property management, leasing, and marketing activities. The company primarily operates in the USA, Australia, New Zealand, and the UK. It is headquartered in Sydney, Australia and employs about 5,000 people.

Mitsubishi Estate Company, Limited

Mitsubishi Estate Company (Mitsubishi Estate) along with its group companies is engaged in real estate development activities that comprise its building business, residential business, urban development and investment management, international business, architectural design and engineering, custom-built housing, hotel business, and real estate service operations.

Sun Hung Kai Properties

Sun Hung Kai Properties (SHKP) is primarily engaged in the development of property for sale and investment. The group is also involved in telecommunications, construction, property management, financial services, property insurance, transport, infrastructure and logistics, waste treatment facilities, apparel business, and department stores. The group primarily operates in Hong Kong. It is headquartered in Wanchai, Hong Kong and employs more than 30,000 people.

Mitsui Fudosan

Mitsui Fudosan is the real estate arm of the Mitsui Group. The company builds, sells, leases, and manages a wide variety of real estates, including office buildings, residential subdivisions, and condominiums. The company primarily operates in Japan.

The company has eight business segments which include leasing, sales of housing, office buildings and land, construction, brokerage, consignment sales and consulting, property management, sales of housing materials and merchandise, facility operations and others.

CONSUMER FINANCE

Concept of Consumer Finance

As per the Wikipedia:

"**Consumer finance** in the most basic sense of the word refers to any kind of lending to consumers."

The consumer finance industry (meaning branch-based subprime lenders) mainly came to fruition in the middle of the 20th century. At that time, these companies were all stand-alone companies not owned by banks and an alternative to banks. However, at that time, the companies were not focused on subprime lending. Instead, they attempted to lend to everyone who would accept their high rates of interest.

Consumer credit is supplied in many forms, ranging from small, unsecured loans to long-term contracts of thousands of rupees protected by valuable collateral. It is sometimes provided on a personalized retail basis and sometimes handled in large-scale bulk operations.

Average finance charges on the consumer credit provided by different groups of institutions vary as per credit outstanding. Most of the variation in finance charges was traced to differences in operating expenses.

Consumer Finance Products

Financing facilities that support consumption and, as a result thereof, improve the living standards of households fall within the broad definition of consumer finance. Their range includes credit cards, short-term loans, finance and operating leases, and housing finance semantics of financial product range; it is treated as a distinct financing product essentially due to its long-term nature.

Role of Consumer Finance in Economy

Consumer finance stimulates demand and consumption that encourage the industry to expand its productive capacity or make fuller use of its existing capacity and cut prices at the retail level besides increasing employment and, possibly, fresh investments in industrial sectors, especially those producing consumer durables. However, the key to sustaining the consumption demand equation without pushing inflation to unsustainable levels is the maintenance of the critical balance between savings, investment, and borrowers' debt-servicing ability.

The big attraction in extending financing facilities to the passive consumer segment is the prospect of earning better interest rate spreads because consumers are softer targets for loan pricing. They are more likely to borrow at higher rates—a convenience no longer available on lending to industrial and commercial borrowers who insist on fine loan rates.

Reasons for Emergence and Growth of "Consumer Finance Industry"

1. Banks made it difficult to obtain personal credit. Banks did not have the wide variety of programs or aggressive marketing that they do today.
2. Many people simply didn't like to deal with bank employees and branches, preferring the more relaxed environment of a consumer finance company.
3. Consumer finance companies focused on lowering the required monthly payment for their customer's debts.

Besides charging a higher interest rate to compensate for their risk, consumer finance companies are usually able to operate successfully because their employees are given more flexibility in structuring loans and in collections than banks.

Operations of a Consumer Finance Company

A sustained trend of depressed demand prevented the development of a sizeable industrial base and reduced the opportunities for investment and employment. Banks are now trying to redress this macroeconomic structural imbalance; but given the historic pattern of market developments, they may be handicapped in their efforts initially, as low interest rates enhance the capacity of middle and upper middle classes to borrow and service consumer loans, not the lower middle class because the demand-pull created by upper income classes pushes up the prices of consumer durables.

The distortion should be a temporary phase, and should vanish as production increases to fill the supply gap. Rising demand encourages new entries, which pushes up competitive stakes for existing suppliers. To sustain their market share, they maximize capacity utilization and pass on the economies of scale in the shape of lower prices.

This is the stage when the lower middle classes enter the consumer goods markets. Banks providing cheap credit to business and industry can exercise a powerful influence on the manufacturing sectors for compensating savers through lower prices. But in markets in which manufacturers lack a sense of social responsibility, this period can sometime become uncomfortably long—a possibility that must be avoided.

Issues of Consumer Finance Industry

There are some issues that hinder consumer finance which are as follows:

Verification of consumers' repayment capacity

First is the lack of institutional arrangements and practices to facilitate verification of consumers' repayment capacity. Verifying the antecedents of the self-employed poses a real problem because many among them don't keep credible records of earnings from their vocations of businesses to permit a reliable assessment of their repayment capacity. Many employers certify very inadequately the status of employees intending to avail consumer finance. Nor do they accept responsibility of informing the financing institution in the event the finance-availing employee leaves, or is laid off. Fewer among them confirm that they have recorded the fact that their employees have availed a financing facility. Unless provisions are made in the relevant labor laws, employers will not provide this information, which they should morally feel bound to provide. Insurance companies could lend a helping hand by providing cheaper loan repayment guarantees to lending banks. Consumer insurance is available; but for many consumers (especially those in the middle and low-income groups) its pricing makes the overall cost of availing consumer credit uncomfortably high. Cheaper availability of such insurance could significantly improve the prospects of expanding the consumer finance market.

Inadequacies of our legal system

This factor limits expansion of consumer finance (especially for those in the middle and low-income groups) and it makes it cumbersome for borrowers to collateralize their unencumbered assets for the satisfaction of lending banks and repossession of financed assets.

Shortcuts in risk assessment of customer

Employing shortcuts in risk assessment to extend micro consumer loans may lumber banks with hundreds of small delinquent loans.

Inabilities of banks to adopt

Retail banks with large branch networks have the potential for succeeding in this business but it will require making alterations in their infrastructure and a change in the focus of investigative effort for assessing repayment capacity. The organization must be pro-active and sufficient in terms of manpower and MIS to ensure a reaction speed that is commensurate with size of its customer base. In this regard, it will be crucially important to ensure that, on a continuing basis, administrative resources are matched with the size of customer base.

Method of lending and risk assessment

Cobb–Douglas function

Cobb–Douglas function is the number of accounts outstanding. This measure, rather than the money volume of loans, is used because branch operations are closely related to the number of loans processed. This can be illustrated by classifying loan branch expenses into one of the following functional cost categories:

1. Acquisition
2. Servicing
3. Risk assumption (default losses)
4. Forbearance (cost of capital)

The latter two categories, risk assumption and forbearance, are excluded from the definition of direct branch operating costs. The acquisition and servicing costs are incurred largely on a per-loan basis because the basic operating procedures for processing loan applications, extending loans, and servicing accounts are very similar for various types of loans, differing mainly in degree or extent of activity involved. Thus, most loans would be expected to have the same basic cost, with variations due to other influencing factors such as the size of the loan and the type of customer or risk class. In comparing two loan branches with the same dollar amount of loan volume but different average loan size and number of accounts, the branch with larger loans (and fewer accounts) is expected to have lower costs; the low-cost condition is directly related to the number of accounts. Since direct operating costs are considered to vary more directly with the number of accounts than with money volume, the number of accounts outstanding is considered to be the more appropriate output measure. Further support for the use of the number of accounts as an output measure is provided by the relationship between the numbers of accounts outstanding (or extended) and the number of applications rejected. Since application processing costs are also likely to be incurred on a per-application basis, there will be a direct relationship between these costs and the number of rejected and accepted applications relative to the number of accounts outstanding. Thus, output and, inferentially, operating scale are measured as the number of accounts outstanding.

The statistical analysis in different researches has supported the hypothesized cost function.

The major empirical results are the finding of

1. scale economies, and
2. a positive relationship between average loan size and direct operating cost per loan.

The scale effect implies that restrictive licensing of loan offices, and the resulting increase in loan office size, should result in lower costs per loan. However, in view of the competitive environment of the small-loan market, and the apparent nature of the small-loan borrower, it is debatable whether any cost advantages would accrue to the borrower. Similarly, recommendations on finance charge rate structures do not necessarily follow directly from the statistical results. Although the test of the loan size–cost relationship clearly supports a graduated rate structure, the advisability of setting legal rate ceilings is less clear because of the difficulties in establishing the appropriate levels. Additional complications are introduced by socio-political considerations: the dilemma lies in the question of the appropriate cut-off rate beyond which no consumer should be permitted (legally) to borrow. This is largely a value judgment which will not be considered here.

Some of the companies in consumer finance business in India

- ICICI Bank
- Reliance Consumer Finance
- TVS
- FIDC
- Tata Capital
- Standard Chartered
- Karnataka Bank
- Muthoot Capital Services
- Yamha India Finance
- Dena Bank
- Allahabad Bank
- SBI
- Axis Bank
- Shriram Transport Finance

INVESTMENT BANKING

Background and Present Status

The investment banking and brokerage industry profile covers financial institutions engaged in investment banking and brokerage services, including equity and debt underwriting, and mergers and acquisitions (M&A) services.

Market values reflect revenues generated through fees and commissions obtained in three key segments: M&A, equities, and fixed income. Any currency conversions used in the creation of this report have been calculated using constant annual average exchange rates. The global investment banking and brokerage sector generated total fee revenues of USD 57.4 billion in 2008, representing a CAGR of 5.5 percent for the period spanning 2004–08. The M&A services segment was the sector's most lucrative in 2008, generating total fee revenues of USD 29.4 billion, equivalent to 51.1 percent of the sector's overall value.

The performance of the sector is forecast to decelerate, with an anticipated CAGR of 5.3 percent for the 5-year period 2008–13.

After a period of strong, double-digit growth, the global investment banking and brokerage sector declined in 2008. Further declines are not expected and the sector is set to recover, posting increasing growth rates toward 2013.

In comparison, the American and European sectors grew over the same period, to reach respective values of USD 26.5 billion and USD 19.2 billion in 2008.

The equity services contributed fee revenues of USD 18.5 billion in 2008, equating to 32.2 percent of the sector's aggregate revenues.

The performance of the sector is forecast to decelerate, with an anticipated CAGR of 5.3 percent for the 5-year period 2008–13, which is expected to drive the sector to a value of USD 74.2 billion by the end of 2013.

Concept of Investment Banking

An investment bank is a financial institution that raises capital, trades in securities, and manages corporate M&A. Investment banks profit from companies and governments by raising money through issuing and selling securities in capital markets (both equity, debt) and insuring bonds (e.g., selling credit default swaps), as well as providing advice on transactions such as M&A. A majority of investment banks offer strategic advisory services for mergers, acquisitions, divestiture, or other financial services for clients, such as the trading of derivatives, fixed income, foreign exchange, commodity, and equity securities.

Investment banking is one of the most global industries and is hence continuously challenged to respond to new developments and innovation in the global financial markets. Throughout the history of investment banking, it is only known that many have theorized that all investment banking products and services would be commoditized. New products with higher margins are constantly invented and manufactured by bankers in hopes of winning over clients and developing trading know-how in new markets. However, since these usually cannot be patented or copyrighted, they are very often copied quickly by competing banks, pushing down trading margins.

Functions of Investment Banking

An investment bank is split into the so-called front office, middle office, and back office. While large full-service investment banks offer all of the lines of businesses, both sell side and buy side, smaller sell-side investment firms such as boutique investment banks and small broker-dealers will focus on investment banking and sales/trading/research, respectively. Investment banks offer security to both corporations issuing securities and investors buying securities. For corporations, investment bankers offer information on when and how to place their securities in the market. The corporations do not have to spend on resources with which it is not equipped. To the investor, the responsible investment banker offers protection against unsafe securities. The offering of a few bad issues can cause serious loss to its reputation, and hence loss of business.

Front office

1. **Investment banking** is the traditional aspect of the investment banks which also involves helping customers raise funds in the capital markets and advising on M&A. Investment banking may involve subscribing investors to a security issuance, coordinating with bidders, or negotiating with a merger target. Another term for the investment banking division is corporate finance and its advisory group is often termed M&A. The investment banking division (IBD) is generally divided into industry coverage and product coverage groups. Industry coverage groups focus on a specific industry such as health care, industrials, or technology, and maintain relationships with corporations within the industry to bring in business for a bank. Product coverage groups focus on financial products, such as M&A, leveraged finance, equity, and high-grade debt, and generally work and collaborate with industry groups in the more intricate and specialized needs of a client.
2. **Sales and trading:** On behalf of the bank and its clients, the primary function of a large investment bank is buying and selling products. In market making, traders will buy and sell financial products with the goal of making an incremental amount of money on each trade. Sales is the term for the investment banks' sales force, whose primary job is to call on institutional and high-net-worth investors to suggest trading ideas (on caveat emptor basis) and take orders. Sales desks then communicate their clients' orders to the appropriate trading desks, who can price and execute trades, or structure new products that fit a specific need. Structuring has been a relatively recent activity as derivatives have come into play, with highly technical and numerate employees working on creating complex, structured products which typically offer much greater margins and returns than underlying cash securities. Strategists advise external as well as internal clients on the strategies that can be adopted in various markets. Ranging from derivatives to specific industries, strategists place companies and industries in a quantitative framework with full consideration of the macroeconomic scene.
3. **Research** is the division which reviews companies and writes reports about their prospects, often with "buy" or "sell" ratings. While the research division generates no revenue, its resources are used to assist traders in trading, the sales force in suggesting

ideas to customers, and investment bankers convince the clients for customers. There is a potential conflict of interest between the investment bank and its analysis in that published analysis can affect the profits of the bank.

4. **Custody and agency services** is the division which provides cash management, lending, and securities brokerage services to institutions. Prime brokerage with hedge funds has been an especially profitable business, as well as risky, as seen in the "run on the bank" with Bear Stearns in 2008.

5. **Investment management** is the professional management of various securities (shares, bonds, etc.) and other assets (e.g., real estate) to meet specified investment goals for the benefit of the investors. Investors may be institutions (insurance companies, pension funds, corporations, etc.) or private investors (both directly via investment contracts and more commonly via collective investment schemes, e.g., mutual funds). The investment management division of an investment bank is generally divided into separate groups, often known as private wealth management and private client services.

6. **Merchant banking** is a private equity activity of investment banks. Current examples include Goldman Sachs Capital Partners and JPMorgan's One Equity Partners. (Originally, "merchant bank" was the British English term for an investment bank.)

Middle office

1. **Risk management** involves analyzing the market and credit risk that traders are taking onto the balance sheet in conducting their daily trades, and setting limits on the amount of capital that they are able to trade in order to prevent "bad" trades having a detrimental effect to a desk overall.

2. **Corporate treasury** is responsible for an investment bank's funding, capital structure management, and liquidity risk monitoring.

3. **Financial control** tracks and analyzes the capital flows of the firm. The finance division is the principal adviser to senior management on essential areas such as controlling the firm's global risk exposure and the profitability and structure of the firm's various businesses.

4. **Corporate strategy**, along with risk, treasury, and controllers, often falls under the finance division as well.

5. **Compliance areas** are responsible for an investment bank's daily operations' compliance with government regulations and internal regulations, often also considered a back-office division.

Back office

1. **Operations** involve checking the data of trades that have been conducted, ensuring that they are not erroneous, and transacting the required transfers.

2. **Technology** refers to the information technology department. Every major investment bank has considerable amounts of in-house software, created by the technology team, who are also responsible for technical support. Technology has changed considerably

in the last few years as more sales and trading desks are using electronic trading. Some trades are initiated by complex algorithms for hedging purposes.

Challenges in Investment Banking

1. Historically, equity research firms were founded and owned by investment banks. One common practice is for equity analysts to initiate coverage on a company in order to develop relationships that lead to highly profitable investment banking business. In the 1990s, many equity researchers allegedly traded positive stock ratings directly for investment banking business. On the flip side of the coin: companies would threaten to divert investment banking business to competitors unless their stock was rated favorably. Politicians acted to pass laws to criminalize such acts. Increased pressure from regulators and a series of lawsuits, settlements, and prosecutions curbed this business to a large extent following the 2001 stock market tumble.
2. Many investment banks also own retail brokerages. Also during the 1990s, some retail brokerages sold consumers securities which did not meet their stated risk profile. This behavior may have led to investment banking business or even sales of surplus shares during a public offering to keep public perception of the stock favorable.
3. Since investment banks engage heavily in trading for their own account, there is always the temptation or possibility that they might engage in some form of front running. Front running is the illegal practice of stockbrokers executing orders on a security for their own account before filling orders previously submitted by their customers, thereby benefiting from any changes in prices induced by those orders.

Developments in Investment Banking

Investment banking is one of the most global industries and is hence continuously challenged to respond to new developments and innovation in the global financial markets. Throughout investment banking history, many have theorized that all investment banking products and services would be commoditized. However, new products with higher margins are constantly invented and manufactured by bankers in hopes of winning over clients and developing trading know-how in new markets. However, since these cannot be patented or copyrighted, they are very often copied quickly by competing banks, pushing down trading margins. For example, trading bonds and equities for customers is now a commodity business, but structuring and trading derivatives is highly profitable. Each contract has to be uniquely structured to match the client's need, may involve complex pay-off and risk profiles, and is not listed on any market. In addition, while many products have been commoditized, an increasing amount of investment bank profit has come from proprietary trading, where size creates a positive network benefit (since the more trades an investment bank does, the more it knows about the market flow, allowing it to theoretically make better trades and pass on better guidance to clients). A derivative is a generic term for specific type of investments from which payoffs over time are derived from the performance of assets (such as commodities, shares, or bonds), interest rates, exchange rates, or indices (such as a stock market index, consumer price index (CPI), or an index of weather).

Vertical Integration: Previously, investment banks had historically assisted lenders in raising more lending funds and having the ability to offer longer term fixed interest rates by converting the lenders' outstanding loans into bonds. For example, a mortgage lender would make a house loan, and then use the investment bank to sell bonds to fund the debt. The money from the sale of the bonds can be used to make new loans, while the lender accepts loan payments and passes the payments on to the bondholders. This process is called securitization. However, lenders have begun to securitize loans themselves, especially in the areas of mortgage loans. Because of this, and because of the fear that this will continue, many investment banks have focused on becoming lenders themselves, making loans with the goal of securitizing them. In fact, in the areas of commercial mortgages, many investment banks lend at loss leader interest rates in order to make money for securitizing the loans, causing them to be a very popular financing option for commercial property investors and developers.

Some notable investment banks include:

- ABN AMRO
- Adams, Harkness, & Hill
- Anderson & Strudwick
- Banc of America Securities
- Barclays Capital
- Bear Stearns
- BMO Nesbitt Burns
- BNP Paribas
- Banque Marocaine pour le Commerce Exterieur
- Bulltick Capital Markets
- Brown Brothers Harriman
- Calyon
- Cantor Fitzgerald
- Canaccord Adams
- Cazenove
- Citigroup
- CIBC World Markets
- Commerce International Merchant Bankers Berhad (CIMB)
- Cowen and Company
- Credit Suisse
- Deutsche Bank
- Dresdner Kleinwort
- Ferris, Baker Watts, Inc.
- Friedman Billings Ramsey
- Genuity Capital Markets
- Goldman Sachs

- Grace Matthews
- Greenhill & Company
- Houlihan Lokey Howard & Zukin
- Jefferies & Co.
- JPMorgan Chase & Co.
- Keefe, Bruyette & Woods
- KeyBanc Capital Markets
- Lazard
- Lehman Brothers
- Macquarie Bank
- Merrill Lynch
- Merriman Curhan Ford & Co.
- Mizuho Corporate Bank
- Morgan Stanley
- Northern Securities
- Newbury Piret
- NIBC
- N.M. Rothschild & Sons
- Nomura Securities
- Oppenheimer of North America
- Peter J. Solomon Company
- Petrie Parkman & Co.
- Piper Jaffray
- RBC Capital Markets
- Robert W. Baird & Company
- Rutberg & Co.
- Rothschild
- Sanford Bernstein
- Stephens Inc.
- SVB Alliant
- Scotia Capital
- Société Générale
- TD Securities
- ThinkEquity Partners, LLC
- Thomas Weisel Partners
- TSG Partners, LLC
- UBS AG
- Wachovia Securities
- Wedbush Morgan Securities
- Wells Fargo Securities
- Westminster Securities Corporation
- William Blair & Company, LLC

Details of some of the investment companies are as follows:

The Goldman Sachs Group, Inc.

Goldman Sachs is a global investment banking, securities and investment management firm that serves corporations, financial institutions, governments, and high-net-worth individuals. The company primarily operates in the USA, Europe, and Asia. The company has offices in more than 25 countries and 40 cities around the world. At the end of the fiscal year 2007 the company's assets under management were valued at USD 868 billion.

Goldman Sachs' research operations, named Global Investment Research (GIR), provide fundamental research on companies, industries, economies, currencies, commodities, and macro strategy research. GIR covers 3,250 companies and over 50 national economies worldwide. Research is conducted globally through the following departments: equity research, credit research, economic research, commodities research, and strategy research.

Goldman Sachs operates through three business segments: trading and principal investments, investment banking, and asset management and securities services.

JPMorgan Chase & Co.

JPMorgan Chase & Co. (JPMC) is a financial holding company. It is a leading global financial services firm and one of the largest banking institutions in the USA. In 2007, JPMC recorded around USD 1.56 trillion in assets and USD 123.2 billion in stockholders' equity. The company is a leader in investment banking, financial transaction processing, asset management, and private equity.

The company operates through the following brands: JPMorgan Chase, JPMorgan and Chase. JPMorgan Chase represents the parent company, which includes all of the firm's subsidiaries; it is also used by the treasury services business. The following businesses of JPMC use the JPMorgan brand: investment bank, worldwide securities services, private banking, asset management, one equity partners, and private client services. The US consumer and commercial banking businesses serve customers under the Chase brand.

JPMC's principal bank subsidiaries are JPMorgan Chase Bank, a national banking association in the USA with branches in 17 states, and Chase Bank USA, a national bank that is the company's credit card issuing bank.

JPMC's principal non-bank subsidiary is JP Morgan Securities, which is the company's US investment banking arm. Its operations are spread across more than 50 countries.

The company operates through seven segments: investment bank, retail financial services, card services, asset management, treasury and securities services, commercial banking, and corporate.

Citigroup Inc.

Citigroup is a diversified global financial services holding company. It has more than 200 million customer accounts in over 100 countries. Citibank, a subsidiary, is Citigroup's arm in commercial banking.

Citibank's principal offerings include consumer finance, mortgage lending, and retail banking products and services, investment banking, commercial banking, cash management, trade finance and e-commerce products and services, and private banking products and services. Citigroup operates in the following regions: North America, Latin America, Asia, Europe, the Middle East, and Africa.

The company operates through five operating segments: global consumer group, markets and banking, global wealth management, alternative investments and corporate and other. Global consumer group provides an array of banking, lending, insurance, and investment services. The segment's distribution network includes 8,527 branches, approximately 20,000 ATMs, and 530 automated lending machines (ALMs), the Internet, telephone and direct mail, and through independent representatives.

Global consumer group comprises the US consumer and international consumer businesses. The US consumer is composed of four businesses: cards, retail distribution, consumer lending, and commercial business. Operating in five geographies, namely, Mexico, Latin America, Europe, Middle East and Africa (EMEA), Japan, and Asia, international consumer sub segment is composed of three businesses: cards, consumer finance, and retail banking.

Morgan Stanley

Morgan Stanley is a financial services firm providing investment banking, conventional banking, securities brokerage, asset management, and credit card services. The company is based in the US and has operations in 28 countries spanning the continents of North America, Europe, and Asia. Outside the USA, Morgan Stanley offers financial services in Europe, the Middle East, Asia, and Latin America.

Morgan Stanley's majority-owned subsidiary, Morgan Stanley Capital International (MSCI), calculates and distributes over 40,000 international and US equity benchmark indices. The company's global research department, named Research, engages in equity and fixed income research.

Morgan Stanley manages and participates in public offerings and private placements of debt, equity, and other securities worldwide. The company is an underwriter of common stock, preferred stock, and other equity-related securities, including convertible securities and American Depositary Receipts.

The company also provides advisory services on M&A, divestitures, corporate defense strategies, joint ventures, privatizations, spin-offs, restructurings, proxy and consent solicitations, tender offers, exchange offers, and leveraged buyouts. The company has three operating segments: institutional securities, global wealth management group, and asset management.

BILL FINANCING

Bill Financing/Discounting

While discounting a bill, the bank buys the bill (i.e., bill of exchange or promissory note) before it is due and credits the value of the bill after a discount charge to the customer's account.

The transaction is practically an advance against the security of the bill and the discount represents the interest on the advance from the date of purchase of the bill until it is due for payment.

Under certain circumstances, the bank may discount a bill of exchange instead of negotiating them. The amount the bank advances to you also depends on your past record and reputation as a drawee.

Usually, the bank may want some conditions to be fulfilled to be able to discount a bill:

1. A bill must be a usance bill.
2. It must have been accepted and bear at least two good signatures (e.g., of reputable individuals, companies, or banks).
3. The bank will normally only discount trade bills.
4. Where a usance bill is drawn at a fixed period after sight, the bill must be accepted to establish the maturity.

Presenting a Bill

Bills may be presented to the nominated bank in two ways:

With recourse

The bank checks the documents and confirms that they comply with the Documentary Credit (DC) terms, and send the bill with the original DC to the nominated bank requesting payment. The nominated bank need not recheck the documents and it can claim a refund from us in the case of an unspotted discrepancy. We pay our customer after receipt of funds from the nominated bank.

Without recourse

We pass the original DC and unchecked documents to the nominated bank on a collection basis, requesting payment. The nominated bank has to check the documents in the normal way. Usually, we present documents to the nominated bank without recourse:

i. when the opening bank is a member of the bank nominated for payment, acceptance, or negotiation;
ii. when the nominated bank has confirmed the DC; and
iii. when the nominated bank is the drawee.

If you have a good standing, we can give you an advance against an Outstanding Bills (OB). You will then have to repay the advance from the proceeds of the bill.

Finance against Collection

You as an exporter may ask the bank for finance against a collection bill. Now, if your buyer will close the sale only if he gets credit, you may involve the bank to arrange for the same. This will allow you to be flexible in the payment terms.

The remitting bank may finance a good creditworthy exporter by purchasing or discounting his collection bills under an "Export Line." However,

1. If the importer refuses a bill the bank has purchased, the bank must be sure of being able to get a refund.
2. The importer must be reliable. The bank usually tries to avoid the risk of refusal by keeping in touch with large banks.
3. The bank always ensures that when a bill is purchased, it is drawn on approved drawees within limits.

Bill discounting is a short tenure financing instrument for companies willing to discount their purchase/sales bills to get funds for the short run, and as for the investors in them, it is a good instrument to park their spare funds for a very short duration. A lot of people believe that bills discounting falls in the purview of banks and financial institutions. While this may be correct to a large extent, it is also true that most of the smaller value bills of big corporates and smaller, but sound, companies are undertaken by retail investors, who have funds to spare for a certain period.

Bills discounting is of two types:

1. Purchase bills discounting
2. Sales bill discounting

A purchase bill discounting means that the investor discounts the purchase bill of the company and pays the company, who in turn pay their supplier. The investor gets his money back from the company at the end of the discounting period.

A sales bills discounting means the investor discounts the sales bill of the company and pays directly to the company. The investor gets his return from the company at the end of the discounting period.

Procedure

The procedure is that a broker will contact you with proposals to discount bills of different companies at different rates of discounting. The better companies command discounting rates of 13 to 15 percent, while the lesser known, by size and by safety, have to pay discounting rates of 17 percent to as high as 28 percent. It is later explained what factors determine the discount rates.

When an investor and the company agree to a particular bill discounting transaction, the following is what the company gives to the investor:

1. the original copies of bills to be discounted;
2. *hundi*/promissory note; and
3. postdated cheque.

The investor simply has to issue a cheque. The amount of cheque is arrived at after deducting the discount rate. The postdated cheque that the company gives is of the full amount of the transaction. This can be better explained with an example as follows.

We see that the investor benefits in two ways.

He gets the interest element at the first day of issuing the cheque, that is, he does not include that part in his cheque amount. Thus, he can earn interest on this interest for a 3-month period.

Discount Rates

The rates depend on the following factors:

- **The Broker:** The broker has a good influence on the rates offered by companies. His relations with the company and the investor do make a difference of a couple of percentage point in discounting rates.
- **Market Liquidity:** Liquidity crunch in the market tends to hike up the rates even in the best of the companies. Since this instrument is a short tenure one, short-term changes in the market liquidity greatly affect the discount rates.
- **Volume/Value of Discounting:** When the volume/value of discounting done by the investor is high, he is looking at security more than returns. The company on its part is looking at savings by way of reduced legal paper work and a higher amount of dedicated funds for a said period and hence on the whole reduced costs to the company.
- **Frequency:** An investor who is regular bills discounter for the company may get up to 1 to 1.5 percent points higher interest rates than a new investor. As for the investor he is trying it out with a new company and will agree to a lesser rate to ensure safety.
- **Company's Finance Resources:** This is one of the biggest factors that decide the discount rates. A public limited company generally tends to have a cheaper source of finance as against any other form of company. Working capital financing of companies to a large extent manipulates the rates the companies are willing to discount their bills at.

Cautions in Dealing with Bill Finance Instrument

The following points need to be remembered when dealing in this instrument.

1. One must have a thorough knowledge of the company whose bills are discounted.
2. The industry, its competitiveness, people at the helm and reputation in the market, as it is going to be the company that is going to pay you from its earnings.

3. There is no legal fallback option in case of default by the company.
4. The company does sign a promissory note, but legal respite through using this will take years to happen.
5. The investor is not a secured creditor for the company nor does he get any preference on winding up of the company. Brokers need to be people who are well known to one. Since most of the deals happen through them, one should know the broker well enough to trust him and his deals. Spurious brokers are plenty out there in the market and a watchful eye must be kept.

RBI's Stringent Norms for Bills Discounting

The Reserve Bank of India (RBI) has permitted banks to sanction limit for bills discounting to borrowers in accordance with the loan policy as approved by their board of directors. In its guidelines on discounting and rediscounting of bills by banks, based on the recommendations of the working group on discounting of bills by banks, the RBI has said banks should lay down a bills discounting policy approved by their board of directors and consistent with their policy of sanctioning of working capital limits.

In a circular issued to all scheduled commercial banks, the apex bank has said the procedure for board approval should include banks' core operating process from the time the bills are tendered till these are realized.

While purchasing, discounting, negotiating bills under LCs or otherwise, banks have been asked to establish genuineness of underlying transaction documents. Accommodation bills should not be purchased, discounted, or negotiated by banks. Banks should be circumspect while discounting bills drawn by front finance companies set up by large industrial groups on other group companies.

Banks may exercise their commercial judgment in discounting of bills of services sector. In order to promote payment discipline which would to a certain extent encourage acceptance of bills, all corporates and other constituent borrowers having turnover above threshold level as fixed by the bank's board of directors should be mandated to disclose "aging schedule" of their overdue payables in their periodical returns submitted to banks.

Banks should not enter into repo transactions using bills discounted/rediscounted as collateral.

Banks should follow the foregoing instructions strictly and any violation of these instructions will be viewed seriously and invite penal action from the RBI.

Bills Discounting Schemes in India

The RBI has announced following bill discounting schemes in India w.e.f. July 27, 1992.

The banks may adhere to the following guidelines while purchasing/discounting/negotiating/rediscounting of genuine commercial/trade bills:

1. Since banks have already been given freedom to decide their own guidelines for assessing/sanctioning working capital limits of borrowers, they may sanction working

capital limit as also bills limit to borrowers after proper appraisal of their credit needs and in accordance with the loan policy as approved by their board of directors.

2. Banks should clearly lay down a bills discounting policy approved by their board of directors, which should be consistent with their policy of sanctioning of working capital limits. In this case, the procedure for board approval should include banks' core operating process from the time the bills are tendered till these are realized. Banks may review their core operating processes and simplify the procedure in respect of bills financing. In order to address the often cited problem of delay in realization of bills, banks may take advantage of improved computer/communication network like Structured Financial Messaging System (SFMS) and adopt the system of "value dating" of their clients' accounts.

3. Banks should open LCs and purchase/discount/negotiate bills under LCs only in respect of genuine commercial and trade transactions of their borrower constituents who have been sanctioned regular credit facilities by the banks. Banks should not, therefore, extend fund-based (including bills financing) or non-fund based facilities like opening of LCs, providing guarantees, and acceptances to non-constituent borrower or/and non-constituent member of a consortium/multiple banking arrangement.

4. For the purpose of credit exposure, bills purchased/discounted/negotiated under LCs or otherwise should be reckoned on the bank's borrower constituent. Accordingly, the exposure should attract a risk weight appropriate to the borrower constituent (viz, 100 percent for firms, individuals, corporates, etc.) for capital adequacy purposes.

5. While purchasing/discounting/negotiating bills under LCs or otherwise, banks should establish genuineness of underlying transactions/documents.

6. Banks should ensure that blank LC forms are kept in safe custody as in case of security items, like blank cheques and demand drafts, and verified/balanced on daily basis. LC forms should be issued to customers under joint signatures of the bank's authorized officials.

7. The practice of drawing bills of exchange claused "without recourse" and issuing LCs bearing the legend "without recourse" should be discouraged because such notations deprive the negotiating bank of the right of recourse it has against the drawer under the Negotiable Instruments Act. Banks should not therefore open LCs and purchase/discount/negotiate bills bearing the "without recourse" clause.

8. Accommodation bills should not be purchased/discounted/negotiated by banks. The underlying trade transactions should be clearly identified and a proper record thereof maintained at the branches conducting the bills business.

9. Banks should be circumspect while discounting bills drawn by front finance companies set up by large industrial groups on other group companies.

10. Bills rediscounts should be restricted to usance bills held by other banks. Banks should not rediscount bills earlier discounted by non-bank financial companies (NBFCs) except in respect of bills arising from sale of light commercial vehicles and two-/three-wheelers.

11. Banks may exercise their commercial judgment in discounting of bills of services sector. However, while discounting such bills, banks should ensure that actual services are rendered and accommodation bills are not discounted. Services sector bills should not be eligible for rediscounting. Further, providing finance against discounting of services sector bills may be treated as unsecured advance and, therefore, subject to the condition that 20 percent of a bank's unsecured guarantees plus the total of its outstanding unsecured advances do not exceed 15 percent of its total outstanding advances.

12. In order to promote payment discipline which would to a certain extent encourage acceptance of bills, all corporates and other constituent borrowers having turnover above threshold level as fixed by the bank's board of directors should be mandated to disclose "aging schedule" of their overdue payables in their periodical returns submitted to banks.

Banks should not enter into repo transactions using bills discounted/rediscounted as collateral.

Review Questions

CHAPTER 1

1. "There are multiple financial institutions working in the country. There is overlapping in their operation. At times, a large section of population is deprived from services of financial institutions." Examine.
2. "The opening up of economy has witnessed tremendous growth in new instruments." Analyze the impact of globalization while highlighting new capital market instruments.
3. "Services are intangibles; however, they are connected in products." Do you agree with statement? Analyze fund based financial services in India.
4. Explain:

   i.   GDRs
   ii. Repo
   iii. Press Note 18
   iv. When-issued market
   v.   Reverse mortgage product

CHAPTER 2

1. "There are multiple regulators often competing and overlapping with each other." What do you infer from the statement? Explain. How is capital market regulated in India?
2. Examine the regulation of banking industry in the country. Explain how regulations of banking companies are different from NBFCs.
3. Write short notes on:

   i. PFRDA
   ii. IRDA

CHAPTER 3

1. Mr Vijay Sharma owns two securities: Reliance and Infosys. Reliance has an expected return of 15 percent with a standard deviation of those returns being 11 percent. Infoys has an expected return of 12 percent, and a standard deviation of 7 percent. The correlation of returns between Reliance and Infosys is 0.81. If the portfolio consists of Rs 60,000 in Infosys and Rs 40,000 in Reliance, what is the expected standard deviation of portfolio returns?

   Solution: Expected return on Reliance E (r1) = 15%
   Expected return on the Infosys Stock E (r2) = 12%
   Standard deviation of returns on Reliance ($\sigma1$) = 11%
   Standard deviation of returns on Infosys ($\sigma2$) = 7%
   Coefficient of correlation (ρ_{12}) = 0.81
   Proportion of investment in Reliance stock (W1) = 0.40
   Proportion of investment in Infosys stock (W2) = 0.60
   Variance of a portfolio of two assets is given by the following formula:

   $$\sigma^2 = W_1^2\sigma_1^2 + W_2^2\sigma_2^2 + 2W_1W_2\sigma_1\sigma_2\rho_{12}$$

   Substituting the given values, we get

   $$\sigma^2 = (0.40)^2 (11)^2 + (0.60)^2 (7)^2 + 2 \times 0.40 \times 0.60 \times 11 \times 7 \ 0.81$$
   $$= 19.36 + 17.64 + 29.94$$
   $$= 66.94$$
   $$\sigma = \sqrt{66.94} = 8.18\%$$

2. Security A offers an expected return of 14 percent with a standard deviation of 8 percent. Security B offers an expected return of 11 percent with a standard deviation of 6 percent. If you wish to construct a portfolio with a 12.8 percent expected return, what percentage of the portfolio will consist of security A?

   Solution: Let the proportion of investment in security A = W
   Then investment in security B = (1 – W)
   Expected return on a portfolio (E (rp)) = W1 E (r1) + W2 E (r2)

   $$12.8 = W \times 14 + (1 - W) \times 11$$
   $$12.8 = 14W + 11 - 11W$$
   $$1.8 = 3W$$
   $$W = 0.6$$

   Thus, investment in security A = 60 percent and investment in security B = 40 percent.

3. Deepak has a portfolio of eight securities, each with a market value of Rs 5,000. The current beta of the portfolio is 1.28 and the beta of the riskiest security is 1.75. Deepak wishes to reduce his portfolio beta to 1.15 by selling the riskiest security and replacing it with another security with a lower beta. What must be the beta of the replacement security?

Solution: Beta of a portfolio = weighted average beta of the constituent securities = $\Sigma wi\ \beta i$

The current beta of Deepak's portfolio = 1.28

Market value of the portfolio = Rs 40,000

Weight of each security in the portfolio = $\dfrac{5,000}{40,000} = \dfrac{1}{8}$

Sum of the betas of eight securities = $1.28 \times 8 = 10.24$

The beta of the portfolio after replacement = 1.15

Sum of the betas of eight securities = $1.15 \times 8 = 9.20$

Since the riskiest security with a beta of 1.75 is replaced, it means

$$10.24 - 1.75 + x = 9.20$$
$$x = 9.20 - 8.49 = 0.71$$

Thus, the beta of the replacement security = 0.71.

4. What do we mean by return? If a company declares a dividend payout of 50 percent on shares (face value Rs 10) issued at a premium of Rs 140, does it mean that investors have earned a return of 50 percent? Discuss.

5. Earnings announcements by companies are followed by changes in the market price of the stock. Given the historical nature of these earnings and the fact that these are accounting figures and not cash flows, why they are so important? Discuss.

6. What is beta? How can a portfolio manager change the beta of his portfolio? Discuss.

CHAPTER 4

1. "Banks provide services. However, these services have now bundled into products. Some banks say that it is our loan products and it is our saving products." What do you infer from the statement? What kind of qualitative changes do you notice in banking services? How will you read the change in attitude of bank persons providing services? Explain.

2. "Marketing of banking services and products have accepted, implemented, and executed the fundamental of basic marketing which includes price, promotion, product, and place along with identification of target market." The statement refers to the emerging practices of marketing of banking products. In view of the both statements, how will you implement AIDA (awareness, interest, desire and action) theory in the marketing of banking products?

3. Write short notes on:
   i. Banca Assurance
   ii. Banks offering non-banking services
   iii. Regulation of banks in India especially in view of recent global crisis
   iv. Financial sector reforms and banking sector

CHAPTER 5

1. Suppose you are an insurance advisor. You have to convince the prospective clients who have no idea about life insurance. What steps will you take to convince about concept, type, and products? How will you market the insurance product to the population which has no faith in insurance? Explain.

2. It is said that insurance industry has now become buyers dominated from sellers dominated. Do you agree with this? Examine the impact of opening up of insurance sector on product, quality, and services while analyzing the emerging trends in insurance industry.

3. Write short notes on:

   i. Insurable interest
   ii. Growth of insurance industry post globalization

4. Examine the following punch lines:

   i. Born to Lead
   ii. *Mera Farz*
   iii. *Sar Utha Ke Jiyo*
   Do these punch lines influence the insurance purchase decision?

CHAPTER 6

1. It is clear that "intermediaries are must for capital market operations." What do you infer from the statement? Examine while analyzing the recent trends in capital market.

2. Explain

   i. Value paid investment
   ii. Demutualization
   iii. MAPIN
   iv. Dematerialization

CHAPTER 7

1. "Mutual funds have emerged as one of the effective tools for small investors as small investors have been hit badly by direct exposure to capital market; therefore, the government has formulated such policies which promotes and motivates small investors to go to mutual funds." Analyze the statement while explaining advantages and disadvantages of investment in mutual fund.

CHAPTER 8

1. Explain the concept of leasing while comparing it with hire-purchase. What factors should one keep in mind while deciding about leasing?
2. Write short notes on:
   i.   Finance lease
   ii. Sale and lease back
   iii. Net, Net, Net Lease
   iv. Hire-purchase and credit sales

CHAPTER 9

1. It is said that "securitization is nothing but conversion of illiquid assets into liquid assets. In this process, the company ensures its liquidity which can be used for more productive purpose." Explain the statement and draw the flow of securitization process.

CHAPTER 10

1. "Rating is indicative but not conclusive evidence of solvency. It simply refers but does not communicate the accuracy." How do you react to this statement? What are the essential features of ratings in India?

CHAPTER 11

1. Examine the concept of venture capital while analyzing the regulatory framework of venture capital in India.
2. It is said that "a venture capital fund is high risk bearing investment opportunity. The risk is inherent with all other ventures." Discuss the elements of risk which are special to venture capital.

Chapter 12

1. "Factoring is way to realize payments from debtors." Explain while analyzing the types of factor.
2. A Ltd has a total sale of Rs 3.2 crores and its average collection period is 90 days. The past experience indicates that bad-debts losses are 1.5 percent on sales. The expenditure

incurred by the firm in administering its receivable collection efforts is Rs 500,000. A factor is prepared to buy the firm's receivables by charging 2 percent commission. The factor will pay advance on receivables to the firm at an interest rate of 18 percent p.a. after withholding 10 percent as reserve. Calculate the effective cost of factoring to the firm.

(CA Final May, 2002)

Total sales:	32,000,000
Average collection period:	90 days
Receivables:	32,000,000 × 90/360
	= 8,000,000

(i) If factor service is not taken
   - Bad debts loss: 1.5% of sales
   - Cost of administration of receivables: 500,000
(ii) If factor service is taken
   - Factor commission payable: 2%
   - Interest on advance payment of receivable: 18% p.a.
   - Factor reserve: 10%

Receivables		8,000,000
Less: 10% advance	800,000	
Factor commission(8000,000 × 2/100)	160,000	960,000
Amount available for advance		7,040,000
Interest on advance(7,40,000 × 18/100 × 90/360)		316,800
Net amount paid to the firm		6,723,200

Evaluation of cost of factoring to the firm

(i)	Savings		
	Cost of administration receivables		500,000
	Cost of bad debts	(320,000 × 1.5/100)	480,000
			(i) 980,000
(ii)	Factoring commission	(8,000,000 × 2/100 × 360/90)	640,000
	Interest charges	(316,800 × 360/90)	1,267,200
			(ii) 1,907,200
	Net cost to the firm		(ii) – (i) 927,200

Effective rate of interest to the firm = 927,200/6,723,200 × 100 = 13.79%

CHAPTER 13

1. Examine the statement, "no doubt the use of plastic money has simplified exchange function but not without cost and complications." Also underline the reason for growing popularity along with future of credit cards in India.

CHAPTER 14

1. Examine the concept of merger and acquisition. How does it help corporates for generating value to stakeholders?
2. "M&A" does not come alone. It has several issues involved. Examine the issues while describing the types of M&A.

Q.1 X Ltd acquires Y Ltd by way of merger. The following data are available.

Particulars		X Ltd	Y Ltd
Earnings after tax	(Rs)	200,000	60,000
No. of equity shares		40,000	10,000
Market value per share	(Rs)	15	12

i. If the merger goes through by exchange of equity share and the exchange ratio is based on the current price, what is the new earnings per share for X Ltd?

Calculation of new EPS of X Ltd

Number of equity shares to be issued by X Ltd
$$= 10{,}000 \text{ shares} \times \text{Rs } 12/\text{Rs } 15 = 8{,}000 \text{ shares}$$

Total number of shares in X Ltd. after acquisition of Y Ltd = 40,000 + 8,000 = 48,000

Total earnings after tax after acquisition = 200,000 + 60,000 = 260,000

$$\text{EPS} = \frac{\text{Rs } 260{,}000}{48{,}000 \text{ equity shares}} = \text{Rs } 5.42$$

ii. Y Ltd wants to be sure that the earnings available to its shareholders will not be diminished by the merger. What should be the exchange ratio in the case?

Calculation of exchange ratio which would not diminish the EPS of Y Ltd after its merger with X Ltd

Current EPS

$$\text{X Ltd} = \frac{\text{Rs } 200{,}000}{40{,}000 \text{ equity shares}} = \text{Rs } 5$$

$$\text{Y Ltd} = \frac{\text{Rs } 60{,}000}{10{,}000 \text{ equity shares}} = \text{Rs } 6$$

Exchange ratio is to be = 5/6 = 1.20

Number of new shares to be issued by X Ltd to Y Ltd = 10,000 × 1.20 = 12,000 shares

Total number of shares after acquisition = 40,000 + 12,000 = 52,000 shares

EPS after merger = Rs 260,000/52,000 shares = Rs 5

Total earnings of Y Ltd = No. of shares × EPS = 12,000 × Rs 5 = 60,000

Q.2 M Ltd is considering takeover of N Ltd. and O Ltd. The financial data for the three companies are as follows:

Particulars		M	N	O
Equity share capital of Rs 10 each	(Rs in lakhs)	450	180	90
Earnings	(Rs in lakhs)	90	18	18
Market price of each share	(Rs)	60	37	46

Calculate:

i. Price earnings ratios

ii. Earning per share of M after the acquisition of N and O separately. Will you recommend the merger of either/both of the companies? Justify you answer.

Calculation of price earning ratios

Particulars		M	N	O
Earnings	(Rs in lakhs)	90	18	18
No. of shares	(Lakhs)	45	18	9
EPS	(Rs)	2	1	2
Market price per share	(Rs)	60	37	46
PE ratio		30	37	23

Calculation of EPS of M Ltd. after acquisition of N Ltd and O Ltd

$$\text{Exchange ratio or rate} = \frac{\text{Buyer's P/E ratio}}{\text{Seller's P/E ratio}}$$

Particulars		M	N	O
Exchange ratio in A Ltd		–	.81	1.30
Value of shares	(Rs in lakhs)	2,700	666	414
No. of A Ltd's share to be given	(Lakhs)	–	666/60	414/60
EPS	(Rs)	–	11.11	6.9
Total earning after acquisition	(Rs in lakhs)	–	108	108
Total number of shares	(Lakhs)	–	56.1	51.9
EPS after acquisition	(Rs)	–	1.93	2.08

Analysis: After merger of O Ltd with M Ltd, O Ltd.'s EPS is higher than M Ltd (Rs 2.08). Hence, merger with only O Ltd is suggested to increase the value to the shareholders of M Ltd.

Q.3 XYZ Ltd is considering merger with ABC Ltd XYZ Ltd's shares are currently traded at Rs 25. It has 2,00,000 shares outstanding and its earnings after taxes (EAT) amount to Rs 4,00,000. ABC Ltd has 100,000 shares outstanding; its current market price is Rs 12.50 and its EAT is Rs 100,000. The merger will be effected by means of a stock swap (exchange). ABC Ltd has agreed to a plan under which XYZ Ltd will offer the current market value of ABC Ltd's shares:

i. What are the pre-merger earnings per share (EPS) and P/E ratio of both the companies?

ii. If ABC Ltd's P/E ratio is 8, what is its current market price? What is the exchange ratio? What will be XYZ Ltd's post-merger EPS?

iii. What must be the exchange ratio for XYZ Ltd so that pre- and post-merger EPS is the same?

iv. Pre-merger EPS and P/E ratio of XYZ Ltd and ABC Ltd.

Particulars	XYZ Ltd	ABC Ltd
Earning after taxes	400,000	100,000
Number of shares outstanding	200,000	100,000
EPS (earnings after tax/number of shares)	2	1
Market price per share	25.00	12.50
P/E ratio (times)	12.50	12.50

v. Current market price of ABC Ltd, if P/E ratio is 8 = Rs 1 × 8 = Rs 8
Exchange ratio = Rs 25/8 = 3.125

$$\text{Post merger EPS of XYZ Ltd} = \frac{\text{Rs } 400,000 + \text{Rs } 100,000}{200,000 + (100,000/3.125)} = \frac{500,000}{232,000} = \text{Rs} = 2.16$$

vi Desired exchange ratio
Total number of shares in post-merged company

$$\frac{\text{Post-merger earnings}}{\text{Pre-merger EPS of XYZ Ltd}} = 500,000/2 = 250,000$$

Number of shares required to be issued = 250,000 − 200,000 = 50,000
Therefore, the exchange ratio is = 50,000/100,000 = 0.50

Bibliography

Achleitner, Kristin Ann (2008), "Employment Contribution of Private Equity and Venture Capital in Europe". Available online at www.evca.eu

Andrade, Gregor, Mark Mitchell, and Erik Stafford (2001), "New Evidence and Perspectives on Mergers", *The Journal of Economic Perspectives*, 15(2): 103–120.

Berkowitch, Elzar and M.P. Narayanan (1993), "Motives for Takeovers: An Empirical Investigation", *The Journal of Financial and Quantitative Analysis*, 28(3): 347–362.

Brealy, R.A and S.C.Myers (2002), *Principles of Corporate Finance*. New York: Tata McGraw Hill.

BSE (2007), *Indian Finance Review*. Annual Report, BSE.

CARE research team (2008), "Indian Banking Sector: Edgy but Resilient". Available online at www.careratings.com

Chandara, Prasanna (2004), *Financial Management: Theory and Practice*. New Delhi: Tata McGraw Hill.

CMIE (2008), *Monthly Bulletin*. Bombay: Centre for Monitoring Indian Economy.

CRISIL research team (2009), "CRISIL India Budget Analysis for Years 2008–09: Detailed Economic Analysis." Available online at: www.crisil.com

CSO (2009), Various Reports, Government of India, New Delhi.

C.S. Kalyansundaram Committee Report (1989), RBI.

Economic Times (2002), "Understanding PSU Valuation Models", ET in the classroom, *Economic Times*, July 14.

———— (2008), "Special feature on 'Banking Technology'", *Economic Times*, August 21.

Elton, J and Martin J. Gruber (1991), *Modern Portfolio Theory and Investment Management*. New York: John Wiley & Sons.

Gaughan, Patrick A. (2002), *Mergers, Acquisitions and Corporate Restructurings (3rd ed.)*. New York: John Wiley and Sons.

Goergen, Marc and Luc Renneboog (2003), "Shareholder Wealth Effects of European, Domestic and Crossborder Takeover Bids", *European Financial Management Journal*, 10(1): 9–45.

ICFAI (1994), *Merchant Banking in Financial Services*. Hyderabad: ICFAI University Press.

IFMR (1982), *Investment Management*. Chennai: IFMR.

IRDA (2009), *Annual Report 2008–09*.

Jensen, Michael C. (1986), 'Agency Cost of Free Cash Flow' Corporate Finance and Takeovers, *The American can Review*, 76(2): 323–329.

Kale, Prashant (2004), "Acquisition Value Creation in Emerging Markets: An Empirical Study of Acquisitions in India", Best Paper Proceedings, Academy of Management, New Delhi.

K.B. Chandrashekhar Committee (2000), Report of K.B.Chandrashekhar Committee on Venture Capital, SEBI.

Kothari, R. and B. Dutta (2005), *Contemporary Financial Management*. New Delhi: MacMillan.

Kishore, Ravi M. (2006), *Financial Management*. Mumbai: Taxman.

Madura, Jeff (2006), *International Financial Management (8th edition)*. Mason, Ohio: Thomson South Western.

Markowitz, Harry Max (1992), "Portfolio Selection", *Journal of Finance*, 7(1): 77–91.

Maheshwari, SN. *Financial and Management Accounting*. Delhi: Sultanchand & Co.

Mukherjee, Tarun K., Halil Kiymaz, and H. Kent Baker (2004), "Merger Motives and Target Valuation: A Survey of Evidence from CFOs, Social Science Research Network". Available online at www.ssrn.com

National Stock Exchange (NSE) (2008), *Annual Report*.

RBI (2006), *Annual Reports*. Publication Division. Available online at http://www.rbi.org.in/scripts/AnnualReportPublications.aspx?Id=909 (last accessed on June 14 2009).

Ross, Stephen, Randolph Westerfield, and Bradford Jordan (2002), *Fundamentals of Corporate Finance*. New Delhi: Tata McGraw Hill.

SEBI (2000), *Mutual Fund Vision Fund*. Mumbai: SEBI.

———— Guidelines on Venture Capital, Investment Management Department, Division of Funds, SEBI.

———— (2008), *Annual Report*.

———— (2009), *Economic Survey*. Ministry of Finance, Government of India, New Delhi.

————. (2009), *Handbook of Statistics on the Indian Securities Market*. RBI: Securities and Exchange Board of India.

Seth, Anju, Kean P. Song, and Richardson Peltit (2000), 'Synergy, Managerialism on Hubris? An Empirical Examination of Motives for Foreign Acquisition of U.S. firms', *Journal of International Business Studies*, 31(3): 387–405.

Shekhar, K.C. (1986), *Banks, Theory and Practice*. New Delhi: Vikas Publishing House.

Suranovic, Steven M. (2008), 'International Trade Theory and Policy', Chapter 40. Available online at www.internationalecon.com

The Economist (2001), 'Effects on Terrorism Coverages in Property Business', *The Economist*, September 27.

Tratwein, Friedrich (1990), 'Merger Motives and Merger Prescriptions,' *Strategic Management Journal* 11(4): 283–295.

TSJ (2007), *Venture Intelligence India*. TSJ Media.

United Nations Conference of Trade and Development (UNCTAD) (2006), *FDI from Developing and Transition Economies: Implications for Development*. World Investment Report. New York/Geneva: United Nations.

Weston, J., Fred Mitchell, Mark L., and J. Havold Mulherin (2004), *Takeovers, Restructuring and Corporate Governance (4th edition)*. New Jersey: Pearson Prentice Hall.

Wubben, Bernd (2007), *German Mergers & Acquisitions in the USA*. Germany: DUV Gabler Edition Wissenschaft.

Index

About the Author

Rajesh Kothari is Professor at the R.A. Podar Institute of Management, University of Rajasthan, Jaipur.

He had been the Dean at the Faculty of Management Studies, University of Rajasthan, Jaipur. Several students have already obtained their Ph.D. under his supervision.

He has twenty eight years of teaching and research experience and has been an advisor to companies like IFCI, Dalal Street Journal, Autolite Industries, Lupin Human Welfare Research Foundation, to name a few. His areas of specializations are strategic finance, risk management, security analysis, and investors education. He has authored three bestselling textbooks: *Contemporary Financial Management*, *Management Account: Concepts and Application*, and *Bhav-Kitna*.